"This volume is an excellent contribution to the literature on Emerging Multinationals. But what I particularly liked about this particular group of essays was that, following four carefully written and analytical robust chapters on the origin and determinants of the foreign activities of Emerging MNEs, there followed eight quite distinctive and original case studies of those new forms of investment by particular home countries. *Inter alia* these revealed that each emerging country has its own particular reasons and agenda for investing outside its national boundaries. Altogether, I found this a first rate and eminently readable group of essays. The volume deserves the widest attention of government, the business community and academic scholars alike."

   John H. Dunning, State of New Jersey Professor Emeritus, Rutgers University, and Emeritus Professor of International Business, Reading University

"Ramamurti and Singh have masterfully engineered a productive confrontation between extant theorizing in international business and the empirical phenomenon of newer multinationals from emerging markets. All scholarship is enriched as a result."

   Tarun Khanna, Jorge Paulo Lemann Professor, Harvard Business School, and author of *Billions of Entrepreneurs: How China and India Are Reshaping Their Future and Yours* (2008).

"Just as every person discovers his own path in life, so too with companies and countries. This is a fascinating book with a comment on the multiple pathways adopted by emerging countries in their quest for globalization. An exhilarating read, a wondrous experience."

   R. Gopalakrishnan, Executive Director, TATA Sons Ltd

"Multinational enterprises from emerging markets are in the process of transforming the world FDI market. This book goes a long way in analyzing the main players in this process and the forces driving it, and does so in a very illuminating way."

   Karl Sauvant, Executive Director, Vale Columbia Center on Sustainable International Investment

"Ramamurti and Singh make an outstanding contribution to understanding the new configuration of world markets and its new competitive structure. As the different country studies show, multinationals from emerging economies share a number of common structural features, as well as the imprinting of specific local experiences. For managers and business practitioners, the book offers valuable tips on how to shape the new international order."

Henrique Rzezinski, Chairman, Brazil–US Business Council

"*Emerging Multinationals in Emerging Markets* is a fascinating and timely volume that will be of great value not only to students of international business theory but also to practitioners heading emerging world multinationals and those in the developed world competing with them. As a long-time executive of an EMNE, and now heading an association of CEOs of EMNEs, I found the case studies in Part 2 to be particularly interesting."

Michael Spicer, CEO, Business Leadership South Africa

Emerging Multinationals in Emerging Markets

Why have so many firms in emerging economies internationalized quite aggressively in the last decade? What competitive advantages do these firms enjoy and what are the origins of those advantages? Through what strategies have they built their global presence? How is their internationalization affecting Western rivals? And, finally, what does all this mean for mainstream international business theory?

In *Emerging Multinationals in Emerging Markets*, a distinguished group of international business scholars tackle these questions based on a shared research design. The heart of the book contains detailed studies of emerging-market multinationals (EMNEs) from the BRIC economies, plus Israel, Mexico, South Africa, and Thailand. The studies show that EMNEs come in many shapes and sizes, depending on the home-country context. Furthermore, EMNEs leverage distinctive competitive advantages and pursue distinctive internationalization paths. This timely analysis of EMNEs promises to enrich mainstream models of how firms internationalize in today's global economy.

RAVI RAMAMURTI is CBA Distinguished Professor of International Business and Director of the Center for Emerging Markets at Northeastern University, Boston.

JITENDRA V. SINGH is Saul P. Steinberg Professor of Management at the Wharton School, University of Pennsylvania. From 2007 to 2009, he was Dean, Shaw Foundation Chair, and Professor of Strategy, Management, and Organization at the Nanyang Business School, Singapore.

Emerging Multinationals in Emerging Markets

Edited by

RAVI RAMAMURTI

AND

JITENDRA V. SINGH

CAMBRIDGE
UNIVERSITY PRESS

CAMBRIDGE UNIVERSITY PRESS
Cambridge, New York, Melbourne, Madrid, Cape Town, Singapore, São Paulo, Delhi, Dubai, Tokyo, Mexico City

Cambridge University Press
The Edinburgh Building, Cambridge CB2 8RU, UK

Published in the United States of America by Cambridge University Press, New York

www.cambridge.org
Information on this title: www.cambridge.org/9780521160186

First published 2009
Reprinted 2010
First time paperback 2010

Printed in the United Kingdom at the University Press, Cambridge

A catalog record for this publication is available from the British Library

ISBN 978-0-521-51386-9 hardback
ISBN 978-0-521-16018-6 paperback

To our families:
  Meena, Bharat, Gita, and Arjun
  Marlies, Ambika, and Katherine

Contents

Figures

Tables

Abbreviations

ASEAN	Association of Southeast Asian Nations
BCG	Boston Consulting Group
BRIC	Brazil, Russia, India, China
CEO	Chief executive officer
CIS	Commonwealth of Independent States
CNOOC	China National Offshore Oil Corporation
CSA	Country-specific advantage
EMNE	Emerging-market multinational enterprise
EU	European Union
FDA	Food and Drug Administration (US)
FDI	Foreign direct investment
FMCG	Fast-moving consumer goods
FOE	Foreign-owned enterprise
FSA	Firm-specific advantage
GDP	Gross domestic product
GNP	Gross national product
IB	International business
IDP	Investment development path
IPO	Initial public offering
IT	Information technology
M&A	Merger and acquisition
MNE	Multinational enterprise
NAFTA	North America Free Trade Agreement
NASDAQ	National Association of Securities Dealers Automated Quotations
OECD	Organization for Economic Co-operation and Development
OEM	Original equipment manufacturer
OLI theory	Ownership-Location-Internalization theory
PMI	Post-Merger Integration
POE	Privately owned enterprise

R&D	Research and development
SARB	South African Reserve Bank
SME	Small and medium-sized enterprise
SOE	State-owned enterprise
3G	Third generation
TWMNCs	Third World multinational corporations
UAE	United Arab Emirates
UNCTAD	United Nations Conference on Trade and Development
WTO	World Trade Organization

Contributors

Yair Aharoni, Professor of International Business Emeritus, Faculty of Management, Tel Aviv University, Israel

Alice H. Amsden, Barton L. Weller Professor of Political Economy, Massachusetts Institute of Technology, US

Afonso Fleury, Professor of Production Engineering, University of Sao Paolo, Brazil

Maria Tereza Leme Fleury, Professor of Economics and Management, University of Sao Paolo, Brazil

Andrea Goldstein, Deputy Director, OECD, France

Donald R. Lessard, Epoch Foundation Professor of International Management, Sloan School of Management, Massachusetts Institute of Technology, US

Rafel Lucea, Assistant Professor of International Business, George Washington University, US

Daniel J. McCarthy, Alan McKim and Richard A. D'Amore Professor of Global Management, Northeastern University, US

Pavida Pananond, Associate Professor, Thammasat University, Thailand

Wilson Prichard, Ph.D. candidate, Institute of Development Studies, UK

Sheila M. Puffer, Professor and Cherry Family Senior Fellow of International Business and Strategy, Northeastern University, US

Ravi Ramamurti, CBA Distinguished Professor of International Business, and Director, Center for Emerging Markets, Northeastern University, US

Alan M. Rugman, L. Leslie Waters Chair in International Business, Kelly School of Business, Indiana University, US

Jitendra V. Singh, Saul P. Steinberg Professor of Management, Wharton School, University of Pennsylvania, and Dean, Nanyang Business School, Singapore

Oleg S. Vikhanski, Dean, Graduate School of Business Administration, Moscow State University, Russia

Louis T. Wells, Jr., Herbert F. Johnson Professor of International Management, Harvard Business School, US

Peter J. Williamson, Visiting Professor of International Management, Judge Business School, Cambridge University, UK

Ming Zeng, Professor of Strategic Management, Cheung Kong Graduate School of Business, Beijing, China, and President of Yahoo-China and Executive Vice-President, Alibaba Group, China

Acknowledgments

This book grew out of a conference organized by Northeastern University and the Wharton School, University of Pennsylvania, in Boston in June 2007. It was sponsored by Northeastern University's Center for Emerging Markets, with funds provided by the Liberty Mutual Foundation, and by the Wharton School's Mack Center for Technological Innovation and the Center for Leadership and Change Management. We are grateful to Deans Tom Moore and Bill Crittenden as well as former Provost Ahmed Abdelal and President Joseph Aoun of Northeastern University for their unstinting support at every stage. We would like to thank the two centers at the Wharton School for part of the financial support for this project. We would particularly like to thank our colleagues Profs. Harbir Singh and Michael Useem for helpful discussions leading up to the conference. In addition, Ravi Ramamurti's sabbatical at the Wharton School in 2006–2007, which led to the collaboration with Jitendra Singh, would not have been possible without the Jeff Bornstein Senior Fellowship.

A book like this is only as good as its contributors. We were extremely fortunate to be working with a truly outstanding group of scholars who reviewed each other's papers meticulously and revised their own chapters several times, while meeting deadlines along the way. At the conference we were joined by a delightful group of thoughtful discussants and chairs from our two universities and from all around the world. Among them were: Nick Athanassiou, Paul Beamish, Dan Danielsen, Charles Dhanaraj, Saikat Chaudhuri, Vit Henisz, Tarun Khanna, Steve Kobrin, Harry Lane, Stefanie Lenway, Gerry McDermott, Marshall Meyer, Suzanne Ogden, Chris Robertson, Ravi Sarathy, Sushil Vachani, Eleanor Westney, and Valery Yakubovich. In addition, several other faculty members from Northeastern University and Boston-area schools participated actively in the discussions. We would like to extend a special thanks to the three doctoral students from Harvard Business School who compiled notes on the conference deliberations: Kjell Carlson, Barbara Zepp Larson, and Markus Taussig. Finally, we would like to thank the three anonymous reviewers engaged by Cambridge University Press for providing very helpful comments on the original manuscript.

An international conference requires a great deal of planning and careful execution. Kathy McCart of Northeastern University handled these duties superbly, with contributions from Carolyn Boviard and Beth Cliff. Don Unger of MIT helped edit the chapters for uniformity and clarity. At Cambridge University Press, we had the pleasure of dealing with one of the most responsive and professional editors in the business, Paula Parish.

RAVI RAMAMURTI
Boston
JITENDRA SINGH
Singapore

PART I

Introduction

1 Why study emerging-market multinationals?

RAVI RAMAMURTI[1]

As developing and transition economies opened up to the global economy in recent years, a number of local firms not only survived the battle for markets at home, they expanded internationally through exports and foreign direct investment (FDI) to become fledgling multinational enterprises (MNEs) in their own right. By 2007, the more prominent emerging-market MNEs (hereafter referred to as EMNEs) included firms such as China's Huawei in telecommunications equipment, Mexico's Cemex in cement, Russia's Gazprom in energy, India's Tata Consultancy Services in information technology (IT) services, and Brazil's Embraer in regional jets. Many more firms in emerging economies were preparing to go down the same path in the future. Business magazines, such as *BusinessWeek* (2006) and the *Economist* (2007), trumpeted this trend with cover stories on "emerging giants" or "globalization's offspring" and illustrated the disruptive effects EMNEs were having on established Western multinationals. Consulting companies, such as McKinsey & Co. and the Boston Consulting Group (BCG), also took notice of these potential clients.[2] There was a parallel increase in studies on EMNEs by international business (IB) scholars, although no consensus emerged on whether and how EMNEs differed from multinationals that had come before.[3]

Why have EMNEs come into prominence in the past decade? What competitive advantages did they leverage as they internationalized? Were they distinctive in any way because they originated in emerging

---

[1] I would like to thank Jitendra V. Singh and other participants in the NU-Wharton conference for useful conversations leading up to this chapter.

[2] See Sinha (2005) in *McKinsey Quarterly* and Boston Consulting Group (2006), which identified 100 global contenders from 12 rapidly growing economies.

[3] Aulakh 2007; Buckley *et al.*, 2007; Child and Rodrigues, 2005; Dunning, 2006; Goldstein, 2007; Khanna and Palepu, 2006; Luo and Tung, 2007; Mathews, 2002; Narula, 2006; Ramamurti, 2004; and Zeng and Williamson, 2007.

economies? What internationalization strategies did they pursue, and why? What impact were they having on their respective global industries? How consistent or inconsistent is the rise of EMNEs with mainstream IB theory? These are some of the questions we explore in the pages that follow.

This project was based on three premises. First, we view the rise of EMNEs starting in the early 2000s as a long-term trend with important consequences for the global economy, rather than a flash in the pan. Like Korean and Japanese companies that came before, emerging-market firms were seen as capable of becoming global giants in a number of industries in due course. By some accounts, EMNEs were already among the world's top twenty firms, in such industries as container shipping (eight firms), petroleum refining (six firms), steel (five firms), mining (three firms), electronics (three firms), and tele-communications (two firms) (UNCTAD [United Nations Conference on Trade and Development], 2007: 123). There was no assurance, of course, that EMNEs would grow steadily in the future as they had in the early 2000s, when, arguably, all the stars were aligned for their ascendance. On the other hand, if the twenty-first century really belonged to emerging economies, as some have claimed (e.g., Wilson and Purushothaman, 2003; van Agtmael, 2007), then these countries could reasonably be expected to spawn many more EMNEs.

A second premise of the project was that IB theory could explain a lot about EMNEs, but not everything of interest to managers and policy makers. Studying EMNEs was therefore seen as a way to enrich existing IB theory, particularly about the process by which firms internationalize and become multinational enterprises. However, to ensure that insights from extant IB theory were taken fully into account in our research, prominent IB scholars participated in the Northeastern University-Wharton School conference at which authors presented their preliminary chapters.

The third premise was that a collaborative research effort would be the most productive way forward, given that EMNEs were relatively new actors on the global stage and hailed from a heterogeneous set of countries – even if those countries were often lumped together under the label "emerging economies." Accordingly, we invited a team of scholars to write papers on EMNEs specifically for this volume. They were leading IB scholars deeply familiar with the countries about which they were writing. All but two of the country studies (Mexico and South Africa) had at least one co-author from the country involved. Our sample covered the famous "BRIC" economies – Brazil, Russia, India, and China – plus four other emerging economies. We hoped that juxtaposing the country experiences and company studies would allow us to discern more clearly the country-level and industry-level variables that shaped the competitive advantage of EMNEs.[4] To be sure, including so many countries and researchers could make it harder to reach conclusions, but given the topic's novelty and complexity we felt alternative approaches would amount to over-simplification. We believed that you had to understand the lay of the land and the facts on the ground before rushing to conclusions about EMNEs or zeroing in on very specific research questions and hypotheses, as some prior studies have done.[5] We expect follow-up studies to be focused more narrowly on particular industries, countries, or issues.

Multinationals from rich and poor countries

In the post-WWII period, most of the world's FDI flowed from one advanced economy to another (see Cell 1 in Figure 1.1). Therefore, even as most of the world's largest MNEs were based in the advanced economies, most of the research on MNEs was about Cell 1 cases – for example, American companies investing in Europe, or European companies investing in the US.

Cell 2 is probably the next most widely researched case by IB scholars, because even in the 1970s, more than 20 percent of global FDI flows went to developing countries, especially after the commodity-price boom of the mid-1970s (Weigel *et al.*, 1998: Figure 2.4, p. 16). The strategies of Western MNEs in developing countries and their stormy relations with host governments, sometimes resulting in outright expropriations by host countries, caught the attention of IB scholars and development economists (e.g., Kobrin, 1977). Cell 2 assumed renewed importance in the 1990s, when many developing

---

[4] This is in keeping with the plea by Tsui (2007: 1358) for developing "context-specific indigenous theories."

[5] For instance, one detects a rush to judgment in consulting company studies such as those by Sinha (2005) and the Boston Consulting Group (2006), and other studies, such as Mathews (2002) or van Agtmael (2007).

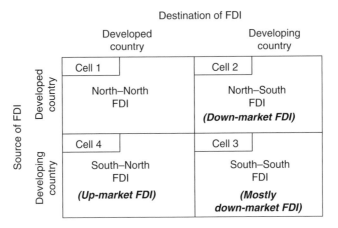

Figure 1.1 Source and destination of FDI.
Note: Down-market FDI refers to investment from a more developed country to a less developed one, and up-market FDI refers to the opposite

countries set aside their hostility to MNEs and welcomed them instead with open arms. At the same time, sweeping reforms in China and other transition economies created vast new opportunities for MNEs. By 2004, FDI from advanced countries to emerging economies accounted for almost 30 percent of global FDI flows.[6] Concomitantly, research on Cell 2 situations grew significantly.

To date, most of the research on FDI has been about Cells 1 and 2, that is, about investment originating in advanced countries. The fact that most research on MNEs was conducted by Western scholars, particularly in the United States, further skewed the research on MNEs towards Cells 1 and 2.

In the late 1970s and early 1980s, however, outward investment from developing countries received attention from IB scholars for the

---

[6] This was estimated from data in *World Investment Report 2006*. Total outward FDI in 2004 from developing and transition economies was $60 billion, excluding outflows from offshore financial centers, almost all of which went that year to other developing and transition economies (p. 118). Subtracting this amount from the total inward FDI into developing and transition economies that year ($275 billion, p. 299), suggests that $215 billion came from advanced countries (Cell 2). Given that worldwide FDI outflows that year (excluding $66 billion from offshore financial centers) was $747 billion, Cell 2's share is 29 percent.

first time, at the same time as the first significant wave of outward FDI from developing countries took place (Wells, 1977). At least two-thirds of that outward investment went to other developing countries (Wells, 1983: 4), that is, they were predominantly of the Cell-3 type, or what is sometimes referred to as South–South investment. Studies from this period shed light on the distinctive aspects of South–South investment (e.g., Wells, 1983; Lall, 1983; Kumar, 1982; Lecraw, 1977), but work on Cell 3 situations petered out as South–South FDI failed to keep pace with overall growth in FDI, partly because the leading source of outward FDI from developing countries – Latin America – got mired in debt crises during the 1980s. Even at its peak, though, outward FDI from developing countries in the 1970s represented only a small percentage of global FDI flows (UNCTAD, 2007). Moreover, since Cell 3 cases did not affect advanced countries, they did not receive much attention in the West.

Of the four cells in Figure 1.1, the least studied was Cell 4, which represented FDI originating in developing countries and destined to advanced countries. To be sure, this neglect was largely justified by the facts. At best, such flows represented one-third or less of the outward FDI flows from developing countries, which itself in past years represented one-tenth or less of overall global FDI flows. And even when it occurred in the 1960s and 1970s, Cell 4 cases were probably seen as aberrations, originating in atypical developing countries, such as Hong Kong, which at the time was an unusually open economy (Lall, 1983, ch. 3). In most other developing countries, Cell 4 investments were a rarity, although they did occur from time to time – for example, when the Indian firm Kiroloskar bought up 48 percent of a German engineering company in 1965 (Lall, 1983: 22).

The second wave of outward FDI from developing countries began in the 1980s in countries such as Hong Kong, Singapore, and Taiwan, but spread to many more countries in the early 1990s. Annual FDI outflow from developing and transition economies peaked at $133 billion in 2000, then fell to one-fourth of the peak, followed by a rally that took it to $174 billion in 2006 (UNCTAD, 2007: 251). Outward FDI from emerging economies (i.e., developing and transition economies) could no longer be ignored. By 2006, the outward FDI stock of emerging economies exceeded $1,600 billion, compared to $149 billion in 1990 (UNCTAD, 2007: 255). In this second wave, the outward FDI from emerging markets represented 14 percent of global

FDI flows, which was substantially higher than in the 1970s. This was all the more impressive because FDI outflows from advanced countries also surged in this period, from $50 billion in 1980 to $218 billion in 1990 and $1,023 billion in 2006.

The share of outward FDI from developing countries going to advanced countries averaged 20% between 1985 and 2004, reaching a high of about 35% in 2000 (UNCTAD, 2007: 118). These Cell 4 investments made headlines in the West, because they belonged to the "man-bites-dog" category of news stories: you had firms from poor, underdeveloped countries investing in rich, developed countries, which puzzled many observers, including FDI scholars. Among the recent headline-grabbing Cell 4 cases were China National Offshore Oil Corporation's (CNOOC) failed bid for Unocal, Lenovo's acquisition of IBM's personal computers business, Mittal Steel's merger with Arcelor of France, Russian Lukoil's acquisition of Getty Oil, and Tata Steel's takeover of Anglo-Dutch Corus Steel, to name just a few examples. There were many more examples of Cell 4 investments, as the country studies in this volume show.

Cell 4 cases are interesting theoretically, because they go against the grain of conventional wisdom about the direction in which capital, technology, and knowledge should flow in the global economy – that is, from advanced economies to emerging economies. Cell 4 is a good example of a situation that extant IB theory fails to explain well.

The focus of this book is on Cells 3 and 4, both of which deserve more attention than they have traditionally received from IB scholars, not because they account for the lion's share of global FDI flows – which they do not – but because they are important to the home countries involved and because of the disruptive effect that EMNEs seem to have on their global industries. The rise of Cemex, Embraer, Huawei, or Tata Consultancy Services (TCS), for instance, caused considerable turmoil for Western MNEs. In the case of Cemex, a tranquil, regional industry was turned into a dynamic, global one, forcing established cement firms such as Holcim of Switzerland and Lafarge of France to quickly bolster their global presence (Ghemawat and Matthews, 2000; Lessard and Lucea, Chapter 10 in this volume). Brazil's Embraer was a real thorn in the side of Canada's Bombardier, which had earlier been the global market leader in regional jets (Goldstein, 2007; and Fleury and Fleury, Chapter 8 in this volume). Huawei's aggressive internationalization was at least one important reason why Siemens and Ericsson pooled their telecom equipment businesses and Alcatel merged with Lucent. And Indian IT firms such as TCS, Infosys, and Wipro forced giants such as IBM and Accenture to rethink their core business models (Palmisano, 2006; Ramamurti and Singh, Chapter 6 in this volume).

EMNEs are also important because they are potentially the Samsungs and Toyotas of the future. In the 1960s, about thirty Japanese companies, and no Korean companies, appeared on the Fortune Global 500 list, but in 2007 companies from these two countries and Singapore held ninety-two spots on the list (for Japanese companies on the list in 1962, see Amsden and Hikino, 1994: 116). Similarly, EMNEs from countries other than South Korea, Singapore, and Taiwan held forty-nine spots on the 2007 list, but could easily double or triple that number by 2020 or 2030. In 1999, China set an explicit goal to get fifty of its companies on to the Fortune Global 500 list by 2010, a target unlikely to be realized, because only twenty-four had made the list by 2007. But China's goal is indicative of its ambitions, and the extent of support for achieving them. For those interested in how new entrants can displace incumbent global giants, EMNEs will provide an interesting domain for further study.

EMNEs have also represented attractive financial investments, compared to their incumbent Western rivals. The point is illustrated by the profitability and valuations of Indian software service firms. In 2006, two such companies, Infosys and Wipro, had sales of only about $2 billion, compared to $18–20 billion for US rivals such as Accenture and EDS; yet, their after-tax profit margins were in the range of 20–25%, compared to 1% for EDS and 5% for Accenture, and their market capitalization was of the order of $30 billion, compared to $22 billion for Accenture and $13.7 billion for EDS (valuations as of January 23, 2007). This was one reason that Goldman Sachs, in its famous report on the BRICs, urged its clients to increase the weight of emerging economies in their global investment portfolios (Wilson and Purushothaman, 2003). Indeed, portfolio investors in emerging markets earned some of the highest returns during the period 2003–2007.

None of the above implies that the rise of EMNEs will be monotonic and permanent. It is quite possible that some of these firms will stumble or even collapse, because of overambitious strategies or poor execution (recall Korean Daewoo's experience after the Asian financial crisis). Emerging economies also face many economic and political risks that could derail their upward trajectories. Rising labor costs or currencies may undermine the low-cost advantage that many EMNEs enjoy in 2008. Protectionism may also rise in the advanced countries, slowing down the internationalization of EMNEs (Aharoni and Ramamurti, 2008). It does not take much imagination to construct negative scenarios of this sort. On the other hand, it is also quite possible that the turn towards free markets among emerging economies, particularly in Asia, will not be reversed, and that rapid domestic-market growth and openness to global competition will produce more EMNEs in the future, not just in low-technology or commodity businesses but quite possibly also in industries employing sophisticated technologies and requiring sophisticated marketing skills.

Research questions and prevailing IB theory

In studying emerging multinationals from developing and transition economies (i.e., Cells 3 and 4 in Figure 1.1), we are interested in answers to the following questions:

(1) What competitive advantages and capabilities do EMNEs leverage in international markets, and how are those advantages and capabilities shaped by the home-country context?
(2) What internationalization strategies do they follow, and why?
(3) What impact is their rise having on global industry dynamics, including established Western MNEs?

The first two research questions are not unlike those asked by researchers who have studied Cells 1 and 2, and they were also probed by researchers studying Cell 3 when the first wave of outward FDI from developing countries occurred in the 1960s and 1970s. The more fundamental question is whether the concepts and theories developed by studying Cells 1 and 2 are equally relevant for Cells 3 and 4. It is possible, a priori, to argue for either side of this issue.

On the one hand, all four cells entail firms making cross-border direct investments, and for that reason a common set of concepts, frameworks, and theories may well explain them equally effectively. Several mainstream IB ideas, such as Dunning's Ownership-Location-Internalization (OLI) framework (Dunning, 1977), the motivations for internationalization (market-seeking, resource-seeking, strategic asset-seeking), the notion of "liabilities of foreignness" (Zaheer, 1995), or the stages-model of internationalization (Johanson & Vahlne, 1977), may apply as well to Cell 3 and 4 situations as they do to Cell 1 and 2 situations. After all, the only difference across the four cells is the state of one contextual variable – a country's level of development. While level of development is clearly important, it may not be so powerful a contextual variable as to nullify the explanatory power of mainstream IB theories for how and why firms become multinational enterprises. This is particularly true of abstract frameworks, such as the OLI framework, which posits a set of general conditions that an organization must meet in order to become multinational. It states, for instance, that a firm cannot become multinational unless it possesses firm-specific or ownership advantages that offset the disadvantages of operating in a foreign country, or that firms expand internationally only if there are location-bound advantages in foreign countries that cannot be exploited without a presence in those countries, or that a firm will internalize international transactions only if alternative arm's-length arrangements for exploiting foreign opportunities are less profitable. These assertions are general enough that they may hold regardless of context. Indeed, in his 1983 work on Third World multinationals, Wells posed the question raised here and came to the following conclusion:

Can the same concepts that have proved useful in studies of the traditional multinationals help in understanding the new foreign investors [Third World multinationals]? My contention is that they can and the process of applying the concepts to the new firms aids in understanding both the concepts and the different kind of multinationals. (Wells, 1983: 6)

On the other hand, context becomes much more relevant if one is interested in substantive answers to the questions that motivated this research project. If one would like specifically to know what ownership advantages multinational firms from different countries enjoy and why, or what the location advantages of different countries are, or what particular internationalization paths firms are likely to follow in different contexts, then context-free frameworks are inadequate. For instance, the ownership advantages most commonly attributed to MNEs from the West include proprietary cutting-edge technologies, marketing prowess, and powerful brand names. None of these is usually a source of competitive advantage for MNEs from developing countries, a point Lall (1983) noted in his study of the first wave of outward FDI from developing countries:

Studies of MNEs have been strongly flavored by the activities of firms from the USA. The literature has barely started to take note of the possibility that the nature of monopolistic advantages of MNEs from other countries may be quite different. (Lall, 1983: 2)

Early work on Third World MNEs suggested a distinctive set of advantages for such firms (Wells, 1983; Lall, 1983; Amsden, 1989), but the relevance of those findings for EMNEs in the changed context of the 2000s is an open issue (see Wells, Chapter 2 in this volume). Recent work on EMNEs suggests a wider range of possible competitive advantages, including the extreme view that EMNEs internationalize to *acquire* competitive advantages rather than to *exploit* pre-existing ones (Mathews 2002), a point also made by Luo and Tung (2007). Narula (2006) offers a passionate rebuttal of the latter argument, while Dunning (2006) concedes that Mathews' view may have some merit. The country studies in this volume shed light on this interesting controversy.

The other half of the first research question brings into focus country- and industry-level variables that shape the competitive advantage of firms. We know from prior work on clusters and the competitive advantage of nations (Porter 1990) that a country's endowments – such as labor, skills, capital, home demand, quality of suppliers and customers, and market-supporting institutions – affect the international competitiveness of its firms. The question is what kinds of distinctive competitive advantages emerging markets may bestow on their firms, because of distinctive contextual factors, such as their lower level of development, their status as late-industrializing countries (Amsden, 2001; Amsden and Chu, 2003), the weakness of their institutions (Khanna and Palepu, 1997 and 2005), or the faster growth of their markets.

The second question was designed to look at the usual aspects of internationalization, such as which foreign markets a firm targets and why, how rapidly it internationalizes, and what modes of entry it uses to enter chosen markets. Of particular interest was the question of when EMNEs target their exports and investments towards other emerging markets and when they do so towards rich-country markets, such as the US, Europe, and Japan. In terms of modes of entry, a question of interest was when an EMNE pursues organic growth and when it engages in cross-border acquisitions, and why.

The internationalization process, again, is an area in which extant literature offers some answers, but the relevance of those findings for EMNEs is unclear. The dominant framework here is the stages-model of internationalization, which grew out of research on Scandinavian manufacturing firms internationalizing within Europe in the 1970s (Johanson and Vahlne, 1977). While offering excellent insights, its contextual parameters were not always recognized in subsequent studies, as a result of which it yielded quite mixed findings when applied, for example, to Japanese firms expanding into the US in the 1980s or to Dot Com firms globalizing rapidly in the 1990s (Rhee and Cheng, 2002). The relevance of the stages-model to EMNEs is brought into question by the fact that emerging economies are different from developed economies in many respects, that EMNEs frequently invest up-market into advanced countries (a scenario not considered in the stages-model), and they are internationalizing at a time when the technological context and economic policy environment are quite different from what prevailed in the 1960s or 1970s.

In summary, a good part of the IB literature consists of context-free generalizations at high levels of abstraction, or context-dependent generalizations at much lower levels of abstraction. The former apply universally, but are too broad to guide managerial decision making or policy making. The latter are much more specific and useful to decision makers, but their applicability is often limited to the particular contexts (space and time) in which they originated. What is needed is theory in between that incorporates contextual variables as contingencies.

Some IB theories explicitly recognize the role of context. An example is the product cycle hypothesis (Vernon, 1966), which grew out of an effort to explain the nature of US exports, outward FDI, and imports, to or from Western Europe and developing countries. Its reasoning included key contextual variables, such as America's lead in per-capita income and technology relative to Europe, and the latter's lead in these same areas relative to developing countries. When America's income and technological lead over Europe narrowed, the original product cycle hypothesis needed modification (Vernon, 1979).

And there's the difficulty with context-dependent models – *they often do not survive unscathed across space (countries) and time.* Countries differ so much from one another on so many dimensions and the world changes so much from one decade to the next that context-dependent theories must be continually revised. It is daunting to develop models that incorporate so many contextual variables, or to distill the complexity down to a parsimonious and stable set of variables.

From our point of view, there are at least four dimensions of context that need to be taken into account in IB research. First, there is the home-country context, one aspect of which is highlighted in Figure 1.1 – that is, a country's level of development. But countries differ along other important dimensions as well, such as their endowment of natural resources, the quality of their institutions, the size of their economies, their human capital, and so on.

Second, to understand firm internationalization, one must recognize industry context, because the globalization potential of industries varies widely, as argued by Yip (1989), and the dynamics of internationalization varies in different stages of the product life cycle, as illustrated by the product cycle hypothesis.

Third, the issues that arise in internationalization are quite different in the early stages of that process, when firms are building global presence, than in the later stages, when the firm has already built a sprawling network of overseas subsidiaries. The impact of the home-country on a firm's competitive advantages, for instance, is more pronounced in the early stages of internationalization than in later stages. It is easy to forget that IB, as a serious field of study, began only in the 1960s, shortly after the Academy of International Business (AIB) was established in 1959; AIB's main organ, the *Journal of International Business Studies*, began publishing only in 1970. By this time, US firms had already built a significant international presence and accounted for 55% of the world's outward stock of FDI, compared to only 6% in 1914 (see Table 1.1). It is only natural that as the IB field took off in the US, researchers would focus on contemporary problems facing large American MNEs, which included managing their global networks, coping with conflicting pressures from different markets and governments, or growing the enterprise at the margin by entering new markets, such as developing countries. Only business historians paid much attention to the question of how large US or

Table 1.1 *Share of selected countries in worldwide stock of outward FDI, various years*

Region/Country	Years				
	1914	1969	1980	1990	2006
Europe[#]	93%	43.2%	41.1%	49.5%[#]	57.0%[#]
UK	50%	16.2%	14.1%	12.8%	11.9%
France		n.a.	4.2%	6.1%	8.7%
Germany }	43%	n.a.	7.5%	8.5%	8.1%
Netherlands		n.a.	7.4%	6.0%	5.2%
United States	6%	55%	37.7%	24.3%	19.1%
Japan	0%	1.3%	3.4%	11.2%	3.6%
Emerging Markets[@]	0%	0%	12.7%	8.3%	12.8%
Worldwide OFDI stock (US$ B)	n.a.	n.a.	571	1791	12474

Notes:
[#] Europe had a secular decline from 1914 to 1980 but then began to reverse course, with the growth of intra-EU (European Union) FDI, following the Single European Act of 1986 and the creation of the euro
[@] Reported as "developing economies" in UNCTAD's FDI statistics
Source: Aharoni and Ramamurti (2008), with 2006 data from UNCTAD (2007: 255)

European MNEs became multinational firms in the first place (see, e.g., Wilkins, 1974; and Franco, 1976). On the other hand, building global presence was the key challenge facing EMNEs in the early 2000s. Even the pioneering EMNEs listed in the first paragraph of this chapter relied heavily in 2007 on exports, and much of their overseas production came into being only after 2000. Thus, studying EMNEs provides an opportunity to revisit the issues that arise as firms internationalize – and that too in a contemporary twenty-first century context.

That brings us to the final contextual factor that IB theory must take into account, namely the temporal context, because the world can change so profoundly from one decade to the next. One important area of change in the past two decades has been the economic policy environment, which in many emerging economies has changed from being highly closed to relatively open, in matters such as domestic regulation, international trade, and international investment. The

international policy environment has also changed in the past two
decades, with agreements such as the Uruguay Round taking effect
and institutions such as the World Trade Organization (WTO) coming into existence. The other profound change has been in the realm of
technology, especially in information, computing, and communications technologies, which have lowered the costs and increased the
benefits of internationalization, while opening up services to international trade in unprecedented ways.

Given that the aim of this project was to obtain substantive answers
to the three research questions we began with, we could not ignore
context, even though the contexts we are interested in are under-
researched (Cells 3 and 4) and manifestly different from the US and
Europe, where mainstream IB ideas were developed. Cell 4, in particular, has not been studied much at all, and it could well warrant
new explanations or significant modification of existing theories.

To sum up, our goal is *to understand how firms originating in
emerging markets and operating in different industries build global
presence in the contemporary economic environment.* In pursuing this
goal, we have to be careful not to fall into the trap of assuming that
Cells 3 and 4 are so unique that none of the past research on Cells 1
and 2 will be relevant to our understanding of them, nor should we
limit ourselves to only those concepts or frameworks developed from
studying Cell 1 and 2 situations.

Overview of the book

Each country study in Part II focuses on the three research questions
mentioned earlier. No particular theoretical lens was prescribed,
although most authors drew frameworks from the IB literature.
Authors were requested to build their country analysis through micro-
level case studies of important firms that had internationalized, rather
than focus just on macro trends, such as the volumes of outward FDI
flow, its sector breakdown, its geographic distribution, and so on.
They were encouraged to explore why certain firms in certain industries in each country were in the vanguard of internationalization.
The studies were expected to be descriptive or positive rather than
normative; no attempt was to be made to assess the effectiveness
of internationalization strategies, using performance metrics such as a
firm's growth rate, market share, profitability, or market capitalization.

In the mid-2000s, the jury was still out on the long-term viability or performance implications of the strategies being pursued by EMNEs.

Our sample of countries includes the famous quartet of Brazil, Russia, India, and China, as well as two other large emerging economies, Mexico and South Africa (see Table 1.2). Notable omissions include Asian economies that opened up to globalization in the 1970s and 1980s – such as South Korea and Taiwan, whose trailblazing experiences would have served as a valuable backdrop for studying the experiences of late-globalizing countries. Unfortunately, authors who we had expected to write on those countries were unable to participate in the project. Nevertheless, Amsden's essay (Chapter 4) draws on the experience of both countries, given her extensive prior work in those settings (Amsden 1989; Amsden and Chu, 2003). On the other hand, our sample includes two countries – Thailand and Israel – that may surprise some readers. We thought Thailand was interesting because it had not spawned many EMNEs, even though it was a high-growth economy, in a high-growth region, and the recipient of considerable inward FDI. Labeling Israel an "emerging economy" is debatable, because its 2006 per-capita income of $23,300 is comparable to that of many industrialized countries and thrice that of the next richest country in our sample, Mexico. Yet, the country's very small size and its exceptional record in spawning EMNEs made it an interesting case for inclusion. In short, while the project's sample selection was mostly deliberate, it was opportunistic at the margin, taking advantage of leading IB scholars willing to collaborate on the project.

The book consists of three parts. The first introduces the topic and the issues surrounding EMNEs. The second, which is the heart of the book, analyzes the experience of fledgling MNEs in eight emerging markets, guided by the project's research questions. The final part presents conclusions and suggestions for future research.

Part I includes an essay by Louis T. Wells Jr., who pioneered research on multinationals from developing countries in the 1970s, resulting in the seminal work, *Third World Multinationals* (1983). Wells' essay highlights areas in which his original work is still valid as well as new issues raised by EMNEs. In the next essay, Alan M. Rugman argues that EMNEs are neither truly novel (compared to MNEs that came before) nor particularly important actors in the global economy, compared to US, European, or Japanese MNEs that

Table 1.2 *Profile of sample countries (in order of appearance in Part II)*

Country (authors)	GDP, 2006 (US$ B)	Per-capita GDP, 2006 (US$)	Population (millions)	Examples of EMNEs discussed in chapter (in alphabetical order)
China (Williamson and Zeng)	2,527	1,914	1,320	China International Marine Containers, Haier, HiSense, Huawei, Lenovo, Pearl River Piano, Wanxiang, Xi'an Aircraft Co.
India (Ramamurti and Singh)	805	712	1,130	Dr. Reddy's, Hindalco, Infosys, Mahindra & Mahindra, Ranbaxy, Suzlon Energy, Tata Group, Wipro
Russia (McCarthy, Puffer, and Vikhanski)	734	5,205	141	Evraz, Gazprom, Lukoil, Norilsk Nickel, Rosneft, Severstal, United RusAL, VimpelCom
Brazil (Fleury and Fleury)	967	5,089	190	COTEMINAS, CSN, Duratex, Embraer, Gerdau, InBev/AmBev, Marcopolo, Petrobras, SABO, TIGRE, Vale (CVRD), WEG
South Africa (Goldstein and Prichard)	201	4,568	44	ABSA, Aveng, MTN, Old Mutual, SABMiller, Sasol, Standard Bank, Telkom, Woolworths Holdings
Mexico (Lessard and Lucea)	743	6,880	108	CEMEX
Thailand (Pananond)	198	3,046	65	Charoen Pokphand Group, Siam Cement Group, PTT, S&P Group
Israel (Aharoni)	140	23,300	6	Check Point Software, Elscint, Scitex, Teva Pharmaceutical Industries

account for most of the world's trade and FDI stock. In Chapter 4, Alice Amsden takes the opposite view to Rugman's, arguing that the developmental implications of indigenous firms in emerging economies are quite different from those of foreign-owned firms.

Part II, which presents the country studies, begins with the two low-income, mega-population economies in our sample – China and India (see Table 1.2). These are followed by five middle-income countries with varying degrees of natural resource endowments: at the high end of natural resource endowment is Russia, followed by the other four countries – Brazil, South Africa, Mexico, and Thailand. The last case, Israel, is unique in that it is both much richer than the other countries and much tinier in terms of population and gross domestic product (GDP). The three parameters used to describe these eight countries – economic size, per-capita income, and natural resource endowment – appeared, a priori, to be important country-level variables that would influence the types of EMNEs produced by countries. China and India, with their vast home markets and low incomes, were expected to spawn quite different EMNEs than South Africa or Russia, with their vast, exportable mineral resources, and still different from those spawned by tiny Israel. However, this initial guess about which country-level variables were important was only a provisional, working hypothesis, to be revisited after the country studies were completed. In the end, other country-specific variables, such as the quality of human capital and the availability of local entrepreneurs, turned out also to be important determinants of whether and how indigenous firms would internationalize.

References

Aharoni, Yair and Ravi Ramamurti. 2008. The Internationalization of Multinationals. In Jean Boddewyn (ed.), *The Evolution of International Business Scholarship: AIB Fellows on the First 50 Years and Beyond*. Amsterdam: Elsevier, pp. 171–201.

Amsden, Alice H. 1989. *Asia's Next Giant: South Korea and Late Industrialization*. Oxford: Oxford University Press.

Amsden, A. 2001. *The Rise of 'the Rest'. Challenges to the West from Late-Industrializing Economies*. Oxford: Oxford University Press.

Amsden, A. and Wan-wen Chu. 2003. *Beyond Late Development: Taiwan's Upgrading Policies*. Cambridge, MA: MIT Press.

Amsden, Alice H. and Takashi Hikino. 1994. Project Execution Capability, Organizational Know-How and Conglomerate Corporate Growth in Late Industrialization. *Industrial and Corporate Change*, Vol. 3, No. 1: 111–147.

Aulakh, Preet S. 2007. Emerging Multinationals from Developing Economies: Motivations, Paths, and Performance. *Journal of International Management*, Vol. 13, No. 3: 235–240.

Boston Consulting Group. 2006. *The New Global Challengers: How 100 Top Companies from Rapidly Developing Economies are Changing the World*. Boston: Boston Consulting Group (May 2006).

Buckley, Peter J., L. Jeremy Clegg, Adam R. Cross, Xin Liu, Hinrich Voss, and Ping Zheng. 2007. The Determinants of Chinese Outward Foreign Investment. *Journal of International Business Studies*, Vol. 38, No. 4 (July): 499–518.

BusinessWeek. 2006. Emerging Giants. July 31.

Child, John and Suzana B. Rodrigues. 2005. The Internationalization of Chinese Firms: A Case for Theoretical Extension? *Management and Organization Review*, Vol. 1, No. 3 (November): 381–410.

Dunning, J. H. 1977. Trade, Location of Economic Activity and the MNE: A Search for an Eclectic Approach. In B. Ohlin, P. O. Hesselborn, and P. M. Wijkman (eds.), *The International Allocation of Economic Activity*. London: Macmillan, pp. 395–418.

Dunning, John. 2006. Comment on *Dragon Multinationals*: New Players in 21st Century Globalization. *Asia Pacific Journal of Management*, Vol. 23, No. 2 (June): 139–141.

Economist. 2007. Globalization's Offspring. April 4.

Franco, L. G. 1976. *The European Multinationals*. New York: Harper & Row.

Ghemawat, Pankaj and Jamie L. Matthews. 2000. *The Globalization of Cemex*. Boston, MA: Harvard Business School Publishing, No. 9701017.

Goldstein, Andrea. 2007. *Multinational Companies from Emerging Economies*. New York: Palgrave-Macmillan.

Johanson, Jan and Jan-Eric Vahlne. 1977. The Internationalization Process of the Firm: A Model of Knowledge Development and Increasing Foreign Market Commitments. *Journal of International Business Studies*, Vol. 8, No. 1: 23–32.

Khanna, Tarun and Krishna Palepu. 2006. Emerging Giants: Building World-Class Companies in Developing Countries. *Harvard Business Review*, Vol. 84, No. 10 (October): 60–69.

Khanna, T. and Krishna Palepu. 2005. *Spotting Institutional Voids in Emerging Markets*. Boston, MA: Harvard Business School Publishing, Note No. 9106014.

Khanna, Tarun and Krishna Palepu. 1997. Why Focused Strategies May Be Wrong for Emerging Markets. *Harvard Business Review*, (July), Reprint 97404.

Kobrin, Stephen J. 1977. Comment. In Tamir Agmon and Charles P. Kindleberger (eds.), *Multinationals from Small Countries.* Cambridge, MA: MIT Press, pp. 157–165.

Kumar, Krishna. 1982. Third World multinationals: A growing force in international relations. *International Studies Quarterly*, Vol. 26, No. 3 (September): 397–424.

Lall, Sanjaya. 1983. (ed.) *The New Multinationals: The Spread of Third World Enterprises.* Chichester, UK, and New York: John Wiley, IRM series on multinationals.

Lecraw, D. 1977. Direct Investment by Firms from Less-Developed Countries. *Oxford Economic Papers*, Vol. 29, No. 3 (November): 442–457.

Luo, Yadong and Rosalie L. Tung. 2007. International Expansion of Emerging Market Enterprises: A Springboard Perspective. *Journal of International Business Studies*, Vol. 38, No. 4: 481–498.

Mathews, John A. 2002. *Dragon Multinational: A New Model for Global Growth.* Oxford and New York: Oxford University Press.

Narula, Rajneesh. 2006. Globalization, New Ecologies, New Zoologies, and the Purported Death of the Eclectic Paradigm. *Asia Pacific Journal of Management*, Vol. 23, No. 3 (June): 143–152.

Palmisano, Samuel J. 2006. The Globally Integrated Enterprise. *Foreign Affairs*, Vol. 85, No. 3 (May/June): 127–136.

Porter, Michael E. 1990. *Competitive Advantage of Nations.* New York: Free Press.

Ramamurti, Ravi. 2004. Developing Countries and MNEs: Extending and Enriching the Research Agenda. *Journal of International Business Studies*, Vol. 35: 277–283.

Rhee, Jay Hyuk and Joseph L. C. Cheng. 2002. Foreign Market Uncertainty and Incremental Market Expansion: The Moderating Effect of Firm, Industry, and Host Country Factors. *Management International Review*, Vol. 42, No. 4: 419–439.

Sinha, Jayant. 2005. Global Champions from Emerging Markets. *McKinsey Quarterly*, No. 2: 27–35.

Tsui, Anne. 2007. From Homogenization to Pluralism: International Management Research in the Academy and Beyond. *Academy of Management Review*, Vol. 50, No. 6: 1353–1364.

UNCTAD. 2007. *World Investment Report, 2007 Transnational Corporations, Extractive Industries, and Development.* Geneva: United Nations.

van Agtmael, Antoine. 2007. *The Emerging Markets Century.* New York: Free Press.

Vernon, R. 1966. International Investment and International Trade in the Product Cycle. *Quarterly Journal of Economics,* Vol. 41 (May): 191–207.

Vernon, Raymond. 1979. The Product Cycle Hypothesis in a New International Environment. *Oxford Bulletin of Economics and Statistics,* Vol. 41, No. 4 (November): 255–267.

Weigel, Dale R., Neil F. Gregory, and Dileep M. Wagle 1998. *Lessons of Experience No. 5: Foreign Direct Investment.* International Finance Corporation and World Bank.

Wells, Louis T. Jr. 1977. The Internationalization of Firms from Developing Countries. In Tamir Agmon and Charles P. Kindleberger (eds.), *Multinationals from Small Countries.* Cambridge, MA: MIT Press, pp. 133–156.

Wells, Louis T. Jr. 1983. *Third World Multinationals: The Rise of Foreign Investment from Developing Countries.* Cambridge, MA: MIT Press.

Wilkins, Mira. 1974. *The Maturing of Multinational Enterprise: American Business Abroad from 1914 to 1970.* Cambridge, MA: Harvard University Press.

Wilson, Dominic and Roopa Purushothaman. 2003. *Dreaming with BRICs: The Path to 2050.* New York: Goldman Sachs, Global Economics Paper No. 99.

Yip, George. 1989. Global Strategy … in a World of Nations? *Sloan Management Review,* Vol. 31, No. 1: 29–41.

Zaheer, Sri. 1995. Overcoming the Liability of Foreignness. *Academy of Management Journal,* Vol. 38, No. 2 (April): 341–363.

Zeng, Ming and Peter Williamson. 2007. *Dragons at Your Door: How Chinese Cost Innovation is Disrupting Global Competition.* Boston, MA: Harvard Business School Publishing.

2 | Third World multinationals: A look back

LOUIS T. WELLS JR.

When I finished the book *Third World Multinationals: The Rise of Foreign Investment from Developing Countries*[1] in 1982, I said that I was finished with the subject. I had described a number of multinationals, proposed some explanations for the phenomenon, provided a little evidence, and hoped that others would pick up on the ideas and do more systematic research. I refused to participate in subsequent conferences on the subject and would not write any more on the topic. With perhaps two very minor exceptions, I have stuck by this commitment for the past twenty-five years.

Nevertheless, the organizers of this conference convinced me to return to the subject. After twenty-five years, it seems like a good time to reflect on early work, to ask which ideas now seem dated, or even wrong, and which might still be relevant. More important is the question of whether more recent Third World Multinational Corporations (TWMNCs) present us with questions that were not addressed in the early research, and whether past research offers broader lessons for today's researchers.

Underlying arguments of earlier work

The books by Sanjaya Lall[2] and myself were not the first pieces of research on the subject of FDI from the developing countries. Ram Gopal Agarwal, Eduardo White, Antonio Casas-Gonzalez, Marcelo Diamand, Carlos Diaz-Alejandro, Carl W. Dundas, and a few others did work in the area in the earlier part of the 1970s.[3] In general, this

---

[1] Louis T. Wells Jr., *Third World Multinationals: The Rise of Foreign Investment from Developing Countries* (Cambridge, MA: The MIT Press, 1983).

[2] Sanjaya Lall, *The New Multinationals: The Spread of Third World Enterprises* (Chichester, UK: John Wiley & Sons, 1983).

[3] See, for example, the work of Ram Gopal Agarwal, including his "Joint Ventures among Developing Asian Countries," UNCTAD TC/B/AC.19/R.7,

work drew less than would later work on the core concepts that had been built by scholars interested in multinational enterprises from the industrialized countries. Looking back, it is interesting to note that much of this work was driven by the enthusiasm of the period for South–South cooperation. One pillar of the proposed New International Economic Order – popular at the time – was the need to strengthen the developing world through various forms of cooperation among the countries of the South. Thus, the work on Latin American multinationals, for example, focused on joint ventures between Latin American enterprises of different nationalities. With the broad political agenda underlying a substantial part of the work, it is perhaps not surprising that the results drew relatively little on existing conceptual frameworks related to multinationals of the North. The fact that this work did not tie its ideas to existing concepts may also explain why it is not heavily referenced today. Here lies a warning for today's researchers: today's work on the subject should be grounded in the general theories of multinationalization if it is to make a lasting contribution.

In the late 1970s and early 1980s, Lall and I were also far from the only researchers examining TWMNCs. During this period, Krishna Kumar and Malcolm McLeod, for example, pulled together some valuable country studies into an edited volume.[4] Students, including Vinod Busjeet,[5] K. Balakrishnan,[6] Carlos Cordeiro,[7] and Dennis Encarnation,[8] took up TWMNCs as thesis subjects – in Cordeiro's case, as an undergraduate honors thesis. Donald Lecraw followed his

1975; and Eduardo White, *Empresas Multinacionales Latinoamericanas: la Perspectiva del Derecho Económico* (Mexico: Fondo de Cultura Economica, 1973). For a more complete list of work done in the early 1970s, see the bibliography in my *Third World Multinationals*.

[4] Krishna Kumar and Malcolm McLeod (eds.), *Multinationals from Developing Countries* (Lexington, MA: Lexington Books, 1981).

[5] Vinod Busjeet, "Foreign Investors from Less Developed Countries," unpublished doctoral dissertation, Harvard Business School, 1980.

[6] Although his thesis was not completed, K. Balakrishnan published some of his findings as "Indian Joint Ventures Abroad: Geographic and Industry Patterns," *Economic and Political Weekly*, Review of Management, May 1976.

[7] Carlos A. Cordeiro, "The Internationalization of Indian Firms: A Case for Direct Foreign Investment from a Less Developed Country," unpublished undergraduate honors thesis, Department of Economics, Harvard College, 1978.

[8] Findings from Dennis J. Encarnation's dissertation were published in his "The Political Economy of Indian Joint Industrial Ventures Abroad: A Study of

dissertation work with several publications on multinationals within Southeast Asia.[9] David Heenan and Warren Keegan produced an article on the subject in the *Harvard Business Review*.[10] Quite a few researchers focused largely on foreign investments into or out of particular home countries. Also during the later period, Ram Gopal Agarwal, Eduardo White, and Jaime Campos continued work that they had begun much earlier. For a more complete list of people working on the subject in the late 1970s and early 1980s, see the bibliography of my book. Of course, most of these researchers met at one or more of the various conferences that were organized on the subject in the late 1970s. The exchange of ideas provided ways of looking at the phenomenon that influenced Lall and me.

Although Lall began and ended his book with challenges to propositions in my book, that may have been largely the result of the fact that I was lucky enough to win the race to get a book out first. With hindsight and careful reading, I believe that our books have much more in common than they have differences. At a broad level, both books reflect efforts to fit the phenomenon of TWMNCs into the main paradigms that had been used to explain the emergence of multinationals from the industrialized countries. In particular, both of us subscribed to the Hymer argument that a firm generally needs some monopolistic advantages in order to survive outside its home country. This argument permeated Raymond Vernon's work on US-based multinationals and then Lawrence's Franko's work on European multinationals and Yoshi Tsurumi's and Michael Yoshino's books on Japanese multinationals. Extending the basic idea to TWMNCs did not seem like a stretch. A twist would emerge, however: the advantage of a particular TWMNC would presumably have to top strengths of potential local competitors in foreign markets and also the more traditional multinational firms from rich countries that served those markets.

Domestic Policies and Transnational Linkages," *International Organization*, Winter 1982, pp. 31–39.

[9] See, for example, Donald Lecraw, "Direct Investments by Firms from Less Developed Countries," *Oxford Economic Papers*, November 1977, pp. 442–457.

[10] David A. Heenan and Warren J. Keegan, "The Rise of Third World Multinationals," *Harvard Business Review*, January–February 1979, pp. 101–109.

Lall and I both assumed that the advantages of a firm were particularly likely to reflect characteristics of the firm's home country, another assumption that had underpinned earlier work on multinationals from the rich countries. Further, we both assumed that firms with an advantage had to have some reason that would lead them to exploit that advantage through owning a foreign subsidiary or branch. Otherwise, they would simply export their product or service from home or, if this was not feasible because of transportation, tariff costs, or the need for a physical presence, sell the advantage to a foreign entity through a licensing arrangement. That is, the literature on "internalization" that had emerged so strongly in the 1970s had affected the thinking of both of us.[11]

Finally, both my work and Lall's contained what, with hindsight, turned out to be a major flaw: neither of us really raised questions about the future of the import substitution policies that we both believed so deeply affected the strengths of many of the TWMNCs that we were observing. Remember, since World War II the fashion in development had been to build local industry by protecting it from import competition through quotas and tariffs. Neither of us predicted the emergence of the Thatcher/Reagan revolution and the subsequent "Washington Consensus" that would mean the end of the dominant development policies of the post-war period. I would like to think that this failure on our part was inevitable, but, again, with hindsight hints of change should perhaps have been apparent to us. It is, I believe, this failure that makes some of our observations seem a bit quaint and it is perhaps what has relegated our books to the shelves of antiquarian book shops. In spite of this flaw, I believe that a substantial part of what we said in 1983 is still applicable today.

Dated ideas

In fact, most of our ideas that have not survived well are connected with our failure to recognize the imminent demise of import substitution.

In my book I emphasized the advantages that some TWMNCs held in the form of technology particularly suited to small-scale and labor-intensive manufacture, and know-how that enabled firms to use

---

[11] This was contributed particularly by Peter Buckley and Mark Casson and Alan Rugman.

locally available materials to substitute for imported materials. Their mastery of small-scale technology had arisen from a need to serve autarchic home markets, safe from imports of mass-produced products from abroad. The small-scale technology was, of course, often an adaptation of technology originally imported from the rich countries. The observed labor intensity of the subsidiaries of TWMNCs was, I argued, associated with small-scale manufacture, because the necessary adaptation to mass production techniques generally substituted labor for capital. Of course, the technology was likely "efficient" in terms of cost only in countries where wages were low. Whether the resulting unit production costs were lower than those of large-scale technologies mattered little as long as tariffs kept out products produced at high volumes in larger markets. Since other developing countries also protected their markets, the special skills of an innovative firm were useful not only in the countries where they were developed, but also elsewhere in the developing world. The advantages of some TWMNCs in having technologies that allowed them to substitute local materials for imported materials had also been developed as a result of import substitution. It was difficult or expensive in many developing countries to import the "right" materials into protected markets. Firms that had generated ways of using locally available substitutes often found themselves with a firm-specific advantage (FSA) that they could exploit in other import-substituting countries.

Lall argued that my data showing that the subsidiaries of TWMNCs were smaller than those of the traditional multinationals did not *prove* the small-scale hypothesis. They did not show that the technology itself was different. I agree that this was not totally convincing evidence. On the other hand, considerable case information supported the hypothesis. I still believe that the hypothesis was accurate at the time.

Lall himself turned to closed home markets for quite similar hypotheses about FSAs. For example, he attributed the strength of Indian-based multinationals in part to their development of technology at home that responded to the closed nature of the Indian market. The firms then exported the technology to countries "needing outdated and simpler but adapted technology."[12] Presumably that need

---

[12] Lall, *The New Multinationals*, p. 254.

might be associated with small markets, but it could also have been associated with the shortage of skills to operate and maintain more sophisticated equipment. Although he was not altogether clear on the characteristics of the technology that was exported to subsidiaries, and perhaps appropriately so, Lall and I were not very far apart.

Of course the decline in import substitution strategies meant the virtual demise of the particular advantages associated with know-how developed for closed markets – whether those advantages were adaptation to scale, labor costs, skill availability, scarcity of the "right" materials, or all four factors. If lower costs were generally associated with large-volume production (to be sure, an assumption), in the new world small markets could and would be supplied from large-volume plants located elsewhere. Or, large-volume plants could be located in smaller countries and rely on export markets elsewhere to utilize their capacity. For sure, some firms in developing countries have continued in their home markets to substitute local materials for imported ones that might otherwise dominate production. For example, Packages Ltd. in Lahore, Pakistan, still uses local materials to substitute for pulpwood in the manufacture of cardboard for boxes. But this kind of skill has become less of an exportable advantage as it has grown easier in most countries to import the more commonly used materials from elsewhere.

Ideas still relevant

Although the special advantages that firms acquired because of their protected home markets have probably largely disappeared with the spread of various versions of the "Washington Consensus," other ideas in the earlier work remain useful.

Search for cheaper labor

Both Lall and I noted the frequency with which labor-intensive *export* manufacturers in East Asia were opening subsidiaries in still lower-wage countries. In fact, it was observing these investors that attracted me to the topic in the first place.

In explaining the proliferation of garment-making subsidiaries of East Asian-based firms, I relied heavily on my belief that the original impetus for this kind of investment had been the network of quotas that had been negotiated with the rich countries under the Multi-Fibre Arrangement. Manufacturers from Hong Kong, in particular, responded to the quotas governing their exports by locating plants in other countries that were not yet subject to quota restrictions or that offered unused quotas. Southeast Asian countries were the early beneficiaries of these investments, but they eventually reached Sri Lanka, Mauritius, and elsewhere.

Although Lall and I both failed to predict the demise of the quota system that controlled garment exports from the developing countries, the phenomenon we were seeing was not solely the result of the restrictions negotiated by the rich countries. It was also caused by rising wages in the rapidly growing East Asian countries, particularly in Korea, Taiwan, and Hong Kong. Lall called the resulting moves from the richer developing countries to the poorer ones a "mini-product cycle." Accordingly, it was a continuation of the product cycle model that had been used to explain the shift of production location from rich countries to lower-income sites as products matured and costs grew increasingly important in the choice of production site.

The original product cycle model, however, did not provide clear explanations as to when FDI would be the vehicle for moving production down the ladder of development. For the Third World garment firms, the explanation surely did not lie in technology. Hong Kong firms used cutting and sewing equipment and techniques that were easily available to, say, an Indonesian entrepreneur who might take up the business. Rather, I argued in *Third World Multinationals*, direct investment was the vehicle through which location shifted because of the relationship that had been established between Hong Kong and other East Asian suppliers with their rich-country buyers. Once a supplier had built a track record for quality production and timely delivery, that supplier had an advantage over potential local competitors in, say, Indonesia or Mauritius. Direct investment was the way to capitalize on that advantage.

Export-oriented investments similar to those for garment manufacture continued to move down the ladder of development even for products that did not face quotas, or after quotas had disappeared. For example, Korean and Taiwanese sports shoe and glove manufacturers located subsidiaries in Indonesia, Thailand, and the Philippines, even though these products were not subject to the Multi-Fibre

Arrangement. In his work, Lall wisely put more emphasis on labor costs as the driving force, while I probably overemphasized the impact of quotas on a phenomenon that quotas likely encouraged, rather than created.

Even today, one can find many cases of TWMNCs that are moving production down the ladder of development. The phenomenon seems to have changed little, although it incorporates more industries than at the time of our earlier work.

Innovation of products for emerging markets

My book reported that TWMNCs also developed innovative products, not only machinery and production techniques, that were particularly suited to emerging markets. The book pointed out the amusingly named Gurgel, a Brazilian automobile that was not only suitable for small-scale manufacture (because of its fiberglass body) but which also came in electric and alcohol powered versions, reflecting the scarcity of petroleum fuels in Brazil. At the time of the study, the company was allegedly exporting a quarter of its output and planning plants in Panama and Ecuador. Yet, the firm eventually failed, in the 1990s. My study similarly described Brazilian manufacturers of household appliances designed to resist the deterioration so common to mechanical equipment in the humid tropics; at the time, the products were being sold in Africa. I have not heard recently of the special Brazilian appliances. It may be that these kinds of innovations were too easily copied by other firms and provided no sustainable advantages on which innovating firms could build.

No doubt innovative products are still being developed by firms in Third World markets and eventually being exported to and perhaps manufactured in other similar markets by their originators. One wonders, however, whether the innovators will become lasting multinationals. If they are to do so, they may have to possess strong marketing skills that will enable them to lock in their technical advantages through brands that lead to consumer loyalty. Neither Lall nor I thought that TWMNCs in the 1970s were strong on the marketing side. If they still lack these skills, they may become temporary multinationals, with their innovations soon copied by others.

Firms have developed other kinds of innovative consumer products for their home markets but which have also appealed to related ethnic groups abroad. Inca Kola, a Peruvian cola producer, was an illustration that I used. It had established bottling plants outside Peru, primarily serving Latin American Diaspora communities. Yet, in 1997 Inca Kola sold at least 50 percent of its equity to Coca Cola. Apparently its marketing skills – adapted as they were to the Peruvian market – were not sufficient to ward off competition from rich-country multinationals. After Coca Cola bought a share in Inca Kola, Coca Cola bottled the Peruvian drink in Ecuador and in New York; the original Peruvian company could no longer accurately be called a TWMNC.

The shortage of marketing skills – particularly in branding – may have affected other TWMNCs in similar ways. Indofood Sukses Makmur, a strong Indonesian producer and exporter of instant noodles and other food products, eventually went into a joint venture with Pepsi for one of its brand-intensive lines. Packages, a TWMNC referred to earlier, sold part of its shares in its Milkpak venture to Nestlé, when the parent added brand-intensive food products to its more commodity-like packaging materials.

Anecdotal evidence suggests that TWMNCs are still weak when it comes to developing brands. TWMNCs have joined with traditional multinationals or even acquired them to obtain marketing skills that they needed. One well-known example is the acquisition by the Chinese firm Lenovo of IBM's PC business. It appears that the goal was primarily the name. I will turn briefly to this and other cases later. Yet, there are some new multinationals from the developing countries that may be exceptions; they may even suggest that the lack of branding skills is disappearing. I hope that some current researchers will look further into the relationship between TWMNCs and marketing – and particularly branding – abilities.

Other conventional explanations

Twenty-five years ago I tried to explain some of the internationalization of Third World companies by pointing out phenomena that were similar to those that had pushed multinationals from the rich countries to establish subsidiaries abroad. Some of these explanations are as relevant today as in the past.

For example, suppliers to firms that set up overseas operations are often compelled to follow their customers. This is true for manufacturers of components – manufacturers of sports shoe components have followed sports shoe manufacturers from Korea to Indonesia – but also for firms that provide services. Banks illustrate. A leading South African bank may see opportunities with domestic customers in neighboring countries, but it seems even more likely that it is driven to set up branches in those countries to service other South African firms that have made direct investments there. In the absence of a multinational network, a bank is likely to lose both foreign and domestic business to its more internationalized competitors.

Another pattern observed at the time was that of successful exporters of certain manufactured goods that felt compelled to set up foreign affiliates to provide services – for distribution, final assembly, or maintenance, for example – to support their exports. This is an old pattern that appears to remain quite important.

Perhaps more controversial are the firms that have tried to source their raw materials abroad. Earlier research identified mining companies in developing countries that had used their skills to operate mines in other countries. Presumably, the more recent acquisition of Inco by CVRD of Brazil simply continues that pattern.[13] But the drive for vertical integration is different, and generally runs counter to the trend among multinationals of the industrialized countries. The phenomenon was, and remains, poorly understood. Moreover, it seems to have become more important with the emergence of investors from China. I will turn to the issue in my later list of questions that call for a good deal more research.

Another phenomenon that seemed to explain some internationalization of firms in the 1970s was the need on the part of owners to diversify their risks. With political instability a possibility at home, some company owners seemed to want to hold assets elsewhere, in case they had to flee. Of course, that begs the question of why they did not satisfy this need through portfolio investment, rather than by engaging in direct investment. The question stood out particularly strongly since, in a number of cases, the foreign holdings had little to do with the parent business.

---

[13] For implications of the acquisition for Goro Nickel, in New Caledonia, see Raphael Minder, "Taking the Caledonian Road to Nickel Riches," *Financial Times*, June 7, 2007, p. 17.

I believe that the drive for diversifying risk had, and still has, a peculiar twist when it comes to TWMNCs. Firms – or, more accurately, their owners – have wanted more assurances than financial assets alone could offer. They desired a business outside their country of residence which they could manage in the event that they had to leave home. At the time I did my research, I noted that a number of such investors were ethnic Chinese Indonesians, based in a country that had in the past turned hostile to their ethnic group. This explanation remained, however, no more than a hypothesis. But it is one that perhaps ought to be resurrected today to explore why so many owner-managed firms from emerging markets – and particularly white owners from South Africa – have undertaken direct investment abroad. Might the motivations be similar?

New phenomena?

Recent expansion of TWMNCs has almost certainly incorporated new phenomena, as well. In fact, news articles report on a number of TWMNCs that do not seem to fit the old hypotheses at all. To be sure, one might find a few early examples of almost anything, but investments similar to some recent ones were sufficiently rare that they attracted little attention from researchers in the past. Some examples follow.

State investment

One noticeable "new" category of TWMNCs comprises firms that are owned by their home government. So important have these new firms become that the *Financial Times* titled an article "How State Capitalism Could Change the World."[14] The article reported on state-owned investments from China, Singapore, and the Middle East. But foreign investment by state-owned firms appears to be a disparate category that researchers will have to disaggregate.

The spread of Chinese state-owned or state-controlled firms abroad may be connected with national strategic objectives that have little

---

[14] Gerard Lyons, "How State Capitalism Could Change the World," *Financial Times*, June 8, 2007.

to do with the usual objectives of private firms. Some of the most publicized is investment in raw material sources. Although this kind of investment may serve the interests of the firm in tying raw materials into their processing facilities, it might also be motivated by a broader national interest. CNOOC's activities illustrate this.

On the other hand, at least some significant part of Chinese investment, or offers of investment by the Chinese, is not directly in raw material projects. In particular, some of the recent proposals made by the Chinese in Africa and in Indonesia include infrastructure projects. Some offers specify very low rates for, say, electricity from the projects. One wonders whether there are broader foreign policy objectives that this investment might support, as well. We simply do not have any systematic knowledge about the motivations that lie behind these investments. In fact, many of them remain just offers.

On the other hand, investments by government or quasi government firms from Singapore and the Gulf States are likely driven primarily by profit goals. In important ways they may be similar to the old "free-standing" companies of Great Britain and elsewhere that exploited their favorable access to capital markets to expand abroad.[15] About 25 percent of the equity of MTC of Kuwait, for example, is owned by the government of Kuwait. Its website emphasizes the large amount of capital at its disposal. Moreover, the company seems to have a track-record that gives it access to International Finance Corporation funds.[16] MTC has used its resources to acquire Celtel, itself an interesting company founded by a Sudan-born Britisher.

In the case of Singapore and governments in the Gulf States, one also wonders why these capital-rich enterprises have invested directly rather than holding tradable securities. To be sure, one could argue that Dubai Ports World has developed exportable skills through its home-country experience and its established relationships with shipping companies. But it remains doubtful that MTC has any real advantages over potential competitors in most of its product lines, beyond its ability to obtain capital. If it indeed has no other

---

[15] For a history of "free-standing" investors, see Mira Wilkins and Harm Schröter (eds.), *The Free-Standing Company in the World Economy 1830–1996* (New York: Oxford University Press, 1998).

[16] Alec Russell, "World Bank to Finance African Phone Networks," *Financial Times*, June 13, 2007.

competitive advantage, one has to ask whether it is likely to be enduring as a multinational enterprise. It was rare for the old British free-standing companies to outlast British colonial rule and the development of capital markets elsewhere.[17] It seems quite possible that firms like MTC will face a fate similar to the old free-standing multinationals.

Search for marketing skills

Most of the firms described in our old studies did not have strong brand names, as I mentioned earlier. I also suggested that the lack of branding and other marketing skills might limit their ability to continue for long to exploit their innovations outside their home countries.

It appears, however, that some TWMNCs have found a way to obtain the needed marketing skills, by collaborating with multi-nationals from the rich countries, or even by acquiring all or parts of them. I have mentioned Lenovo's acquisition of IBM's PC business; Packages' sale of some of its equity in Milkpak to Nestlé; Inca Kola's equity sale to Coca Cola; and Indofood Sukses Makmur's tie with Pepsi. Although we do not know a great deal about these purchases or joint ventures, they appear to have been important ways to address the need for marketing know-how on the part of TWMNCs.

We also know little about how the cell phone companies that have spread through Africa obtained their marketing skills. Vodacom, based in South Africa, presumably adapted the know-how of its affiliate, Vodafone, to Third World markets. And maybe Celtel was an exception that developed its marketing from its original home market, but it did initially have connections with MCI, another possible source. This is a fertile field for research, especially for scholars with a strong interest in marketing.

---

[17] In fact, the demise of some of the old free-standing companies led directly to a few TWMNCs. Malaysians, for example, acquired one or more British plantation companies. In doing so, they bought not only Malaysian estates but also estates in other countries, creating TWMNCs. Thus, Malaysians acquired Guthrie, which in turn acquired Uniroyal's plantations in Malaysia. In the acquisition, Guthrie also ended up with plantations in Indonesia, Liberia, and elsewhere.

Relocation

A number of TWMNCs have "relocated," moving their official seat
from a developing country to, for example, London. In particular,
several South African firms, including Anglo American, illustrate. We
do not know exactly why these relocations occurred. They do seem to
be influenced by something different from what drove some Chinese
firms to seek overseas (usually Hong Kong) identities in the past.
Those firms wanted to avail themselves of the legal and tax advantages that a foreign firm had over a domestic enterprise when it
invested inside China. This "round tripping" was common. Although
South African firms must have faced different drives, they may have
escaped some South African exchange controls. I doubt, however, that
this was sufficient motivation for such major changes.

One might look at the argument of Jordan Siegel, as an alternative
explanation. His research argues that firms from developing countries
have intentionally subjected themselves to the tighter discipline of
corporate governance in, say, London in order to increase their
credibility with investors.[18] Listing on foreign exchanges was Siegel's
focus, but relocating the firm's seat might be an extreme version of the
phenomenon. On the other hand, there may well be other causes at
work that we need to understand.

Non-national

A perhaps related type of firm that has appeared more frequently than
in the past is the business from the developing country that has taken
on an international identity. For sure, this is also not an entirely new
phenomenon. Just one example: in the 1920s, the Bolivian tin baron
Simón Patiňo bought out the Chilean interests in his Bolivian mining
company and then acquired tin smelters in England and Germany.
He moved to Europe, then New York, and later Buenos Aires. By the
time of his death, the national identity of his company had become
quite blurred.

---

[18] See, for example, his "Can Foreign Firms Bond Themselves Effectively by
Renting U.S. Security Laws?" *Journal of Financial Economics*, Vol. 75, 2005,
pp. 319–359.

But even in that case, the blurring of identity was hardly as strong as that of Lakshmi Mittal's international steel group today. Although Lakshmi Mittal started by managing the international division of his family's steel company in India, in the mid-1990s he split off the operations and directed them from London. With the acquisition of Arcelor in 2006, the firm clearly established itself as a multinational, but its nationality was far from clear. Lakshmi Mittal grew up and got his business start in India; he lived in and managed from London; but the holding company was registered in the Netherlands Antilles and Mittal Steel shares were listed in New York.

The nationalities of the Indonesian-born firm Indofood Sukses Makmur and particularly of its parent, First Pacific, have become similarly unclear. First Pacific is a diversified Hong Kong firm with interests in a number of countries. First Pacific is itself controlled by Indofood's founding family (now by Anthony Salim, the son of the founder, Liem Sioe Liong, an ethnic Chinese Indonesian).

We do not have good classification systems for these firms that had their origins in the developing world but which now belong to expatriated owners or expatriated corporations. I will return particularly to Lakshmi Mittal's steel business, because it raises other interesting questions as well.

New service firms

Banks and other firms that serviced multinationals were not the only examples of service firms that grew into multinationals from developing countries. The earlier research looked at construction firms, for example. They seemed to transport low-cost labor from one developing country to provide construction services elsewhere, but mainly in other developing countries. More recently, firms from developing countries appear to have gone abroad to provide services to customers from the rich countries as well. Software and consulting multinationals illustrate.

The reasons for the internationalization of some of the software and consulting firms may be a mix of earlier phenomena. Some firms may be driven to other developing countries when skilled labor at home becomes too expensive. Tata, for example, may have gone to Latin America as low-cost technical skills became more difficult to find in

India. These motivations parallel the factors that drove the earlier garment firms abroad.

In other cases, firms appear to have gone abroad because they had to be near their customers. In this, they may be much like the earlier firms that set up subsidiaries in the rich countries to provide maintenance and repair to exports from their home countries.

Some additional research questions

There are other interesting research questions that ought to be addressed today. For example:

(1) What happened to the TWMNCs that made the wrong bet on import substitution in the past? Did they retreat to their home markets, as Packages seems to have done? Were some able to adapt in other ways to the new environment? And, if so, how?

(2) What has happened to the firms that went abroad for textile quotas? It appears that locally owned firms displaced some of the Hong Kong subsidiaries in Mauritius, but I do not believe that a similar phenomenon occurred in Indonesia. If the observation is correct, what differentiates the two sites?

(3) What happened to firms that had little in the way of advantages anyway? In particular, one might ask the question about those firms that went abroad mainly to diversify owners' portfolios in case they had to flee.

(4) A particularly important question is, how do we explain the international competitiveness of some of today's strong TWMNCs that grew out of protected markets? After all, import substitution is supposed to lead to uncompetitive firms; that was one of the principal charges that made it unpopular. But clearly, a number of successful Indian and South African multinationals, for example, were born and raised in highly protected markets. If we could understand why these firms – and not others – became competitive, there might be important implications for the development strategies of African countries today. Did more of them have managers who had been trained abroad, or did they face international exposure from exports even during import substitution days? If one can answer these questions, one might conclude that a little bit of import substitution might not be a disaster, at least in larger countries. Of course, it might take some real nerve to make this kind of suggestion.

(5) Are the Chinese wise in their efforts to own resources abroad as a way of gaining security? Some Japanese companies tried this strategy for a period, but they largely backed off.[19] With today's open markets for most raw materials, one might question the necessity and the wisdom of tying up resources through direct investment. Of course, the Chinese are not alone in the effort. Mittal is going against the historical trend of the past few decades as it tries to balance its controlled sources of iron ore with its steel-making capacity. In the case of China, however, control of the Strait of Malacca might be much more important to energy security than who owns the oil producing companies in Sudan.

(6) Do the governments of developing countries have any preference for firms from other emerging markets? In the 1970s, the politically correct answer was "of course, because they are much more sensitive to local needs." But, the facts may show otherwise. Note, for example, the problems that Brazilian investors have faced in Bolivia; Argentine investors, in Venezuela; and Chilean investors, in Argentina. Similarly, Indonesians have begun to question Singaporean ownership of Indosat, a major Indonesian telecommunications company, just as Thais have questioned the Singaporean company Temasek's holdings of a Thai telecommunications firm. Foreign ownership may be a sensitive issue whether the foreigner is from another developing country or from a rich country.

Warnings for research in the area

One advantage of presenting one's research as history is the possibility to pontificate "wisely." I will take the opportunity to pontificate, wisely or not.

Go beyond the country studies

Many of the studies of TWMNCs done in the 1970s and 1980s focused on investors from single developing countries. A number of other studies dealt with only a single host country that had attracted

---

[19] To be sure, Bridgestone is reestablishing a vertically integrated rubber industry at a time when most tire companies are content to buy their natural rubber on the world market, from unaffiliated suppliers.

investment from other developing countries. Too many researchers went no further than country studies. Country-specific research was extremely useful in providing data and ideas for the research that attempted to draw broader generalizations about the multinationalization of firms from the developing world. Without the broader work, however, I am afraid that we would remain lost in the specific details of individual countries. It remains important to go beyond country studies to look for general patterns, although those patterns might be contingent on country characteristics.

Study industries

The earlier work on TWMNCs did not include major studies of particular industries, with the possible exception of textiles. I would be tempted today to undertake a few industry studies. I would turn, for example, to the steel industry. I would start with the fact that rich-country steel companies almost never became multinationals, except through vertical integration. Yet, some developing-country steel firms have expanded internationally and become true multinational enterprises. As illustrations, note that Tata Steel took over Corus Steel, a British-Dutch steel producer; Techint, an Argentine conglomerate, controls a steel producer in Venezuela (as well as other diversified and international assets, including hospitals in Italy). Its steel company, Ternium, operates in Mexico and Argentina, as well. Lakshmi Mittal, whose enterprise we have already found difficult to classify, now holds a vast multinational steel and iron ore network. And Lakshmi Mittal's brother turns out to be a rival who has also sought to build a multinational steel enterprise.

There are dozens of questions in this complex network of TWMNC steel companies. Most important, why have Third World firms become multinationals in an industry where companies from the rich countries remained largely national? Are there real advantages to being a multinational that we have not really understood? And is vertical integration again becoming a viable strategy in such industries? Perhaps the TWMNCs are showing the way for others.

Consider the incomplete Darwinian process

Finally, there are some special problems in looking at relatively new phenomena like TWMNCs. Most of the empirical research on multinational enterprise has relied on a version of a Darwinian process. The usually unstated assumption of empirical researchers is that what we observe is what makes economic or financial sense. We assume that the mistakes have been largely weeded out; we look for rational explanations of the investments that we see.

Although the assumption is accurate enough for research on multinationals that have been established for a long time, it can be a dangerous one when many of the observations are really of quite new multinational enterprises. The data may be overwhelmed by mistakes: firms that, for example, followed a fad in investing abroad, but which do not have advantages that will allow them to survive for long periods. Time would weed them out, but time has been too short.

I am not sure what to do about this problem, but it does suggest some care in drawing the conclusion that what we see today as TWMNCs always reflects good business reasons. My bet is that there are many TWMNCs today that have invested abroad for poor reasons and will not survive long. But that is a question for researchers to address, in other chapters in this book and elsewhere.

3 | Theoretical aspects of MNEs from emerging economies

ALAN M. RUGMAN[1]

What is the current theoretical research agenda regarding the theory of latecomer or emerging economy MNEs? Currently the world's 500 largest MNEs dominate world trade and investment. In terms of FDI the world's largest firms account for 90 percent of the world total. In terms of trade they account for approximately half of world trade, as they often have a hundred or more foreign subsidiaries around the world. These data are well known to scholars in international business (see Rugman 2000 and 2005). It is through the activities of this set of very large MNEs that less developed countries are being integrated into the world's economic system.

The basic logic for this position is explained below in the next section where more details are provided about the nature and scope of the world's 500 largest MNEs. This is followed by data showing that these firms perform mainly on an intra-regional basis (rather than globally) and by data examining the specific activities of the relatively small set of large MNEs from emerging economies. These data are then integrated with the orthodox theory of MNEs to examine how MNEs from emerging economies can succeed in the world economy and act as flagship firms leading economic development.

Recent research in international business shows that FDI and the activities of MNEs are two-way streets. In terms of MNEs the traditional view is that North American, European, and Japanese MNEs build upon their strong home-region, FSAs and expand these into other regions through networks of overseas subsidiaries (Rugman 1981, 1996). More recently it has been found that the foreign

[1] I am pleased to acknowledge the excellent research assistance, in the preparation of data for many of the tables, of Dr. Chang Hoon Oh of Brock University, Canada. I also received helpful comments from participants at the Northeastern University-Wharton School Conference on MNEs from Emerging Markets, Boston, June 22–23, 2007.

subsidiaries of MNEs in emerging economies help to improve the host country macroeconomic infrastructure. In turn, this leads to the emergence of local MNEs which benefit from the upgraded infrastructure. In many ways this process mimics the Canadian history of MNEs. Canada relied upon inward FDI (mainly from the United States) for many years until in the 1980s it developed a set of world-class Canadian-owned MNEs. This transition, and the emergence of world-class Canadian MNEs, has been examined by Rugman (1987; Rugman and McIlveen, 1985).

A similar transition to a two-way system of both inbound and outbound FDI is possible in many of the world's less developed economies. There is evidence that it is already taking place in India, Korea, Singapore, Taiwan, and even in China itself. The manner in which Western MNEs have upgraded the macroeconomic infrastructure of these economies leading to the emergence of new MNEs from these host economies is discussed by Rugman and Doh (2008).

One difficulty in this research is that data are only available on publicly traded companies which are required to issue annual reports to provide information to shareholders. Thus, the list of the world's 500 largest firms is confined to those providing such information. Indeed, the rankings are done by size, namely the annual consolidated sales of each company. While for Western economies the list captures virtually all large companies, in many less developed countries there are missing firms. These include private companies, family-owned firms linked by informal networks, state-owned enterprises (SOEs), and others failing to disclose information about their activities and performance. However, the number of very large firms (with sales of $12b or more) excluded in this manner is probably relatively small.

This approach also excludes small and medium-sized enterprises (SMEs), of which there are many in less developed economies. Again, the influence of such SMEs is not a significant determinant of economic development. Many of these firms, especially the more entrepreneurial ones, need to grow and are then bought up by the larger MNEs, both foreign and domestic. To summarize, the world's 500 largest MNEs dominate world business. Logically, the set of the world's largest MNEs from emerging economies, along with the foreign MNEs in such emerging economies, will dominate business in these countries. The MNEs often serve as flagship firms that operate at the centers of large business networks and clusters, so another aspect of this is to examine the ways in which less developed countries can build manufacturing- and/or service-based clusters that will both attract foreign MNEs and also, in time, generate their own MNEs. We now turn to a more specific analysis of the data on the world's 500 largest MNEs and those in emerging economies.

The world's largest multinationals

The focus of this chapter is to identify and analyze the set of MNEs registered and based in the world's emerging markets. To do this, I take as the relevant population the world's 500 largest firms, ranked by total revenues, as compiled annually in the Fortune Global 500. This entire set of 500 firms (most of which are MNEs) was analyzed in Rugman (2005). In that study the focus was on an examination of data on the regional sales of MNEs from the "broad" triad markets of Europe, North America, and the Asia Pacific, which accounts for nearly all of the 500 firms. The total number of MNEs from the "core" triad of the EU, United States, and Japan in 2001 was 428 of the 500. In this chapter attention is paid to the MNEs from emerging markets in the list of the 500, which numbered 32 in 2001 (and 44 in 2004).

The chapter will proceed to identify this set of 32 (or 44) MNEs from emerging markets. As most of these are from the Asia Pacific, the substantive theoretical analysis of their performance will focus upon a set of Chinese MNEs. The 16 Chinese MNEs already in the 2004 list of the world's 500 largest firms provide perhaps the most interesting challenge to theories of international business, international economics, and explanations of FDI. In order to apply the relevant theory I shall adapt the basic firm- and country-level matrix (Rugman 1981) to analyze the performance of China's MNEs.

China is home to a set of large firms that can now be classified as MNEs. An MNE is defined as a firm with some foreign sales and some foreign production, usually 10 percent or more. The foreign production takes place in a wholly owned foreign subsidiary, and an MNE is also defined by having foreign subsidiaries in three or more countries (Rugman 1981). Using these definitions, basically all the firms in the Fortune Global 500 are MNEs. In the list of the world's 500 largest companies, ranked by sales for 2001, Rugman (2005) found that there were 11 Chinese MNEs. In 2004, there were 16 Chinese firms in the list. These large MNEs are discussed here as the basic set of firms that will determine the success of China in developing MNEs. This theory and analysis can be generalized to all MNEs from emerging markets.

The regional aspects of multinational enterprises

The performance of the world's 500 largest MNEs has been examined in Rugman (2005). The world's 500 largest firms, ranked by revenues, account for approximately 90 percent of the world's stock of FDI. They also account for over half of the world's trade (Rugman 2000). Recent research has shown that the vast majority of these large MNEs operate on an intra-regional basis. This information is summarized in Table 3.1. The geographic basis for the broad regions of the triad is developed and explained in Rugman (2005). Of the world's 500 largest firms a total of 379 provide data on the geographic dispersion of their sales across the three broad regions of the triad. As shown in Table 3.1, the 75 MNEs from Asia have an average of 77.9% of their sales in their home region. This is somewhat above the average for the 379 MNEs, which is 74.6%. Otherwise the 75 Asian MNEs have average revenues of $27.4b, which is only slightly less than the average for North American MNEs of $28.8b and the $31.1b for the European MNEs. In summary, the regional performance of Asian MNEs parallels that of the regional nature of business of their competitor MNEs from North America and Europe.

The asymmetric pattern of classifications reported in Table 3.1 is based on the data for year 2001, in Rugman (2005). Some petty criticisms of this book have been advanced to the effect that these data present a snapshot and do not reveal a trend towards regionalization. In fact, in Rugman (2005) it was demonstrated that these data were consistent over the time period for which firms reported their geographic distribution of sales, basically starting with fewer than 200 of the 500 largest in the late 1990s. Indeed, for 2002 data, the same pattern emerged as for 2001. To further address the nature of the need for longitudinal data, Rugman and Oh (2007) provided data for 2001–2005, which showed a stable percentage of intra-regional sales over a five-year period.

For year 2004 there were seven global firms and thirty-three bi-regionals (of which seven were host-region oriented). The vast majority (271) of the 311 firms for year 2004 were home-region

Table 3.1. *Intra-regional sales of the 500 largest firms, 2001*

	Number of MNEs	Average revenue (US$b)	Intra-regional sales (%)
Total	379 (500)	29.2 (28.0)	74.6
N. America	186 (219)	28.8 (28.5)	78.6
Europe	118 (159)	31.1 (29.0)	66.4
Asia	75 (122)	27.4 (25.8)	77.9
Emerging economies	5 (34)	23.3 (21.8)	70.4

Notes: Values in parentheses are for the entire set of the 500 largest MNEs in 2001. Only 379 MNEs' intra-regional sales can be identified. The emerging economies only include Brazil, China, Malaysia, Mexico, Republic of Korea, Russia, Singapore, and Venezuela.
Source: Based on Rugman (2005).

oriented. Of these 271 firms, their average home-region sales were 77 percent. The conclusion to be drawn from Table 3.1 (and for 2001–2005 data) is that the world's 500 largest firms operate predominately on an intra-regional basis, not globally, and that this picture is consistent over time.

Multinationals from emerging markets

In this section data are reported on MNEs from emerging markets. For year 2001, as reported in Rugman (2005), there were thirty-two such MNEs, mainly from the Asia Pacific region. Only two were from Europe: the Russian firms Gazpron and Lukoil. Another three were from the Americas: Pemex and Carso Global Telecom from Mexico, and one oil firm from Venezuela. In contrast, there were twelve firms from the Republic of Korea. Another eleven were from China, with another two from Taiwan, one from Singapore, and one from Malaysia.

Relatively few of the set of thirty-two firms from emerging economies in year 2001 provide data on the geographic dispersion of their sales. Using the 2001 data and the methodology in Rugman (2005), the following facts emerge. First, five South Korean firms provide data which show that all of them are home-region oriented. For example, POSCO has 91.9% of its sales in Asia Pacific, while Hyundai Motor has 81.6% of its sales in Asia Pacific and 18.1% in North America. The remaining three Korean firms are close to being bi-regional, but need to be classified as home-region based since more than 50% of their sales are in Asia Pacific. These include Samsung Electronics, which has 60.6% of its sales in Asia Pacific; 20.8% in North America; and 18.3% in Europe. Then LG Electronics has 60.4% of its sales in Asia Pacific; 23.6% in North America; and 11.7% in Europe. Finally, Hyundai (different from Hyundai Motor) has 56.3% of its sales in Asia Pacific; 24.2% in North America; and 10.5% in Europe.

Only one of the thirty-two firms from emerging markets is a global firm. This is Flextronics of Singapore. It has only 19.8% of its sales in its home region, but 44% in North America, and 36.2% in Europe. This firm is clearly an exception. In contrast, all other multinationals from emerging economies reporting data on regional sales are home-region based. Some of the most extreme examples come from China, although the data are sketchy. China Telecommunications has 100% of its sales at home. The Bank of China has 98.41% of its sales in Asia Pacific, and Sinopec has 90% or more in the Asia Pacific region. A related firm, Cathay Life, from Taiwan, has 100% of its sales in its home region. The pattern of dependence on sales in the home region for Asian MNEs is followed by Pemex of Mexico, which has 91.7% of its sales in North America.

Table 3.2 reports the firms from emerging markets for year 2004. The number has increased to a total of forty-four. There are now three from Russia, with one from Turkey and another from Saudi Arabia. There are still two from Mexico. Otherwise the MNEs from emerging markets are all from the Asia Pacific, including five from India. There are sixteen from China, and again two from Taiwan, one from Singapore and one from Malaysia. There are eleven from Korea. Due to the emergence of a large number of potential and actual multi-nationals from China in recent years the remainder of the chapter will focus on this group.

The data on the regional sales of these 44 MNEs from emerging markets for year 2004, in Table 3.2, shows much the same picture as the 2001 data. There are now twenty-five firms providing some evidence that they are home-region based. Only five firms are bi-regional (mostly the Korean firms, plus Flextronics). However, Flextronics is no longer a global firm, as its sales to North America have fallen below the 20% threshold to 13.83%. It is now like Samsung

Table 3.2. *The world's forty-four largest MNEs in emerging markets, 2004*

(Rank refers to rank in Fortune Global 500 based on total revenues for year 2004)

Company name	Industry	Country	Revenue (US$b)	(%) NA	(%) EUR	(%) AP
Sinopec	gas	China	75.1	na	na	>90
Samsung Electronics	electronics	Korea	71.6	23.18	21.76	54.61
State Grid	electricity	China	71.3	na	na	>90
China National Petroleum	gas	China	67.7	na	na	na
Pemex	gas	Mexico	63.7	>58.05	na	na
Hyundai Motor	motor	Korea	46.4	25.08	11.59	63.33
LG Electronics	electronics	Korea	37.8	25.24	15.60	51.16
SK	gas	Korea	37.7	na	na	na
Petronas	gas	Malaysia	36.1	na	na	>90
OAO Gazprom	gas	Russia	35.1	0.00	100.00	0.00
Indian Oil	gas	India	29.6	na	na	96.08
Lukoil	gas	Russia	28.8	na	>21.97	na
China Life Insurance	insurance	China	25.0	na	na	na
China Mobile Comm.	telecom	China	24.0	na	na	na
Ind. & Comm. Bank of China	banking	China	23.4	na	na	na
UES of Russia	electricity	Russia	22.6	na	>99.47	na
Samsung Life Insurance	insurance	Korea	22.3	na	na	na
China Telecommunications	telecom	China	21.6	0.00	0.00	na
POSCO	steel	Korea	20.9	2.21	na	93.75

Company	Industry	Country				
Korea Electric Power	electricity	Korea	20.9	na	na	na
Sinochem	chemical	China	20.4	na	na	>90
Shanghai Baosteel Group	steel	China	19.5	na	na	>90
China Construction Bank	banking	China	19.0	na	na	na
China Southern Power Grid	electricity	China	18.9	na	na	100.00
Sabic	chemical	Saudi Arabia	18.3	na	na	na
Bank Of China	banking	China	18.0	na	na	>98.41
Hutchison Whampoa	telecom	China	17.3	13.81	33.62	52.57
Hon Hai Precision Industry	electronics	Taiwan	16.2	na	na	na
PTT	gas	Thailand	16.0	na	na	>90
Flextronics International	electronic	Singapore	15.9	13.83	40.86	45.31
Koc Holding	manufacturing	Turkey	15.6	na	na	na
Hanwha	chemical	Korea	15.4	na	na	na
Agricultural Bank of China	banking	China	15.3	na	na	>90
Chinese Petroleum	gas	Taiwan	15.2	na	na	na
KT	telecom	Korea	14.9	na	na	na
Reliance Industries	gas	India	14.8	na	na	>78.24
CFE	electricity	Mexico	14.5	na	na	na
Bharat Petroleum	gas	India	14.4	0.00	0.00	100.00
COFCO	food, cereal	China	14.2	na	na	>90
Hindustan Petroleum	gas	India	14.1	0.00	0.00	100.00
Samsung	trading	Korea	13.9	3.04	3.97	93.00
SK Networks	telecom	Korea	13.8	na	na	>82.01
China First Automotive Works	motor	China	13.8	na	na	>90
Oil & Natural Gas	gas	India	13.8	na	na	>91.33

Note: NA = North America; EUR = Europe; AP = Asia Pacific
Source: Based on Rugman (2005) and annual reports for each company

Electronics, which is a bi-regional firm, with over 20% of its sales in each broad-triad region, but over 50% in its home region. Overall, the data show that the firms from emerging markets are mainly home-region based.

Before exploring the implications of the data on emerging economy multinationals, the next section reviews the relevant theory needed to analyze MNEs from such emerging markets.

Internalization theory and emerging economy MNEs

The literature in international business analyzes the growth and foreign expansion phase of MNEs. The starting point of this theory of the MNEs (Rugman 1981, 1996) is the proposition that an MNE goes abroad to further expand on its FSA. In this so-called internalization theory the FSAs are proprietary to the firm, and they can be technology based, knowledge based, or they can reflect managerial and/or marketing skills (Rugman and Verbeke 2003). Further, the large MNEs often serve as "flagship" firms at the hub of large business networks where key suppliers, distributors, and businesses in the non-government infrastructure all come together in a cluster to help promote foreign sales (Rugman and D'Cruz 2000).

There are two building blocks in the basic matrix used in international business to analyze the nature, performance, and strategies of MNEs (Rugman 1981, 1996). First, there is a set of firm-specific factors that determine the competitive advantage of an organization. We call these firm-specific advantages (FSAs). An FSA is defined as a unique capability proprietary to the organization. It may be built upon product or process technology, marketing, or distributional skills. Second, there are country factors, unique to the business in each country. They can lead to country-specific advantages (CSAs). The CSAs can be based on natural resource endowments (minerals, energy, forests) or on the labor force, and associated cultural factors.

Managers of most MNEs use strategies that build upon the interactions of CSAs and FSAs. They do this so that they can be positioned in a unique strategic space. The CSAs represent the natural factor endowments of a nation; they are based on the key variables in its aggregate production function. For example, CSAs can consist of the quantity, quality, and cost of the major factor endowment, namely resources.

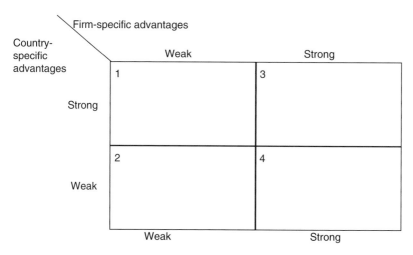

Figure 3.1 The FSA/CSA matrix

The FSAs possessed by a firm are based ultimately on its internalization of an asset, such as production knowledge, managerial, or marketing capabilities over which the firm has proprietary control. FSAs are thus related to the firm's ability to coordinate the use of the advantage in production, marketing, or the customization of services (Rugman 1981).

Using Porter's terminology, the CSAs form the basis of the global platform from which the multinational firm derives a home-base "diamond" advantage in global competition (Porter 1990). Tariff and non-tariff barriers to trade and government regulations also influence CSAs. Building on these CSAs, the firm makes decisions about the efficient global configuration and coordination between segments of its value chain (operations, marketing, research and development [R&D], and logistics). Skill in making such decisions represents a strong, managerial, firm-specific advantage (FSA).

To help formulate the strategic options of the MNE, it is useful to identify the relative strengths and weaknesses of the CSAs and FSAs that they possess. Figure 3.1, the FSA/CSA matrix, provides a useful framework for discussion of these issues. In Figure 3.1, quadrants 1, 2, and 3 can incorporate the major strategies. Quadrant 1 firms are generally the cost leadership ones; they are generally resource-based and/or mature, internationally oriented firms producing a commodity-type product. Given their late stage in the product life cycle, production FSAs flowing from the possession of intangible skills are less important than the CSAs of location and energy costs, which are the main sources of the firm's competitive advantage. Quadrant 2 firms represent inefficient, floundering firms with neither consistent strategy, nor any intrinsic CSAs or FSAs. These firms are preparing to exit or to restructure. Quadrant 2 can also represent domestically based SMEs with little global exposure. Firms in quadrant 4 are generally differentiated firms with strong FSAs in marketing and customization. These firms usually have strong brands. In quadrant 4 the FSAs dominate, so in world markets the home-country CSAs are not essential in the long run. Quadrant 3 firms generally can choose to follow any of the strategies listed above because of the strength of both their CSAs and FSAs.

It is useful to note the following two points. First, if the firm has a conglomerate structure it should be more useful to situate each division or product line individually, recognizing that different units of the diversified firm would use different generic strategies. Second, changes in the trading environment, such as the EU 1992 single-market measures, or the EU 1999 single currency, or the United States–Canada Free Trade Agreement and the North America Free Trade Agreement (NAFTA), will affect the relative CSAs of the firm. To the extent that CSAs are improved, the firms will tend to move to quadrant 3, and, to the extent that the CSAs are hampered, the firm or some of its product lines may move to exit, as in quadrant 2.

The FSAs and CSAs of emerging economy MNEs

We can analyze the role of Chinese MNEs as an example of emerging economy MNEs in general. A case can be made that the recent economic development of China is almost entirely due to FDI. The opening of the Chinese economy to foreign MNEs, first in the Special Economic Zones in the 1980s, followed by the opening of most coastal cities in the 1990s, introduced market-based efficiency to a command economy. While China is still dominated by SOEs and collectives, by 2005 foreign-owned firms accounted for one-third of production and 50 percent of exports (Thun 2005). The foreign MNEs operate on a world-class basis of competition, and they have developed efficient supply networks. Much of the privatized sector of SMEs in China has affiliated to the MNEs. Together the MNEs and SMEs are now driving forward the economic development of China. The inefficient and protected SOEs are beginning to reform and are starting to adopt more market-based strategies in the face of this new type of MNE-led domestic competition. Through this process, efficiency-based thinking is spreading from the coastal cities throughout China. In this sense, foreign MNEs are the agents of economic development for China.

This raises the question: when will China generate its own world-class MNEs? The answer is – not for ten to twenty years. While eleven Chinese firms are in the Fortune Global 500, the evidence we have suggests that none of them are truly internationalized. Indeed, these large Chinese firms are mainly SOEs, and well over 95 percent of their sales are within China (although only partial data are available for eight firms). They are still largely in the protected banking, natural resources, and telecom sectors; they show few signs of developing any proprietary FSAs which would allow them to compete internationally even on an intra-regional basis.

Indeed, when the Chinese SOEs do go abroad they build on CSAs in natural resources or they try to acquire technology. However, they are not doing well through acquisitions. Lenovo bought an obsolete IBM line of business; Baosteel bought up iron ore supplies in Brazil; Shanghai Motors bought the technologically laggard Rover of the UK; TLC bought Thomson TV and has found it difficult to upgrade. None of these acquisitions is due to a Chinese firm's FSAs; all are explained by China's CSAs. Overall, these Chinese acquisitions reveal a search for the technology, management, and strategy skills missing in Chinese firms. The objectives appear to be to secure natural resources and market access, but no useful technologies have been acquired. The Chinese MNEs still lack the internal managerial capabilities to integrate foreign acquisitions to develop anything resembling dynamic capabilities. They suffer from a Penrose effect of a lack of top management talent. This competitive disadvantage in management will take about a decade to remedy, before Chinese SOEs are competitive with Western MNEs.

Related work by Nolan (2004) finds that Chinese firms have failed to develop FSAs and are lagging well behind Western firms, especially in their lack of technology. Nolan finds no evidence that Chinese firms can develop knowledge of the systems-integration skills that characterize successful Western MNEs. The Chinese firms are protected, resource based, labor intensive, low technology, and inefficient firms. The potentially efficient SMEs are now linking to foreign MNEs, rather than to the inefficient and uncompetitive Chinese-owned SOEs. Japanese and Korean MNEs have developed FSAs whereas Chinese firms have not.

The World Bank (1993) categorized eight Asian countries into three groups: first, Japan; second, the first-generation, newly industrialized countries (Republic of Korea, Hong Kong, Taiwan, and Singapore); third, the second-generation, newly industrializing countries (Malaysia, Indonesia, and Thailand). Even though those Asian countries have experienced fast-growing and export-oriented economic growth, they have different MNEs based on CSAs.

Debrah, McGovern, and Budhwar (2000) show that Singapore's CSAs lie in skilled labor, advanced technology, advanced physical infrastructure, and advanced commercial infrastructure, while Indonesia and Malaysia have advantages in cheap (unskilled) labor and natural resources. The three other first-generation countries (and Japan) have advantages similar to those of Singapore.

Nelson and Pack (1999) explain the successful growth of the Republic of Korea and Taiwan via technology assimilation. They argue that individual firms had strong incentives to improve their efficiency-based FSAs to enable them to export rather than to engage in rent seeking in the domestic market. Brouthers, O'Donnell, and Hadjimarcou (2005) show that emerging market firms achieve higher levels of export performance when they mimic the product strategies of Western MNEs in triad nation markets rather than when they enter emerging markets or when they develop other product strategies in triad nation markets.

Due to geographical, cultural, institutional, and historical similarities the internationally successful Korean and Japanese firms can be models for Chinese firms. In contrast to the Chinese firms discussed earlier (Haier, Lenovo, etc.), Korean MNEs have acquired foreign technologies (but not really strong FSAs); for example, Samsung Electronics acquired Harris Microwave Semiconductor in 1993, and LG Electronics purchased 57.7 percent of the stock of Zenith Electronics in 1995.

Japanese firms are linked to firms in the newly industrialized Asian countries as markets for final electrical and electronic products and as customers for Japanese-made components. The first-generation, newly industrialized countries developed their technological capabilities relying on Japanese firms' FSAs. Korean and Taiwanese electronic firms acquired technology mainly through licensing and contracting arrangements with Japanese firms such as Sony, Sanyo, Matsushita, etc., between 1970 and 1980 (Hobday 1995).

Asia's multinationals

There are only sketchy data on the regional sales of firms from Asia. The home-country base of the forty-five Asian MNEs providing data on their sales in each region of the triad for 2001 data represented in Rugman (2005) shows that this set is dominated by the thirty-seven MNEs from Japan, which average 74.6% of their sales in Asia, 14.8% in North America, and 7.3% in Europe. While there are eleven Chinese MNEs in the dataset analyzed by Rugman (2005), none of them report their geographic sales across each region of the triad. The only firm from China-Taiwan reporting has 100% of its sales in Asia. I would anticipate that the other eleven MNEs from China would also have close to 100% of their sales in Asia. Table 3.3 lists the 16 Chinese firms in the top 500 for 2004, arranged by industry group.

In order to explore this, Table 3.4 reports data on the regional sales of the eight Chinese firms that provide some data on the geographic dispersion of their sales for year 2004. In Table 3.4 we can see that China Telecom and China Southern Power have 100% of their sales in Asia (indeed, virtually all of these within China itself). The Bank of China has 98.4% of its business in Asia. With the exception of Hutchison Whampoa, the other five Chinese firms have over 90% of their sales in Asia. Overall these eight large Chinese firms, most of which have the potential of being classified as MNEs, average 93.1% of their sales in Asia. I do not see that this number will fall below 90% for many years. Indeed, it is likely to be at least ten to fifteen years before the largest fifteen Chinese firms have intra-regional sales close to the world average of about 75%. Until then, the Chinese MNEs will continue to experience strong sales within China itself, with a gradual increase in foreign sales, but mostly within the Asian region.

Table 3.3. *List of Chinese MNEs in the world's 500 largest firms, 2004*

Industry	Company name	Revenue (US$b)
Banking and insurance (5)	China Life Insurance	25.0
	Industrial & Commercial Bank of China	23.4
	China Construction Bank	19.0
	Bank of China	18.0
	Agricultural Bank of China	15.3
Utility (4)	State Grid	71.3
	China Mobile Telecommunications	24.0
	China Telecommunications	21.6
	China Southern Power Grid	18.9
Natural resource manufacturing (3)	Sinopec	75.1
	China National Petroleum	67.7
	Shanghai Baosteel Group	19.5
Other manufacturing (3)	Sinochem	20.4
	COFCO	14.2
	China First Automotive Works	13.8
Other (1)	Hutchison Whampoa	17.3
Average (16)		29.0

Source: Adapted and updated from Rugman (2005). Data adapted from Fortune Global 500

Applying the FSA/CSA matrix in Asia

The logic of this chapter is that MNEs contribute to the economic development of nations, although the distribution of those benefits may vary. MNEs bring FDI, transfer technology, increase national income, provide more skilled jobs, pay taxes, and otherwise contribute to the overall macroeconomic growth of host economies. In an interesting and novel twist to this, MNEs from emerging economies build on the improved macroeconomic infrastructure created by foreign MNEs. In turn, these new indigenous emerging economy MNEs grow and help improve the prosperity of their countries as has

Table 3.4. *Regional sales of eight Chinese MNEs, 2004*

Company name	Revenue (US$b)	Regional sales(%)			
		N. America	Europe	Asia	Unidentified
Sinopec	75.1	n.a.	n.a.	> 90.0	< 10.0
China Telecom	21.6	n.a.	n.a.	100.0	0.0
Sinochem	20.4	n.a.	n.a.	> 90.0	< 10.0
China Const. Bank	19.0	n.a.	n.a.	> 90.0	< 10.0
China Southern Power	18.9	n.a.	n.a.	100.0	0.0
Bank of China	18.0	n.a.	n.a.	> 98.4	< 1.6
Hutchison Whampoa	17.3	14.0	33.0	53.0	0.0
Agri. Bank of China	15.3	n.a.	n.a.	> 90.0	< 10.0
Average	25.7 (29.0)	n.a.	n.a.	88.9	5.2

Notes: Value in parentheses is for all 16 Chinese MNEs in 500 largest MNEs in 2004. Only six of them report their regional sales. n.a. stands for not applicable. If values are larger than 90 percent, 90 percent is used for calculation.
Source: 2005 annual report for each company

occurred with the "yang" MNEs in Korea, Singapore, Taiwan, and China (see Rugman and Doh 2008). It is anticipated that the virtues of yang multinationals will also apply to MNEs from India, Latin America, Russia, and other emerging economies.

This analysis leads to two key conclusions. First, MNEs from the advanced triad economies of Europe, North America, and Japan serve to foster the development and growth of economies in poor countries. Second, building upon this improved macroeconomic infrastructure the emerging economies generate their own MNEs, thus further enhancing their growth and prosperity. This can be seen in a retroactive study of Figure 3.1 which combines the country-level and firm-level factors relevant to MNEs.

On the basis of analysis of the Chinese and Korean MNEs appearing in the list of the world's 500 largest firms, Rugman and Doh (2008) came to the following conclusions. Of primary importance is that the success of Chinese MNEs is almost entirely due to favorable country factors. Chinese MNEs are successful because they build upon abundant cheap labor, which can lead to economic efficiency in terms of cost competitiveness and low prices across a variety of manufacturing and routines-based service sectors. Such firms develop FSAs that are strongly dependent upon the nature of China's CSAs. Thus Chinese MNEs may develop economies of scale (a type of FSA), but this is determined by the country factor of cheap labor rather than any inherent proprietary FSAs. This means that the competitiveness of Chinese manufacturing relies on country factors not firm factors.

Chinese MNEs are also successful due to relatively cheap money. In order to help process the large balance of trade surplus with Western economies such as the United States, the Chinese banking system (with government guidance and support) has provided cheap financing to Chinese businesses. This has led to outward FDI in the form of takeovers and acquisitions of foreign firms especially in the natural resource sectors. In the past few years Chinese MNEs have been active in FDI in the energy sector and in the acquisition of minerals in Africa. Again, this is a quadrant 1 strategy in Figure 3.1.

In contrast, Korean MNEs are located in quadrant 3 of Figure 3.1 (see Rugman and Doh [2008]). Firms such as Samsung Electronics have developed knowledge-based FSAs, building upon the improved macroeconomic infrastructure of Korea. Indeed, Samsung Electronics now outsources much of its basic manufacturing and assembling to plants in China. In other words, Korean MNEs are now performing in the same manner as leading Western MNEs in the sense that they rely on strong firm-driven factors that build upon a set of country-specific attributes.

There is little evidence to support the existence of emerging economies in quadrant 4 of Figure 3.1. In other words, there are few (if any) purely knowledge-based emerging economy MNEs. Instead, the existing ones combine country and firm advantages in quadrant 3. As yet there are no emerging economy MNEs with pure brand-name marketing FSAs, or pure technology-based FSAs where these are independent of their home-country infrastructure. Furthermore, there is no evidence that there is asset-seeking FDI. Instead, the emerging economy MNEs making takeovers and acquisitions do so by building upon strong home-country advantages, such as cheap money in China.

A case in point is the Lenovo acquisition of the IBM computer assembly division. With this acquisition Lenovo has acquired the existing routines in computer assembly, but not the intangible brand name and knowledge-service advantages of IBM. Thus, the Lenovo acquisition is not asset-seeking in the host economy but is driven by country factors in the home economy. (An alternative view appears in Zeng and Williamson 2007.)

The emergence of IT and services offshoring and outsourcing, however, may begin to change this dynamic. Offshoring is an important economic and social phenomenon that has generated considerable attention in practitioner outlets, the popular press, and in political circles; however, its impact on the development process is not yet clear. What *is* clear is that worldwide trade in services is growing at a rapid rate, and services are accounting for increasing shares of domestic and global output. Initially driven primarily by cost, it now appears that offshoring is evolving to become a more complex phenomenon with broad implications for economic and management theory and practice. Of relevance is the emergence of IT and business process outsourcing MNEs in India – such as Infosys, Wipro, Tata Consultancy, and others. This may point to the emergence of a more knowledge-based services sector in developing countries. Yet to date, these firms – like the Chinese MNEs – are dependent primarily on CSAs. However, some appear on the verge of developing genuine FSAs related to business process outsourcing. Despite these signs, it is still too soon to determine the scope and impact of this trend on MNEs and development.

Conclusions

The best way to integrate less developed countries into the world economy is through the promotion of market-based reforms which promote business activity. The most useful type of business activity is that generated by MNEs. A sequential process is required. First, less developed countries need to engage in internal market reforms to attract FDI. As Western MNEs build subsidiaries in the host economies of less developed economies, they help to improve the macroeconomic infrastructure. The foreign MNEs provide transfers of technology, training for more skilled workers, new managerial and marketing skills, the development of high-quality supply chains, and, in general, improved network linkages. In time this leads to the emergence of local MNEs. Thus, the second phase of economic development policy for less developed countries is to facilitate the development of indigenous MNEs. Ultimately, such emerging economy MNEs need to develop their own world-class FSAs. There is some evidence that this is occurring in Asia, where MNEs from countries such as Korea and Singapore are now world class. The Chinese MNEs still have a long way to go before they acquire knowledge-based FSAs. There are also successful MNEs from India, but there is little publicly available information reported on these firms. The remaining challenge for economic development is the pace at which MNEs develop in Eastern Europe, the Middle East, and Africa. So far, no data are available providing evidence that these areas are generating a set of world-class MNEs.

The focus of this chapter is upon the world's most important (the largest) MNEs. The 500 largest MNEs account for 90 percent of the world's stock of FDI and well over half the world's trade (Rugman, 2000). Across this set, as shown above, there are several dozen MNEs from emerging economies. These are mainly from China, Korea, and India. There are only a handful large enough to be included in this set from other emerging economies, such as Russia, Mexico, Singapore, and countries in the Middle East. Of course, there are hundreds, indeed thousands, of small MNEs from emerging economies. Other chapters in this book pay attention to these small MNEs. Yet, the total sales of all the small MNEs outside of the world's top 500 probably sum to less than the $14b cutoff for inclusion as a top 500 firm.

This is not to say that studying small MNEs is irrelevant, only that it is of little economic significance compared to the role of large MNEs in the top 500. All the evidence we have from the field of international business suggests that membership in the top 500 club confers leadership in international business activity. Progress is being made, as now there are more MNEs from the currently defined emerging economies in the top 500 than were present ten or fifty years ago. Of course, fifty years ago, the definition of emerging economies included those from Japan, while today Japanese MNEs are regarded as highly developed and part of the core triad. MNEs from the core triad of Japan, the EU, and North America account for well over 400 of the world's 500 largest firms. In short, it is necessary to focus upon the world's 500 largest firms in order to gain an accurate perspective on the importance of emerging economy MNEs.

The key theoretical conclusion in this chapter is that, based on the evidence to date, emerging economy MNEs appear to be building upon their home CSAs. There is little evidence that emerging economy MNEs have developed sustainable FSAs, especially the knowledge-based FSAs in systems integration and internal managerial coordination which are now important for the success of differentiated network Western-type MNEs. Indeed, the relatively few examples of emerging economy MNEs in the top 500 firms, which are mainly from China, India, and Korea, appear to be centralized and hierarchical in their organizational structures. That is, the large emerging economy MNEs are rather like the Western MNEs of the 1960s and 1970s, which were also generally centralized and hierarchical before they developed differentiated networks and the knowledge-based transnational solution popularized by Bartlett and Ghoshal (1989).

This observer of emerging economy MNEs remains skeptical that any new theory is required to explain their activities. If they are mainly centralized and hierarchical, and their FSAs build upon home CSAs, then the international business theories of the 1970s and 1980s are undoubtedly adequate to explain their growth, performance, and contribution to economic development. The traditional (or orthodox) theory of FDI is internalization theory, for example, popularized by Rugman (1981). To the extent that emerging economy MNEs have FSAs, they will be based upon their home-country CSAs of cheap labor and the ownership of natural resources. In the case of Chinese MNEs and some government-owned (or sovereign equity) funds from the Middle East, there may be CSAs in cheap money such that overseas mergers and acquisitions are possible. However, the empirical evidence to date suggests that emerging economy MNEs lack knowledge-based FSAs and that such FSAs as they possess are related to their CSAs. This is perfectly well explained by orthodox internalization theory and so no new theory is required to explain MNEs from today's emerging economies.

References

Bartlett, C. A., and Ghoshal, S. 1989. *Managing Across Borders: The Transnational Solution*. Boston, MA: Harvard Business School Press.

Brouthers, L. E., O'Donnell, E., and Hadjimarcou, J. 2005. "Generic Product Strategies for Emerging Market Exports into Triad Nation

Markets: A Mimetic Isomorphism Approach," *Journal of Management Studies* 42(1): 225–245.

Debrah, Y. A., McGovern, I., and Budhwar, P. 2000. "Complementarity or Competition; The Development of Human Resources in a South-East Asian Growth Triangle: Indonesia, Malaysia and Singapore," *International Journal of Human Resource Management* 11(2): 314–335.

Fortune Global 500. 2004. http://money.cnn.com/magazines/fortune/global500/

Hobday, M. 1995. "East Asian Latecomer Firms: Learning the Technology of Electronics," *World Development* 23(7): 1171–1193.

Nelson, R. R., and Pack, H. 1999. "The Asian Miracle and Modern Growth Theory," *The Economic Journal* 109: 416–436.

Nolan, P. 2004. *China at the Crossroads*, Cambridge, UK: Polity Press.

Porter, M. E. 1990. *The Competitive Advantage of Nations*, New York: Free Press, MacMillan.

Rugman, A. M. 1981. *Inside the Multinationals: The Economics of Internal Markets*, New York: Columbia University Press. Reissued in 2006 as *Inside the Multinationals, 25th Anniversary Edition*, New York: Palgrave Macmillan.

Rugman, A. M. 1987. *Outward Bound: Canadian Direct Investment in the United States*, Toronto: C. D. Howe and Prentice-Hall of Canada.

Rugman, A. M. 1996. *The Theory of Multinational Enterprises*, Cheltenham, UK: Edward Elgar.

Rugman, A. M. 2000. *The End of Globalization*, London: Random House.

Rugman, A. M. 2005. *The Regional Multinationals: MNEs and Global Strategic Management*, Cambridge, UK: Cambridge University Press.

Rugman, A. M., and D'Cruz, J. 2000. *Multinationals as Flagship Firms: Regional Business Networks*, New York: Oxford University Press.

Rugman, A. M., and Doh, J. 2008. *Multinationals and Development*, New Haven, CT: Yale University Press.

Rugman, A. M., and McIlveen, J. 1985. *Megafirms: Strategies for Canada's Multinationals*, Toronto: Methuen.

Rugman, A. M., and Oh, C. H. 2007. "Multinationality and Regional Performance, 2001–2005," in A. M. Rugman (ed.), *Regional Aspects of Multinationality and Performance*, Research in Global Strategic Management series, Vol. 13, Oxford, UK: Elsevier, pp. 31–43.

Rugman, A. M., and Verbeke, A. 2003. "Extending the Theory of the Multinational Enterprise: Internalization and Strategic Management Perspectives," *Journal of International Business Studies* 34: 125–137.

Thun, E. 2005. *Changing Lanes in China: Foreign Direct Investment*, Cambridge, UK: Cambridge University Press.

World Bank 1993. *The East Asian Miracle: Economic Growth and Public Policy*, New York: Oxford University Press.

Zeng, M., and Williamson, P. J. 2007. *Dragons at Your Door: How Chinese Cost Innovation is Disrupting Global Competition*, Boston, MA: Harvard Business School Press.

4 | *Does firm ownership matter? POEs vs. FOEs in the developing world*

ALICE H. AMSDEN

The nationality of a firm's owner doesn't matter for economic development in perfectly competitive markets. A foreign-owned enterprise (FOE) from a developed country or a privately owned enterprise (POE) from a developing country are equally capable if both have access to the same inputs and marketing opportunities (ignoring SOEs and tiny enterprises). Where the theory of free competition reigns, developing countries should open their arms to investments from all types of firms in order to maximize jobs, as many Asian countries did using export processing zones. Ownership, measured by votes of shareholders or boards of directors, is immaterial to performance.

Matters change drastically, though, when competition depends on monopolistic assets and market theory no longer rigorously holds, as in "mid-tech" industries such as shipbuilding, steel, and heavy machinery, and "mature" high-tech industries, such as calculators, computers, and cell phones, after millions of units from advanced countries have already been sold but demand is still booming. Knowledge, brand names, political clout, and other sources of market power vary by firm and influence market outcomes. The outsourcing that now characterizes mature high-tech is predicated on the existence of POEs. Outward foreign investment also requires them. Then, ownership matters.

Because FOEs have controlled more competitive assets than POEs since the First Industrial Revolution, they have gained the upper hand and the respect of the elite business schools, that tend to view them as the best policy choice for backward countries to follow. FOEs are highly productive, the argument runs, and somehow transfer knowledge (measured by "spillovers") to local enterprise, so invite them into your midst.

But this outlook has turned out to be extremely short run. FOEs can "crowd out" POEs. They can break their back before they have a chance to acquire their own assets, and the acquisition of their own assets may be far better for economic development than FDI, or joint ventures. "Foreign firms" do pass on important information to new-comers, but not through FDI. Foreign firms that are teachers tend to be vendors of parts and components located in third countries. They help by giving all their customers a roadmap of their industry. FOEs in direct competition with POEs are not necessary for economic development to flourish, and it is dangerous for a promising POE to confront a privileged FOE in its own back yard, often with the backing of the FOE's powerful government (a role Washington played in the foreign-dominated Latin American automobile industry, for example).

Because assets differ systematically between FOEs and POEs in their respective stages of evolution, we would argue that FOEs may not contribute more to economic development in monopolistic industries than POEs. For one, they can't create the highest man-agerial talents, which are always kept at home in corporate head-quarters. The skills and salaries of the chief executive officer (CEO) and other top managers are never located abroad. Nor can FOEs "globalize" a developing country in the form of outward foreign investment. In order for a developing country to invest abroad, it must have its own companies. To win outsourcing contracts a POE must be a local entity, setting a high national standard.

I would argue that the best of POEs in the fastest growing emerging economies (e.g., Korea's Samsung, India's Tata, and Brazil's Embraer) tend to be more *entrepreneurial* than FOEs. FOEs today are *bureau-cratic* – they operate with relatively dense levels of management and continue to cookie-cut a single model throughout the world that has proved to be highly lucrative for them but not necessarily for emerging economies. Bureaucracy can be measured by number of signatures, review boards, management layers, or people thrown at a problem. For now, during a growth phase when most POES enjoy *both* family ownership and professional management, they display a highly dyna-mic entrepreneurship. Akin to what Schumpeter said, they formulate novel ideas (locally); coordinate resources; enter and exit "new" (for them) industries at lightning speed (a highly profitable skill unmen-tioned by Schumpeter); and restructure industries in a creative way that in labor abundant countries doesn't involve the mass layoffs typical of American retrenchments (China's restructuring, say, of the First Auto Works, involved only modest redundancies).

The thin layer of bureaucracy in POEs improves information flows. With fast transmissions of information, POEs have perfected the asset of *short time to market*, especially in Asia (Kwak, 2008). They are super-quick in picking new industries to enter and then designing the integration of parts and components to win the global race to market. In the case of one POE in the Indian pharmaceutical industry, it reached the market faster than the Indian subsidiary of the multinational that had invented the drug in the first place (Mourshed 1999). POEs, not FOEs, should take credit for industrialization in the developing world. Industry by industry, they diversified forcefully and fast. In the process, they themselves became highly diversified as business groups.

Business groups

POEs have tended to take the form of diversified business groups because, unlike specialized firms in advanced countries with revolutionary technology, POEs from developing countries are still competing without world-class products and know-how. It is too risky for them to specialize in a single technology family. In almost every market, they are behind the technological frontier and must move from industry to industry as opportunities arise. To do so, POEs must develop alternative skills, not just to do battle with FOEs but also to compete against other POEs from developing countries, all of which depend on low wages to compete. Long hours and voluntary or involuntary overtime help developing countries reach consumers at record speed, but only skills, not hours of work, differentiate the best.

The diversification process itself holds the key to group success. The more groups diversify, the greater their experience and acquired skills at diversification (or "project execution," from buying technology to starting up operations; Amsden and Hikino 1994). This allows them to get a head-start over other entrants into the "new" industries (and services) that their governments open or that they capture from overseas. Groups can enter these "new" industries with great speed and low cost aided by project execution skills, in a virtuous circle.

The greater the scope of their operations, the greater the visibility of a group, and the greater its ability to attract the best talent to reach world norms of productivity at the industry-wide level. This talent brings the diversified firm the production know-how that specific industries require. Expertise in many industries gives groups an advantage with large, multi-product vendors that provide them with further knowledge and better industry-level capabilities.

The swiftness of POEs, which raises profitability, stems partly from their membership in a business group that is managed by a single owner, who knows where resources lie and who can transfer them from one subsidiary to another. The fungibility of resources among the subsidiaries of a single group, especially capital ("cross-investments"), makes it difficult for FOEs to engineer takeovers of POEs, which is why they are disliked on Wall Street (Lawrence 1993). Instead of searching for the right person for a job on the market, which takes time in the developing world, the group can find a cachet internally from one or another subsidiary. Groups even harbor a captive market for individual subsidiaries. The employees of Korea's groups bought their life insurance and their automobiles from sister subsidiaries.

Groups benefit from the inter-sectoral learning made possible by the absence of operating in a single market (Dosi 1988). Paint problems in automobile making can benefit from the experience of solving paint problems in the shipbuilding industry – both within the scope of a group such as Korea's Hyundai.

A business group in the developing world today is typically in its first, second, or third generation of family ownership (a sixty-year cycle roughly). It is free from bureaucracy at the top while enjoying professional management at the bottom and middle. Joint ventures are regarded in much of the business school literature as a compromise between FOE and POE, good for both, but the protracted negotiations that joint ventures typically involve slow decision making. Decision making is far faster in a diversified group, or an alliance of national domestic groups, than in a foreign joint venture: compare the speed of entry and operations in China's automobile industry of Cheri, a national champion, and joint ventures involving General Motors and Volkswagen.

POEs tend to have more knowledge of the local business environment than FOEs. Charles Kindleberger argued as early as 1970 that proximity creates advantages for the national investor. But he was writing before the mass migration of Third World managers and engineers to study, live, and work in advanced countries, permanently or temporarily. This coming-and-going between continents has given leading POEs *two types of knowledge,* not just one. The people who know their own native environment *also know the richest economies abroad.* Managers born in India or Brazil, for example, who then study or work in the United States, acquire a unique take on globalism that Americans, knowing only one culture and one language, don't have.

Diversified business groups have excelled especially in mature high-tech industries, or industries with advanced technology whose demand is still growing but whose profitability has begun to fall. When RCA invested in Taiwan and Mexico to manufacture TVs in the 1950s, it opened its own subsidiaries. When Nokia goes to Taiwan today to lower the production costs of its cell phones, it outsources production to Taiwan-owned companies. Taiwan's POEs have their own skill sets, and ramp up quickly to achieve volume in the face of falling profit rates, not least of all by creating internal construction and automation arms to hasten the conversion of old factories (e.g., in textiles) to new ones (in cell phones). Taiwan's POEs excel in integrating the hundreds of parts and components bought outside that comprise, say, a notebook, given their skills in modularity and design (and weakness in designing a single advanced component). Within hours or days rather than weeks, a product made by a POE can reach a FOE, making the wholesale relocation of manufacturing activity to developing countries all the more likely (Amsden and Chu, 2003).

This is the gist of the argument that crowding out of POEs by FOEs in monopolistic industries (mid-tech and mature high-tech) is not development friendly. To celebrate FOEs is to close one's eyes to the knowledge-based assets of POEs. Now that POEs are growing, their speed-to-market, project execution skills, and capabilities in assembly make it easier to answer the question of whether or not they can ultimately reach the world technological frontier. Why not, given their assets?

Below, we try to answer the question "why are POEs more evident in some emerging economies than in others?" The answers possibly lurk in a few facts of colonialism and de-colonization, one of the great events of the twentieth century.

De-colonization and the destiny of FOEs

Some say colonialism was indispensable to enlighten backward people (Ferguson 2003); others say it retarded progress once colonial peoples understood foreign ways. Pre-World War II manufacturing experience arose in only a few colonies, so as a system of development, colonialism clearly had its limits. Among countries with prewar manufacturing experience, only a few succeeded after de-colonization in freeing themselves *not only from foreign rule but also from foreign firms*. Those that succeeded in freeing their industries from FOEs became the most successful in the developing world after 1950.

POEs were a scarce institution in the colonial world. Manufacturing experience, involving not just physical dexterity but the embodiment of that dexterity in a "firm" – a complex social entity with knowledge of accounting, finance, labor management, and marketing – was the key to economic development but a scarce competitive asset. No developing country after World War II entered the orbit of modern industry without prewar manufacturing experience, measured by the share of a country's manufacturing in GDP (excluding countries where manufacturing comprised only a single industry, as in the textile industry of Egypt and Pakistan, the oil industry of Venezuela, and the processed foods industry of the Philippines). Only one dozen developing countries managed to acquire diverse prewar manufacturing experience, *and POEs arose only in these countries* (Argentina, Brazil, Chile, China, India, Indonesia, Korea, Malaysia, Mexico, Taiwan, Thailand, and Turkey; Amsden 2001, Amsden 2007).

Manufacturing experience derived from three sources: premodern know-how that pre-dated Western influence (in China, India, Mexico's woolen industry, and possibly Ottoman Turkey); émigrés, who brought business acumen with them to Latin America (from Europe and the US) and the Pacific Basin (from China); and colonial companies, which built industries in their own conquered territories. Japan's co-prosperity sphere was a hub. Korea was industrialized to act as a bridgehead to Manchuria. Taiwan was belatedly industrialized to help Japan conquer Southeast Asia. As Japan's war drums beat louder, the UK introduced defensive industry in Malaysia, and the Dutch and Americans did the same in Indonesia and the Philippines respectively. Fascist governments in both Japan and Thailand in the 1930s collaborated to build military-related industries.

Latin American émigrés were probably the most successful in transferring know-how, because Latin America had the highest per capita income in the developing world after World War II. But postwar decolonization wrought radical change.

Decolonization didn't affect Latin America at all because Latin America had gained its independence in the early nineteenth century. After World War II, the same powerful political groups and the same

FOEs survived as before (Pirelli was the first multinational to arrive in Argentina in 1917, and still exists). This inertia left Latin America with relatively little space for POEs (or land reform, which exploded amidst decolonization in Asia). Industrial leadership was lethargic until a developmental state arose. Only then did Brazil, for example, create Embraer, Petrobras, and other SOEs.

Starting with India in 1947, colonies slowly got their independence. The first African colony to cast off colonial ties was Ghana in 1957, and the last was South Africa in 1989. But the countries that became fertile crescents for POEs, mostly in Asia, not only shed colonial rule but also *kicked out colonial companies*. China expropriated them. India drove them out by fear or competition. Korea and Taiwan acquired Japanese properties, especially subsidiaries of big banks. Indonesia inherited around 400 Dutch companies. Malaysia bought British properties on the London Stock Exchange (Amsden 2001; Amsden 2007).

In one way or another, these former colonies "crowded out" foreign firms and created space for their own national POEs to flourish. Those that didn't create this space – the Philippines, for example, got rid of American foreign rule but was stuck with uninventive American companies – performed badly.

Virtually all POEs took the form of diversified groups, but there is disagreement about why this business model arose in such a wide range of poor countries. Disagreement has tended to be narrow and one-sided, especially if groups are analyzed as market phenomena, without the goal of economic development directly in mind (Khanna and Yafeh 2007).

To let in some fresh air, it is helpful to think of groups as either money machines, that mobilize finance for development (the market approach), or as institutions that build knowledge, skills, and technological capabilities (the institutional approach). Some say groups arose to pool family savings when financial markets were weak. But this assumes that savings were scarce rather than "shy" (savers awaited the appearance of firms with profitable skills to invest in). Others argue that to stay independent from the sorties of FOEs, the group form emerged – as it had done in Japan much earlier – and empowered itself by building knowledge-based assets.

If a country runs a persistent surplus in its balance of payments such that savings exceed investment, as in India from 1835 to 1946, then capital shyness may be said to exist (Das 1962; Banerjee 1963; Maddison 1971; Bagchi 1972). There was no scarcity of investment capital in India, however poor; it was exporting capital. Alternatively, shyness can mean the excess product that a country either does or can produce above subsistence (Riskin 1975), as in pre-industrial China. As early as the 1840s, there was substantial qualitative evidence that when profitable opportunities in India and China arose, capital came out of the woodwork, and that the family form of business is not tightly tied to how capital is raised. In the case of India:

The early textile mills were not exceptionally costly ventures by local standards. A company could get into operation in Bombay for an investment of Rs. 500,000 to Rs. 1 million or about £50,000 to £100,000 at prevailing exchange rates.[1] This covered cost of land, buildings, equipment and inventory. Many other types of enterprise projected in the same period involved sums as great or greater. Shares were issued in units of Rs. 2,500 or, more typically, Rs. 5,000. These were not amounts intended to attract the small investor. Yet *the number of people in Bombay with sums to risk in promising enterprises was sufficiently great* so that when the Oriental mill was floated in 1854 with paid-up capital of Rs.1,250,000 divided into 500 shares of Rs. 2,500, *no one was permitted to subscribe for more than four shares.* (Morris 1983: 575; emphasis added)

According to a partner of Tata Sons and Company, India's largest group: "The public in India, especially in Bombay, are ever ready to put their money in mill concerns started by individuals or firms who

---

[1] The low cost of entry into India has been debated. According to one study, Rs. 500,000 amounted to a lot of money and the fact that cotton and jute mills and tea companies required independent managements added to their financial burden (Rungta 1970). As for the cost of entry into other countries, Japanese mill entrepreneurs were usually rich farmers or local manufacturers of soy sauce or wine who entered textile manufacture "out of a sense of patriotic duty." However, "mill manufacture forced them into unexpectedly high expenditure." The amount required to start an enterprise was already at the limit of their ability (Nakaoka 1991: 293). In China (1904–1908), some cotton mills were on the low end of the spectrum of authorized capital (in taels), and some were in the middle. The most expensive investments tended to be railroads, mining and smelting, and modern-type banks (Feuerwerker 1958: 3). On the other hand, by the early 1930s out of a total of twelve industries in Shanghai, cotton textiles was found to have had the highest average capitalization per factory (Lieu 1936). Per contra, the capital requirements of the First Industrial Revolution were modest; entry into mechanized textile spinning or weaving was supposedly within the grasp of a typical artisan (Mathias 1973).

have a reputation for honesty and efficiency, and who have a good deal of mill experience" (Chandavarkar 1994). With a successful business in textiles, Tata was able to raise money from the private sector in 1907 for a large steel mill. "The total Capital of the new Company was subscribed by the Indian public in a remarkably short space of a few weeks, the number of shareholders being about 7,000" (Fraser 1919).

China's potential economic surplus in 1933 was also estimated (by Riskin 1975) to be very large, possibly more than 25 percent of gross national product (GNP). Given the operations of "compradors" (merchants to foreign business), "contrary to the generally held view, an important reason for China's relatively slow economic development in the nineteenth century was not the scarcity of capital, because large amounts of Chinese funds were readily available" (Hao 1986: 348). The Chee Hsin Cement Company, for example, allegedly had no trouble raising capital after the turn of the century. Its twenty-nine shareholders held diversified portfolios, with interests in other industries, commerce, and banking (Feuerwerker 1967).

Rather than being dirt poor, the problem was high risks from low skills. In India, only five of the pioneering textile firms of the nineteenth century survived until World War I. Out of a total of ninety-seven mills erected in Bombay between 1855 and 1925, twelve were burnt down or else were closed and dismantled, sixteen transferred their managing agencies voluntarily and forty-five went into liquidation and were reconstructed under other names (Rutnagur 1927). There occurred a very large number of company failures, with the result that "*the Indian investor, habitually shy, became shyer still*" (Das 1962: 162; emphasis added).

Causality thus seems to run from "no skills" to "no money" rather than the reverse, both before and after de-colonization. Shyness of capital seems to characterize much of Africa today, according to studies of Canada's North-South Center in Ottawa.

There was huge speculation before World War II, even in Japan, but in commodities such as cotton and silk, not financial instruments. After World War II, the stock markets in India boomed. But this only goes to show that groups could get the capital they wanted without family strings attached.

Skill-intensity differentiated groups in developing countries from conglomerates in the US, which regarded their affiliates as an asset to buy and sell. The business groups of the developing world, by contrast, regarded their affiliates as long-term commitments, to be nursed to health rather than put up for adoption if sick. Few affiliates until very recently could be bought or sold.

Thus, most group characteristics don't fit the market paradigm, but have proved to be development friendly despite an enormous amount of angry criticism of their structure and strong government ties. The developing countries where POEs became strongest were the developing countries with the longest history of manufacturing experience and not trade or free markets. Decolonization was most developmental when it included the expulsion of FOEs *as replaced* by group-organized enterprises.

Services

As manufacturing migrated in ever increasing numbers to developing countries, the FOE found a sanctuary in services. It had a helping hand from the Great Powers, ranging from the US Treasury, which pressured emerging economies to open their financial markets and allow foreign takeovers, to the most expensive business schools, which supplied the rationales for doing so, to the WTO, which rewrote the regulatory rules for privatizing government-owned services and universalized Western accounting roles. How did POEs fare, when their own presence in the service sector of FOEs was negligible, a hindrance to their imitative learning?

Three points about national ownership in the service sector emerge from Taiwan. First, the Taiwanese government promoted national ownership in services as it had done in manufacturing, despite global cries for laissez-faire. It bet on the speed of learning and skill formation of its groups to keep services in national hands. It won from the US government a five-year reprieve before some services were opened to FOEs. This gave POEs time to catch up.

Second, the big national players in services became mainly old business groups, not specialized national service providers. (The top ten companies in retail, wholesale, and department stores, the largest service sub-sector, were all groups.) Third, many groups transferred know-how to services from traditional industries (Amsden and Chu 2003).

In the case of cell phone services, all groups built up their operating systems within a year, and then, three months later, entered into fierce price competition with each other. "Ramp-ups and start-ups were extremely fast by world standards," an advantage gained from older industries (Amsden and Chu 2003, p. 137). In sectors where financial assets were lacking, local firms allied with each other. Foreign joint ventures grew, but alliances were viewed as a faster route to market entry, especially in financial services and telecommunications.

A company in the textile and construction industry, Ruentex, founded RT-Mart International, along the lines of Costco, the American mass wholesale warehouser. After it opened its first store and bought two others, Ruentex quickly ramped up to a total of sixteen stores to acquire brand-name recognition and good vendor service. A year later it opened its first outlet in China, which soon expanded to eleven outlets in all. Speed came from Ruentex's traditional construction and development arm, which designed and built Ruentex's retail outlets. Capital to finance diversification into services came from Ruentex's old textile business, which had also invested in a financial securities company and then, the first global Taiwan fund. Once in finance, Ruentex formed a partnership with Aetna Insurance and then bought shares in the Sinopec Bank.

The old economy thus became a bridgehead to services, given the suppleness of business groups. Due to differences in skills, some services became completely foreign dominated (advertising) while others fell mostly under local control (fast foods). Overall, POEs kept their grip on the local economy, which maintained steady growth and low unemployment at a time when manufacturing was migrating en masse to the Mainland. As Taiwan's service sector built up capacity in China, service businesses in Taiwan were strengthened. Just as national capital in manufacturing helped entry into services, so national capital in services helped entry into the Chinese market. Around 60 percent of total foreign investment in China comes from overseas Chinese POEs.

Conclusion

Outside perfectly competitive industries, FOEs and POEs are different animals, at least when POEs are still in their first, second, or third generation of family ownership. The POE is entrepreneurial and the FOE, especially from the US, tends to be bureaucratic (an assertion I have not dealt with in this paper). The evidence favors the POE rather than the FOE as the agent of industrialization in the developing world, diversifying from the simplest industries to the most complex, on the basis of latecomer types of skills, especially related to project execution and speed to market.

POEs became strongest in developing countries with prewar manufacturing experience, whose de-colonization involved not just kicking out foreign rulers but also kicking out foreign firms (China, India, Korea, Taiwan, Malaysia, Indonesia, etc.). Space was made for domestically owned POEs to spread their wings, thereby crowding out FOEs and creating the opportunities for developing countries to reach the highest levels of skills and salaries, and to expand overseas. Countries can globalize only on the basis of nationally owned companies. Where the crowding out of FOEs failed to happen, as in the Philippines and Brazil (which never experienced postwar decolonization and where multinationals stayed put), POEs were weaker as an agent of growth.

The diversification pattern of national economies was mirrored in the diversification pattern of business groups, the most popular form of POE. As groups repeatedly diversified, they became good at diversifying – that is, they mastered the skills bundled in project execution – ranging from acquiring technology to starting up operations. With few levels of bureaucracy, the group's most talented professional engineers were known to top management, and could be mobilized for new ventures quickly, rather than sought on the market. With speed and know-how in starting up new operations, groups became extraordinarily fast to market, from ramping up new facilities to integrating parts and components. Today, countries such as Korea and Taiwan can deliver different varieties of notebooks and cell phones to world markets in a matter of hours. Speed is an indigenous asset.

All developing countries after World War II were capital-scarce, which suggests that the group form of business emerged to mobilize capital on a family basis. But in many countries like India and China (and in many African countries today), capital was more shy than scarce. Capital came out of the woodwork as groups acquired knowhow and lowered perceived risk. This attracted the capital of nonfamily members. The rise of the group form of business in the developing world is best understood in relation to knowledge-based assets, not finance.

In former colonies that ejected foreign firms and at the same time built new entrepreneurial enterprises, globalization began to take the form of brain drain, and then reverse brain drain. POEs soon became blessed with two types of knowledge compared with FOEs: they knew intimately their own native environment and language, and they knew the environments of FOEs, where they studied, worked, and happily lived, and learned English. This contrasts with the limited learning of the US and Japan, which know intimately only their own language and way of doing business. The deep, dual knowledge of the POE argues in favor of its long-run success.

A third type of animal is the joint venture between FOE and POE, and it appears as an attractive mutant for economic development. But joint ventures tend to have protracted negotiations between partners and to move slowly (compare the entry of Cheri on the one hand and General Motors and Volkswagen on the other into the Chinese automobile industry). Nor is history in their favor. After all, no joint venture is known to have emerged between David and Goliath.

References

Amsden, A. H. (2001). *The Rise of "the Rest": Challenges to the West from Late-Industrializing Economies*. New York, Oxford University Press.
Amsden, A. H. (2007). *Escape from Empire: The Developing World's Journey Through Heaven and Hell*. Cambridge, MA, MIT Press.
Amsden, A. H. and W. W. Chu (2003). *Beyond Late Development: Taiwan's Upgrading Policies*. Cambridge, MA, MIT Press.
Amsden, A. H. and T. Hikino (1994). Project Execution Capability, Organizational Know-how and Conglomerate Corporate Growth in Late Industrialization. *Industrial and Corporate Change* 3(1): 111–147.
Bagchi, A. K. (1972). *Private Investment in India, 1900–1939*. Cambridge, UK, Cambridge University Press.
Banerjee, A. K. (1963). *India's Balance of Payments: Estimates of Current and Capital Accounts from 1921–22 to 1938–39*. Bombay, Asia Publishing House.
Chandavarkar, R. (1994). *The Bombay Cotton Textile Industry*, 1900–1940. Cambridge, UK, Cambridge University Press.
Das, N. (1962). *Industrial Enterprise in India*. Bombay, Orient Longmans.
Dosi, G. (1988). Sources, Procedures, and Microeconomic Effects of Innovation. *Journal of Economic Literature* Vol. 26, No. 3: 1120–1171.
Ferguson, N. (2003). *Empire: The Rise and Demise of the British World Order and the Lessons for Global Power*. New York, Basic Books.
Feuerwerker, A. (1958). *China's Early Industrialization: Cheng Hsuan-Huai (1844–1916) and Mandarin Enterprise*. Cambridge, MA: Harvard University Press.

Feuerwerker, A. (1967). Industrial Enterprise in Twentieth-Century China: The Chee Hsin Cement Co. *Approaches to Modern Chinese History*. A. Feuerwerker, R. Murphey and M. C. Wright (eds.). Berkeley and Los Angeles, CA, University of California Press: 304–341.

Fraser, L. (1919). *Iron and Steel in India*. Bombay, Times Press.

Hao, Y.-p. i. (1986). *The Commercial Revolution in Nineteenth-Century China: The Rise of Sino-Western Mercantile Capitalism*. Berkeley, CA, University of California Press.

Khanna, T. and Y. Yafeh (2007). Business Groups in Emerging Markets: Paragons or Parasites? *Journal of Economic Literature* Vol. 45: 331–372.

Kwak, J. (2008). Time to Market. Ph.D. dissertation. Cambridge, MA, Massachusetts Institute of Technology.

Lawrence, R. Z. (1993). Japan's Low Levels of Inward Investment: The Role of Inhibitions on Acquisitions. *Foreign direct Investment*. K. Froot (ed.). Chicago, University of Chicago for the National Bureau of Economic Research.

Lieu, D. K. (1936). *The Growth and Industrialization of Shanghai*. Shanghai: China Institute of Pacific Relations.

Maddison, A. (1971). *Class Structure and Economic Growth: India and Pakistan Since the Moghuls*. New York, W. W. Norton.

Mathiar, P. (1973). Capital, Credit and Enterprise in the Industrial Revolution. *Journal of European Economic History* Vol. 2: 121–143.

Morris, M. D. (1983). The Growth of Large-Scale Industry to 1947. *The Cambridge Economic History of India*. Vol. 2 D. Kumar and M. Desai (eds.). Cambridge, UK, Cambridge University Press.

Mourshed, M. (1999). Technology Transfer Dynamics: Lessons from the Egyptian and Indian Pharmaceutical Industries. *Urban Studies and Planning Ph.D. thesis*. Cambridge, MA, Massachusetts Institute of Technology.

Nakaoka, T. (1991). The Transfer of Cotton Manufacturing Technology from Britain to Japan. *International Technology Transfer, Europe, Japan and the USA, 1700–1914*. D. J. Jeremy (ed.). Aldershot, UK, Edward Elgar: 181–198.

Riskin, C. (1975). Surplus and Stagnation in Modern China. *China's Modern Economy in Historical Perspective*. D. H. Perkins(ed.). Stanford, CA, Stanford University Press: 49–84.

Rungta, R. S. (1970). *The Rise of Corporations in India, 1851–1900*. Cambridge, Cambridge University Press.

Rutnagur, S. M. (1927). *Bombay Industries: The Cotton Mills*. Bombay, The Indian Textile Journal, Ltd.

PART II

Country Studies

5 | *Chinese multinationals: Emerging through new global gateways*

PETER J. WILLIAMSON AND MING ZENG

Chinese companies have begun to 'go global'. High-profile examples include: Lenovo's $1.75 billion takeover of IBM's personal computer business in 2004; Huawei, which has implemented its telecommunications network equipment solutions in over a hundred countries, maintains a network of twelve R&D centres around the world, and in 2007 bid for 3Com in partnership with Bain Capital; and appliance maker Haier, whose brand ranked 86th in the top 500 most influential global brands (World Brand Lab, 2006). Less widely recognized, however, is the fact that scores of other, little-known Chinese companies have begun to carve out significant, sometimes even dominant, global market shares in numerous industries as diverse as port machinery, medical equipment, and pianos (Zeng and Williamson, 2007, p. 19).

In analysing this recent emergence of Chinese multinationals, this chapter begins by outlining how leading companies from China have parlayed their CSAs into the FSAs (Rugman, 1981) that equip them to successfully compete in the global market. We then compare and contrast the strategies Chinese companies have used to leverage these FSAs globally with the typology introduced by Ramamurti and Singh to describe the emergence of multinationals from India. The remainder of the chapter focuses on how these strategies are allowing Chinese firms to harness the new 'gateways to entry' (Verdin and Williamson, 1994) that the globalization of the world economy is opening up, to build new multinationals with surprising speed. These gateways to entry include: the rise of outsourcing; the modularization of global value chains; the codification of knowledge; the gradual concentration and globalization of retailing; the more fluid international market for talent and professional services; and the increasingly open market for corporate control in many countries around the world.

We show that by analysing the interaction between these gateways to entry and the generic strategies we can reach a more complete understanding of how and why such strategies are effective. The analysis also suggests an additional generic strategy being adopted by some Chinese firms as they globalize: what we term the 'demand wedge'. We conclude by considering how the emergence of multinationals from developing countries in an era of globalization not only harnesses the new global gateways, but might also reshape the nature of global competition.

Cost innovation: From country-specific to firm-specific advantage

If Chinese companies were to succeed in going global they clearly needed a source of competitive advantage that not only set them apart from established global players, but also compensated for their disadvantages as newcomers – handicaps that include a relative lack of knowledge of international markets, limited stocks of other intangible assets (such as proprietary technologies and brand equity), and a paucity of other resources (including capital and tangible assets). Their Chinese home base provides a number of CSAs. Perhaps most important among these is the benefit of a large pool of low-cost, low-skilled labour that can be parlayed into low manufacturing cost. But this alone is insufficient as a source of competitive advantage in the global market because foreign companies are also readily able to exploit this low-cost labour advantage either by setting up manufacturing in China or outsourcing manufacturing and other basic operations to domestic companies in China.

Nor do potential CSAs deriving from widespread state ownership provide a sustainable source of competitive advantage capable of underpinning Chinese companies going global. Chinese companies often have hybrid shareholding structures that involve substantial ownership by a variety of national, provincial, and local governments, mixed together with publicly listed shares, and equity held by management. State interests have provided many of the leading Chinese companies with initial advantages in the form of hard assets, capital, and intellectual property made available to them more cheaply than the prevailing value of these assets on world markets. But beyond this initial endowment, significant ongoing subsidies or special support from the state cannot be relied upon for most companies. Rather, once restructured and partially privatized, they are generally forced to stand on their own feet and often compete in the market against other firms with hybrid ownership (Zeng and Williamson, 2003).

Chinese companies wishing to succeed globally, therefore, have been forced to find radical new ways of using Chinese cost advantages so as to parlay their CSA into FSAs which would be difficult for rivals, both foreign and domestic, to replicate. They have achieved this through what we term *cost innovation* (Zeng and Williamson, 2007). Within the broad strategy for creating FSA, leading Chinese companies (who we have termed 'Chinese dragons') have innovated along some combination of three dimensions:

- First, they have developed strategies and organizational routines (Nelson and Winter, 1982) that have allowed them to offer customers high technology at low cost. Computer maker Dawning, for example, has worked to put supercomputer technology into the low-cost servers that are the everyday workhorses of the world's IT networks. This novel strategy is difficult for established firms to replicate because their own internal processes are designed to deploy high technology into a restricted range of high-end products and segments. Established global competitors also have a disincentive to imitate this strategy for fear of interrupting the cycle whereby they maximize their profits along the product life cycle by only slowly migrating new technology from high-priced segments toward the mass market.
- Second, the emerging Chinese multinationals are finding processes that enable them to offer customers a wide choice of product varieties or customization at prices that are competitive with incumbents' standardized, mass-market offerings. Goodbaby, for example, offers a product line of over 1,600 types of strollers, car seats, bassinets, and playpens – four times the range of its nearest competitor – all at mass-market prices.
- Third, Chinese companies are developing strategies that use their low costs to reduce the break-even point of producing specialty products. This enables them to reduce the risk of trying to 'explode' hitherto niche markets into volume businesses by dramatically lowering prices. For example, consumer appliance maker Haier has transformed the market for wine-storage refrigerators from the preserve of a few wine connoisseurs into a mainstream category sold through America's Sam's Club, at less than half the then-prevailing price of

comparable products. Haier has captured a 60 per cent market share of the expanded US market (measured by value). Incumbents have found it difficult to match this FSA because it would require them not only to access CSAs in China, but also to completely re-engineer their existing business models which are based around the assumption that specialty products must forever remain low volume and high priced.

As we have argued in detail elsewhere, this cost innovation approach has been quite successful in permitting the Chinese dragons to build FSAs that are allowing them to break into the global market and begin to build viable multinationals capable of competing in a variety of industries across different market segments well beyond the bottom end (Zeng and Williamson, 2007).

This contention is supported by China's rising world share of high-technology exports. In 1995 China exported $6 billion worth of goods and services classified as 'high technology'. By 2005 that figure was $217.6 billion, representing 28.6% of China's total exports. In Shenzhen, which started as a Special Economic Zone across the border from Hong Kong producing cheap clothes, toys, and athletics shoes, high-technology exports have been growing at more than 45% per annum in recent years. By 2005 Shenzhen exported $47 billion in high-tech goods (Government of Singapore, 2006). Even more significantly, some 57% of high-technology production was based on intellectual property owned by Chinese firms. In 2004 alone, Shenzhen companies applied for 14,918 patents. Today 90% of China's growing investment in R&D is made by the corporate sector.

Some specific examples of this successful emergence of Chinese multinationals include: Galanz, which now supplies more than one in two microwave ovens sold in the global market; Wanxiang, the world's largest producer of universal joints, which has established an industry fund to buy US firms in auto components (it is already talking to struggling Delphi); BYD, the world's second largest maker of rechargeable batteries; CIMC (China International Marine Containers), which controls 55% of the global container industry across all segments from low to high end; Shanghai Zhenhua Port Machinery Company, which has a 54% share of the world market for harbour cranes; and the Pearl River Piano Group, which has won 15% of the

US market (40% in upright pianos) in just five years, and is the global volume leader, producing around 100,000 pianos every year.

Strategies for leveraging cost innovation advantages

Individual Chinese companies have used different strategies to leverage the competitive advantages they have built by focusing on cost innovation. In part these differences reflect variations in the FSAs across the spectra from capabilities to deliver high technology at mass-market volumes and prices, to offer a wide choice of varieties or customization to potential buyers at little or no price premium, or to explode niche segments into volume markets. Choice of strategy is also influenced by cross-industry differences in industry structure, conduct, and the nature of the competitive advantages enjoyed by incumbents (Caves and Porter, 1978). Nonetheless, in the sample of fifty Chinese companies we studied (Zeng and Williamson, 2007), it is possible to distinguish a number of generic strategies that Chinese companies are adopting as they seek to globalize. Interestingly, these closely parallel the generic strategies identified by Ramamurti and Singh among emerging multinationals from India. As we will see, however, there are differences both in the relative popularity of different generic strategies between the Indian and Chinese cases and in the fact that some Chinese companies have adopted an additional generic strategy (the demand wedge) so far not seen in India.

In what follows we briefly discuss some examples of how the Chinese dragons are using each of Ramamurti and Singh's generic strategies.

Local optimizer

This strategy focuses on leveraging FSAs based on the capability to deliver products and processes optimized for emerging markets. HiSense, now one of China's leading exporters of television sets, epitomizes this strategy. Proudly displayed in the exhibition room at company headquarters is a TV that the company customized especially for an African distributor when the company received its first international order in the early 1990s. It doesn't seem much out of the ordinary until you turn it on: this TV has a special capability to automatically adjust its brightness according to the light intensity in the room.

In Africa, TVs are used in a wide variety of situations – in bright sunshine and black storms, sometimes outdoors. Such a capability therefore made perfect sense. But most of the companies the African customer originally contacted refused even to entertain the idea because, far from being straightforward, such a function required R&D, redesign of the circuitry, and installation of new production equipment.

Even though the market was dominated by Japanese and Korean competitors, HiSense was able to use its low-cost R&D and design capabilities to create a product that could still be profitable in a low-price emerging market despite requiring customization that competitors found too expensive. This turned out to be the market breakthrough HiSense was looking for. On the back of the light-adjusting TV's success, their air conditioners and refrigerators started to enter the market. Sales jumped from a few thousand to twenty-five thousand appliances per month. The company became the second largest player in the African market.

Lost-cost partner

This strategy seeks to exploit factor cost arbitrage more effectively than competitors and hence a potential FSA rooted in superior local knowledge of how to minimize factor costs (and hence one of China's key CSAs), combined with process excellence. This basic cost advantage may be augmented by green-field expansion or downstream acquisitions overseas to enable the emerging multinational to move up the value curve. It is arguably one of the most common strategies adopted by the emerging Chinese dragons, including companies such as BYD (global number-two supplier of rechargeable batteries), Chint (a maker of transformers and other accessories to power portable consumer electronics products), and auto components maker Wanxiang. Each of these companies has focused on building process excellence that can be parlayed into FSAs, offering customers increased variety and customization at low cost (Zeng and Williamson, 2007, Chapter 2).

Wanxiang is a good example of a company that has pursued this strategy to move up-market from low-end auto components to become a tier-one supplier to major, global car companies. The company's name, which translates to 'universal joint', is a reminder of the way it was able to enter the world market by focusing all of its limited resources on just one product – universal joints – courtesy of the global auto makers that chose to outsource this humdrum component. Wanxiang was able to concentrate on manufacturing universal joints and still be economically successful, because falling barriers and more efficient transportation meant it could run just one large-scale operation to serve global market demand; this was in the remote town of Ningwei, where it enjoyed the world's lowest costs but where foreign competitors probably lacked the local knowledge or willingness to operate. Focusing all of its human and financial resources on building a company specializing in universal joints allowed Wanxiang to pull in front of its rivals. With relentless attention to improving quality and reducing cost in this narrow product range, Wanxiang was able to win the business outsourced by first-tier auto suppliers such as Delphi, Bosch, and Visteon in forty countries, to become the largest supplier of universal joints in the world, producing over 25 million units per annum.

One part at a time, Wanxiang then gradually expanded its product offers from universal joints to other parts of the driveline, and then to parts of the brake system, and subsequently to the whole chassis. Fast growth in the United States based on its cost and process advantages helped Wanxiang to quickly graduate from a third-tier supplier of a minor component to become a tier-one supplier of subassemblies to Ford and GM.

Since 2003, Wanxiang has also run the American Manufacturing Fund, an investment vehicle that is devoted to acquisitions of auto components makers in the United States. It then extended its acquisition strategy to other parts of the world. By 2005, Wanxiang had acquired, merged with, or established thirty companies (eighteen of which it controls outright) in eight countries, including the United States, UK, Germany, Canada, and Australia.

Global consolidator

This generic strategy is characterized by FSAs in operational excellence combined with restructuring/turnaround capabilities. Ramamurti and Singh identified a number of successful proponents of this approach emerging from India. Although epitomized by Lenovo, which has acquired both IBM's personal computer business and Packard Bell (a major player in Europe), the *global consolidator* strategy is, as yet, less common in the case of the emerging Chinese dragons. A handful of Chinese companies have, however, deployed it with impressive results. One such example is CIMC, which, as noted above, controls 55 per cent of the global market across a wide range of container types with sales six times greater than its nearest competitor. Its range includes products with sophisticated refrigeration, state-of-the-art electronic tracking, internal tanks, folding mechanisms, and customized features.

Taking advantage of new regulations that opened the way for initial public offerings (IPOs) in China, they floated the company on the Shenzhen Stock Exchange in 1993 and used the money to buy up Chinese competitors that were struggling as the demand cycle suffered a downswing. These acquisitions enabled CIMC to expand to five massive plants; by 1996, it was number one in China. Given the huge size of the Chinese market, this already made it one of the largest players in the world. In the wake of the 1997 Asian financial crisis, it was able to acquire Hyundai's plant in Qingdao at a bargain price – under $20 million. The deal gained CIMC production facilities with an estimated replacement value of $180 million, added a line for producing refrigerated containers, and effectively removed a major competitor from the market. In 2004 CIMC acquired a 60 per cent stake in Clive-Smith Cowley, the British company that invented the proprietary Domino technology that allows empty containers to be 'folded' for ease of back-hauling. In 2005 it bought up seventy-seven patents from a bankrupt competitor, Graaff – ironically the German firm from which CIMC had licensed its first refrigeration technology back in 1995. All of these acquisitions were rapidly integrated into CIMC's operations and then capacity in the segments they served was massively expanded to provide scale economies and force further consolidation in the global industry.

Global first-mover

This strategy for international expansion is based on the emerging market company becoming a global innovator, leveraging a low-cost home base and large home demand. Given the importance of cost innovation capabilities in creating their FSAs, many of the Chinese dragons could be seen as at least partially adopting this approach. For a few companies, such as telecoms equipment maker Huawei, this *global first-mover* strategy has been at the core of their international expansion. To some, the idea of a multinational from an emerging market betting its future on becoming a global innovator might seem unlikely. But although in many ways still a 'developing economy', China had built up a formidable base of high technology even prior to its opening up in 1978, much of it associated with defence requirements. As this technology has increasingly been transferred from government research institutes into the commercial sector, therefore, it is less surprising that a global first-mover strategy can be viable.

Up until 1995 Huawei still made most of its then-modest $200 million total sales to telecoms operators in rural China. However, even at that time its chairman, Ren Zhengfei, already had an ambitious goal for Huawei to 'become a world-class, leading global telecoms equipment manufacturer' (interview with authors, Shenzhen, April 2005). Huawei's first target was a small provider of mobile telephony services in Hong Kong, the then-fledgling Hutchison Telecom. Hong Kong was also the first region in the world to demand that consumers be offered number portability – the ability of users to change to a new telecoms provider while keeping their existing number. Re-engineering the telecommunications equipment and software to accommodate this then-novel requirement posed challenges. Hutchison found itself boxed into a corner because the best offer Hutchison's European equipment suppliers had come up with was a six-month implementation time. Huawei saw its chance to become a first-mover: it committed to complete this innovative application in just three months and at a lower cost than its competitors. By dedicating a large team of Chinese engineers looking for a cost-innovative solution to Hutchison's problem, Huawei kept its promise. With its first satisfied customer outside mainland China, albeit an operator in tiny Hong Kong, Huawei was launched on the road to globalization.

Huawei continued to target new entrants among the telecom operators who were prepared to try innovative approaches and technologies in order to stretch their limited funding and in the hope of gaining a competitive advantage over their established rivals by breaking the rules. A good example is AIS in Thailand, a maverick

company that had been set up by entrepreneur Taksin Shinawatra –
a retired police chief later to become Thailand's billionaire prime
minister.

In 1999 Huawei installed and tested equipment to support AIS's
novel prepaid service in just sixty days. Following this success, Huawei
went on to supply AIS with the equipment and support to increase its
network capacity eightfold, to become the largest mobile telecommunications company in Thailand. In the course of these expansions,
Huawei developed more than eighty unique features, tailored to meet
AIS's particular needs. And it continued to deliver each, up and run-
ning, in record time, allowing AIS to be consistently first to market
with new, value-added services for users, helping it to go on winning
market share.

Huawei then looked for an opportunity to parlay its experience
with peripheral markets and new players into sales in the mainstream,
developed world. An important stepping-stone was a deal with
Etisalat, the operator in the wealthy United Arab Emirates (UAE).
The country has a population of just 2.4 million, but it provided an
opportunity to prove Huawei's capability in an advanced, 'third
generation' (3G) mobile application. Pitted against the global majors
like Motorola and Ericsson in a parallel equipment trial (or 'test-off')
Huawei used its cost advantage to put an incredible number of
engineers (200) on-site in the UAE, with many more supporting staff
back in China, to continually evaluate and improve its technology.
After one year, Huawei's equipment came out top of the performance
league and Huawei won the contract for full-scale implementation.
This was the world's first project commercializing R4 technology,
an emerging switching technology that effectively substituted flexible
software for less flexible and more expensive hardware, and that
Huawei was betting on heavily to catapult it to technology leadership.

With the UAE as reference site in the bag, it went on winning
contracts to build entire 3G mobile networks at SUNDAY in Hong
Kong, Emtel in Mauritius, and TM in Malaysia. Once its track record
of experience, success, and volume was firmly in place, Huawei then
began to move in on more mainstream developed markets, starting
with Europe.

Its first European contract to build a 3G Universal Mobile Telecommunications System to provide mobile broadband access to the
Internet and services such as video telephony was with Telfort BV of

the Netherlands, previously an Ericsson customer and reported by the media to be worth between $265 and $530 million. During the signing ceremony, Ton aan de Stegge, CEO of Telfort, observed: 'Telfort's strategy is to challenge the established norms of the mobile industry, and this contract, which is the first of its kind in Europe, is exactly in line with that. We are confident that Huawei will help us to develop innovative and cost effective data solutions for our customers and look forward to a prosperous relationship with them' (cited in Normile, 2005).

By following this global first-mover strategy, Huawei became a potent global competitor that was able to beat both Motorola and Britain's Marconi to win a share of British Telecom Group plc's $19 billion 21st Century Network.

Each of the four generic strategies identified by Ramamurti and Singh in their analysis of India's emerging multinationals, therefore, can also be observed among Chinese emerging global dragons. We postulate that one reason for these similarities is that these strategies allow emerging multinationals from both emerging economies to take advantage of the new gateways to entry that are being opened up by increasing globalization of the world economy.

Globalization opens new gateways to entry

The gateways being opened up by globalization of the world economy that have enabled multinationals from emerging economies to quickly become a potent force in global competition, despite being latecomers with a 'liability of foreignness' (Zaheer, 1995), include:

- the increasing use of 'outsourcing' by established multinational companies;
- the increasing modularization of products and services from automobiles to software and financial services;
- the so-called 'Global Knowledge Economy' and the drive to codify more and more of the world's knowledge so that it can be handled by IT and communications systems;
- concentration and globalization of retailing;
- a more fluid international market for talent and professional services;
- a more open market for corporate control, allowing the Chinese to acquire foreign companies.

In the following sections we explore how each of these trends is acting to open opportunities to speed up the process, and reduce the risks, of building multinationals from emerging economies using the generic strategies described above.

Outsourcing opens the gates

As global competition heats up, the cost pressures on US, European, and Japanese firms have led to a boom in their use of outsourcing (Brown and Wilson, 2005). Established multinationals are concentrating on the activities whose returns are most attractive and where they see the potential to build competitive advantage, leaving other pieces of the chain – both basic manufacturing and routine services – to be supplied by others. This drive toward more focused businesses in the West has also led to the global value chain being cut into ever-finer slices.

Carving up the global value chain and outsourcing less attractive activities makes a lot of sense as a way of boosting profitability. But it is also having an important side effect: outsourcing is opening up a new gateway through which Chinese dragons can penetrate into the heart of the world economy.

In the past, when established multinationals were much more vertically integrated than they are today, a new entrant was faced with replicating an entire complex system of activities in order to compete effectively. In today's de-integrated global value chains, where many of the participants concentrate on just one or two activities and the integrators at the top of the chain use a plethora of subcontractors and outsourced services, Chinese companies can get a foothold in the industry by capturing just one slice. Globalization and de-integration of supply chains have had the side effect of reducing the barriers to entry for newcomers like the Chinese dragons. Once they have established a beachhead, they can then use the weight of their cost advantage and capabilities for rapid learning to relentlessly expand into other activities along the chain. Starting out as junior partners, they can eventually become major players.

A recent study of a typical 'American' car by the WTO, for example, found that of a vehicle notionally made in the United States, 30% of the value was accounted for by Korean subassembly suppliers, 17.5% by Japan for specialized components and advanced technology,

7.5% by Germany for design, 4% by Taiwan and Singapore for minor parts, 2.5% by the United Kingdom for advertising and marketing services, and 1.5% by Ireland and Barbados for data processing. In total, the US auto manufacturer accounted for just 37% of the value-creating activities (World Trade Organization, 1998, p. 36).

The rise of the auto parts maker Wanxiang (described above) is a good example of how these high levels of outsourcing in the auto industry have opened gates through which the Chinese have been able to enter, even while their capability bases are still narrow. This outsourcing gateway to entry is a key to enabling the *low-cost partner* strategy to be pursued successfully.

Modular products and services

Another gateway being opened up by globalization is the modularization of value chains (Fleury and Fleury, 2007). In some industries, the slicing and dicing of the global value chain is so far advanced that the chain has come to resemble a series of 'plug-and-play' modules. This kind of modularity is a familiar principle in the computer business, for example. Different companies can independently design and produce components, such as disk drives or operating system software, and those modules will fit together into a complex and smoothly functioning product because the module makers obey an accepted set of design rules. When a dominant design emerges in a particular industry, modularity increases efficiency and speed of innovation. But modularization, like outsourcing, also helps frame a well-defined gateway through which emerging Chinese firms have entered the global market even while they have a limited set of capabilities.

Creating a mobile phone handset, for example, used to be a black art known only to a few global players, so entry of the Chinese dragons was forestalled. For years the big three producers – Motorola, Nokia, and Ericsson – together controlled around 80 per cent of the Chinese market, while other foreign manufacturers, including Philips, Alcatel, Siemens, and Sony, shared the rest. Chinese companies only started to enter the market in 1998 and in the first few years struggled to gain a foothold in their home market, let alone break into the business abroad.

Since 2000, however, as the technology has matured the value chain has been broken down into different modules, from radio frequency circuits to RISC (reduced instruction set computing) chips and applications software. The interactions between each of these modules are now regulated by a codified set of standards available to all. Specialist companies such as Wavecom of France, which makes radio frequency modules, and Bellwave of Korea, which specializes in mobile phone design, offer the core building blocks of mobile phones. This means new entrants can launch a phone by 'picking and mixing' these modules to create a distinctive product.

The Chinese competitors grabbed the opportunity opened up by modularization with both hands. Companies such as Ningbo Bird, Amoi, TCL, and Konka launched attractive phones by combining third-party modules with the help of Korean design houses. Modularization has allowed the dam that had held back the Chinese for a decade to be broken; Chinese handset producers captured 55% of the Chinese market in 2003, up from a mere 8% in 2000. By 2006 Ningbo Bird announced that it had signed contracts to sell customized handsets to ten global operators, including Vodaphone and AT&T. Meanwhile, it was rapidly penetrating emerging markets for handsets, such as in Mexico, where it was selling phones at the rate of 300,000 per annum. Global leaders such as Nokia and Motorola are fighting back aggressively against the expansion of Chinese handset competition – obviously the game is far from over. But the message is clear: modularization provided the key that opened the global market to Chinese competition using both the *local optimizer* and *low-cost partner* generic strategies.

The codification of knowledge

The corollary of global supply chains becoming modular is that knowledge becomes more codified. And once knowledge that used to be tacit becomes codified, it can be digitized. It is then only a short step into the global knowledge base and onto the information superhighway. Increased codification of knowledge and rapid advances in communications, not least the emergence of the Internet, mean that it is much easier for Chinese firms to fill information gaps and to keep up with leading-edge developments anywhere in the world. The CEOs of Chinese high-tech firms we interviewed, such as those at Dawning and TechFaith, all explained that they were now just a few months behind the global industry leaders in knowing what was happening on the cutting edge. For knowledge that is still not accessible by digital means, it is now much easier for Chinese companies to establish subsidiaries to act as their 'eyes and ears' in hotbeds of new technology, customer applications, or competitor intelligence around the world. Many of the emerging dragons have therefore established a network of overseas offices for just this purpose. Huawei, for example, maintains a R&D centre just down the street from Ericsson's headquarters in Stockholm.

The increasing codification of knowledge is relevant to helping multinationals from emerging markets successfully execute all of the generic strategies discussed above; but it is particularly important in enabling the global first-mover strategy, because of the need to access knowledge available around the world to compliment local technologies in ways that enable the company to become a global innovator.

Concentration and internationalization of retailing

Increasing concentration of the retail sector has also reduced the barriers Chinese companies face in penetrating global markets. In the past – when reaching the final customer meant navigating fragmented, multilayered wholesaling and retailing in every individual country – building distribution channels took years. Today, Wal-Mart alone buys more than $18 billion worth of goods in China each year. Once a Chinese company cracks the Wal-Mart account, it is automatically on the shelves of thousands of stores in the string of countries in which the retailer operates. And because the world's retailers are under relentless pressure from customers and competitors to provide greater value for money, they are prepared to assist budding Chinese multinationals with the world's lowest costs by teaching them how to upgrade and customize their products to enhance value to the consumer. Working directly with Chinese manufacturers in this way, the retailers can cut out the middlemen and shorten the chain to remove dead-weight costs.

The story of how Haier broke into the mass market in the United States market is a good example. Haier's CEO, Zhang Riu Min, recalled:

I set my US general manager the target of half of the top ten retail chains in the United States. He said it was impossible – it took famous brands like General Electric, Whirlpool, and Maytag decades to do that. Eventually we

came up with a way forward: we erected a huge billboard displaying the
Haier brand and some of our products on the road outside Wal-Mart's
headquarters in Arkansas. Seeing the advertisement from his office window,
Wal-Mart's head of purchasing began to enquire into Haier and its capabilities. (*Dialog*, 2003)

This led to Haier working closely with Wal-Mart to fine-tune its
product designs and marketing. As well as getting product onto US
shelves, the relationship with Wal-Mart helped the Chinese company
overcome its lack of in-depth understanding of the United States
and learn to better tailor its products to fit US consumer needs. In
exchange, Wal-Mart reaped benefits from adding a new supplier
capable of offering products with outstanding value for money. Today
a large proportion of Haier's US sales come from the top ten retailers –
Wal-Mart, Lowe's, Best Buy, Home Depot, Office Depot, Target,
Sam's Club, Costco, Circuit City, and Sears. The pattern is the same in
Europe and Japan, where Haier's sales are concentrated in the top five
retailers. From a standing start twenty-five years ago, Haier is already
global number four in white goods, just behind the leaders from the
United States, Europe, and Japan, each with more than a hundred
years of history.

The ongoing consolidation of global retailing to create giants like
Wal-Mart, Carrefour, or Tesco, acting in their own self-interest, is
opening up a new gateway for Chinese dragons to enter the global
market, helping them reduce the barriers to entry that they would
otherwise face. It is a particularly important enabler for the global
consolidator strategy.

Globalization of the markets for talent and services

Another important trend that is powering Chinese firms' ability to
mount an attack on world markets, despite their lack of international
experience and gaping holes in their knowledge bases, is the increasing
globalization of the markets for talent and business services.

A decade ago, it was very unusual to find an experienced Western
expatriate working for a Chinese company. But as the global market
for talent becomes more fluid, Chinese companies now employ dozens,
sometimes hundreds, of foreign experts both to fill their knowledge
gaps in China and to help establish their subsidiaries abroad. Take the
example of the Pearl River Piano Group. Pearl River was established

in 1956 in the southern city of Guangzhou (at that time, known in the West as Canton). For decades it was just another SOE. But in the early 1990s, as China's modernization gathered speed, Pearl River became aware that it was only earning one-third of the price for its pianos in China that foreign piano makers were earning. It also came to the painful realization that the quality of its instruments was, quite simply, poor.

With piano making hardly top of the priority list for government support, Pearl River's CEO, Tong Zhi Cheng, recognized that he would have to upgrade. His first step was to search the world for expertise. His first hire was Charles Corey, former general manager of US company Wurlitzer's piano plant. Corey's background had been in quality control, and he was regarded as a world expert. Pearl River's first foreign consultant, he ended up working with the company for more than ten years, helping it, as Tong put it, to 'overcome dozens of technological problems' (*Yangcheng Evening News*, 2004). In 1993 Pearl River hired two German experts to assist in improving the quality of their tuning process. The quality improvements they achieved allowed Pearl River to raise prices by 10 per cent. Over time, the company hired more than ten world-class consultants to assist in improving every aspect of piano making, from design to production to finished instrument. Looking back, Tong observed:

Without the help and guidance of these foreign experts there are some obstacles in piano making that we probably wouldn't have solved by our-selves in a lifetime! The fees of these foreign experts were extraordinarily high compared with the salaries of local people, but the technology and know-how they brought is the accumulation of hundreds of years of experience. After absorbing these insights we can use them generation after generation. No matter how high the price, it is worth it. We had to tighten our belt, learn the technology first, and then eat. (*Yangcheng Evening News*, 2004)

Likewise, as the market for corporate control has become more open throughout much of the world, and especially in developed economies, the dragons have increasing opportunities to use mergers and acquisitions to accelerate their international expansion and to capture assets, capabilities, and know-how that would otherwise take years to replicate. When it acquired IBM's PC business, Lenovo not only quadrupled its sales from $3 billion to $12 billion per annum, catapulting it into the number-three slot worldwide (behind Dell and Hewlett-Packard), it also gained the distribution networks that IBM had built up over decades in 116 countries. As part of the acquisition Lenovo also secured a broad-based strategic alliance with IBM that gave it the right to use the IBM trademark on its personal computers under licence for a period of five years. Lenovo also acquired full ownership of the 'Think' family of brands. Along with these benefits came the assets of IBM's personal computer division, including over 10,000 IBM employees, 40% already located in China, 25% stationed in the United States, and 35% elsewhere. IBM also agreed to ongoing marketing-support and demand-generation services through its existing sales force of 30,000 professionals and through IBM.com. IBM Global Financing and IBM Global Services – the number-one IT services organization in the world, with powerful existing enterprise channels – are preferred providers to Lenovo for leasing and financing services, and for warranty and maintenance services, respectively.

Of course, as US congressional disquiet – over the attempted acquisition of the American oil and gas company Unocal by CNOOC in 2005, and Haier's early interest when Maytag came up for sale – has demonstrated, the market for corporate control is not yet fully open to Chinese companies, even in the self-styled citadels of the free market. But the dragons will continue to knock at the doors of companies coming up for sale as they seek to use acquisitions to speed up their push into global markets. And there is mounting evidence that the door to Chinese global expansion through acquisitions is opening. The German consulting firm Klein and Coll found that Chinese firms acquired 278 German companies in 2003 alone. Most were small, with revenues of between $1 million and $10 million, but possessed know-how, patents, respected brands, and distribution relationships that their Chinese buyers hope to use to shortcut some of the slower stages of their global capability building agenda (Rabe and Hoffbauer, 2005).

The internationalization of professional service firms has also opened a new gateway through which Chinese companies can catch up with world best practice. McKinsey & Company, for example, has large offices in both Beijing and Shanghai. Over two-thirds of their assignments are for Chinese clients. Lenovo has a $200 million brand-building and PR contract with Ogilvy & Mather, part of the global WPP advertising and marketing services group. Since 1997, Huawei alone has spent more than $70 million in consulting fees to hire IBM, Hay Group, Towers Perrin, PricewaterhouseCoopers, and FhG to help it build up management systems, introduce best practices, and improve operation efficiency in many areas. Such investment in upgrading its processes and management capabilities has been invaluable in helping Huawei maintain its fast-paced growth. Many of the world's leading accounting and law firms are also working for Chinese companies.

Because China is the world's fastest-growing market for machinery and equipment (between 2000 and 2004 it accounted for nearly two-thirds of the global growth in fixed capital investment), suppliers of capital goods are falling all over themselves to get a share of the Chinese market. This buying power means many Chinese companies are able to demand that their suppliers provide extraordinary levels of technical advice and support. This gives the Chinese a golden opportunity to absorb new technology and learn world best practice, accelerating the pace at which they can catch up with established multinationals.

These diverse aspects of globalization are all converging on at least one point: they are jointly breaking down the barriers that Chinese companies would otherwise face in their quest to become global players and opening up new gateways through which they can enter the global game. These gateways are particularly important in enabling the global consolidator and global first-mover strategies, as both rely on a relatively open international market for corporate control, talent, and services to access the intangible assets on which these strategies depend.

Overall, because the Chinese are entering a world economy that is already highly globalized, they have the potential to quickly build multinational enterprises more powerful and more pervasive across industries and markets than anything we have seen in the past – Japanese and Korean giants such as Toyota and Samsung included.

Weaknesses of the emerging Chinese multinationals

Despite the impact of globalization in reducing barriers to inter-nationalization faced by the Chinese dragons, they do have significant weaknesses. These weak points include: a limited capability to run complex, systemic businesses; a lack of strong brands; the limitations of cost innovation where industries are in the early stages of the product life cycle; and difficulty in penetrating businesses where the market is immature or nonexistent in China or the developing world. We briefly explore the impact of these weaknesses in turn.

Limited size of the Chinese and developing markets

Where the Chinese market is small, the dragons don't have much opportunity to build volume and experience at home before venturing into the global market. Worse still, if developing country markets for a product or service are small or nonexistent, Chinese competitors can't use a strategy of building volume in peripheral, emerging markets where skills honed in China are most applicable and competition from established multinationals is arguably less intense. The limited size of the Chinese and developing markets compared with the global market, therefore, acts as an impediment to the dragons to challenging global incumbents.

The investment banking sector, especially merger and acquisition (M&A) services, is a good example. Just five years ago regulatory restrictions meant the M&A market in China was virtually non-existent. By 2005, China still accounted for less than 2% of global M&A activity by value, while total M&A in the developing world was only 5% (Dealogic, 2006). As a result, Chinese banks and financial services companies had little or no opportunity to develop their skills, experience, and volume in this sector. With the US market accounting for nearly half of global activity and the EU countries a further 40%, the outside-in strategy simply wouldn't work for M&A services. Not surprisingly, the Chinese cost innovation wedge hasn't even scratched the surface in the market for investment banking services.

The small size of the Chinese and developing country markets compared with global demand has historically blunted the Chinese cost innovation wedge in other product markets, such as automobiles. For example, China's leading auto maker, Chery, historically produced little more than 100,000 vehicles per year. Volume at Tianjin First Autoworks was only modestly higher; Geely's output was even lower. These volumes paled into insignificance compared with global volumes of over 8 million cars per annum each for Toyota, General Motors, and Ford. Even Hyundai, the global number seven, churns out over 3 million vehicles per year. While the Chinese market remained small relative to the global market, the growth of Chinese multinationals was forestalled.

As a critical element in three of Ramamurti and Singh's generic strategies – global consolidator, global first-mover, and local optimizer – industries where the Chinese and developing markets account for only a small percentage of global demand will prove difficult territory for these strategies to succeed.

Immature industries

Chinese cost innovation also has less potential as a source of FSA where a dominant technology has not yet emerged. Without a dominant technology it is difficult to climb aboard an experience curve that leads to reduced costs through economies of scale and learning. As a result, even when the Chinese come up with cost innovation ideas, they have trouble leveraging them up. Moreover, when a new business is emerging and early adopters are the target customers, it is novel functionality that drives the demand, rather than value for money. Technological uncertainty and an immature market comprising early adopters, therefore, expose limitations as to where the dragons' cost innovation strategy can be applied.

These impediments are aptly demonstrated by the lack of Chinese penetration in the mobile phone handset business early in its product life cycle. While proprietary base technologies were competing for pre-eminence, the Chinese competitors were at a disadvantage to their established global rivals. They lacked sufficient knowledge and strength in the base technology and the global experience to drive proprietary approaches into the market. While the pace of technological change remained rapid – a characteristic of the early product life cycle – Chinese firms struggled to get reliable products out in a timely manner. The Chinese cost innovation wedge was blunted by an inability to keep up with a fast-moving product life cycle and the cost penalties associated with the need to buy key bits of proprietary technology from their Western competitors. Not surprisingly, the dragons' fire was sapped and, despite investing (and losing) a great deal of money, they made little headway in gaining market share.

Immature technology, therefore, will tend to be an important impediment to successful application of all of Ramamurti and Singh's generic strategies with the possible exception of local optimizer.

Successfully executing a global first-mover strategy in such an environment will be particularly difficult. This implies, in turn, that multinationals from emerging economies are only likely to succeed as global first-movers either when technological advances spring from an already established technology base, or when first-mover advantage can be gained in other dimensions such as customization, new distribution methods, or dramatically improved value for money.

Systemic businesses

A third industry characteristic that exposes the limitations of the dragons' cost innovation strategy and impedes their advance is what economists call a *systemic* value network – in other words, industries in which a successful competitor needs to manage a complex, largely indivisible system of activities in order to deliver an attractive offering to the customer. Fast-moving consumer goods (FMCG) industries such as ready-made foods, snacks, or personal care products are a good example. These industries generally don't involve particularly high technology. But getting them right involves coordinating a complex, interrelated system that brings together sophisticated market research and product development; global sourcing of nonstandard, natural raw materials; manufacturing processes that must work as a continuous flow; and complex logistics that must take account of product variations (such as the shelf-life of different foods) and sophisticated marketing campaigns. The value delivered to the final consumer is only as good as the weakest part of this systemic network. Because a successful competitor must orchestrate the entire system to get the right result, it isn't clear where the Chinese can insert their cost innovation wedge. This is a key reason that multinational firms such as Procter & Gamble, Unilever, L'Oréal, and Henkel have dominant positions in many FMCG sectors such as personal care products and cosmetics, even in China.

The drug business is another example. Traditional approaches to drug development used by the pharmaceutical industry are highly systemic, involving research, development, and clinical testing teams working together to use their tacit knowledge of interrelated, often proprietary processes.

The weakness of the dragons in these systemic industries is that they can't easily 'slice and dice' the value chain into separate activity modules that require only simple interfaces and minimal coordination to deliver value to the end customer. Chinese companies can't break in by applying cost innovation to just one part of the chain. Instead they would have to tackle the complete complement of activities at once, with the risk of failure caused by the handicaps they face in other activities or the fact that their limited resources would be spread too thin. This tends to undermine the Chinese multinationals' competitive traction, whichever of the generic strategies discussed above they choose.

Intangible assets

The final factor that impedes the advance of Chinese competition is the importance of intangible assets, such as brands or proprietary technology and experience that are costly to build and require as well a significant investment of time. Where these assets are critical to competitive success, the Chinese, as latecomers, are disadvantaged.

The power of cost innovation tends to be blunted in businesses where the bulk of customers won't even try a new supplier if they don't recognize the brand. Offering high technology, variety, or specialized products at low cost isn't enough if customers never recognize these benefits or aren't prepared to take the risk that such seemingly attractive Chinese offers might turn out to be a mirage.

Retailing is a prime example of the kind of industry in which Chinese companies face considerable intangible asset barriers. In addition to the importance of a strong retail brand – enjoyed by the likes of Wal-Mart, Carrefour, or Tesco – success in retailing involves a plethora of intangible assets including relationships, knowledge about supplier management, logistics, shelf-space control, display, merchandising, and sales-force training.

Since labour costs are mostly driven by local wage rates, it's difficult for the Chinese to transfer the cost advantage to retail operations overseas. Meanwhile the scope for cost innovation is probably limited (although in consumer electronics retailing Chinese competitors have developed an innovative 'while-you-wait' system where, after discussing a customer's requirements, a technician will assemble a customized PC or home theatre to suit those exact needs from basic components in-store).

One reflection of the intangible asset advantage enjoyed by the international players over their emerging Chinese competitors is the fact that all of the fifty largest global retailers have entered the Chinese market (e.g., Carrefour has sixty-eight stores and Wal-Mart is close behind with sixty-two). While local competitors are fast imitating the capabilities of the global retailers, it is unclear that Chinese retailers will be able to develop significant sources of FSA beyond the CSAs of local knowledge and low overhead. This will impede their ability to expand into the global market outside China.

An additional generic strategy: The demand wedge

It is clear that while globalization of the world economy is opening up gateways that the Chinese dragons can use to increase the probability and speed of successful internationalization, some important barriers to the success of the generic strategies that we have discussed above in gaining competitive advantage in the global market still remain. These barriers are highest in industries where Chinese and developing country demand is limited relative to the size of the global market, where a dominant technology has yet to emerge, where intangible assets that take time to build and are difficult to acquire are critical for competitive success, and where the value chain is systemic (rather than modular). Faced with these barriers, however, we observe the Chinese dragons adopting an additional generic strategy beyond those identified by Ramamurti and Singh: the demand wedge – the use of China's clout as a large and rapidly growing buyer in the global market to secure a position for Chinese companies where their learning can be maximized, and so overcome the barriers they would otherwise face. In this way, the dragons use China's importance on the demand side of the global market (not only on the supply side) as a wedge to drive their global penetration into systemic businesses, those with immature technologies, or those with a heavy dependence on intangible assets that would otherwise be hard to crack.

This use of demand-side leverage, of course, is not a new phenomenon. Since 1978, when China began to open the doors to foreign investment, Chinese policy makers have used the potential of their local market as a lever to promote the transfer of foreign technology to Chinese organizations and individuals. In recent years, however, this strategy has been applied to successively higher technology areas.

Once they have absorbed the foreign technology, Chinese companies have increasingly begun to apply their cost innovation capabilities to build new types of FSAs around the technological core.

Using the demand wedge

Take the example of the massive hydropower-generation turbines used in major dams. In 1997, the Three Gorges Dam project invited bids for power-generation equipment. The specifications demanded turbines capable of generating 700 megawatts per unit – some of the largest, heaviest, and most powerful machines in the world. Just a handful of global suppliers such as General Electric, Siemens, and Mitsubishi had the know-how to design, manufacture, and install this complex equipment. Even they had installed only twenty-one machines of this size and complexity in the world.

At the time, the barriers faced by the Chinese players in entering this industry looked insurmountable. Chinese firms were only able to produce 320-megawatt machines, and were decades behind in technology. So the Chinese government announced that it would accept bids only from consortia comprised of a lead foreign company and Chinese firms. It further stipulated that, during the project, the winning foreign firms must actively transfer core technology to their Chinese partners. Faced with such an onerous condition, in effect requiring the multinationals to surrender their technology and know-how in order to win a single contract, the global players would normally have walked away. But the contract the Chinese were putting out to tender was for fourteen machines, a single order equal in size to two-thirds of the total capacity previously installed worldwide. With such massive prospective global sales up for grabs, the bidders lined up, despite having to share their proprietary technology and know-how with future potential competitors.

Once the Chinese government had used its massive buying power to help the putative Chinese dragons pry open the market for its local companies, the dragons were quick to learn. By 2005 the Chinese firms were capable of producing the 700-megawatt machines independently and at lower costs; in consequence, they won a 67 per cent share of the orders put out to tender in the second phase of the Three Gorges Dam. The dragons' next horizon, of course, would be to take their cost advantage into the global market. This is exactly what happened in 2006. A consortium of four Chinese firms, of which three were involved in the original Three Gorges deal, won a contract to build power stations with 10 million-megawatt output over the next three years in Indonesia. This project is worth between $7 billion and $8 billion – equivalent to one-third of the total installed power station capacity in Indonesia.

In those industries where the Chinese cost innovation wedge alone isn't effective in breaking down the barriers around the global market, therefore, beware the possibility that a demand wedge might take its place. The pattern has been repeated in other sectors where the dragons face high barriers because of complex, systemic value chains and limited potential for labour cost advantage. Take the example of petrochemicals. Sinopec, the largest integrated petrochemical company in China, has sales of $75 billion per annum (ranking it 31 in the Fortune Global 500). When such a powerful global buyer says it would like to join as a partner in a foreign oil or gas project from which it can gain invaluable knowledge and experience to build its own capabilities, few are willing to demur. Using this demand wedge, Sinopec now has active participation in oil and gas development in six countries. Meanwhile its state-owned rival, China National Petroleum Corporation, with a turnover of $68 billion, has been invited to invest in more than forty projects across twenty countries. It is only a matter of time before the cycle of learning and cost innovation kicks in, and their entry into the global market as independent competitors follows.

Another industry where this strategy is at work is aircraft manufacturing. Coordinating an aircraft's value chain is the epitome of system complexity, the global market is controlled by a handful of players, each with massive stocks of proprietary high technology, and the product life cycle begins anew almost every time a new model of aircraft, using the latest materials, is introduced. Lagging decades behind global leaders such as Airbus and Boeing, surely the Chinese don't have a chance.

Even in aircraft manufacturing, however, the Chinese dragons are starting to catch up. Their strategy involves three stages. First, they find a pressure point where they can participate in global value chains on the basis of even their narrow cost advantage. Thus, quite a few Chinese firms have become subcontractor component suppliers or subassemblers for minor pieces of Boeing and Airbus planes.

Once they have travelled some way down the experience curve and have a better understanding of how the complex system that delivers an aircraft works, the Chinese firms bid to supply higher-value components and subsystems. The fact that China is now one of the largest markets for aircraft, and that offering to increase local content is often decisive in the politicized world of aircraft procurement, helps the emerging dragons win a disproportionate share of the business. This, in turn, creates opportunities for further learning. Airbus, for example, recently awarded contracts to the Chinese company AVIC (Aviation Industries of China) equivalent to 5 per cent of the total work involved in producing its new narrow-body jet, the A350. As part of the deal, Airbus agreed to set up a joint R&D centre with AVIC in China.

At the same time, Chinese firms have learned how to build a complete aircraft. For instance, using the demand wedge, they convinced McDonnell Douglas to have the Chinese deliver 70 per cent local content for two models of their long-haul MD-90 jet in late 1980s. By the time McDonnell Douglas discontinued the relationship – shortly after it was taken over by Boeing – much of the necessary systemic know-how had already been absorbed by its Chinese partners.

Using what they learned through the Airbus and McDonnell Douglas deals the same Chinese firms or their associates are now targeting the market for regional jets. By applying a dose of cost innovation, Xi'an Aircraft Co. has developed a sixty-seat regional jet that costs 30 per cent less than competing aircraft on the market. While still meeting global standards in safety and reliability, Xi'an's plane also offers customers 10 per cent lower operating costs relative to comparable aircraft.

AVIC, meanwhile, is investing $600 million to develop the ARJ21 – a 110-seat regional jet. Again, its weapon is cost innovation, so instead of using leading-edge design concepts to try to produce a more sophisticated aircraft, it has taken the same advanced technology and applied it to the problem of how to build a uniquely cost-competitive plane using mostly standard components from a mature supplier base.

The resulting plane will start commercial operation in 2008. AVIC's target? To sell 300 planes in China and 200 globally within the next twenty years. Using the demand wedge may not be subtle, but it seems to be effective in allowing the dragons to overcome their lack of intangible assets to break into complex businesses. Once through the door, they are proving adept at using cost innovation to win market share.

Conclusion: The emergence of Chinese multinationals will reshape global competition

In this chapter we have described how emerging Chinese multinationals are successfully parlaying China's CSAs into FSAs in cost innovation: delivering high technology at affordable cost to mass markets, offering variety and customization at little or no price premium over a standard offering, and using their low break-even to seek to 'explode' niche markets for specialist goods into volume businesses. We compared and contrasted the generic strategies identified by Ramamurti and Singh in the case of India with the strategies being adopted by Chinese dragons. We found a high degree of commonality at the level of these generic strategies.

Our subsequent analysis went on to show how these generic strategies were taking advantage of new gateways to entry being opened up as world markets increasingly globalize. We concluded that this interaction was greatly speeding up the rate and scale at which Chinese companies were able to emerge as globally competitive multinationals. At the same time, we identified some important barriers that these generic strategies found it difficult to overcome – barriers that varied significantly and systematically across industries. In those industries where impediments to success were high we found that emerging Chinese multinationals were adopting an additional strategy – the demand wedge – to break in. After gaining scale and experience through this approach, they were then able to apply their cost innovation FSAs to grow share.

Yesterday's competition from China might have come in the form of basic functionality at the lowest possible price. But because of the forces of globalization in the world economy discussed above, and the gateways to entry they open up, the competitive challenge posed by China's budding global players is increasing rapidly. Incumbent multinationals and national champions worldwide, that used to be protected because their products were differentiated by offering high technology, a wide variety of models to choose from, or specialized features, will increasingly be confronted by competitors that use cost innovation to create FSAs that allow them to match many of these benefits while simultaneously offering better value for money. We therefore expect the continued emergence of Chinese multinationals to have a powerful, disruptive impact on the shape of the global competitive landscape.

References

Brown, D. and S. Wilson (2005), *The Black Book of Outsourcing: How to Manage the Changes, Challenges, and Opportunities*, Hoboken, NJ: John Wiley & Sons Inc.

Caves, R. E. and M. E. Porter (1978), 'Market Structures, Oligopoly, and Stability of Market Shares', *Journal of Industrial Economics*, Vol. 26 (June), pp. 289–308.

Dealogic (2006), www.dealogic.com.

Dialog (2003), 'Interview with Zhang Rai Min', CCTV 2, 14 December.

Fleury A. and M. T. Fleury (2007), 'Evolution and Reconfiguration of Production Systems', *Journal of Manufacturing and Technology Management*, Vol. 18, No. 8, pp. 946–965.

Government of Singapore (2006), www.csc.mti-mofcom.gov.sg

Nelson, R. R. and S. G. Winter (1982), *An Evolutionary Theory of Economic Change*. Cambridge, MA: Belknap Press/Harvard University Press.

Normile, D. (2005), 'Chinese Telecom Companies Come Calling', *Electronic Business*, 1 February.

Rabe, C. and A. Hoffbauer (2005), 'Chinesische Firmen drängen auf den deutschen Markt', *Handelsblatt*, 9 June, p. 1.

Rugman, A. (1981), *Inside the Multinationals*, New York: Columbia University Press.

Verdin, P. and P. J. Williamson (1994), 'From Barriers to Entry to Barriers to Survival', in *Building the Strategically Responsive Organisation* (H. Thomas, ed.), Chichester, UK: Wiley, ch. 15.

World Brand Laboratory (2006), www.brand.icxo.com/

World Trade Organization (1998), *Annual Report 1998*.

Yangcheng Evening News (2004), 'Pearl River Piano Will Strike a Strong Tone of Global Brand', 7 June, p. 2.

Zaheer, S. (1995), 'Overcoming the Liability of Foreignness', *Academy of Management Journal*, Vol. 38, No. 2, pp. 341–363.

Zeng, M. and P. J. Williamson (2003), 'The Hidden Dragons', *Harvard Business Review*, Vol. 81, No. 10 (October), pp. 92–99.

Zeng, M. and P. J. Williamson (2007), *Dragons at Your Door: How Chinese Cost Innovation is Disrupting Global Competition*, Boston, MA: Harvard Business School Press.

6 Indian multinationals: Generic internationalization strategies

RAVI RAMAMURTI AND JITENDRA V. SINGH[1]

Indian firms expanded outward in two waves, the first occurring in the 1970s and 1980s, and the second occurring after 1995, shortly after India had opened up to the global economy in 1991 following economic reforms. The second wave was not only bigger in terms of the scale and speed of outward FDI, but the firms involved used a broader range of strategies. One especially interesting feature was that in the second wave 60–70 percent of the outward FDI went "up-market" (i.e., to highly advanced countries), unlike the first wave in which almost the same proportion went "down-market" (i.e., to countries less developed than India; Lall, 1983). In addition, there was some evidence that in 2006 and the first half of 2007, Indian firms may have invested more abroad than foreign MNEs invested in India – a surprising result for a poor country, although the data underlying these claims need more careful sorting out (Dunning and Narula, 1996).[2,3]

---

[1] We thank Yair Aharoni, Saikat Chaudhuri, Charles Dhanaraj, Devesh Kapur, Tarun Khanna, Don Lessard, and other participants at the NU-Wharton conference for helpful comments.

[2] Indian inward FDI was underestimated for many years, because, for instance, reinvested earnings were not counted as inward FDI, even though this was standard international practice. (This was remedied starting in 2000–2001.) In 2006–07, inward FDI reached $19 billion (*Economist*, 2007a, p. 35). In calendar year 2006 outward FDI was estimated at $9.9 billion, while in the first four months of 2007, that figure rose to $24.4 billion, thanks to two large acquisitions by Tata Steel and Hindalco (*Economist*, 2007b, p. 2). However, a large part of the acquisition funds was raised overseas by both companies, as a result of which official outward FDI figures are likely to be lower. Data compiled by Thomson Financial on outward M&A deals by Indian companies also registered a big increase from 2005 to 2006 (Accenture 2006, pp. 8, 13).

[3] A newspaper report (*Financial Express*, June 18, 2007), quoting from a study of outbound and inbound FDI by the Federation of Indian Chambers of Commerce and Industry (*Financial Express*, June 18, 2007) and Ernst & Young, stated: "For [the] Indian corporate sector, 2006 was a watershed year in terms of mergers and acquisitions as Indian companies went shopping across the globe. The total outbound deals, which were valued at $4.3 billion in 2005, crossed the

In this chapter, we try to get beneath these intriguing macro outcomes by looking at the underlying micro phenomena at the firm level. Among other questions, we ask: Which Indian firms were at the vanguard of internationalization, and why? What international competitive advantages did they enjoy, and why? How did they internationalize? Which firms directed their investment to the advanced countries, and why? And finally, what impact did Indian firms have on the structure and dynamics of the global industries in which they participated?

It turns out that India, unsurprisingly, is a somewhat unique country. It is poor on average, but quite rich and advanced in specific pockets. Its technical capabilities, built over the many decades before and after independence in 1947, were leveraged in unanticipated ways in the second wave of outward expansion. India's institutions, especially its capital markets, were also more sophisticated than one might usually expect for a poor country. All this, combined with a low-cost base, a strong entrepreneurial tradition, a large, booming internal market, and a seasoned, high-quality managerial class, helped to launch a new breed of Indian multinationals in the first decade of the 2000s.

These multinationals did not follow one monolithic strategy for internationalization, as was the case in the 1970s and 1980s (see Lall, 1983; and Wells, 1977 and 1983). Instead, they took a few different paths. We identify in this chapter four such paths, which we here term generic internationalization strategies, each based on a different set of competitive advantages, governed by a different logic, and resulting in a different choice of target markets and modes of entry. We hope that bringing these generic strategies into focus, and highlighting the organizational demands and strategic dilemmas each is likely to present, will be helpful to future managers as they take their companies global.

It is worth noting that these generic strategies identified here are not unique to Indian firms or to India; they are relevant for MNEs from other emerging markets as well. As a group, nevertheless, these generic strategies are unlikely to be pursued by firms in advanced

---

$15 billion mark in the following year and it could well breach the $35 billion level this year." In the fiscal year 2007–2008, the estimated $35 billion in outbound FDI deals would likely exceed the target of $30 billion for inbound FDI.

economies because they are rooted in conditions peculiar to emerging markets, such as low-income consumers, low-wage workers, high-growth domestic markets, and underdeveloped hard and soft institutions (on the latter, see Khanna and Palepu, 2006, and Khanna, Palepu, and Sinha, 2005). At the same time, distinctive aspects of each emerging economy will make some generic strategies more viable than others.

In particular, we believe India's experience was influenced by four distinctive characteristics: the large size of its economy; the country's stock of human capital (technical and managerial); its stronger institutions such as capital markets and the rule of law, at least when compared with other countries at comparable stages of development; and its historically rooted entrepreneurial traditions – none of which factors typically are present in every emerging economy. These factors may explain why many Indian firms have fared quite well in the post-liberalization period and why they were more prone to up-market FDI, compared to firms in many other emerging economies.

In terms of the several possibilities for FDI flows presented in the opening chapter, and reproduced here in Figure 6.1, India provides a good setting for exploring the least studied case – that is, Cell 4, which refers to South–North FDI flows. Despite its low per-capita income (under $1,000 per person), 60–70 percent of India's outward FDI in the second wave, through 2006, went to the advanced countries, contrary to predictions of the product cycle model (Vernon, 1966, 1979). For discussion purposes, we call Cell 4 cases "up-market FDI," contrasting them with "down-market FDI" (Cells 2 and 3), wherein firms invest in host countries less developed than their home countries (Indian firms still initiate down-market FDI, although that is not our main focus here). It is quite possible that in the coming decade Indian firms will not only maintain but even accelerate their up-market FDI.

India may also be unique in another sense: Despite being a low-income country, by some accounts, in 2005 and 2006 it had more outward FDI than inward FDI, an outcome that contradicts the predictions of the investment development path (IDP) model (Dunning and Narula, 1996). Although short-run trends of the sort, even if true, can be reversed by one or two giant deals going the other way, we suspect that India has a higher propensity to invest abroad and a lower propensity to attract inward FDI than countries of similar size and per-capita income, perhaps reflecting the strength of the local private

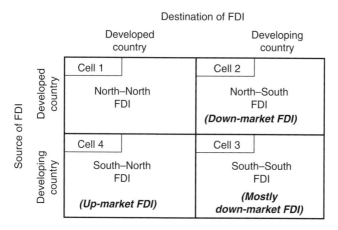

Figure 6.1 Source and destination of FDI

Note: Down-market FDI refers to investment from a more developed to a less developed country, and up-market FDI refers to the opposite

sector. A little known fact is that India exhibited the same pattern in the 1970s, when the first wave of outward FDI occurred: Through August 1980, cumulative overseas investment by Indian firms in projects completed and under way was $115.8 million, compared to cumulative inward FDI from 1969 to 1980 of $70 million (Lall, 1983; p. 22; both at 1980 exchange rates). When a surprising result of this sort is observed not once but twice in a country's brief history, it suggests the possibility that there may be something distinctive about the Indian example.

India's first and second waves of outward FDI

About the first wave of outward FDI from developing countries in the 1960s and 1970s, Lall (1983, p. 1) said: "In very recent years ... the number of foreign ventures by genuinely indigenous firms from a wide range of developing countries has increased dramatically. Not only this – the size of the foreign ventures has increased, their spread internationally has widened, and the sophistication of activities has greatly increased."

This same comment could have been made about the second wave of outward FDI from developing countries in the 1990s and 2000s. In many ways, the second wave of outward FDI from countries like India is merely a scaled-up version of what transpired in the 1970s and 1980s. The size of Indian foreign ventures has increased since the late 1970s and early 1980s; their investments are more dispersed than before, and the sophistication of activities has greatly increased. Yet, in some other respects, the second wave has been quite different from the first, at least as far as India is concerned. Based on what we know of India's second wave of investments and Lall's observations about the first wave in his 1983 work, several important differences stand out:

(1) Whereas in the first wave (Lall, 1983) 80% of outward FDI went to other *developing* countries (Cell 3), in the second wave almost 70% went to *developed* countries (Cell 4). While Indian firms made a large number of investments in other developing countries in the second wave, the value of investments going to developed countries was much higher.

(2) Whereas in the first wave more than 80% of all outward FDI was in manufacturing (Lall, 1983), in the second wave only 36% was in manufacturing, while services accounted for 62%, and software alone accounted for nearly 30% (up to 2001, according to EPW Research Foundation, 2006, pp. 1–2). However, updating these numbers through 2007 is likely to increase significantly the share of manufacturing.

(3) Whereas in the first wave greenfield investments were the norm, acquisitions played a far more important role in the second wave.

(4) Whereas in the first wave Indian firms worked principally through joint ventures, usually with minority equity positions, as required by the government of India, in the second wave they went in for many more majority-owned or wholly owned subsidiaries.

(5) Whereas in the first wave most of the outward FDI took the form of investments in kind (such as technology or know-how), in the second wave it more often took the form of cash or stock.

(6) Some of the same firms – the same business groups – that were prominent investors in the 1970s were also prominent in the second wave (e.g. Birla, Tata, and Mahindra groups), but several new names also appeared in the 1990s and 2000s, including companies such as Dr. Reddy's, Infosys, Ranbaxy, Reliance, and Wipro.

The second wave was just getting under way in 2007, and there was no telling if this wave would gather further momentum over the following decade, or fizzle out if the results of the initial investments were disappointing, as they well could turn out. But, as of 2007 there was no question that collectively the differences listed above were substantial enough to suggest that something new was afoot. Indian firms were clearly moving abroad more aggressively, in terms of the pace of expansion, the degree of control they sought, and the kinds of markets they targeted (rich vs. poor countries).They were also seizing new opportunities in services that were not available in the first wave. And they had vastly improved access to foreign exchange, not only from the Reserve Bank of India, but from private sources, such as foreign equity markets in London and New York (often accessed by firms through the use of American deporitary receipts/global deporitary receipts), commercial banks, private equity firms, pension funds, and insurance companies, because the government gave them much greater discretion in such matters.

In hindsight, it is hardly surprising that the second wave would have different characteristics than the first. The context changed significantly after the 1970s on at least three fronts. First, the domestic economic policy environment was much more open than in the 1970s. Government policy towards imports, exports, domestic regulation, inward FDI, outward FDI, exchange rates, and the role of big business changed dramatically. As a result, firms had greater freedom to pursue strategies governed by their own goals and judgment, even as the threat of competition from foreign products and firms intensified. The policy reforms also raised India's growth rate from 3% per year in the 1970s to 8–10% per year in the 2000s, which bolstered the scale, competitiveness, and global standing of Indian firms.

Second, the international policy context also changed. Most developing countries also opened up their economies in the same way that India did. If the old economic policy relationship between India and other developing countries was closed–closed, in the 2000s it was open–open. At the same time, the Uruguay Round greatly reduced the ability of developing countries to adopt protectionist policies, and it required them to put in place significantly stronger intellectual property laws, while the new dispute settlement mechanism made sure that countries lived up to their trade commitments. This set of changes required new strategies for internationalization by Indian firms, and it also reduced the scope for the Indian government to pursue industrial policies to promote national champions in specific industries. Thus, Indian firms globalizing in the 1990s and 2000s had to do so more through the strengths of their own resources and capabilities, and less with government help or subsidies than might have been available at an earlier time.

Third, technology has changed significantly in the thirty-five years since the first wave of outward FDI, resulting in much cheaper computing and long-distance communication, while digitization of products and services and improvements in connectivity have expanded the opportunity to "slice and dice the value chain" in ways that were not possible before. The combined effect of these changes was to open up opportunities for Indian firms to export services that would have been inconceivable in the first wave.

From an evolutionary perspective, it would be surprising if such profound changes in the policy and technological environment did not transform the internationalization strategies of Indian firms.

Emerging Indian multinationals

There are many places one can turn to identify lists of emerging multinationals in India's second wave of outward FDI (see Table 6.1). One such source is the Fortune Global 500 list of the world's largest non-US firms, which in 2006 included only six Indian companies, compared to twenty companies from China (*Fortune*, 2006): these were Bharat Petroleum, Hindustan Petroleum, Indian Oil Corporation, Oil and Natural Gas Corporation, Reliance Industries, and the State Bank of India. Firms made this list based on their worldwide sales, regardless of how much of that came from abroad. The striking feature of the Indian six is that all but one is in the petroleum sector. All but Reliance Industries also happened to be state owned. Some of these firms (Indian Oil Corporation, Oil and Natural Gas Corporation, and Reliance) had made large foreign investments by 2007, but on the whole they were less internationalized, in terms of sales, assets, or employees, than many other smaller Indian companies.

UNCTAD's 2006 list (not included in Table 6.1) of the world's 100 largest transnational corporations from developing countries (based on 2004 data) is similarly skewed towards large firms, this time towards firms with large *foreign* assets (UNCTAD, 2006, pp. 283–285). In 2006, only one Indian firm (Oil and Natural Gas Corporation) made that list, which was dominated by firms from Hong Kong, Korea, and Singapore. China had ten companies on this list. The

Table 6.1. India's emerging multinationals, according to various sources

Enterprise	Industry	Fortune (2006)	Boston Consulting Group (2006)	EPW Research Foundation (2006)	IBEF (2006)
Indian Oil Corporation	oil	X			
Reliance Industries	chemicals	X	X	X	
Bharat Petroleum#	oil	X			
Hindustan Petroleum#	oil	X		X	
Oil and Natural Gas Corporation#	oil	X	X	X	
State Bank of India#	banking	X			
Bajaj Auto	auto equipment		X		
Bharat Forge	auto equipment		X	X	X
Mahindra & Mahindra	auto equipment		X	X	X
Tata Motors Ltd.	auto equipment		X	X	X
TVS Motor Co.	auto equipment		X		X
Crompton Greaves	engineered products		X		
Larsen & Toubro	engineering services		X		X
Infosys	IT		X	X	X
Satyam Computer Services	IT		X	X	X
Tata Consultancy Services	IT		X	X	X
Wipro	IT		X	X	X
Cipla	pharmaceuticals		X		
Dr. Reddy's Laboratories	pharmaceuticals		X	X	X

Table 6.1. (*cont.*)

Enterprise	Industry	Fortune (2006)	Boston Consulting Group (2006)	EPW Research Foundation (2006)	IBEF (2006)
Ranbaxy Pharmaceuticals	pharmaceuticals		X	X	X
Hindalco	nonferrous metals		X	X	
Tata Steel	steel		X	X	X
Tata Tea	food/beverages		X	X	X
Videocon	consumer electronics		X	X	X
VSNL@	telecom		X	X	

Notes: See Appendix to Table 6.1 at the end of this chapter for details on how the above lists were compiled.

#Majority or largely state-owned enterprise

@Formerly state-owned, since privatized and acquired by the Tata group

Fortune and UNCTAD lists show that Indian firms were, by and large, still not big enough to qualify in such rankings.

The most useful lists for our purposes come from a Boston Consulting Group (BCG; 2006) report on the top 100 internationalizing firms in a dozen "rapidly developing economies," all of which are emerging economies, and from a EPW Research Foundation (2006) report. Twenty-one Indian companies made BCG's list, compared to forty-four from China. BCG's criteria, which are explained in the Appendix to Table 6.1 (on p. 165), considered multiple factors, some of which were qualitative, and whose relative weights were unspecified. Most firms derived at least 10 percent of their sales from abroad. BCG's list picked up firms whose internationalization was quite visible in the Indian media, but also a few other early-stage internationalizers.

The EPW Research Foundation list, released in December 2006, was based on Indian companies making major overseas acquisitions, as reported in annual reports and media sources. It listed twenty-six firms, sixteen of which were also on BCG's list (see Table 6.1). The additional ten firms on the EPWRF list were in pharmaceuticals or healthcare (five), software (one), and process industries (four).

Many of the firms on the BCG or EPW Research Foundation lists would not meet the definition of "multinational enterprise" used, for instance, in Harvard's path-breaking study of American MNEs (Curhan *et al.*, 1977). Firms on the BCG list have significant international operations, often in the form of exports, with varying amounts of foreign investment and assets. Most were really in the early stages of building their international presence and becoming multinational enterprises. In 2006, even a company such as Dr. Reddy's Laboratories, which had made some of the largest overseas investments (until 2007), had only 22 percent of its property, plants, and equipment abroad.[4] (See Table 6.2 for major overseas acquisitions by Indian firms through 2005 and Table 6.3 for the countries towards which their investments were directed.) Yet another list of Indian multinationals was put together by the India Brand Equity Foundation (IBEF, 2006), using unspecified criteria. As of 2006, it included thirty-three companies, of which fourteen appeared on BCG's list.

[4] Out of Rs. 9.09 billion in total property plant and equipment, only Rs. 2.02 billion was located overseas, all but 2 percent of it in North America and Europe (Dr. Reddy's Laboratories Ltd., 2006, p. 201).

Table 6.2. Major acquisitions by Indian companies, 2001–2005 (approx.).

Acquirer	Industry	Acquired company	Country	Deal value (US$ M)
Dr. Reddy's	pharmaceuticals	Betapharm	Germany	570
Ranbaxy	pharmaceuticals	Terapia SA	Romania	324
		RPG (Aventis)	France	n.a.
Aurobindo Pharmaceuticals	pharmaceuticals	Milpharm	UK	n.a.
Matrix Laboratories	pharmaceuticals	Docpharma NV	Belgium	263
Nicholas Piramal	pharmaceuticals	Rhodia's IA	UK	14*
		Avecia	UK	
Wockhardt	pharmaceuticals	CP Pharmaceuticals	UK	18
Cadila Health	pharmaceuticals	Alpharma SAS	France	5.7
Mahindra & Mahindra	automotive	Jiangling Tractor	China	8*
Tata Motors	automotive	Daewoo Comm. Vehicle	S. Korea	118
		Hispano Carrocera		
Bharat Forge	auto parts	Carl Dan Peddinghaus	Germany	49*
Subex Systems	IT	Azure Solution	UK	140
Tata Consultancy Services	IT	Comicrom	Chile	23*
		FNS	Australia	26*
Satyam Computer	IT	Citisoft	UK	23.2*
Infosys	IT	Expert Information	Australia	3.1
Wipro	IT	Nerve Wire Inc.	USA	18.5
Videocon	electronics	Thomson SA	France	290

Company	Sector	Target	Country	Value
VSNL	telecoms	Teleglobe	Canada	240
		Tyco	USA	130
Reliance Industries	chemicals	Flag Telecom	Bermuda	212
		Bermuda Trevira	Germany	95
Tata Chemicals	chemicals	Brunner Mond	UK	177
ONGC Videsh	oil & gas	Brazilian oilfields from Shell Oil	Brazil	1,400
HPCL	oil & gas	Kenya Petroleum Refinery	Kenya	500
Tata Tea	FMCG	Tetley	UK	407
		Good Earth	USA	50
		JEMCA	Czech R.	12.5
		Energy Brands: Glaceau	USA	
Hindalco Aditya Birla	metals	Straits Ply	Australia	58.4
		Dashiqiao Chem	China	8.5
United Phosphorus	fertilizers	Oryzalin Herbicide	USA	21.3

Source: EPW Research Foundation (2006) and authors' estimates from press reports of deal values in some cases (*marked with asterisk)

Table 6.3. *Country-wise approvals issued, April 1995–March 2005*

Country	No. of approvals	Equity	Loan	Guarantee	Total
USA	2268	1762	163	234	2159
UK	633	584	101	92	777
British Virgin Is.	87	769	19	136	924
Bermuda	34	503	5	181	689
Hong Kong	126	102	98	345	544
Russia	32	1757	5	1	1763
Mauritius	388	682	182	174	1038
Sudan	5	964	–	–	964

Source: EPW Research Foundation (2006), Table 4

For our purposes it is not necessary to compile a census of emerging Indian multinationals but rather to obtain a good sense of which firms, in which sectors, have become active internationally via exports and FDI. Combining data from the BCG and EPWRF lists, we think that emerging Indian multinationals cluster into five broad groups. The first group consists of energy-related firms, particularly oil and gas, which are among the largest Indian firms and have made some of the largest individual foreign investments. However, these firms sell most of their output in their home market, and their foreign investment, as a share of total assets, is not particularly high.

The other four clusters consist of firms in IT services, pharmaceuticals, engineered goods, and natural-resource based manufacturing firms. These sectors account for more than half of BCG's and India Brand Equity Foundation's lists. In terms of international revenues (i.e. exports from India plus overseas sales by foreign subsidiaries), some of them are very dependent on foreign markets – for example, software, which probably ranks at the top, followed by pharmaceuticals, and engineered goods. In terms of the ratio of foreign assets to total assets, the ranking probably runs from pharmaceuticals to software to engineered goods, although individual firms rank higher or lower than their industry grouping. Finally, in terms of the share of employees located abroad, the ranking probably runs from IT to pharmaceuticals to engineered goods.

In this chapter, we focus on all but the energy-related firms. Unlike China, where more than two-thirds of the forty-four firms on BCG's roster were state owned or state controlled, there was only one state-owned firm on BCG's Indian list – and that was in the natural resources category (Oil and Natural Gas Corporation). This sector is strategically important to the country, but analytically the other sectors are more interesting, because they are not sectors in which one would expect developing-country firms to emerge as international players. These were also the sectors in which India stood in contrast to China, despite order of magnitude similarities in the two countries' size and per-capita income.

Based on this list of emerging multinationals, India's revealed comparative advantage was not principally in natural-resource based industries, such as in Brazil or Russia, nor in labor-intensive industries, such as in Hong Kong (in the 1970s), Taiwan, or China, but in skill-intensive products and services (Kapur and Ramamurti, 2001). Even in manufacturing, the internationally competitive Indian firms made products with substantial embedded, skilled services, such as pharmaceuticals and engineered goods. Another feature of India's emerging MNEs was that they were almost all private firms, rather than SOEs, even though each of the sectors identified earlier had one or more state-owned players: in IT/software there was historically the Computer Maintenance Corporation, which was sold to Tata Consultancy Services; in pharmaceuticals there was Indian Drugs & Pharmaceuticals Ltd., which subsequently went bankrupt; in engineered goods there were several prominent SOEs, including Bharat Heavy Electricals Ltd., Heavy Engineering Corporation, Bharat Heavy Plates & Vessels, and Bharat Earth Movers Ltd.; and in metal industries, such as steel and aluminum, there were SOEs such as the Steel Authority of India, which was not nearly as aggressive in expanding internationally as its private-sector counterparts, Tata Steel or Essar Steel.

In India, unlike China, SOEs played a peripheral role in internationalization, with the exception of the oil and gas sector. Apparently, state ownership inhibited internationalization, as Vernon (1979) predicted. The Indian government made no concerted attempt to build SOEs into global champions, even under a coalition federal government supported by two Communist parties. After more than four decades of government-led economic development, the Indian government was taking a surprisingly hands-off approach at the firm level. Indian firms were internationalizing in the 2000s largely in response to domestic and international market forces. This, too, stood in contrast to China, where the state was more deeply engaged at the microeconomic level.

Strategies for internationalization

The internationalization of (state-owned) firms in oil and gas followed the path of vertical integration seen in Western firms in this industry. Given India's energy shortfall, and the booming economy, SOEs such as Oil and Natural Gas Corporation and Indian Oil Corporation scoured the world for energy supplies. The only thing different about how these firms internationalized, compared to their Western predecessors, was that, as late-movers, their choices were limited to countries that Western firms had avoided in the past – countries such as Kazakhstan and Sudan.

As mentioned above, in this chapter, we focus on the more surprising and interesting cases of internationalization by Indian firms in sectors such as IT services, pharmaceuticals, metals, and engineered goods. In looking at these sectors, we take a different approach from Lall (1983) or Wells (1983) in their landmark studies of Third World multinationals, which drew conclusions about the unique competitive advantages of these firms, as a group, compared to Western multinationals, and their motivations and methods of international expansion. The Lall-Wells approach yielded many useful insights that have informed subsequent research, but it did not tell us which firms had what competitive advantages, and whether particular competitive advantages were associated with particular methods of internationalization, such as the markets targeted or the modes of entry used.

It would appear from Lall and Wells' studies that in the 1960s and 1970s MNEs from developing countries pursued minor variations of a single strategy, regardless of country or industry. This strategy was built on competitive advantages such as: low-cost, small-scale production; products tailored to developing-country needs; labor-intensive technologies; and the substitution of imported inputs with local inputs. These advantages were then exploited in other developing countries through exports, followed by FDI. Neither Lall (1983) nor Wells

(1983) devoted much space to Cell 4 situations, even though Hong Kong was one of the five countries studied in depth in the Lall volume.[5]

Given the market-driven environment in which Indian firms operated in the 2000s, they seemed to enjoy more degrees of freedom and more routes to internationalization than similar firms in the 1970s. Consequently, in the 2000s there was more than one way for an Indian firm to expand and compete internationally. They were no longer limited to minor variations of the Lall–Wells strategy. Therefore, we present our findings as a menu of generic strategies for internationalization that Indian firms have recently pursued. At least three of the four generic strategies speak specifically to Cell 4 situations – that is, South–North investments.

We view the generic strategies that follow as Weberian ideal types. No firm may pursue them in their pure form as described, or do so to the exclusion of other generic strategies. However, it is conceptually useful to specify the pure form strategies and discuss their properties. We illustrate each generic strategy with examples of Indian companies that have come closest to pursuing that strategy. A single firm may pursue more than one generic strategy, and firms in the same industry need not pursue the same internationalization strategy, which is why neither firm nor industry is a useful unit for organizing our findings. Many Indian firms are parts of larger business conglomerates, and it should come as no surprise that different business units of the same conglomerate often pursue different internationalization strategies, although this reality and its implications may not be fully recognized by the conglomerates themselves. We found in some cases a single firm simultaneously pursuing three generic strategies, resulting in predictable difficulties in implementation. Our hope is that by bringing the generic strategies into sharper focus, identifying the logic behind each one, and highlighting the organizational demands and strategic dilemmas each is likely to present, we will make it easier for managers to navigate the internationalization process.

The generic strategies described below apply to firms in the early stages of internationalization, when their competitive advantages are

---

[5] There is only a brief discussion in Wells (1983, p. 75) on Hong Kong firms that invested in industrialized countries to undertake the last stages of fabrication, to save on transport costs and tariffs, and to be closer to customers and local competitors.

Table 6.4. *Comparing generic internationalization strategies*

Dimension	Strategy			
	Local optimizer	Low-cost partner	Global consolidator	Global first-mover
International competitive advantage (FSA)	• Products and processes optimized for emerging markets	• Factor cost arbitrage • Process excellence • Project management	• Operational excellence • Restructuring/ turnaround capabilities	• Global innovator, leveraging low-cost home base and large home demand • Global sourcing
National roots of competitive advantage (CSAs)	• Technological absorptive capacity, developed in prior decades (during import-substituting industrialization) • Cheap brainpower • Entrepreneurial tradition			
	• Low-income consumers • Underdeveloped hard and soft infrastructures • Low-cost production	• Low wages • Skill supply	• Large, high-growth home market in "mature industry" • Access to capital • Barriers to acquisition of local firms by foreign firms	• Large, high-growth home market in emerging industry • Low-cost production and research base • Access to capital
Industry conditions	• Mature industries • Products not standardized across income, culture, etc.	• Mostly mature industries, but possible also in emerging industries	• Mature industries • Relatively standard products and processes across income, cultures, etc.	• Emerging industry (globally) • Relatively standard products and processes across income, culture, etc.

Value-chain scope	• Functionally integrated	• Narrow and specialized	• Functionally integrated • International horizontal and vertical integration	• Functionally integrated • Globally dispersed value chain
Target foreign markets	• Other emerging economies	• Developed countries	• Global	• Global
Modes of international expansion	• M&As and JVs* for downstream operations in other emerging markets	• Supply-base diversification into other low-cost countries • Downstream M&As in developed countries for moving up the value curve	• Large M&As in advanced economies, likely themselves to be MNEs • Upstream M&As and JVs* for raw materials and other inputs	• Strategic-asset seeking M&As in developed countries • Greenfield capacity addition in other low-cost countries

Notes: * Joint ventures

largely shaped by capabilities and assets built in their home markets. Issues arising at this stage include how to leverage domestic competitive advantages into foreign markets, which stages of the value chain to focus on, which foreign markets and regions to enter, what modes of entry to use, and how rapidly to internationalize. As the firms become more international, their competitive advantages are likely to be less dependent on their home-country roots. Distinctions made here between the generic strategies are also likely to blur with increased internationalization, as these firms begin to look and act like established MNEs from Western countries. In due course, top management's attention will be consumed by many of the same issues that preoccupy established MNEs, such as how best to manage multinational firms, how to transcend their national roots to become polycentric organizations, or how to balance demands for global integration and standardization with those for local responsiveness (Rosenzweig and Singh, 1991).

We also compare the four generic strategies that follow along several dimensions in Table 6.4.

Generic strategy 1: The local optimizer

This generic strategy bears the closest resemblance to the Lall-Wells type of strategy and comprises three key features.

First, the ownership advantages of firms following this strategy result from optimizing products and processes for the special conditions of the Indian market. Specifically, this includes designing products that meet two unique conditions of emerging markets – namely, low-income consumers who prefer products that offer a different price-feature mix than high-income consumers in the rich countries, and underdeveloped hard and "soft" infrastructures that require unique product or service features. Some examples of the latter include poor physical infrastructure, which requires products to be extra rugged, or poor after-sales support, which requires that products be easily maintained by relatively low-skilled technicians. In addition to optimizing products for the home market, firms optimize production methods to lower costs or increase reliability in the difficult operating environment that usually accompanies developing countries. Kobrin (1977) referred to this as "intermediate technology." Among its other capabilities is project execution, which, as Amsden (2001) and

Amsden and Chu (2003) have noted, allows firms to quickly and cost-effectively set up new capacity, often with technology obtained from diverse foreign sources.

Second, firms that have successfully optimized products and processes as described above can often exploit those capabilities in other emerging markets. Therefore, such firms gradually expand into other emerging markets where local firms lack the requisite capabilities, using some combination of exports and local production. Western MNEs may be as capable technically as Indian firms at optimizing products and processes for local markets but rarely pursue that option fervently; they are more likely to tweak existing products and processes for emerging markets than to optimize them for each national market. Note, however, that in decentralized MNEs it is quite possible that national subsidiaries operating in developing countries might match local firms in local optimization, one example being Unilever's subsidiary in India in the FMCG business (Prahalad, 2005; pp. 171–239). But, on average, the best local firms are likely to "out-optimize" Western MNEs in the local market and thus build a set of capabilities and competitive advantages that can be exploited in other emerging markets with similar income levels or equally underdeveloped hard and soft infrastructures.[6]

Third, a firm pursuing the local optimizer strategy is likely to be integrated across several functional areas, such as design, production, and marketing/distribution, not only in the home market but also in the foreign markets it enters. It is likely to cover several stages of the value chain and to own the brands under which its products are sold. In individual foreign markets the scope of the value chain may be narrower than at home – for example, scale-sensitive production and R&D may be concentrated at home, while final-stage production or

---

[6] Broadly consistent with an important theme in earlier research writings by one of us (Singh), we think it is conceptually useful to think of diverse national environments, including both institutional and market contexts, as selection regimes. The pressures imposed by such selection regimes and the concomitant adaptive responses from firms responding to these pressures are largely responsible for the development of unique capabilities by firms over time. This may also explain why it is considerably more difficult for MNEs from developed countries to develop such capabilities. This argument fits well, we think, with the development of capabilities of Indian IT/software service firms. We intend to pursue this theme in later work.

marketing, distribution, and after-sales service may be replicated in foreign markets.

We think this local optimizer generic strategy is fundamentally similar but not identical to the Lall-Wells strategy, because the Indian policy environment in the 2000s was quite different from the environment in the 1960s and 1970s. Some of the local optimization tactics of the earlier period were much less important in the 2000s. For example, substituting local inputs for imported inputs was far less important in an era of freer trade, as was the ability to lobby government for favors and special privileges. But other types of local optimization were just as relevant in the 2000s as in the 1970s – for example, optimizing the price-to-feature ratio or making products that were rugged or easy to maintain in the challenging emerging-market environment.

However, not all emerging economies have firms capable of optimizing products and processes in this manner. This requires sufficient absorptive capacity to master technologies purchased from advanced countries and a degree of innovation and production-engineering capability to optimize designs and processes. Most Indian firms built these capabilities during the era of import-substituting industrialization, often starting with licensed technology. The currently prominent Indian pharmaceutical firms built their capabilities in the decades when India had a weak intellectual property regime, which made it easier for them to copy Western drugs before they came off patent in the US or Europe; similarly, most leading Indian IT firms got their start soon after IBM was encouraged to leave the country in the mid-1970s.

Before expanding abroad in the 2000s, these firms had to reinvent themselves by reengineering production methods, upgrading quality, developing new suppliers, and improving productivity – mainly to survive the anticipated onslaught of new foreign competition in the Indian market. By 2007, sixteen years after India began its now historic economic reform process, it was apparent that the best Indian firms were not only holding their own in the home market in the post-reform era, they had become strong enough to venture into foreign markets. It appears likely that this positive long-term fallout of the economic reforms is far from over.

Although firms following the local optimizer strategy generally expand into other emerging markets (Cell 3 in Figure 6.1), occasionally there may also be opportunities for them to exploit their capabilities in specialized niches in the rich countries, resulting in some up-market FDI (Cell 4), though this is seldom easy. One of the appeals of this internationalization strategy is that it represents continuity in what firms were doing in the pre-reform period; one of its frustrating aspects is that firms find it difficult to extend this strategy into the much larger (and therefore more attractive) markets of advanced economies in which they could potentially leverage their low-cost Indian assets and capabilities.

Illustrative example

Mahindra & Mahindra is a $3 billion diversified group whose most important products are automotive vehicles (50%) and tractors (25%). We think its success in the mid-2000s with an SUV called the Scorpio illustrates quite well the local optimizer strategy. On commencing jeep production in the early 1950s, Mahindra entered into technical collaborations and joint ventures with several Western European and Korean firms for a broad range of vehicles and components (see Khanna, Lal, and Manocaran, 2005, p. 6). As these agreements expired, Mahindra absorbed their technologies and sold products in India under its own brand names. This accumulated capability allowed Mahindra in 1997 to design the Scorpio from scratch, under the leadership of a senior designer lured away from General Motors (US). It was a stylish SUV targeted at India's middle-to upper-income urban consumer. It leveraged Mahindra's reputation for making sturdy vehicles, such as the famous Jeep, which were ideal for India's rugged roads. Yet, the petrol version of Scorpio was designed to the tougher Euro III emission standards rather than the Euro II standards applicable in urban India, to facilitate exports in the future. Mahindra kept the design costs low by farming out development work to its Indian suppliers and by leveraging its in-house low-cost engineering talent, which is estimated to have cost one-twentieth of what it would have cost in Europe or the US. Mahindra reportedly also turned more readily to low-cost, less famous Asian suppliers in countries such as Korea, which were as good as, but cheaper than, suppliers preferred by Western auto companies. Mahindra built one-third as many prototypes as Western MNEs would have done to test the Scorpio, because "there was a law of diminishing returns – we may have achieved 97–98% of their [Western MNEs'] robustness at one-third the cost" (Khanna, Lal, and Manocaran, 2005, p. 10). Mahindra's capital outlay per unit of capacity was also 40–50 percent lower than Ford's comparable Indian plant, despite being less than half the size.

On the whole, Mahindra was able to coordinate the design of a new vehicle at substantially lower cost than Western competitors, despite operating on a much smaller scale. This capability to design and manufacture products at a fraction of the cost, despite volumes that are substantially lower, is shaping up to be an important competitive advantage of many Indian firms.

When Mahindra decided to follow Scorpio's success in the home market with forays abroad, it targeted mainly other emerging markets. Initial sales were in Sri Lanka, Nepal, and Bangladesh, followed by Iran and Kuwait in the Middle East, and Uruguay in South America because "they had road conditions that were comparable to India," according to the head of the automotive group (Khanna, Lal, and Manocaran, 2005, p. 12). In 2004, Mahindra made a big push into South Africa, which was to be the gateway to the rest of Africa, creating a subsidiary to undertake final assembly. The company's 2005–2006 annual report explained its export strategy as follows:

Your company has intensified its efforts to identify niche markets for its automotive products throughout the world, *especially geographic areas that have similar sales, distribution, and marketing conditions as India.* (Mahindra & Mahindra Ltd., 2006, p. 6; emphasis added)

As of 2007, Scorpio's exports appeared to be almost entirely into other emerging markets.[7] Modest sales were recorded in Europe. In November 2006, the company announced plans to sell an upgraded Scorpio, and a pick-up version, in the US market, and by June 2007 had given an American company exclusive rights for US distribution. The company hoped to sell in the US a total of 10,000 units by 2010 (Reed, 2007). It will be instructive to follow Mahindra's experience of

---

[7] Mahindra's annual report does not report geographic breakdown of sales for each business segment. It only reports geographic breakdown of sales across all businesses, which indicated that in 2005–2006 the Mahindra group derived 18.8% of its sales from exports. Separately, the CEO reports that the company sold 5,534 vehicles in overseas markets, or about 4.3% of their total vehicle production (Mahindra & Mahindra Ltd., 2006, p. 6).

trying to break into the US market – and thus break out of the confines of the local optimizer strategy. The contrast with tractors, Mahindra's other line of business, will also be interesting, inasmuch as Mahindra was the leader in that segment in India.

Mahindra's experience illustrates the competitive advantages, internationalization paths, and the strategic dilemmas faced by firms following the local optimizer strategy. In the 2000s, that strategy entailed more outsourcing and importing of ideas than was typically the case in the 1960s and 1970s. Mahindra also internationalized at a much faster rate in the 2000s, compared to the earlier period; the company had entered only two foreign markets by 1982 – Iran and Greece (Lall, 1983, p. 43).

At its core, however, Mahindra's strategy was similar in both waves of outward FDI – namely, to develop products and processes optimized for the Indian market and then leverage them in other, less industrialized, emerging markets. Internationalization began with "down-market" exports and FDI, following a pattern consistent with the product cycle hypothesis. Firms such as Mahindra may discover that the market is much larger in the rich countries but may find that products and processes optimized for India are not optimal for advanced economies – especially complex, differentiated products such as automobiles, unlike standardized commodities, such as steel or cement.

In the future, we think it likely that many more Indian firms will adopt the local optimizer strategy for internationalization. Thus far, it has been more profitable for many Indian firms to focus on the booming Indian market than to pursue international opportunities, but this is bound to change. Among firms with untapped internationalization potential are those that cater to "bottom of the pyramid," low-income consumers, such as Narayana Hridayalaya (pediatric open heart surgery), Aravind Eye Hospital (cataract operations), or Jaipur Foot (prosthetics; Prahalad, 2005). Others include firms in "cultural products," such as Bollywood movie producers, media firms such as Zee TV, entertainment content producers such as Balaji Telefilms, or ethnic food manufacturers such as Kohinoor Foods. In the latter cases, exports and FDI will be directed at countries with a cultural affinity for Indian products (South Asia, Middle East, parts of Africa and Latin America) or at the non-resident Indian (NRI) segment in these and other countries.

Generic strategy 2: Low-cost partner

This generic strategy leverages India's low-cost advantage, particularly in labor, to serve the needs of firms and consumers in rich countries. The most notable Indian examples are in the field of services, such as IT support, software development, R&D outsourcing, call center operations, and many other forms of business process outsourcing and knowledge process outsourcing. And this strategy differs significantly from the local optimizer strategy.

First, the competitive advantage of firms pursuing this strategy is not based on optimizing products or processes for the Indian market but on helping overseas customers optimize their products or processes for *their* global operations. Indian firms are better able to exploit India's locational advantages in providing these services, because their capabilities at managing in the Indian environment are superior to that of Western firms, particularly in managing human resources, handling government relations, or coping with unreliable suppliers and with underdeveloped hard and soft infrastructures. However, these advantages will weaken over time, as India's hard and soft infrastructure improves and as Western firms gain experience operating in India.[8] Therefore, the more successful low-cost partners no longer depend for their competitive advantage solely on India's quirks or locational advantages (which, in theory, are available equally for foreign firms to exploit), but have used their head start to build new FSAs, such as economies of scale and scope, sophisticated project management skills, and, increasingly, reputation and brands. They also leverage various forms of late-mover advantages – for instance, they started with a clean slate, organizationally speaking, compared to their foreign competitors, who were saddled with legacy costs and could not easily redeploy resources or streamline organizational culture and business processes.

---

[8] By early 2008, Indian IT firms, for the first time in many years, showed slowing growth rates in revenues and profits. While a full explanation of this slowing is very likely complex, involving the strengthening of the Indian rupee against the US dollar, the slowing down of the US and global economies, among other reasons, we believe it also supports our argument, particularly since global firms such as IBM, Accenture, and EDS had mounted significant Indian operations, paralleling the business models of the top Indian firms such as Tata Consultancy Services, Infosys, and Wipro.

Second, the internationalization path of these firms is quite different from local optimizers. Whereas other emerging economies are the main target markets for local optimizers, low-cost partners target their services at advanced countries. Exports to these countries are followed by FDI, to strengthen onsite customer support and integration, or to move up the value curve by acquiring local firms with advanced skills or complementary assets, such as customer relations and brands. These firms also invest in other emerging economies, but not so much to serve those markets as to broaden the number of low-cost countries from which they can serve rich-country customers.

Third, unlike local optimizers, the low-cost partner specializes in a few specific stages of the value chain. It can be an original equipment manufacturer (OEM) supplier, working behind the scenes to help its overseas customers succeed, and not primarily a functionally integrated firm that designs, produces, sells, and distributes products under its own brands.

This last point is one of the frustrating aspects of the low-cost partner strategy. The firm is not as likely to have products carrying its own brand and must be content being a behind-the-scenes partner. On the other hand, the low-cost partner can be more profitable than its customers, who must make risky investments in R&D, branding, and distribution. Indeed, efforts to build brands, which some such firms have tried in the pharmaceuticals industry, for instance, can create the potential for conflict with their global partners.

The low-cost partner strategy is similar to what many Asian firms did in the past to become multinational enterprises (e.g. Sony, Samsung, Acer, Tatung, etc.). They began as suppliers to American or European firms, focusing on a few stages of the value chain in which their home country had a cost advantage. Most of those firms focused on manufacturing, whereas most Indian firms pursuing the low-cost partner strategy have typically focused on services, although this may change as India gains competitiveness in manufacturing.[9] As costs rose at home, these Asian firms shifted some production to other

---

[9] By 2007, manufacturing firms such as Sundaram Fastener and Bharat Forge were already following the low-cost partner strategy successfully, and exports of engineered goods from India grew by 29 percent in the first half of 2006–2007, compared to the same period in the year before (Government of India, Ministry of Commerce, 2007).

low-cost countries, such as Thailand, Malaysia, Indonesia, and, since the mid-1980s, China and Vietnam. Meanwhile, they also worked to extend the value chain and move up the value curve, with some of them eventually covering enough stages to design and sell products under their own brands. A similar progression may eventually occur with Indian firms pursuing the low-cost partner strategy, and when they do, they will face the same challenges that firms such as Acer faced in moving up the value curve (Mathews, 2002, pp. 55–82).

Illustrative examples

India's software services companies, such as Infosys and Wipro, are perhaps the best-known examples of companies following the low-cost partner strategy.[10] These two firms began with quite different goals. In the 1970s and 1980s Wipro was much more focused on computer hardware than software, and more on the home market than exports – that is, it was a local optimizer – but gradually the export of software services became the most important business for both companies. Initially, both firms engaged in labor market arbitrage, sometimes known as body-shopping – that is, sending low-cost Indian programmers on short stints to work in the US or Europe on customer premises. Both availed themselves of opportunities like the Y2K crisis and Euro-conversion to build international revenues and customer relationships. Subsequently, more and more of the work was moved to India, where costs were even lower. As costs in India rose, and competition became fiercer, Infosys and Wipro moved up the value curve, offering more sophisticated services, including a "global delivery model," in which costs were optimized across onsite and offsite locations in India as well as third countries.

The competitive advantage of these firms began with India's low-cost programming talent, but evolved to include significant firm-specific scale and scope economies and late-mover advantages. Scale economies came from spreading fixed costs across a larger number of employees than their customers required for their limited internal

---

[10] There is a vast literature on the Indian software sector, including, notably, Arora and Gamberdella (2005), which includes an excellent chapter on India by Athreye, the original work by Heeks (1996), as well as Bagchi (1999) and Arora *et al.* (2001).

needs. Scope economies arose from serving firms in many industries and countries, allowing for ups and downs in demand to be smoothed out so that staff utilization was higher overall and making it affordable to house highly specialized skills.

But both firms also enjoyed late-mover advantages relative to their Western competitors, because they began with a clean slate and from the beginning could build their staff in low-cost India, whereas firms such as IBM, Accenture, or EDS entered the offshoring revolutions with large staff and legacy costs in high-cost countries. N. R. Narayana Murthy, one of the founders of Infosys, estimated that some US competitors were burdened with as much as 16 percentage points of extra costs on selling, general, and administrative expenses alone (interview with authors, April 2007). The Indian firms also created processes that ensured the highest quality and reliability of software development, earning the highest rating from Carnegie Mellon University's Software Engineering Institute on their Capability and Maturity Model (CMM). By the late 1990s, there were more CMM Level-5 (the highest CMM level) certified firms in India than in the US; apparently it was harder for established firms that were not as focused on software development as the Indian companies to meet SEI's high standards. Given India's poor image and reputation in the 1980s and 1990s, SEI certification was far more important for Indian companies as a way of signaling quality than it was for US firms with strong brands and connections to Fortune Global 500 companies (Ramamurti, 2006).

Infosys and Wipro also enjoyed important advantages relative to their Western rivals in operating in the Indian environment. A great deal has been written about the ability of Indian software firms to attract and retain talent on a large scale, which by 2007 meant adding about a thousand new employees every month. Accenture, EDS, and IBM only began to ramp up their Indian headcount in the 2000s, by which time the Indian firms had built a very strong brand image in the labor market. Accenture and EDS may have had stronger brands among US customers, but not among potential Indian employees. As one senior executive heading the Indian IT subsidiary for a US company remarked, "We devote as much effort building our brand in the [Indian] labor market as we normally do in building our brand with customers."

Infosys and Wipro also enjoyed advantages in dealing with the government – for instance, in complying with regulations or obtaining permits and approvals. They were better able to find a way around India's decrepit infrastructure, which required firms such as Infosys and Wipro to supply public services that in the West would be outsourced – services such as back-up water and power supply, overnight housing, or transportation for employees.

The second feature of the low-cost partner strategy is that most of the overseas investments by firms such as Infosys and Wipro went to advanced countries or regions, such as the US and the EU. Besides opening offices in these locations (and in Japan), these firms acquired SMEs in the West through which they sought access to higher end work, which could be progressively shifted to low-cost India. By 2007, both firms had also made some investments in other emerging economies such as China and the Philippines, but the motivation here was to develop additional low-cost production sites rather than to penetrate their domestic markets (with the exception of China). Also interesting is that none of the leading Indian software firms attempted to acquire or take over a leading US competitor, even though their market capitalization was high enough to make this possible. Wipro's CEO, Azim Premji, dismissed this option by asking, "Why buy yesterday?"

Finally, Infosys and Wipro both focused only on particular stages of the value chain, leaving it to their customers to make final products for sale to end users under proprietary brand names.[11] Unlike OEM suppliers in manufacturing, they supplied software "components" or back-office support to their customers, rather than tangible products or subassemblies. Chief information officers and chief technical officers of Fortune 1000 companies were their target market, the former for IT-related services and the latter for R&D-related services.

Many other Indian firms are internationalizing through the low-cost partner strategy, including dozens of other software firms. Beyond software, there are many firms in the business process outsourcing space, particularly in the call center business (e.g. WNS, 24/7 Customer), in back-office support services, such as accounting or legal assistance, or in document preparation (e.g. Tracmail, OfficeTiger) that play the low-cost partner game. A host of companies provide help

---

[11] There were some exceptions to this, however. For instance, Infosys built a successful branded banking package, Finacle, which had a worldwide customer base.

with medical transcription (Acusis), clinical trials and pharmaceutical contract research (GVK Biosciences, Nicholas Piramal) and manufacturing (Emcure Pharmaceuticals), financial research, management consulting research (Evaluserve), and so on.

Many, though not all, of the firms following this strategy are post-1991 start-ups, often started by returning non-resident Indians or by senior executives who quit existing firms to pursue a purely cost-arbitrage strategy (GVK Biosciences). Several such firms were "born global," in the sense that they were born with a sales and marketing base in rich-country markets, usually the US, and a production base in India (e.g. Tracmail, OfficeTiger, and Cognizant, the latter being technically a US incorporated company with operations in India, rather than the other way around). Others, such as Infosys and Wipro, were born in the pre-liberalization era but adapted their strategies quickly and successfully to the new policy environment. Wipro, for instance, discovered it was much more profitable to be a low-cost partner to foreign firms than to serve its historical markets at home (computer hardware and software).

In each IT-enabled services area, at the low end, smaller firms often competed largely on price; these firms were unlikely to earn high returns or to have sustainable competitive advantages. But in every category, other firms worked hard to move up the value curve and to shift the foundation of their competitive advantage from generic India-based advantages that were available to all players to firm-specific assets and capabilities that were much harder for competitors to replicate.

Notably, the more sophisticated firms in each segment, like Infosys and Wipro had some distinctive characteristics: They derived the bulk of their revenues from exports rather than sales in the domestic market; they obtained most of their exports from customers in the advanced countries; they specialized in a few stages of the value chain that usually did *not* include branding; and they invested modest amounts in front-end offices or in small acquisitions in the advanced countries (Cell 4 situations) to serve customers more effectively and to move up the value curve. On all these points, the low-cost partner was almost the exact opposite of the local optimizer, which derived most of its revenues from domestic sales, directed most of its exports to emerging markets, covered many stages of the value chain, including branding, and invested in production and/or distribution in other emerging markets.

Generic strategy 3: The global (or regional) consolidator

The global consolidator, as the name indicates, is an Indian firm that consolidates an industry globally, often, though not always, beginning with the home market, followed by horizontal acquisitions in other emerging markets, and culminating in acquisitions in rich-country markets. Such a firm encompasses both Cells 3 and 4 in Figure 6.1. Some of the best examples of this strategy are non-Indian companies such as Cemex (Mexico), Lenovo (China), and South African Breweries. Perhaps the best Indian example is Arcelor-Mittal, if, because of Lakshmi Mittal's national origin, one can count it as an Indian firm at all. At any rate, Arcelor-Mittal seems to have inspired Indian companies in steel and other metals industries (e.g. aluminum, copper) to embark on similar strategies, although Mittal Steel internationalized at a slower pace, and acquired assets at lower prices, than did Indian companies in 2007.

The viability of the global consolidator strategy is shown by the high valuation of companies such as Cemex and Arcelor-Mittal, but the sustainability of this strategy was an open issue in 2007 for companies such as TCL, Lenovo, Hindalco, or Tata Steel, which embarked on the strategy much later. Other examples of acquisitions by global consolidators included the $12 billion purchase in May 2007 of GE's plastics business by Saudi Arabia Basic Industries Corporation, or the $1.2 billion acquisition of Swift & Co., an American meat processor, by Latin America's biggest meat producer, J&F Participacoes SA of Brazil, to create the world's largest beef and pork processor. But, in 2007, the global consolidator strategy was still in the early stages of execution in India, unlike the first two generic strategies, and, therefore, our conclusions about this strategy in the Indian context are somewhat more tentative.

The global consolidator strategy builds on the fact that in some industries growth had matured in the rich countries but was booming in emerging markets such as India. The competitive advantage of Indian firms arose partly from this difference in market momentum. Faster growth required the addition of new capacity, which could be undertaken with the latest technology and the largest plant-sizes then on the market. Equipment could be procured at bargain prices, because stagnant demand in the advanced countries made suppliers desperate to win business in booming emerging markets. Indian firms that had built up production and project execution skills in the era of import-substituting industrialization used this period to consolidate their technical skills and production efficiencies. The threat of greater competition from foreign suppliers and competitors, which Indian firms took quite seriously, forced them to upgrade existing plants and operations. They cut costs, improved quality, initiated Six Sigma programs, ramped up labor productivity, and paid greater attention to marketing and customer service. In the process, some firms discovered that they had become quite internationally competitive. As India's economic growth accelerated to 8–9 percent in the middle of the first decade of the 2000s, and as world prices rose for many commodities, the profit margins and cash flow of Indian firms making steel, copper, and aluminum, among others, rose sharply. The larger firms in these businesses then had the financial muscle to shop abroad for other companies.

Two country-specific factors also helped here. The first was the size of the Indian market. Even if the country is poor, its aggregate demand for certain products is quite high, even in relation to many advanced economies, especially given the growth acceleration. This gave local firms a global scale advantage. Second, India enjoyed a low-cost advantage, because of its cheap labor and, in some industries, cheap raw materials (e.g. iron and steel). Together, these factors provided a tailwind for Indian firms internationalizing through the global consolidator strategy.

In terms of markets, the global consolidator, like the local optimizer, is likely to find that its production and project execution capabilities, and its experience of working in the difficult Indian environment, are transferable to other emerging economies. The firm may also make upstream investments to secure raw materials to meet booming domestic demand; this too is likely to occur in emerging economies rather than advanced economies.

The global consolidator's competitive advantages described up to this point overlap considerably with those of the local optimizer. The distinguishing feature of the global consolidator, however, is that its competitive advantages can be leveraged in both emerging economies *and* advanced countries, resulting in the potential for up-market exports and FDI (Cell 4). Why the difference, one might ask?

We believe that the answer lies largely in industry-specific factors – specifically, in the degree to which products and production processes can be standardized across countries, regardless of per-capita income, wages, or cultural differences. The local optimizer is limited by the fact that its products and services do not easily migrate from low-income to high-income countries. On the other hand, many firms pursuing the global consolidator strategy make products (e.g. aluminum, copper, and steel – or cement, chemicals, plastics, etc.), and use production processes (e.g. continuous production), that are relatively invariant across countries. Another cluster makes products that are less standardized across countries (e.g. beverages, consumer durables, auto parts, or finished automobiles). In these cases, the global consolidator strategy may be harder to pull off.

There is another part to this strategy that must be recognized – namely, the plight of firms in these industries in the advanced countries. Whereas emerging-economy firms were booming, expanding, modernizing, and gaining technical and financial muscle, their counterparts in the advanced economies were often staid old firms, saddled with legacy costs, old technologies, undersized plants, excess capacity, weaker finances, and strained labor–management or union–management relations. Whereas Indian firms panicked and restructured when the economy opened up following the reforms of 1991, few firms in the advanced economies worried that some day they would be takeover targets for upstart emerging-market firms. As a result, by the mid-2000s the more aggressive firms in large emerging markets, such as India, were starting to acquire vulnerable firms in their industries in Europe and North America, despite the latter's advanced technological capabilities and strong home-market positions. To be sure, a farsighted Western firm could have acquired firms in its industry in emerging markets well before those firms became strong enough to threaten the opposite. However, few Western firms made pre-emptive strikes of this sort in India. Quite on the contrary, multinationals like Alcan divested stakes in their ventures in India, thereby strengthening the hands of Indian firms in those industries. Even if these global firms had tried to acquire Indian counterparts, they might have found the going difficult, because many of the firms in question were either SOEs or family-controlled firms and therefore not easily acquired, even if they were publicly listed.

Illustrative examples

Several Indian firms, including Bharat Forge, Tata Steel, and Hindalco, an aluminum manufacturing firm belonging to the Aditya Birla Group, illustrate quite well the global consolidator strategy. After India opened up, each of these firms established, or consolidated, a strong position in the Indian market, then acquired or set up new facilities in other emerging markets, in Europe or North America, to become international players. As of mid-2007, Tata Steel's $11 billion acquisition of the Anglo-Dutch steelmaker Corus Group, and Hindalco's $6 billion acquisition of Canada's Novelis, a multinational manufacturer of rolled aluminum products, were the two largest single overseas acquisitions by Indian firms. Indeed, firms following the global consolidator strategy accounted for the lion's share of overseas FDI by Indian firms, and most of their overseas investments were of the South–North, Cell 4 type (see Figure 6.1).

Hindalco's evolution illustrates how the global consolidator strategy plays out. The company was the flagship enterprise in the Aditya Birla Group, whose worldwide turnover of $24 billion in 2006–2007 came largely from industrial commodities, such as aluminum, copper, and cement. The firm started as a small private aluminum maker in 1958 with one plant with a capacity of 20,000 metric tons per year. Like many other Indian firms, its growth was lethargic until India liberalized its economy in 1991. Then, recognizing that competition was likely to become fierce, the company sought to scale up domestic operations and get costs in line with international benchmarks through process improvements and scaled-up production. It embarked on a program of greenfield expansion, domestic acquisitions, and forward integration into rolled and fabricated products, leading eventually to international investments and acquisitions. The company expanded its original aluminum plant ten-fold in 1998, and acquired a controlling share in Indian Aluminum Company, a joint venture with Alcan, in 2000. Four years later, Indal merged with Hindalco. In 2005, a $2.5 billion greenfield plant was launched in the bauxite-rich state of Orissa for alumina refining and smelting, using captive power generation. In 2006, another greenfield aluminum smelter project was announced in Madhya Pradesh. By 2007, Hindalco was the only company in the world that was simultaneously working on four greenfield aluminum projects that would collectively take its total capacity to over 1 million tons of aluminum per year.

These new plants used the latest technologies and one of them had a smelter capacity of 325,000 metric tons per year, making it one of the largest such plants in the world. Even though Hindalco's total aluminum capacity was still only a third or a quarter that of giants such as Alcoa or Alcan, its unit costs were reportedly in the top quartile of low-cost producers.

The firm's international competitive advantage appeared to rest on three pillars. First, Hindalco benefited from being vertically integrated, from ore to aluminum products. India had excellent bauxite resources, while abundant coal allowed for the production of captive power, which accounted for as much as 40 percent of the cost of production. In this regard, Indian aluminum firms apparently had an edge over Chinese producers, who relied, at the margin, on imported bauxite. Second, Hindalco enjoyed an international cost advantage not only because Indian labor was cheap but because its technological capabilities allowed it to minimize capital and operating expenses in ways that Western – or even Chinese – firms usually did not, or could not. Indian firms, unlike Chinese firms, financed their expansions with internal resources or private capital rather than from the government or from state-owned banks. According to Hindalco's CEO, Debu Bhattacharya, an Indian plant could be built at a capital cost that was 40–50 percent lower than similar plants in the developed world, and possibly at lower costs than plants even in China – a significant competitive advantage in a capital-intensive industry. Similar advantages, though less pronounced, were reportedly also enjoyed in operating expenses (interview with authors, June 2007). Third, India's growing demand and large market potential gave a tailwind to its expansion plans. While demand grew at 2–3% in the industrialized countries, it grew at 6–8% in India; yet, per-capita consumption of aluminum in India was still only one-third of China's and one-twentieth America's, suggesting ample room for further growth. As the largest private integrated aluminum producer in the whole of Asia, Hindalco was well positioned to profit from India's growth. During the period 2001–2006, Hindalco's sales and profits grew at more than 30 percent per year. By 2003–2004, the Aditya Birla group was generating free cash flow of $600–700 million per year, and had reportedly built a substantial war chest for future acquisitions and investments (Surendar, 2004).

It was against this background that, in 2007, Hindalco acquired Novelis, a downstream unit spun off from Alcan in 2005 that made rolled aluminum products, such as aluminum foil and cans. Novelis had sales of $9.8 billion, almost 13,000 employees, and thirty-three facilities in eleven countries, including Canada, the US, Germany, and Brazil. It had a 19 percent worldwide share in aluminum rolled products and supplied cans to blue-chip companies such as Coca-Cola on four continents. In its lines of business, Novelis was number one in Europe, Asia, and South America, and number two in North America (Novelis, 2007). The acquisition was met with skepticism by financial analysts, because Novelis was losing money at the time, Hindalco had paid a premium of 49.1 percent relative to Novelis' stock price before takeover rumors surfaced, and Hindalco was forced to borrow to finance its largest-ever acquisition. The company's stock fell almost 14 percent when the acquisition was announced. Company officials viewed Novelis' losses as temporary, because unprofitable fixed-price contracts signed before the spin-off were set to expire by 2010. Further, some synergies were anticipated, because Hindalco would be able to supply low-cost aluminum to Novelis, and Novelis' expertise in aluminum-can manufacturing could be transferred profitably to India, where the packaging industry was still in its infancy. Hindalco might also be able to improve Novelis' operations and streamline its costs, but Hindalco played down these prospects, possibly to assuage fears that the takeover might result in job losses.

The acquisition put Hindalco among the top ten to twelve firms in the industry worldwide, just as the Corus acquisition put Tata Steel among the world's top five steel companies. In May 2007, Hindalco was rumored to be bidding for Alcan, when the latter was facing a hostile takeover attempt by Alcoa. Eventually, though, Alcoa was acquired by Rio Tinto of Australia.

The logic of the global consolidator strategy is also illustrated by a Chinese paper company, privately owned Nine Dragons Paper, which grew from almost nothing into the world's third most valuable paper company in just twelve years (*Economist*, 2007c, p. 76). Although Nine Dragons had not internationalized like the Indian steel or aluminum companies, it illustrates perfectly how a potential global consolidator gathers momentum by aggressively consolidating and expanding capacity to meet the insatiable demand for products in China's large, booming home market. By 2008, Nine Dragons' capacity was expected to exceed International Paper's, making it the world's largest paper company. Moreover, with a net profit margin of 20 percent, quite possibly the highest in the world, Nine Dragons was perfectly placed to gobble up floundering paper companies around the world, if and when demand leveled off in China, and the firm turned its attention to international expansion.

Generic strategy 4: The global first-mover

The global first-mover, as the name suggests, is a firm that creates a global business in a new industry or segment. Its first-mover status could result from spotting a new business opportunity before other firms, or from pursuing a novel business model in an existing industry, or even from technological innovation. The firm adopting this strategy is innovative either in what it does, or how it does it, relative to competitors both at home and abroad.

At first glance, it may be hard to picture firms from emerging economies as global first-movers. Yet, such examples do exist, one of which we describe below. Although we cannot say how common this case is compared to other generic strategies, it is qualitatively different from those strategies and is potentially a lucrative route to internationalization. Once again, this strategy entails FDI by emerging-market firms in advanced countries (Cell 4 in Figure 6.1), rather than just other emerging economies (Cell 3). We anticipate that in the future more firms from emerging markets, especially from large economies such as China and India, will internationalize as global first-movers.

The global first-mover strategy is founded on three country-specific strengths: first, a large and rapidly growing home market in the relevant industry, which serves as a springboard for internationalization; second, the technical capability to absorb, acquire, integrate, and improve borrowed technologies, which allows the firm to assemble the essential business elements globally; and third, India's low-cost advantage in selected operations, which gives its firms a leg-up against foreign competitors whose value chain may be concentrated in high-cost countries. While the global consolidator strategy is also founded on some of these same CSAs and industry-specific advantages, such as globally standardized products and production processes, the key difference is that in this case the industry is growing in *both* developed and emerging markets, not just in the latter. Here, the focal firm is not a late-mover somehow making good (as in the case of the generic strategies discussed earlier) but among the first-movers in an emerging global business.

The end result in this case, as in the global consolidator case, is a firm with a global footprint, a functionally integrated but globally dispersed value chain, and its own global brands and distribution.

Illustrative example

Suzlon Energy, an Indian wind-power company, was created by Tulsi Tanti, a textile manufacturer which invested in a wind-turbine generator in 1990 to augment the unreliable electricity supplied by the state-owned utility. He was so impressed with wind power's potential that he divested the textile business and put all his resources into starting a wind-power company in 1995, figuring it must have a bright future in India. Based on his own experience, he also decided that Suzlon should offer Indian customers a "total solution" – that is, take care of everything from site evaluation, equipment supply, installation, and commissioning, to operations and maintenance, and project financing. He licensed technology for producing 0.35 megawatt wind-turbine generators from a German company (Sudwind) and set up a manufacturing operation in Pune, India.

By its fourth year, Suzlon had absorbed Sudwind's technology and obtained rights to sell that product all over Asia. Subsequently, Suzlon developed its own designs for larger wind-turbine generators up to 2 megawatts in capacity. In 2001, it set up an R&D unit in the Netherlands and a year later bought Sudwind, which was in financial distress, to create an R&D base in Germany. By this time, the company seems to have become well established within India, and was looking for orders abroad. A private equity placement in 2004, followed by a very successful IPO in India in 2005, fueled its internationalization. A string of larger acquisitions followed: in 2006, Suzlon bought Belgian gear-box manufacturer Hansen for 465 million Euros, and in May 2007, after an extended bidding war, Suzlon acquired the German company, REPower, for 1.34 billion Euros, which gave it a stronger position in Europe and access to technology for 5 megawatt wind-turbine generators, including offshore wind-power generation. In 2007, Suzlon was setting up a rotor blade manufacturing operation in the US, an integrated manufacturing operation in China, and three more component manufacturing plants in India. Suzlon shifted its global management headquarters to Amsterdam, and Tanti hired an American executive from GE to serve as global CEO.

In 2006, Suzlon sales were $867 million, net income was $172 million (19.8% of sales), return on net worth was 42%, and its market capitalization was about $8 billion. Tanti, whose family owned 70 percent of Suzlon, was instantly catapulted onto *Forbes*' list of the world's billionaires (*Forbes*, 2007). Suzlon's global market share of 9% (including REPower) was much lower than industry leader Vestas' (Denmark) share of 28%, but only four percentage points lower than the number two firm, General Electric. The other two firms in the top five were from Germany and Spain. (Vestas was only eight years older than Suzlon.) Shortly after the REPower acquisition, Tanti told a reporter that Suzlon could well become the number one firm in the industry by 2010 or 2011 (Moneycontrol.com, 2007).

Whether or not Tanti is eventually proved right, what is notable is that in just one decade, Suzlon came from nowhere to become the world's fourth ranked firm in the global wind-energy business, with the distinct possibility of rising further in the rankings if it could surmount the operational challenges it faced in 2008. Should we be surprised by this story?

One thing we should *not* be surprised by is that an Indian firm went after the wind-energy business; Suzlon's entry was stimulated by local demand for wind power – indeed by Tanti's own need for, and experience with, using it. The Suzlon story is entirely consistent with the view that entrepreneurs innovate in response to problems and opportunities in their immediate surroundings.

Also, we think it unsurprising that Suzlon benefited enormously from India's large market for wind power: In 2006, India was the third largest market in the world, with annual demand of 1,840 megawatts, compared to 2,454 megawatts in the largest market (USA), 2,194 megawatts in the second largest market (Germany), and 1,145 mega-watts in China (YES Bank, 2007, p. 8). Given India's chronic power shortages, high electricity prices for industrial users, and vast areas without public electricity supply, wind energy had understandable appeal. The country's over-reliance on domestic coal and imported oil and gas prompted the government to subsidize wind energy, and several state governments stipulated targets for renewable-energy use by their electricity companies. For all these reasons, Suzlon was able to build in India the world's largest wind farm (1,000 megawatt capacity). Furthermore, Suzlon was the number one firm in India for eight years in a row, with a 50 percent market share and high profit margins. Winning within India was the critical first step in Suzlon's evolution. The other leading wind-energy firms were also from countries with large home demand, such as Denmark, which met 20% of its energy needs from wind power (compared to the global average of 1%), as well as Germany, Spain, and the US.

Both India and China were among the top five markets for wind power. It should be no surprise that for certain products, large emerging economies, particularly China and India, have domestic demand that rivals the domestic demand of advanced countries. This was true in the 2000s in low-tech products, such as cement, steel, oil, and coal; it was also true of some high-tech products, such as cell phones, telecommunications gear, and power plant equipment. The Suzlon experience shows how demand on that scale can propel emerging-market firms on to the global stage.

But should we be surprised that Suzlon has built such a strong position in a technology-intensive industry? Not really, because the industry is in fact not very high-tech, as evidenced by Vestas' R&D spending of only 3 percent of sales (Vestas, Wind Systems A/S 2007, p. 11) and Suzlon's even lower R&D spending (Suzlon Energy Ltd., 2007, p. 88). Suzlon made no claim of having developed state-of-the-art technology for any subsystem of the wind-turbine generators in India, be it rotors, turbines, generators, gear boxes, or controls. What it *had* done successfully was to get hold of state-of-the-art technologies in these areas through acquisitions and occasional greenfield R&D centers in Western Europe. Suzlon did not invent anything new, but it combined existing technologies and capabilities in creative ways to serve an emerging global market.[12] Within India, it seems to have developed larger wind-turbine generators (up to 2 megawatt capacities) after only four years of making much smaller wind-turbine

---

[12] It is worth remembering that Joseph Schumpeter, the renowned economist, included in his definition of innovation novel recombinations of existing ideas or technologies (Schumpeter, 1932).

generators based on imported designs. This is quite remarkable – but it is in keeping with a capability that other Indian companies have demonstrated – namely, a strong capacity for absorbing, adapting, and extending imported technology through internal efforts (seen also, for instance, in the local optimizer and global consolidator strategies). In the longer term, it is quite possible that Suzlon may develop improved designs based on European know-how and lower-cost Indian scientific and engineering talent.

One of the more surprising elements of the Suzlon case is Tanti's audacity in thinking that a tiny Indian firm could become a global leader in wind power, and then achieving that goal by aggressively acquiring foreign technologies and customers. In the process he created a company that optimized the global value chain in ways that its Western counterparts did not: Suzlon leveraged the technological know-how of leading European nations, coupled with low-cost manufacturing and engineering in China and India; it targeted all the major markets of the world, including Europe, the US, China, and India; and it leveraged the Indian stock market, Indian private equity, and foreign banks to finance growth.

In that regard, Suzlon was somewhat ahead of competitors such as Vestas and Gamesa (Spain), which were more Europe-centric in their outlook. Europe, after all, was where the industry originated, and it represented 50 percent of the world market even after the spike in energy prices raised demand for wind energy in other parts of the world. In 2007, about 7,000 of Suzlon's 9,000 employees were located in low-cost India, whereas the vast majority of Vestas' employees and manufacturing operations were in high-cost Europe, and 85 percent of Gamesa's staff were in Europe and the US (Gamesa, 2006, p. 9). In 2005, Vestas launched a three-year strategic plan entitled "The Will to Win" – a surprising title for the plan of a company that was the industry leader and had twice the global market share of its nearest rival (Vestas Wind Systems A/S, 2005). In fact, the title signaled Vestas' vulnerability as a high-cost player that had lost money for the two previous years, following a major acquisition. It therefore set out to downsize its headcount in Europe, cut costs and overheads, and improve customer service, which by its own admission was in bad shape (Vestas Wind Systems A/S, 2006). Two years later, the company's after-tax profit margin was still only 2% (2007), compared to Suzlon's 20% (2006), and its market capitalization was only $12.9

billion, compared to Suzlon's $9.2 billion (June 4, 2007), despite being five times as large. Gamesa too reported after-tax margins of only 8% (2006).

In other words, Suzlon's business model combining a low-cost Indian base with European technology and global marketing seemed to be yielding higher returns than the Europe-centric models of its larger rivals. More than three-quarters of Suzlon's $746 million capital expenditure budgeted for 2007 was for adding or expanding facilities in India. Suzlon's Western rivals may have underestimated not only the market opportunity in India, but also the cost advantage of locating parts of the value chain in low-cost countries such as China and India.

As in the case of global consolidators, the global first-mover strategy worked in Suzlon's case because, once again, the product was standardized across countries. Some countries may have preferred smaller capacity wind-turbine generators than others, or offshore solutions over onshore solutions, but for any given product, its design and production were globally standardized. Wind was wind, everywhere, and so was the output, electricity. If demand were less standardized across emerging and advanced economies, Suzlon's experience in India might have been transferable only to other emerging economies, in which case its internationalization would have been limited to Cell 3 (Figure 6.1), and Suzlon might have missed out on the three-quarters of world demand for wind power in advanced economies.

A second important enabling factor was the availability of finance. In the 1970s, a firm like Suzlon would not have been able to raise money from venture capitalists, private equity firms, the local stock market, or foreign banks, to launch the firm or bankroll acquisitions in advanced countries. Even if private capital had been forthcoming, which would have been unlikely, the government of India would have barred access to it. The new environment of the 2000s, with more open markets and greater access to capital by emerging-market firms, made the global first-mover strategy possible.

The point is often made that firms in developing countries are unlikely to come up with innovations on the technological frontier, because of their technological backwardness, even if they take on technical challenges that are Herculean by local standards (e.g. Amsden and Chu, 2003). The Suzlon experience was consistent with this view, but it did show that Indian firms were capable of combining existing technologies and knowledge to create new businesses – even if the underlying technologies were created elsewhere. While the capacity to develop new frontier technologies is valuable for emerging markets, many jobs and considerable shareholder wealth can also be created by firms like Suzlon that help commercialize cutting-edge technologies developed elsewhere.

India may be unique in having the wages of a low-income country but the technical skills of a middle-income country such as Israel or Taiwan, coupled with a strong entrepreneurial tradition. If true, India ought to spawn more global first-movers like Suzlon Energy in the future. The passage of time should provide a test of this assertion that we have made here.

Combining or morphing across generic strategies

The generic strategies described above are not mutually exclusive, and we make no claim that they are collectively exhaustive. (For instance, one additional generic strategy we have deliberately not dwelt on, as noted in the beginning, is international vertical integration by natural-resource based firms seeking either upstream resources or downstream markets.) Firms may also pursue more than one generic strategy at the same time. In the diversified Tata group, for instance, we believe Tata Consultancy Services employed the low-cost partner strategy, Tata Motors, with its small-car project, employed the local optimizer strategy, and Tata Steel and Tata Tea employed the global consolidator strategy. We think similar statements could be made about the Mahindra & Mahindra group or the Aditya Birla group.

A single company may also pursue multiple generic strategies in parallel, possibly to preserve options for future growth and internationalization. Good examples are to be found in the pharmaceutical industry. For instance, one part of Dr. Reddy's Laboratories focused on reverse engineering drugs for sale under its own brand in India and other emerging economies (local optimizer strategy); another part provided R&D services or bulk drugs to foreign drug firms as a low-cost partner; and a third part challenged the patents of leading pharmaceutical firms in the US in the hopes of securing a 180-day exclusivity period for selling generic equivalents or on discovering new molecules for sale under its own brand globally (global first-mover strategy; see Jha and Chakravarthy [2004] and the company website). Ranbaxy also employed these three strategies simultaneously, but with a less formal internal division of labor (Ranbaxy Laboratories Ltd. [2005] and company interviews, 2006). In contrast, GVK Biosciences, started by an ex-Ranbaxy CEO, focused single-mindedly on the low-cost partner strategy. Ranbaxy and Dr. Reddy's were led by owner-managers committed to making each of their firms, as Ranbaxy put it, "a research-based, globally respected pharmaceutical organization" (Ranbaxy Laboratories Ltd. 2005, p. 9). This led them to make large R&D investments on molecule discovery or new drug-delivery methods; yet the local optimizer strategy dovetailed more smoothly with their historical strategy of reverse-engineering drugs for the local market (generics), and the low-cost partner strategy was probably more profitable than the other two strategies, at least in the short run.

Firms pursuing different generic strategies simultaneously may have difficulty focusing the organization on a clear set of goals, resulting in internal confusion and flip-flopping, especially if contradictions between the different strategies are not explicitly recognized and carefully managed, both internally and externally (e.g. with the investor community).

The low-cost partner strategy, for example, might require the drug firm to court Western firms to win offshore R&D work or to manufacture bulk drugs for them in India, while the global first-mover strategy might require fighting them tooth and nail to nullify their patents or to beat them in introducing new, branded drugs in the advanced economies. Another potential contradiction was between the need to make long-term, risky investments for molecule discovery or new drug-delivery methods, while satisfying the quarterly expectations of investors, who preferred the higher and surer margins of the low-cost partner strategy. Given that the leading pharmaceutical firms were publicly listed in India (and Dr. Reddy's, for instance, was also listed on NYSE), investor pressures for steady profit growth were a constant damper on their grandiose ambitions.

The difficulties of pursuing multiple strategies simultaneously are illustrated by the following remarks by the CEO of Dr. Reddy's:

How can we be an imitator [in the generics business], *and* an innovator [in the drug discovery business] at the same time? We have to maintain a fine balance between producing profits today and investing in future growth. The company just cannot invest in specialty and drug-discovery and then wait for returns...it has to deliver year-on-year results. We need to take care of our legacy businesses. But then, how can we forge out-licensing alliances with large pharmaceuticals [in the drug discovery business] *and* at the same time challenge their patents around the world [in the specialty and generics businesses]?

Some may argue that we really cannot manage imitation and innovation under one roof, that the two business models are different, and we should separate bulk activities and generics business from the specialty and new drug discovery business. My challenge is to prove them wrong. (Quoted in Jha and Chakravarthy, 2004, p. 11; emphasis in original)

Pathways for strategy migration

Pursuing multiple generic strategies *simultaneously* may be difficult, but sometimes it can yield positive synergies, provided the contradictions among the strategies are recognized and managed carefully. However, pursuing multiple generic strategies *sequentially* can be both feasible and desirable. We know from the literature that a firm's strategy evolves as it acquires new capabilities, partly as it adapts to environmental changes. We illustrate this point here by suggesting a few dynamic paths through which one generic strategy can morph into another.

Consider, for instance, the two internationalization strategies that emerging-market firms are most likely to begin with: the local optimizer strategy or the low-cost partner strategy. A firm could pursue one of these and discover that the capabilities thus created provide a gateway for pursuing the other.

To illustrate: A firm might adapt imported technology to cater to the home market and in so doing build scale, quality, or expertise in particular stages of the value chain that can later be used to become a low-cost subcontractor to a US or European firm. The firm could thus morph from a pure local optimizer into one that is internationalizing also as a low-cost partner. This is in fact what many Indian firms founded in the pre-liberalization era did in the post-liberalization era, including IT/software firms such as Wipro and HCL, pharmaceutical firms such as Dr. Reddy's and Cipla, and auto component firms such as Sundaram Motors and Bharat Forge. The Taiwanese firm Acer evolved in a similar fashion, from making low-end PCs for the Taiwanese market to becoming a low-cost assembler for PC giants such as IBM

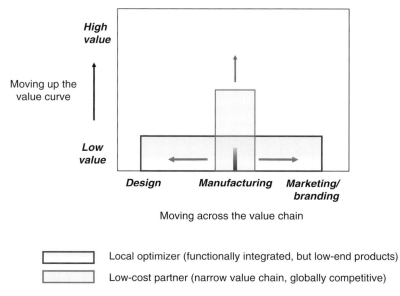

Figure 6.2 Capability building by local optimizers and low-cost partners

and HP. This kind of strategic evolution is feasible because the emerging-market firm and the Western firm do not compete head-on for the same customers: typically, the Western firm targets end-users in the advanced countries, while the emerging-market firm targets end-users at home or in neighboring emerging markets.

Conversely, a firm that started out as a subcontractor to a foreign firm (low-cost partner) is likely to expand its value addition along two dimensions (see Figure 6.2): On the one hand, it is likely to broaden the stages of the value chain that it performs in-house for foreign customers (OEMs), so as to strengthen its strategic relationship with them, build new capabilities, and improve margins; on the other hand, it is likely to move up the value curve, to take on activities that are more sophisticated, and therefore more profitable, especially if margins are under pressure as home-country wages and costs rise over time. These two tendencies have quite different strategic consequences in the long run.

The first tendency – performing more stages of the value chain in-house – is likely to enable the emerging-market firm to launch branded products for sale to end-users in the domestic market. At some point, the firm will decide that this is worth doing because of the additional revenues and profits it can generate, not to mention reducing over-dependence on Western OEM customers. Strategic morphing of this sort occurred with Taiwanese firms such as Yue Yuen, which expanded from making footwear for Nike, Reebok, and other Western brands to setting up 600 retail stores in China for selling sporting goods, including its own brand of footwear (van Agtmael, 2007, p. 117).

The other tendency – moving up the value curve – allows the low-cost partner to gain bargaining power over OEM customers, to the point that it sometimes gains the upper hand in the relationship, especially if it invests in R&D and retains ownership of the intellectual property. This has certainly been the case with Indian companies such as Infosys, Wipro, and TCS, and non-Indian companies such as Flextronics (Singapore) and Li & Fung (Hong Kong), whose profit margins and market capitalization have been more impressive than those of many of their customers (on Li & Fung, see Hagel and Brown, 2005, pp. 25–26).

Some companies, such as Taiwan Semiconductor Manufacturing Corporation, moved up the value curve without integrating across the value chain – in order to reassure customers credibly that they had no intention of ever turning into a competitor. However, firms like Acer moved along both axes (see Figure 6.2) with the intent of becoming a global first-mover.

As discussed earlier, the local optimizer can also morph into the global consolidator if products and production processes are globally standardized and the industry is mature in developed countries but growing in emerging markets. This is what Indian companies such as Tata Steel, Tata Tea, and Hindalco were starting to do in the mid-2000s. The key skills such firms leveraged internationally were operational excellence and restructuring capabilities, both of which were more easily transferred across borders if products and processes were globally standardized. However, transferring these capabilities internationally is hardly an easy task, because of differences in institutional contexts, especially between emerging and developed economies. Yet, companies such as Cemex and Arcelor Mittal seem to have managed that successfully, although more research is needed to understand precisely how they did so.

Non-Indian examples

The generic strategies identified in the Indian context have relevance for other emerging economies inasmuch as all emerging economies share certain characteristics (or CSAs), such as rapid economic growth; low- to moderate-income consumers; low to medium wages; and underdeveloped hard and soft infrastructures. The initial international competitive advantages of emerging-market MNEs are likely to be shaped by these distinctive characteristics. At the same time, because emerging economies differ among themselves in important ways, some strategies are more likely in some settings than in others. For instance, countries well endowed with natural resources are unlikely to develop MNEs of the kind described in this chapter and more likely to spawn large, vertically integrated, natural-resource MNEs (e.g. see the Russia chapter in this volume). Similarly, large countries are more likely to spawn global consolidators than smaller countries, and low-income countries are more likely to spawn low-cost partners than middle-income countries (e.g. Brazil or Israel produce few low-cost players; see the chapters on those countries in this volume).

We have already alluded to several non-Indian examples of the generic strategies discussed. To cite more examples, Embraer of Brazil is an interesting case of a local optimizer that slowly expanded beyond Cell 3 to niche markets in advanced countries (Cell 4), until it eventually captured almost 50 percent of the global market for regional aircraft. By 2007, it was at the technological frontier of designing regional jets, on par with its only global rival, Canada-based Bombardier, and had graduated to become a global first-mover in that segment.

Several firms in Hong Kong and Taiwan internationalized using the low-cost partner strategy, and some developed an international footprint of supply locations for Western firms (e.g. Flextronics of Singapore, or Wistron of Taiwan). Most of these firms had moved beyond the low-cost partner stage to become high-value-adding entities; they hold valuable lessons for Indian firms following the same path two or three decades later. (Acer's experience, for instance, illustrated the difficulties of transitioning from low-cost partner to becoming an independent, branded, global player.)

The larger emerging economies have spawned global or regional consolidators in several mature industries, including cement (Cemex), steel (Arcelor-Mittal), beverages (SAB-Miller, AmBev), PCs (Lenovo), white goods (Haier), microwaves (Galanz), consumer electronics (TCL), and meat products (JBS SA of Brazil). Finally, in the global first-mover category, Williamson and Zeng (see Chapter 5 in this volume) suggest several examples from China, including telecommunications equipment maker Huawei, which was on its way to introducing a new generation of 3G equipment based on a Chinese standard.

Summary and some future directions

Several broad themes emerge from our study of the Indian case. One is that Indian firms internationalized in the 2000s using more than one strategy, each of which had its own antecedents and consequences. It is an over-simplification to depict all Indian firms as using the same approach to internationalization, even when the firms belong to the same industry.[13]

Table 6.4 sums up our main ideas about India's emerging MNEs. It shows four generic strategies for internationalization, the main competitive advantages on which each is based, the national roots of those advantages, their implications for the boundaries of the firm (i.e. which stages of the value chain are internalized), and their implications for how the firm will internationalize. Further, it identifies two industry variables – degree of standardization of products and processes across countries, and industry life-cycle stage – that influence the likelihood that firms can morph from the local optimizer or the low-cost partner strategy to one of the other strategies. We have offered some thoughts on how this morphing might occur, but the question deserves more research, because, among other things, it can add to our understanding of internationalization processes in general.

[13] This kind of over-simplification is sometimes applied to all firms in an industry (e.g. "Indian software firms have these competitive advantages and internationalize in this way...") and, occasionally, to all firms in all emerging economies, as in van Agtmael (2007), where the author advances a single model for why twenty-five firms from several emerging markets turned out to be world-class players. Likewise, Bartlett and Ghoshal (2000) propose a common set of principles for all late globalizers, and Mathews (2002) speaks of "a new model for global growth" that explains the success of his sample of emerging-market firms.

We also believe that the generic strategies described here are relevant to other emerging economies, particularly large ones such as the BRICs.

A second theme is that the competitive advantages of Indian MNEs centered on low-cost production and design capabilities, process excellence, and restructuring capabilities. None of these competitive advantages is usually regarded as the FSAs leveraged by Western firms to become MNEs. In turn, those advantages were rooted in India's technological absorptive capacity, built over several prior decades, its cheap brainpower, its seasoned managerial class, and a historically rooted entrepreneurial tradition. Completing the picture in the 2000s was India's large and booming economy that lent momentum to Indian firms, and unprecedented access to capital that fueled their growth. These are the competitive foundations of India's emerging MNEs, and they explain why Indian firms engaged in so much up-market FDI (Cell 4 in Figure 6.1).

A third theme, related to the last point, is that in the 2000s emerging-market firms faced international opportunities and constraints that were different from those faced in the 1970s and 1980s, and different from those faced by Korean or Japanese firms when they had internationalized decades earlier. For instance, the role of government was quite different in contemporary India than it had been in Japan or Korea when the latter had created home-grown multinationals; in the 2000s Indian firms internationalized under the watchful eye of private investors, rather than government bureaucrats. The domestic and international regulatory environment was also quite different in the 2000s. Indian firms had to craft original internationalization strategies, tailored to the times, because history offered no role models – at least not suitable ones.[14]

From a theory standpoint, we have tried to integrate several IB concepts and insights into a coherent whole around the notion of generic internationalization strategies. Each generic strategy combines in distinctive ways IB concepts such as ownership advantage, location advantage, motivations for internationalization (market-seeking vs.

---

[14] This did not stop Indian firms from periodically viewing Western MNEs, or Japanese and Korean firms, or even contemporary Chinese firms as role models for their own globalization.

resource-seeking), target market selection, speed of international-ization, and modes of entry. Many IB studies look at these variables piecemeal, but we believe it is more useful to look at them in an integrated, strategic way. Not only does that make IB research more accessible and useful to practitioners, it also helps develop IB theories at a level where the literature is quite thin – that is, between the highly abstract level, where we ask questions such as why multinationals exist, and the highly tactical level, where we ask questions such as which entry mode is best for a particular country or how overseas operations should be staffed.

Finally, we would like to place the above discussion of the generic strategies of Indian multinationals in the broader theoretical con-text of an evolutionary perspective on organizations (Singh, 1990; Burgelman, 1991; Baum and Singh, 1994; Bryce and Singh, 2001; Moldoveanu and Singh, 2003; Singh, 2006). We believe that there is considerable untapped potential in asking what insights an evolu-tionary perspective can provide regarding the strategies of Indian multinationals. It is not our purpose here to provide a complete, or for that matter even partial, answer to this question. However, we want briefly to highlight some of the directions in which such an inquiry may lead us.

Bryce and Singh (2001, pp. 163–165) summarized some key fea-tures of an evolutionary perspective: It involves dynamic change over time; the evolving entities are subject to selection pressures broadly in inverse proportion to their fitness to the selection environment; the evolutionary trajectory is history or path dependent – that is, future steps depend on previous states attained; the selection processes involve the interplay of ecological and genealogical entities (Baum and Singh, 1994); and selection processes involve multiple nested levels of analysis such that different nested entities are simultaneously subject to selective influence. As we observed above, the capabilities developed by Indian multinationals have been inevitably shaped by and in response to the selection regime, comprised mainly, though not solely, of institutional and market forces, in which they found them-selves. Thus, it is not meaningful to speak of the capability develop-ment by Indian firms without noting specific aspects of their selection environments. Interestingly, some of the greatest strengths of the successful survivors were the capabilities built in response to unfavorable local conditions.

We believe that some new and productive lines of inquiry will be opened up by asking related questions in the context of Indian multinationals. Thus, how are the strategies of Indian multinationals changing dynamically over time? What is the nature of the selection environment of Indian multinationals and how has that changed over time? Clearly, even as the internal Indian context changed dramatically starting in the early 1990s, the firms that have gone international are competing on a different landscape than more domestically oriented firms. What strategic transitions are *more* likely to occur, given that an evolutionary approach suggests that not all transitions are equally likely? Indeed, some will *not* occur. What are some of the ecological and genealogical processes involved in the evolution of these strategies? And, finally, what are some of the complex interplays of selection forces operating both on entire firms as units and within firms?

References

Accenture. 2006. *India goes global: How cross-border acquisitions are powering growth*. (Location unspecified.)

Amsden, A. 2001. *The rise of 'the rest'. Challenges to the West from late-industrializing economies*. Oxford UK: Oxford University Press.

Amsden, A. and Wan-wen Chu. 2003. *Beyond late development: Taiwan's upgrading policies*. Cambridge, MA: MIT Press.

Arora, Ashish, V. S. Arunachalam, Jai Asundi, and Ronald Fernandes. 2001. The Indian software services industry. *Research Policy*, Vol. 30: 1267–1287.

Arora, Ashish and Alfonso Gamberdella. 2005. *From underdogs to tigers: The rise and growth of the software industry in Brazil, China, India, Ireland, and Israel*. Oxford: Oxford University Press.

Bagchi, Subroto. 1999. India's software industry: The people dimension. *IEEE Software*, May/June: 62–65.

Bartlett, Christopher A. and Sumantra Ghoshal. 2000. Going global: Lessons from late movers. *Harvard Business Review*, March–April: 132–142.

Baum, J. A. C. and J. V. Singh (eds.) 1994. *Evolutionary dynamics of organizations*. New York: Oxford University Press.

Boston Consulting Group. 2006. *The new global challengers: How 100 top companies from rapidly developing economies are changing the world*. Boston, MA: BCG.

Bryce, D. J. and J. V. Singh 2001. The future of the firm from an evolutionary perspective. In Paul DiMaggio (ed.), *The twenty-first century firm: changing economic organization in international perspective* (pp. 161–185). Princeton, MA: Princeton University Press.

Burgelman, R. A. 1991. Intraorganizational ecology of strategy making and organizational adaptation: Theory and field research. *Organization Science* Vol. 2, No. 3: 239–262.

Curhan, J. P., W. H. Davidson, and R. Suri. 1977. *Tracing the multinationals: A sourcebook on U.S.-based enterprise.* Cambridge, MA: Ballinger Publishing.

Dr. Reddy's Laboratories Ltd. 2006. *Annual report 2005–2006: Creating a global enterprise.*

Dunning, John H. and Rajneesh Narula. 1996. The investment development path revisited: Some emerging issues. In John Dunning and Rajneesh Narula (eds.), *Foreign direct investment and governments: Catalysts for economic restructuring* (pp. 1–41). London and New York: Routledge.

Economist. 2007a. India's acquisitive companies: Marauding maharajahs. March 29.

Economist. 2007b. Multinationals: Globalization's offspring: How the new multinationals are remaking the old. April 4.

Economist. 2007c. Face value: Paper queen. June 9, p. 76.

EPW Research Foundation. 2006. Current economic statistics and review for the week ended December 9, 2006 (50th weekly report for 2006. See www.epwrf.res.in/includefiles/THEMES%20LIST.HTM

Financial Express. 2007. FDI outflow may touch $ 35 billion study. June 18. Available online at www.financialexpress.com/news/FDI-outflow-may-touch-35-bn-study/140558

Forbes. 2007. Special report: The world's billionaires, March 8.

Fortune. 2006. Fortune's Global 500 list. July 24. Also available at http://money.cnn.com/magazines/fortune/global500/2006/full_list/

Gamesa, 2006. *Gamesa annual report 2005–2006.* Vitoria-Gasteiz, Spain.

Government of India, Ministry of Commerce. 2007. Engineering goods emerge as largest contributor to India's merchandise exports. Press release, January 21. See http://demotemp279.nic.in/PressRelease/pressrelease_detail.asp?id=1929

Hagel, John III and John Seely Brown. 2005. *The only sustainable edge: Why business strategy depends on productive friction and dynamic specialization.* Boston, MA: Harvard Business School Press.

Heeks, R. 1996. *India's software industry: State policy, liberalization, and industrial development.* Thousand Oaks, CA: Sage Publications.

IBEF (India Brand Equity Foundation). 2006. *Going global: Indian multinationals.* Gurgaon, India: IBEF (October, according to website: www.indiabrandequityfund.org/artdisplay.aspx?cat_id=410&art_id=13725).

Jha, Anand and Balaji Chakravarthy. 2004. *Dr. Reddy's Laboratories Ltd.: Chasing a daring vision*. Lausanne, Switzerland: IMD, Case No. IMD216.

Kapur, Devesh and Ravi Ramamurti. 2001. India's emerging competitive advantage in services. *Academy of Management Executive*, Vol. 15, No. 2: 20–31.

Khanna, T. and Krishna Palepu. 2006. Emerging giants: Building world-class companies in developing countries. *Harvard Business Review*, Vol. 84, No. 10 (October): 60–69.

Khanna, Tarun, Rajiv Lal, and Merlina Manocaran. 2005. *Mahindra & Mahindra: Creating Scorpio*. Boston, MA: HBS Publishing, Case No. 9705478.

Khanna, T., K. Palepu, and J. Sinha. 2005. Strategies that fit emerging economies. *Harvard Business Review*, Vol. 83, No. 6 (June): 63–76.

Kobrin, Stephen J. 1977. Comment. In Tamir Agmon and Charles P. Kindleberger (eds.), *Multinationals from small countries*. (pp. 157–165). Cambridge, MA: MIT Press.

Lall, Sanjaya. 1983. (ed.) *The new multinationals: The spread of Third World enterprises*. Chichester: John Wiley, IRM series on multinationals.

Mahindra & Mahindra Ltd. 2006. *2005–2006 annual report*. Mumbai, India.

Mathews, John A. 2002. *Dragon multinational: A new model for global growth*. Oxford and New York: Oxford University Press.

Moldoveanu, M. and J. V. Singh 2003. The use of evolutionary logic as an explanation generating engine for the study of strategic organization. *Strategic Organization*, Vol. 1, No. 4: 439–449.

Moneycontrol.com. 2007. I want to create wealth for my country: Tanti. June 2. www.samachar.com/showurl.php?rurl=http://news.moneycontrol.com/india/newsarticle/stocksnews.php?autono=284596&news=I%20want%20to%20create%20wealth%20for%20my%20country:%20Tanti&pubDate=Mon%2C + 04 + Jun + 2007 + 03%3A10%3A02 + GMT&keyword=money_biz

Novelis, 2007. *Novelis 2007: A world leader in aluminum rolling and recycling*. Company document, available at www.novelis.com/NR/rdonlyres/8C464163-EAC4-41BF-83C9-70A341136115/0/NOVsel178 10_OverviewLO.pdf

Prahalad, C. K. 2005. *The fortune at the bottom of the pyramid: Eradicating poverty through profits*. Philadelphia, PA: Wharton School Publishing.

Ramamurti, R. 2006. Internationally competitive clusters in developing countries: India's IT industry. In Subhash Jain and Sushil Vachani (eds.), *Multinational corporations and global poverty reduction* (pp. 318–336). Cheltenham, UK: Edward Elgar.

Ranbaxy Laboratories Ltd. 2005. *Annual report 2005: Vision beyond tomorrow.*

Reed, John. 2007. M&M targets SUV market in UK. *Financial Times* (June 5). Online at http://us.ft.com/ftgateway/superpage.ft?news_id=fto 060520071902128992&page=1

Rosenzweig, P. and Jitendra V. Singh. 1991. Organizational environments and the multinational enterprise. *Academy of Management Review*, Vol. 16, No. 2 (April): 340–361.

Schumpeter, Joseph A. 1932. *A theory of economic development.* Cambridge, MA: Harvard University Press.

Singh, Jitendra V. 1990. *Organizational evolution: New directions.* Newbury Park, CA: Sage Publications.

Singh, Jitendra V. 2006. Ecology, strategy, and organizational change. In Joel A. C. Baum, Stanislav Dobrev, and Arjen van Witteloostuijn (eds.) *Ecology and Strategy: Advances in Strategic Management, Vol. 23* (pp. 177–215). Oxford, UK: Elsevier/JAI.

Surendar, T. 2004. Kumar's big bets. *Businessworld*, September 27, 2004. Reproduced at www.adityabirla.com/media/press_reports/20040920_kumars_big_bets.htm#

Suzlon Energy Ltd. 2007. *Annual report 2005–2006.*

UNCTAD. 2006. *World investment report, 2006.* Geneva: United Nations.

van Agtmael, Antoine. 2007. *The emerging markets century.* New York: Free Press.

Vernon, R. 1966. International investment and international trade in the product cycle. *Quarterly Journal of Economics*, No. 80: 190–207.

Vernon, Raymond. 1979. The product cycle hypothesis in a new international environment. *Oxford Bulletin of Economics and Statistics* Vol. 41, No. 4: 255–267 (November).

Vestas Wind Systems A/S. 2005. *Annual report 2004.* Copenhagen, Denmark (March 30, 2005).

Vestas Wind Systems A/S. 2006. *Annual report 2005.* Copenhagen, Denmark. (March 29, 2006).

Vestas Wind Systems A/S. 2007. *Interim financial report: First quarter 2007.* Copenhagen, Denmark (May 15, 2007).

Wells, Louis T. Jr. 1977. The internationalization of firms from developing countries. In Tamir Agmon and Charles P. Kindleberger (eds.), *Multinationals from small countries* (pp. 133–156). Cambridge, MA: MIT Press.

Wells, Louis T. Jr. 1983. *Third world multinationals: The rise of foreign investment from developing countries.* Cambridge, MA: MIT Press.

YES Bank. 2007. *Suzlon Energy Ltd: Global leadership in green innovation.* Mumbai, India: Yes Bank, Sustainability series.

Appendix to Table 6.1

Fortune's ranking is based on total worldwide sales, regardless of how much of that comes from outside the home country (*Fortune*, 2006).

BCG's list was compiled by starting with the largest companies in each country; in India, for instance, they relied on *Businessworld*'s list of the 500 top companies (BCG, 2006, p. 8). Of these, only firms with annual revenue of at least $1 billion in 2004 were considered, but in the end "twenty companies that did not meet this revenue threshold were nonetheless included." Then, they excluded firms whose international business presence (not defined) amounted to less than 10 percent of revenue but "made an exception for companies that were close to 10 percent and whose international business activity had grown swiftly in the recent past." Finally, firms that passed these criteria had their globalization credentials evaluated along five dimensions:

the international presence of the company, as indicated by its owned and operated subsidiaries, sales networks, manufacturing facilities, and R&D centers; major international investments it had pursued in the last 5 years, including M&A; its access to capital for financing international expansion, whether through free cash flows, stock markets, or other sources; breadth and depth of its technological and intellectual property portfolio; and the international appeal of its existing offerings and value propositions.

Thus, BCG's list included an imprecise combination of size, international presence, and activity (as judged by foreign sales and FDI), a requirement that the firm have at least some foreign subsidiaries, along with some vague notions of technical or intellectual property ownership (i.e. "intangible assets"). No financial firms appear on the list – presumably they were not considered, although this is not stated explicitly. But several service firms (in IT, construction, telecommunications, and engineering services) did make the list.

The EPW Research Foundation list, included in a December 2006 report (EPW Research Foundation, 2006) is based on Indian companies that had made major overseas acquisitions, as reported in "company annual reports and media sources." Its start and end dates are not specified.

India Brand Equity Foundation's list comes from a report (IBEF, 2006) titled *Going Global: Indian Multinationals*. It, too, seems to use the criterion that selected firms should have made significant overseas acquisitions, but its other criteria, if any, are unstated. Surprisingly, it does not include four companies on BCG's list that have made significant overseas investments: Reliance, ONGC, Hindalco, and VSNL. However, it includes the following twenty-two companies not on BCG's list: Amtek Auto, Arvind Mills, Ashok Leyland, Asian Paints, Aurobindo Pharmaceuticals, Dabur India, Glenmark Pharmaceuticals, Gokuldas Exports, ITC, Marico Industries Ltd., Motherson Sumi Systems, Nicholas Piramal, Rico Auto Industries, Sterlite Industries, Sundaram Fasteners, Indian Hotels, Thermax Ltd., Titan Industries, United Phosphorus, Voltas, Wockhardt Ltd., and Zee Telefilms.

UNCTAD's list (UNCTAD, 2006; not included in Table 6.1) had only one Indian firm, Oil and Natural Gas Corporation, among the top 100 non-financial transnational corporations from developing countries. UNCTAD's sole criterion is a firm's foreign assets in 2004. The smallest firm to qualify had $699 million in foreign assets.

7 | Russian multinationals: Natural resource champions

DANIEL J. MCCARTHY, SHEILA M. PUFFER, AND OLEG S. VIKHANSKI

Of the 63,000 multinational corporations in the world in 2006 (Lodge and Wilson, 2006), a relatively small, but increasingly visible number were from Russia. This was despite the country having ranked only 62nd out of 125 countries on the 2006–2007 Global Competitiveness Index (World Economic Forum, 2006). Russia's ranking fell from 53rd in 2005 due in large part to the increasingly pervasive role of the state in the economy. Still, the importance of these large multinationals is underscored by the fact that SMEs in Russia accounted for only 12 percent of the country's GDP in 2006 (Fallico, 2007). The future competitiveness of these MNEs, however, will depend substantially on continued positive developments in the Russian economy in which they play so important a part. And it is clear that their competitiveness will also be determined in large part by the role that the government plays in the economy. Since virtually all important Russian MNEs are in the natural resources area, when applying dominant theoretical ideas from the international business literature an examination of the vertical downstream integration strategies pursued by these companies, with their high asset specificity and attendant uncertainties such as price and supply, will be key. This concept is discussed more fully later, in a section on corporate growth strategies. We begin with an overview of the Russian economy, including the strong points and potential weaknesses, such as "the Dutch Disease," which derive from its energy-driven character. The role and priorities of the Russian government in the economy are then discussed, including government ownership of key MNEs during the Putin administration. The next section traces the rise of Russian MNEs as well as the industries in which they operate, and is followed by a discussion of MNE corporate goals. Corporate growth strategies for building international presence are the focus of the next section, which includes not only MNEs' competitive strategies, but also an examination of how successful firms overcame late-entry challenges, their competitive advantages, and obstacles to their development emanating from the national context in which they operate. This section is followed by one that discusses the sustainability of that presence. How the rise of these MNEs has changed global dynamics is the next topic addressed. The chapter conclusion examines implications for various parties of the entrance of Russian MNEs into the global economy.

The Russian economy

Russia's GDP has continued to increase each year since President Putin was elected in 2000, with annual GDP growth averaging around 6.8 percent since that time (Bush, 2007a), reaching approximately $980 billion in 2006 (IMF, 2007; World Bank, 2007). The percentage of GDP coming from the private sector decreased from 70% in 2004 to 65% in both 2005 and 2006 (EBRD, 2007), although the percentage of employment attributable to the private sector increased to more than 54% in 2005, up from less than 52% in 2004 (Goskomstat, 2006). Although per capita income reached nearly $7,000 in 2006 (IMF, 2007), moving 20 million more citizens above the poverty level (Chazan, 2007), the country ranked only 97th on per capita income according to the World Bank. In February 2007, compared to a year earlier, real disposable income rose by 12.5%, while real wages rose 17.5%, and the Consumer Price Index rose only 2.8% from January to February, compared to 4.1% a year earlier (*Moscow Times*, 2007, March 27).

However, as the strong ruble continued to make imports attractive, Russia's foreign trade surplus decreased by 25.5% to around $18 billion in the first two months of 2007, even as revenue from foreign trade grew to an estimated $68 billion, up 10% from the previous year. Still, the vibrant, growing economy convinced Russian companies to increase their capital investment by almost 20 percent in February 2007 compared to a year earlier (*Moscow Times*, 2007, March 27). And growth opportunities have also attracted FDI, which increased from around $10 billion in 2004 to over $18 billion in 2006, increasing the cumulative FDI stock from $36 billion to almost $80 billion by mid-2007 (Goskomstat, 2007; *Moscow Times*, 2007, October 17). Among the leading providers of FDI from 2004 through

2006 were the Netherlands, Austria, Switzerland, France, Germany, and the UK. Additionally, Cyprus, the Bahamas, and the Virgin Islands were among the leaders, likely as a result of the repatriation of earlier flights of capital. The US was conspicuously absent from the top of the list, in contrast to earlier years. FDI had generally been aimed heavily at the energy sector, but decreased in that sector from over 42% in 2004 to 33% in 2006 (Goskomstat, 2007), due in part to governmental restrictions placed on foreign investments in that sector. One positive result of these policies has been a shift of FDI to other sectors in need of investment. In fact, domestic investment has been far more important for Russia since the total investment in 2006 was $164 billion (*Moscow Times*, 2007, May 2).

The currency's strength has limited exports of products and services that are not raw-material intensive, and attracted relatively high levels of imports. Russian MNEs, however, are largely found in the energy and raw materials sectors, and have not likely been hurt by the strong ruble due to global demand for most commodities. Unlike the artificially set level of the Chinese RMB, Russian government policy has allowed the ruble to continually gain strength against the dollar as well as a basket of currencies utilized by the Russian Central Bank. From 2004 through 2006, the ruble–dollar exchange rate fluctuated in a narrow range between 27.75 and 26.33. And although this policy has made Russian exports relatively expensive and could slow the economy's growth, it has helped to stem inflation, a serious concern of policy makers; the rate decreased from 10.9% in 2004 to 9.7% in 2006, after spiking to 12.6% in 2005 (IMF, 2007).

Energy-driven

Because of its abundance of natural resources, particularly energy, Russia has a dominant global position in that sector, controlling over 6% of the world's oil resources, as well as 27% of gas from which it provides over 25% of Europe's needs (Lagorce, 2007). The country is also a major world exporter beyond Europe, and has not only realized positive trade balances with most countries, including the US and those of Europe, but amassed huge amounts in gold and foreign currency reserves. Those reserves reached over $330 billion in late March 2007, third in the world only to China's level of just over $1 trillion and Japan's $900 billion (Shuster, 2007a). "This sector [oil and gas] represents 65 percent of both exports and the total value of Russian companies" (Shuster, 2007b: 8). Oil and gas exports reached $170 billion in 2006, compared to $28 billion in 1998 (Bush, 2007a). Of that total, oil contributed $100 billion (Rodrigues, 2007). Adding coal, energy exports in 2006 reached $190 billion (Federal Customs Service of the Russian Federation, 2007). Federal tax revenues were $240 billion in 2006, compared to $40 billion in 2000 (Bush, 2007a), and the energy sector in total accounted for 45 percent of the government's 2006 budget revenue (Rodrigues, 2007). In part due to the government policy of gaining substantial control over the energy sector, by late 2006 the state controlled around 30% of oil production and 90% of gas production (*Russia Business Watch*, 2006–2007).

However, this excessive dependence on energy exports has produced a worrisome situation in the eyes of many analysts, one indication being that funding for nearly half of the federal budget came from energy exports. A drop in the price of petroleum and/or natural gas could have seriously negative effects on the economy, a scenario noted by many economists as well as Russian officials. This situation has sometimes been referred to as having the potential to incur the "Dutch disease," a syndrome in which the abundance of energy resources, and the associated windfalls, diverts a country from developing a more balanced and diversified economy. The need for Russia to diversify its economy has been sounded by many international bodies such as the World Bank and the International Monetary Fund.

Government policies may have mitigated the potential effects of such a decrease, one factor being that the state budget is based on energy prices substantially lower than those of 2006. Also, "a strong safety net already exists, moreover, after the tight fiscal policy of the past four years helped the state save up the windfalls" (Shuster, 2007b: 8). A positive result of those fiscal policies has been the build-up of a stabilization fund to well over $100 billion in 2007, a hedge against falling world oil prices. Moreover, the country's debt has been reduced to less than 10 percent of GDP, and, as noted earlier, the Central Bank had amassed gold and foreign currency reserves of well over $300 billion. All of these positive impacts provide a solid shield against an energy-triggered economic collapse, at least in the medium term. Still, the long-term continuation of the country's economic growth will necessitate a more diversified economy. As one analyst observed, "In the long run, Russia will be better off with an oil price of $35 rather than $60. Policy makers will have to work much harder. They will have no choice but to diversify the economy" (Shuster, 2007b: 8).

Role of the government

The government's priorities in its nationalization and quasi-nationalization policies during President Putin's second term have been clearly signaled by the industries in which there has been increasing government ownership and control. By 2007, the Putin government had designated forty industrial sectors as being strategic to the country's security and future. The announcement came amid increasing government ownership of companies in some of those industries, particularly petroleum, natural gas, and military equipment and weapons. These have become the major source of the country's exports and tax revenues, and the government's increasing presence in these industries has raised the prospect of further nationalization of at least some companies in all strategic industries.

Beyond the strategic industries mentioned above, the list generally included industries involved in all aspects of nuclear power and materials; cryptographic equipment; military equipment, firearms, and ammunition; space research, manufacturing, and operations; aviation; certain mining operations; and manufacturing, service, and sales in areas designated as natural monopolies. But the strategic list also included the automotive, and even the diamond, sectors. Many such industries have been consolidated under the state-owned arms exporter Rosoboronexport, which has essentially become a holding company for such firms.

As Russia's transforming economy has evolved since privatization, the government's role has varied. A laissez-faire approach was followed under President Yeltsin throughout the 1990s, a period often referred to as producing Wild West capitalism. These policies gave rise to flagrant abuses during the privatization of the country's enterprises, including the immense power amassed by oligarchs, a small group of businessmen who gained control of most of the country's valuable companies and resources, ushering in a period widely known as oligarchic capitalism (Hoffman, 2002). Yeltsin's policies were replaced by a vastly increased government influence on the economy under

President Putin, especially during his second term that began in 2004. His policies about the government's role in the economy have been described as state-managed, network capitalism (Puffer & McCarthy, 2007). The Putin government employed various methods to intrude into the private sector, the most highly publicized being the 2004 Yukos affair in which the government put the owner-CEO and other executives on trial, and seized the assets of that major oil company. The assets were then auctioned off, and ended up in the hands of Rosneft, a then little-known state-owned organization that has subsequently become one of the country's leading oil companies. An important aspect of the government's ownership of key and attractive industries has been the opportunity to sell part of its ownership in IPOs, which has brought hundreds of millions of dollars into the state's coffers. Examples include Rosneft, Gazprom, the bank VTB, and the prospect of others including Alrosa, a firm that produces one-quarter of the world's diamonds, second only to De Beers.

One analyst had earlier noted: "The game without rules that previously reigned in Russian business is over. The Kremlin is writing a new rule book. Businessmen may not like these rules, but they will have to play by them. The predictability that was conspicuously absent in the past is worth a lot" (Zubkov, 2004: 16). However, other sources have questioned the level of predictability and institutional stability. A late 2004 Standard & Poor's study, in criticizing Russian business for not making progress in corporate governance, noted: "This has been particularly aggravated by the recent Yukos affair that has severely undermined the stability of ownership rights and the nascent trust that had been developing between business and the state" (cited in MN-Files, 2005).

Still, President Putin had consistently voiced his support for a market economy, such as when in his January 2006 annual press conference he emphasized that the state was not planning a major renationalization of key industries, adding that the state welcomed private investors in the oil sector. Noting that there were about ten large private oil companies, including LukOil, Surgutneftgaz, and TNK-BP, he declared: "No one is planning to nationalize them. They will develop according to market conditions as private companies" (cited in Levitov and Korchagina, 2006: 8). Putin's statements were supported by an independent financial executive, Alfa Bank's chief strategist, Chris Weaver, who concluded: "The state does not want or need to extend its controlling interest in companies beyond the biggest company in each of the strategic industries" (8).

This could be an accurate assessment: in spite of growing government ownership of key enterprises in these industries, a vibrant market economy still exists in the consumer, retail, food processing, and telecommunications sectors, and is emerging in others such as financial services. And Kremlin-connected oligarchs still privately control a huge percentage of most raw materials industries, including nickel, steel, aluminum, forest products, and precious metals and gems. So, Russia exhibits a form of economic dualism rather than a purer form of Western capitalism (Puffer, McCarthy, and Wilson, 2007). One result of Putin's willingness to let a market sector develop is that retail trade saw annual growth of about 13% in 2004, 2005, and 2006 (Chazan, 2007), and the $99 billion food retailing sector was forecast to continue a 10% annual growth rate through 2011 (*Moscow Times*, 2007, March 30).

Still, the prospect of additional government control remains. For instance, Russian energy expert Richard Paterson of PricewaterhouseCoopers concluded that foreigners would likely not be allowed to gain control of new projects in strategic sectors, and that even current contracts might not be honored (*Russia Business Watch*, 2006–2007). Yet, a very positive light was shed on President Putin's approach to the economy in early 2006 when a Pew Research Center survey reported that "two-thirds of Russians see a strong leader, and not democratic government as best for their country, and an overwhelming majority see a strong economy as more important than a good democracy" (*Moscow Times*, 2006, January 10: 3). So the Putin government clearly has strong popular support to dictate the terms of the Russian economy, including the future of the country's MNEs.

In some respects, the Kremlin's political relations with other countries could be a major determinant in whether Russian MNEs will be accepted as legitimate members of the global community. The need for Russia's government to establish mutual trust with other nations was emphasized in spring 2007, when the EU foreign minister postponed negotiations for a new trade agreement with Russia, largely due to Russia's hostile policies toward newly admitted Eastern European EU members, Lithuania and Poland (Dempsey, 2007). It should be clear that political actions taken by the Russian government can result in supply problems for various European MNEs requiring

Russian energy. But the reciprocal result could be actions by other countries against Russian MNEs.

The rise of Russian MNEs

Origins in the 1990s privatization era

Russian MNEs were able to develop global markets rather quickly by taking advantage of globalization's opening up new "gateways to entry" at a relatively early stage of their own development, similar to the Chinese MNE experience detailed by Williamson and Zeng in Chapter 5. Whether government controlled or privately held, Russian MNEs had their beginnings during the turbulent privatization period of the early 1990s which evolved into the era of oligarchic capitalism referred to earlier. That designation describes the period of the 1990s when virtually the entire Russian economy, except for small businesses and the black market sector, was dominated by a relatively small number of businessmen (oligarchs) who had gained control of the country's most valuable enterprises. These huge enterprises were carved out of the industrial ministries of the centrally planned Soviet economy and within a decade and a half became the country's most influential MNEs, although some were basically renationalized.

The enterprises were mostly in natural resource industries and the oligarchs amassed huge fortunes after securing these privatized assets at a fraction of their value. Their empires consisted of companies in various of these industries with a bank at the center. They became known as financial-industrial groups or FIGs, and resembled in some ways the Korean chaebols or Japanese kieretsus. Many still operate today as global competitors, although competition is somewhat limited because of the nature of their commodity markets.

The unabated influence of the oligarchs lasted nearly until the mid-2000s, when Putin's second term began, although a few oligarchs fell from power before that time. But the turning point was 2004. After the Yukos case, the Putin government persuaded many oligarchs to sell key assets, particularly energy holdings, to government companies. The oligarchs understood well the potential threats to their empires and could hardly resist governmental pressure to purchase their assets. For instance, Vladimir Potanin in late 2005 sold his 26 percent stake in the largest Siberian oil field to the state-controlled oil company Rosneft. Also that year, Roman Abramovich sold his substantial ownership in oil firm Sibneft to the majority state-owned energy giant Gazprom. They certainly anticipated that the state was planning to become the dominant player in the energy sector, one of the earliest designated strategic industries.

Still, years later, a number of Kremlin-favored oligarchs retained substantial power and economic holdings, mostly in major commodity industries. Anatoly Chubais, Roman Abramovich, Vladimir Potanin, Mikhail Fridman, and Oleg Deripaska were ranked by journalists as being among the fifteen most influential Russian businessmen in 2005 (*Ekonomika i Zhizn'* survey reported in *Economic Newsletter*, 2005), and most were billionaires. Some had invested beyond natural resource companies through early ownership of such assets, or by later following a diversification strategy. Mikhail Fridman, for instance, was a major owner of a leading bank, Alfa Bank, as well as of the country's second largest cellular network, VimpelCom. And Oleg Deripaska, who had made his initial fortune in aluminum, had diversified to become a major force in the country's booming construction industry. Their diversification strategies were in part a defense against a government takeover of their energy and possibly other raw materials holdings.

The government's role in operating MNEs had moved beyond the energy sector. For instance, in early 2006, the owner of a 30 percent stake in the world's largest titanium producer, VSMPO-Avisma, commented on the state's apparently increasing interest in gaining control over natural resource-based companies: "I understand that 2006 is the year of a quiet nationalization of Russian assets" (Vyacheslav Bresht, cited in Pronina and Humber, 2006: 5). By the end of that year, the company had been taken over by the government and folded into Rosoboronexport, the defense company that the government had designated to take over other companies from many "strategic" industries (*Moscow Times*, 2007, March 19). These companies came to be run by Kremlin-appointed officials, many of whom retained their positions within the government, a situation that came to be known as siloviki capitalism (Puffer and McCarthy, 2007).[1] It had become clear by 2006

---

[1] "Siloviki" is a Russian term referring to the network of former intelligence officers, dating back to the Soviet KGB which, under Putin, has come to play a dominant role in Russian society in general and specifically in the economy.

that a key objective of President Putin was to develop national champions in natural resource sectors to compete in the global economy (*Moscow Times*, 2006, November 28), seen by some to have its genesis in Putin's Ph.D. thesis during his program at the St. Petersburg Mining Institute (McKenna, 2007).

Putin government's economic strategy supports MNEs

In the background of corporate strategies supporting the development of an international presence of Russian firms are the international economic strategies pursued by the Russian government. An example is Russia's growing relationship with China, including designating 2007 as "The Year of China" in Russia, following "The Year of Russia" in China in 2006. One outcome was the March 2007 signing of an agreement by the state-owned oil giant Rosneft to supply a major China petrochemical company with 60,000 barrels of crude oil per day. In fact, trade between the two nations has been described by the chief economist of Russia's MDM Bank as "one of the fastest-growing bilateral flows" (Smolchenko, 2007a: 2). The Russian government estimated that bilateral trade reached $29 billion in 2006, and the two countries expected to nearly triple that level by 2010. To support the increasing levels of trade, Chinese banks agreed to lend major Russian banks $1.5 billion specifically aimed at supporting Russian exports to China (Smolchenko, 2007a). Understandably, most exports will be from the energy and raw materials sectors.

A number of European countries are also important trading partners, and President Putin has met with many of their leaders – including the president of Italy in early 2007 – to stimulate Russian exports. Italy is a major trading partner, with bilateral trade having grown to almost $31 billion in 2006, a 31.4 percent increase from 2005, and Russian exports to Italy making up $25 billion of that amount (Fallico, 2007). Putin also met with Germany's leader, Angela Merkel, after her election, since Germany also is a major trading partner. Such political collaboration supports the global outreach of Russian MNEs and helps solidify their presence in the international arena. Both President Putin and Russian MNEs have a strong advantage in the fact that Russia is a major energy supplier to many Western European countries, and is expected to become even more so due to the need to fuel economic growth in that region and Russia's immense energy resources.

MNE industry sectors

Thus far, most Russian MNEs, whether government or privately owned, are in various natural resource sectors, with energy predominating. Table 7.1 lists the twenty-five largest Russian companies by revenue, with oil and gas companies comprising five of the top six in 2006, the largest being state-owned Gazprom. As the table shows, twenty-four companies could be called multinationals, with fifteen having extensive international operations, and nine being in the early stages of building an international presence. The one exception, as well as the only non-oil or gas firm within the top six, is the domestic electrical utility monopoly RAO UES, ranked third (*Ekspert* 400, 2006). Five of the top seven companies were majority state-owned, number seven being Sberbank, the country's largest bank. Of the remaining eighteen largest companies, the government had majority ownership of four. Most of the private-sector companies, however, remained closely held by one or a few individuals including various oligarchs, or by an international company such as BP, even though many had become public companies through offerings on the London, New York, or Russian stock exchanges.

Virtually all the energy companies realized between 70 and 85 percent of revenues from international operations, primarily exports. Their markets were primarily Eastern and Central Europe and the countries of the Commonwealth of Independent States (the fifteen former Soviet Republics except the Baltics), as well as China, Western Europe, and to a lesser degree North America. The sixth energy company, coal producer SUEK, ranked twenty-third and earned approximately 20 percent of revenues from exports, primarily to Asia and Western Europe, and through an export subsidiary it recently opened branches in countries including Poland, Taiwan, and Switzerland.

Beyond energy, other natural resource-based companies (primarily steel) comprised nine of the top twenty-five. Notably, UC RusAl in 2007 became the world's largest aluminum producer until later in the year when Canada's Alcan agreed to be acquired by Rio Tinto of the UK, giving that company the number one position. Other Russian

Table 7.1. *MNEs dominate Russia's top twenty-five firms*

Rank by 2006 revenues (*Ekspert* 400, 2006)	Company	Industry	MNEs with extensive international sales and operations	Firms with a growing international presence	Essentially domestic firms
1	Gazprom	oil and gas	X		
2	LukOil	oil and gas	X		
3	RAO UES	electric power			X
4	TNK-BP	oil and gas	X		
5	Rosneft	oil and gas	X		
6	Gazprom Neft	oil and gas	X		
7	Sberbank	banking		X	
8	Severstal	iron and steel	X		
9	MTS	mobile telecoms	X		
10	Nornickel (Norilsk)	nonferrous metals	X		
11	Evraz	iron and steel	X		
12	UC RusAl	nonferrous metals	X		
13	Magnitogorsk	iron and steel	X		
14	AvtoVAZ	motor vehicles		X	
15	Novolipetsk (NLMK)	iron and steel	X		
16	Michel	iron and steel	X		

#	Company	Sector		
17	Alrosa	precious stones	X	
18	VimpelCom	mobile telecoms		X
19	GAZ	motor vehicles		X
20	VTB	banking		X
21	Aeroflot	airlines	X	
22	Megafon	mobile telecoms		X
23	SUEK	coal		X
24	Ilim Pulp	forest products		X
25	Ingosstrakh	insurance		X

MNEs are involved in such areas as diamonds and forest products. Three of the top twenty-five companies by revenue were in the mobile telecommunications sector, although only one, MTS, had significant international revenues of around 26 percent. Three other companies, all state-owned, were in the transportation sector and included Aeroflot in airlines, which realized around three-quarters of its revenues from international operations, and AvtoVAZ and GAZ in motor vehicles, which realized 15% and 19% of 2006 revenues respectively from exports. As noted earlier, both AvtoVAZ and Alrosa, which ranked fourteenth and seventeenth, were state-owned under the umbrella of Rosoboronexport, the major arms exporter. The remaining three of the top twenty-five firms were in the financial services sector and included Sberbank and VTB in banking and Ingosstrakh in insurance.

MNE corporate goals

Leading Russian MNEs have recently expanded globally, acquiring companies and expanding operations in Eastern and Western Europe, North America, Latin America, Africa, and Asia. In the process, private Russian MNEs as well as state-owned energy MNEs, appear to be seeking enhanced market power and control in the natural resource industries in which they operate. Their activities are clearly aimed at growth through occupying higher value-added positions on their value chains, and attaining higher profit margins. State-owned energy MNEs could be and have been accused of being instruments of Kremlin foreign policy. Gazprom's withholding of gas supplies to countries such as Ukraine and Belarus in 2006 and 2007 is one oft-cited example. Non-state-owned MNEs, almost exclusively owned by oligarchs, could achieve other benefits through their global expansion. Many have sought to increase firm legitimacy and attractiveness to investors through the transparency involved in their international acquisitions and operations, effectively increasing the value of the firms and the wealth of the oligarchs.

Both the firms and the oligarchs might also have defensive goals such as decreasing their dependence on the state, since the Kremlin is less likely to become more involved in activities of firms with substantial international operations, given the potential political ramifications. Related to this is the goal of protection from state claims against the companies' shareholders that could arise from questionable activities and actions in the 1990s privatization period, when the oligarchs gained control of their substantial assets. And although hostile takeovers of large companies are becoming difficult in Russia, global operations and transparency build additional defenses against such prospects.

An additional important goal expressed by a number of the major MNE executives is the access to advanced technology and managerial expertise acquired through their global operations. For instance, these objectives were noted at the time of the Canadian acquisitions made by Basovyi Element with its Magna International deal and Norilsk Nickel with LionOre, as well as US acquisitions by Severstal and Evraz of Victory Industries and Oregon Steel respectively. Access to such technology, knowledge, and skills is especially important to these Russian MNEs with their inexperience in the value chain positions into which they have diversified, as discussed below. However, President Putin cautioned against the increasing number of foreign executives which might restrict the rise of Russian nationals to such positions, noting: "In our big, leading and today almost global companies, mostly in the raw materials sector, you know that the thin layer of top management is mostly made up of foreign specialists" (Delany and Elder, 2007). Still, these objectives and actions seem consistent with the approach of Mexico's Cemex, the world's leading cement company, which, after consolidating the domestic industry, gained new technology and best practices through strategic global acquisitions (see Chapter 10 in this volume).

Growth strategies for building international presence

Most Russian oil and gas companies, when entering global markets, follow a strategy of selling products manufactured in the upstream sector in Russia. This is particularly true of the two major state-owned energy companies, Gazprom, in the natural gas sector, and Rosneft, in the oil industry. However, Gazprom's subsidiary, Gazpromneft, operates in the oil sector as well. All of these companies are primarily energy exporters, with Gazprom in 2005 exporting over 70% of its production primarily to Commonwealth of Independent States (CIS) and Western European countries, while its subsidiary exported about the same percentage of its oil to the same regions. Rosneft in 2005 exported over 80% of its production mostly to the same areas. The state-owned companies seem to pursue strategies of moving to the closest downstream position in the value chain, such as oil refining or liquefying natural gas, while private oil companies such as LukOil move closer to the end consumer by opening retail gas stations.

The primary growth strategy for non-government-owned MNEs has been to pursue downstream positions by engaging in both domestic and international M&As, primarily aimed at developing a value-added growth strategy leading to higher profit margins. In 2006 Russian companies spent $13 billion overseas in M&As to help fulfill this strategy, up from $1 billion in 2002, while total FDI from Russia totaled $18 billion, five times that of 2002 (Bush, 2007a). The UK, the Netherlands, the US, and Iran were major destinations, along with Cyprus and Gibraltar, which may reflect capital flight to offshore subsidiaries of some Russian companies. In the energy sector, LukOil has engaged in downstream acquisitions by acquiring the Getty gas station business in the US, as well as others in Eastern Europe, to expand its retail operations to eighteen countries. The company has also engaged in major projects in nine countries, including geological exploration in Latin America and the Middle East.

Russian mining and metals companies have typically followed a global strategy of vertical integration involving both upstream and downstream activities aimed at securing additional resources, as well as value-added businesses. Steel giant Severstal (controlled by Alexei Mordashov) in the spring of 2007 became the fourth largest steelmaker in the US when its subsidiary, Severstal North America, bought Michigan-based Victory Industries. That company specialized in machining, welding, and fabricating services – all downstream, value-added uses of steel (*Moscow Times*, 2007, March 16a: 6). And Evraz, another Russian steel major, operates steel mills in Italy, the Czech Republic, and also the US with its Oregon Steel operations. Norilsk Nickel produces many commodities, such as nickel, copper, and platinum as well as more basic ones such as coal. In 2003, the company acquired majority ownership of Stillwater Mining Company, the only producer of platinum in the US, and in July 2007 reported purchasing Canada's nickel giant, LionOre Mining International, for $6.4 billion. The diamond giant Alrosa also has operations in Angola, and in 2007 planned to extend its cooperation with De Beers in several value-added areas such as mining, geological prospecting, and technologies in mining and processing (*Moscow Times*, 2007,

May 11a). Ilim Pulp's basic strategy was to expand downstream in the forest products industry to produce pulp and paper products, value-added activities closer to the consumer (McCarthy, Puffer, and Shekshnia, 2004).

UC RusAl briefly became the world's largest aluminum company as the result of the 2006 merger of two of Russia's largest aluminum enterprises, RusAl and Sual, as well as Glencore International of Switzerland. UC RusAl also acquired bauxite resources in the Caribbean in an upstream move to solidify its supply sources for that crucial raw material. By spring 2007, it had operations in seventeen countries on five continents. UC RusAl is a prime example of the high concentration of ownership in Russian MNEs. In 2007 Oleg Deripaska had 66% ownership, while his partners Viktor Vekselberg and Leonid Blavatnik owned nearly 15% (*Moscow Times*, 2007, March 22: 6).

In the telecommunications sector, Russia's mobile telecoms companies have actively expanded into CIS countries. Two of the industry's Big Three – VimpelCom and MTS, and, to a lesser degree, Megafon – have done so primarily by buying out local operators and consolidating the domestic industry. In its international expansion plan, in March 2007, VimpelCom started selling services in the former Soviet republic of Georgia, opened a sales office, and planned to open seventy more there by the year's end (*Moscow Times*, 2007, March 16b: 6). Sistema, a diversified holding company with substantial telecoms assets, proposed in late 2006 to obtain 10 to 20 percent of Germany's Deutsche Telekom, in part by swapping its MobileTele-Systems unit, a deal that required German government approval as DT's major shareholder. Also in late 2006, the Russian communications operator, Comstar-UST bought a majority stake in a key Greek internet provider, Hellas On Line, from Greece's Intracom Holdings.

In the financial services sector, state-owned VTB, the former Vneshtorgbank, is becoming an important financial institution within the CIS and Central and Eastern Europe, as well as within Russia. Its operations extend beyond these regions into Western Europe: into France, Germany, Austria, and the UK. Its primary business in these countries is to facilitate business for companies from Russia and CIS and Central and Eastern European countries. In a different arena, the bank, acting as a surrogate for the state, in 2006 acquired 5 percent of EADS, the parent company of Airbus. Additionally, majority state-owned Sberbank, the country's largest bank, made its first foray into international markets through its 2006 acquisition of a major bank in Kazakstan. In the insurance area, Ingosstrakh, which is the former state insurance enterprise but now privately owned, has operations through its international group, Ingos, in a number of CIS countries such as Kazakstan, Azerbaijan, and Ukraine, and some Western European countries such as Finland and the Netherlands, as well as India and China.

These are examples in the few areas outside natural resources where Russian companies are attempting to become more international, but it will likely be a long time before they could be considered important global players. The same is true for virtually any Russian company without a natural resource base, since most are relatively young smaller- to medium-sized firms, while most older manufacturing companies from the Soviet period are still striving to operate efficiently and to compete domestically. These companies would be well advised to consider the alternative strategies for succeeding in their domestic setting before moving beyond national borders, such as some Indian companies have done.

Finally, it is important to address the arms and weapons sector, represented by the government-owned holding company Rosoboronexport. That firm has been designated by the government to coordinate not only arms and weapons exports, but other areas of strategic interest such as the largest (also government-owned) automotive company, AvtoVAZ. Russia has actively exported military equipment, with China and India being the two largest customers for Russian weapons (Smolchenko, 2007b).

Sustainability of MNE competitive advantages

Russian MNEs have experienced marked success in the global arena for one basic reason: they provide products badly needed in the expanding global economy. Most Russian firms that have become multinationals are engaged in various raw materials sectors including petroleum, natural gas, forest products, and many industries in the metals and minerals sectors. These are all commodity industries in which there is a ready market at prices set by global forces. Russia is abundantly rich in natural resources. It has already become the world's second largest producer of petroleum and is among the leaders in the world's oil reserves. The same is true of its natural gas resources, and the country is the world's number one exporter, supplying not only former Soviet republics and Eastern European countries, but also 25 percent of the EU's needs. With such an abundance of natural riches, it is not surprising that Russian MNEs operating in these industries have been able to overcome the usual disadvantages of a late entry into the global economy.

Their competitive advantage is based solidly on the global supply and demand equation, and thus far the demand side has substantially exceeded the supply, all to the benefit of these Russian MNEs. Obvious advantages have accrued to the MNEs themselves from the immediate acceptance of their products in the world market, including their growth and profitability. The country has also benefited from the successful exporting by these MNEs which has produced the lion's share of national tax revenues as well as being the source of the world's third largest store of gold and foreign currency reserves. However, this positive picture could give way to a far more negative scenario if the Russian economy does not diversify in a reasonable period of time. The country is, in the eyes of many experts, in serious danger of succumbing to the earlier-mentioned Dutch disease that is associated with countries that fail to diversify beyond their abundance of natural resource-based exports. This prospect remains a significant obstacle that could prevent the further positive development of Russian MNEs in the global arena. Without diversification and relying for too long on the export of energy and other raw materials, Russia could conceivably become a colony for the global economy with little sustainability beyond the life of its raw materials. At this point in time there are few Russian MNEs outside of the raw materials sector.

We believe that an examination of many of the factors that make up the 2006–2007 *Global Competitiveness Report* (World Economic Forum, 2006) points to an overall weakness in Russia's productivity and competitiveness, and that many of those same factors undermine the competitive sustainability of the country's MNEs. The report's nine factors are institutions, infrastructure, macroeconomy, health and primary education, higher education and training, market efficiency, technological readiness, business sophistication, and innovation. In analyzing some of these factors, we have concluded that they constitute serious obstacles to sustainability. The country's institutions and the infrastructure that is so critical for sustaining economic growth and global competitiveness are notably weak. In addition, the softer institutional aspects including cultural traditions and values (North, 1990; Puffer and McCarthy, 2007) have hampered Russian companies doing business internationally since they include minimum trust of outsiders, and have created inconsistencies in ethics and values, all resulting in a tarnished reputation for many Russians doing international business. We must emphasize again the extensive role of the Russian government in the economy and business which supports an oppressive bureaucracy for business, an extraordinary level of bribery, and the likely reduction of sustained competitiveness for Russian business, including MNEs (Adelaja, 2007).

We have also noted that the macroeconomy is excessively dependent on energy which has produced a seriously unbalanced economy that again brings sustainability into question. Health and education have been badly neglected since the beginning of privatization and constitute severe obstacles to sustainability. In late 2006 they began to receive attention under the major projects initiative of the Putin administration; this will require continuing attention if they are to reverse their position hampering sustained growth and competitiveness (Bush, 2007b).

When we consider market efficiency, technological readiness, business sophistication, and innovation, these are found more often in the non-MNE market sector, where domestic Russian firms compete with one another as well as with many major foreign firms. High-tech parks and liberal economic zones, such as Nizhnyi Novgorod, are intended to stimulate such competitive attributes. Possessing these attributes is the only way that domestic firms will be able to sustain competitiveness, and acquiring these attributes is critical to the competitive sustainability of Russian MNEs as opposed to relying on supplying raw materials to the rest of the world.

One way of acquiring such technology is from Western firms like Microsoft that locate in Russia to tap the country's intellectual technical prowess by employing scientists and engineers (*Moscow Times*, 2007, March 14); another is the earlier-mentioned M&As undertaken by many Russian MNEs.

The large natural resource MNEs, mostly state and oligarch owned, have basically been shielded from most of the problems and obstacles noted above due to their size, connections to the government, and the ready acceptance of their materials in global commodities markets.

How long this advantage will last, however, makes the sustainability of their favorable positions questionable. Many have mitigated this risk by adopting a strategy of vertical integration to move beyond simply supplying raw materials.

Russian MNEs have changed global dynamics

The rise of Russian MNEs has occurred largely through their consolidating domestic Russian industries to gain scope and scale for entry into global markets, similar to Cemex's strategic approach in Mexico as a precursor to going global (see Chapter 10 in this volume). This domestic strategy established the platform for some Russian MNEs to become important global players, which in turn has been an impetus for further consolidation of various world natural resource-based industries, including steel and aluminum. UC RusAl's emergence in 2007 as the world's largest aluminum company, for instance, was a major reason for Rio Tinto's acquisition of one of its major competitors, the Canadian aluminum giant Alcan, which resulted in Rio Tinto's becoming the world's largest aluminum company. An earlier offer by Alcoa had prompted a bidding war for Alcan that involved companies from a half-dozen countries, including UC RusAl (Daniel, 2007).

The increasing global reach of Russian steel companies such as Evraz and Severstal will likely have the same effect in the global steel industry. In January 2007, Evraz, primarily owned by Roman Abramovich, bought Oregon Steel in the US for $2.3 billion, and a majority stake in South Africa's Highveld Steel and Vanadium for $238 million. As a result, Evraz became the world's leading player in vanadium, an element used to strengthen steel (*Moscow Times*, 2007, May 8). Over time, the global automobile industry could also be affected since in May 2007 a unit of Oleg Deripaska's holding company, Basovyi Element, acquired Canada's Magna International, a world-leading auto parts firm, for $1.54 billion (McKenna, 2007). Deripaska's holdings already included GAZ, Russia's second largest automotive company. The move was seen as helping to make GAZ more competitive in the burgeoning domestic automobile market by incorporating more Western technology. But it could also be a prelude to his bidding to acquire AvtoVAZ, Russia's largely government-owned and largest domestic automotive company (*Moscow Times*,

2007, May 11b). Such speculation arises because of Deripaska's close relationship with the Kremlin and the government's favorable view of Magna's cooperation with, and contributions to, companies like AvtoVAZ. Still, the fear of the Russian government becoming even a minority shareholder in Magna was noted in a 2007 company memorandum filed with the US Securities and Exchange Commission (Smolchenko, 2007c). Basovyi Element's oligarch owner, Oleg Deripaska, may have other personal objectives in diversifying his holdings, including the purchase of nearly 5 percent of General Motors Corporation in August 2007 (*Moscow Times*, 2007, August 8).

The most important effect that Russian companies have had on global market dynamics is Russia's emergence as a preeminent energy power. After the fall of the Soviet Union in 1991, the economy was in a shambles, and it took Russia over a decade to take advantage of its huge energy resources in world markets. By the mid-2000s, the country's MNEs ranked at or near the top of petroleum exporters and the country possessed among the largest reserves in the world. Additionally, Russia was the world's largest producer of natural gas, and had the world's largest reserves. The Putin government recognized energy's potential to catapult Russia back onto the world stage not only as an economic, but also as a political, force. Under the state's program of designating thirty-nine industries as strategic to the country's sovereignty and economic competitiveness, energy came to the forefront. By 2007, the government, exercising what some have called increasing statization (McCarthy, Puffer, and Naumov, 2000), had engaged in renationalization and quasi-nationalization that resulted in control of around half of the country's petroleum production. And through Gazprom, the government has continued to control most of the country's gas production.

These government actions, along with the activities of privatized petroleum firms, have changed the balance of power among nations, at least regarding the supply and demand of energy. Energy has always had a political component, and Russia has been accused of using energy to exert its political muscle not only within Eastern Europe, but also in Western Europe where it supplies around 25 percent of energy needs. Russia has also begun exporting energy to the US, which often criticizes its alleged lack of democratic processes, causing tension between the two countries. But Russia's position as a potential major supplier of energy to the US will undoubtedly continue to influence that relationship. And the country's dominant position in other natural resources, particularly metals such as nickel, titanium, gold, aluminum, and steel, as well as diamonds, puts Russia in a position of world importance, particularly for countries like China and Japan that lack such natural resources.

Another politically charged reality is the fact that one of Russia's major exports is arms, munitions, military vehicles, and aircraft, and the country is also a nuclear power. As such, it is often seen as an important player in global conflicts. For instance, it has been viewed as a key party in negotiating with less developed nations like North Korea.

In March 2007, Russia ceased work on Iran's $1 billion nuclear reactor and withheld supplies of nuclear fuel until that country agreed to suspend uranium enrichment, a demand of the United Nations Security Council. Russia had also been extending its influence in African nations where both Russian firms and the government have been increasing investment. Thus, adding to its extensive influence due to huge energy and other natural resources, these more politically oriented activities have brought Russia back to the center of the world stage, changing both economic and political global dynamics.

Implications of Russian MNEs' global strategies

For emerging-market firms

It has been noted throughout this chapter that Russian MNEs are generally limited to natural resource industries. Accordingly, the most important strategic lesson that they might provide to their counterparts from other emerging economies is the necessity to diversify beyond one activity on the value chain if company growth is to be sustainable. Implicit in this strategic approach is the need to reinvest earnings emanating from initial profitable activities of supplying raw materials. This is particularly true since such activities do not generally add substantial value in the chain, a position generally necessary for sustainable growth. Many Russian MNEs seem to have learned this lesson and have begun to diversify beyond producing basic materials, sometimes seeking positions upstream, but particularly downstream, to strengthen their competitive positions through value-adding activities. Although many Russian MNEs have only begun such diversifications, they operate in a number of industries including oil, natural gas, steel, and aluminum. Although these lessons might be derived from the experience of Russian MNEs, Khanna and Palepu (2006) offer a broader view, including alternative strategies for building world-class companies in emerging economies.

In spite of the fact that leaders of these Russian firms have understood these lessons, many of them do not yet have sufficient expertise to operate in downstream activities that require additional higher-level capabilities beyond their experience. For instance, RusAl began operations to produce aluminum foil, but had to withdraw temporarily when management found the challenges beyond the company's capabilities at the time. To gain such capabilities, Russian MNEs have used M&As as the primary vehicle for global expansion, growth, and entering new strategic positions on the value chain. And for the most part, they have looked beyond Russia to Eastern and Western Europe as well as to the US, Canada, Australia, and some Asian and African countries.

Another lesson for MNEs in other emerging economies is the domestic strategy followed by many Russian MNEs. Before engaging in M&As, and in many cases before going global, these leaders sought to consolidate the domestic industries in which they operated, or at least to gain enough critical mass to enter the global market as a major player. Examples can be found in energy, steel, aluminum, nickel, titanium, gold, and forest products.

Beyond such competitive strategies, many Russian MNEs have recruited senior executives and managers from outside of Russia who understand the dynamics of international business, particularly from Europe and North America. Ilim Pulp, for instance, recruited a Canadian as its chief operating officer in order to gain technological and managerial expertise for its forest products operations. The incentives for such executives can be substantial, as in the case of Western investment bankers who in 2007 were paid at twice the level as in their own countries (Martinuzzi and Prince, 2007). Such hirings can enhance company credibility, corporate governance, and reputation in global markets. Additionally, however, these firms will have to find and develop indigenous executives who have, or are open to acquiring, new skills and approaches to managing their businesses in a competitive fashion (McCarthy, Puffer, Vikhanski, and Naumov, 2005). The same requirement is undoubtedly true for MNEs from other emerging economies where there is inevitably a dearth of market-oriented, globally experienced executives and managers.

For Western and Japanese MNEs

So far, Russian MNEs have not yet become a threat to MNEs from developed countries such as Germany, Japan, and the US, since those economies emphasize value-added products, high-tech offerings, and services, especially in the case of the US.

For natural resource-reliant MNEs

For these MNEs, Russia's position as a key supplier of crucial raw materials could influence their growth and progress. Russia is the largest producer of many such materials, without which MNEs from more developed economies could not easily continue to grow or to extend their global reach. If the cost of such materials for developed-country MNEs were to increase significantly due to price increases by Russian companies, their product prices in turn would increase, potentially slowing their growth and progress. Thus, MNEs in developed countries must maintain an awareness of the relative concentration of pricing power within Russian firms for many important resources.

An additional concern is the pervasive role of the Russian government in that country's economy, which could at any time affect the actions of Russian MNEs, possibly reflecting political objectives rather than free market forces. Russia's credibility as a reliable supplier has been a major issue and underestimating the close linkage of politics and business in Russia would be shortsighted on the part of MNEs from developed nations. The need to "reestablish trust" in Russia as a reliable supplier was emphasized in 2007 by a EU official while discussing the dominant role of Gazprom as an energy supplier for Europe (Lagorce, 2007).

For natural resource-based MNEs

The major concern for such MNEs is the potential for Russian competitors to affect and even destabilize world prices for major commodities, including energy, minerals, and other raw materials. In many cases, Russian MNEs are the major source of such crucial natural resources, as well as having the largest reserves. And in addition to their abundance of such resources, they have access to low-cost labor and are subject to limited environmental regulations. Those owned by Kremlin-friendly oligarchs enjoy freedom of operation that others may not, and enjoy the opportunity of having the government cooperate with them in various business ventures such as developing and commercializing sources of natural resources. Such advantages could in time erode world market shares of competitors from more developed countries, despite the fact that the government has not as yet provided other more direct help such as subsidies and domestic protection to most of these MNEs.

Strengthening their positions in the world commodity markets, some Russian MNEs, in aluminum and steel, for instance, have acquired firms in the US, Canada, Eastern and Western Europe, and other locations. Their primary objective, as noted earlier, has been to enhance their value-added, downstream activities, as evidenced by LukOil's acquisition of Getty's gas stations in the US and Hungary. Additionally, Russian natural resource-based MNEs have acquired companies specializing in related extraction and processing industries, such as UC RusAl's acquisition of a major bauxite mining company in the Caribbean. Their objective of becoming world players at various levels on the value chain is clear.

For non-natural resource-based MNEs

At best, Russian companies in this category are only beginning to become involved in international operations, and they are generally found in telecoms, IT, and, to a lesser extent, banking and investment banking. Given their nascent international involvement, these companies need to build credibility and also need investment to fund their growth. Thus they present an opportunity for developed countries' MNEs in their industries to partner with or invest in these companies while they are in their early stages of internationalization. Many European companies, for instance, have established relationships with, partnered with, or invested in Russian firms in the financial services sector, primarily to gain early entry into the attractive Russian market. But the next step for their activities could be to extend these businesses into the international arena, either as partners or as separate entities. Russia appears to present numerous opportunities for developed countries' MNEs to increase their presence in Russia, as well as to cooperate with Russian partners for international growth.

For Russian public policy makers

Many would argue that governments should let business people run their businesses with limited government involvement. However, Putin's policy of significant government involvement might be viewed as reasonable, at least in the short run, because of the tumultuous years of transition before he assumed the presidency in early 2000. However, increased government involvement in the strategic industries could have major effects on the development of Russian multinationals. Most of these companies are in industries that are already, or are likely to become, designated as strategic sectors. The question remains whether the government will be content with nationalizing only the largest company in each strategic industry, or whether many or all companies in those sectors might be targeted. And as mentioned earlier in the case of Canada's Magna International, and the more publicized activities of Gazprom cutting off gas supplies, there is some fear that Russian MNEs, through their foreign activities, are becoming instruments of Russian government foreign policy. The extent of government involvement has implications for international competitiveness and growth of Russian multinationals. It is generally recognized that government-operated industries are typically less competitive in the global arena. Over time, then, more extensive government involvement could be an obstacle to Russian MNEs in the global economy.

Certainly, the Russian government should not repeat the destruction of private businesses such as Yukos by whatever means, even though that company's assets became the basis of the state oil giant, Rosneft. Rather than increasing direct involvement in business, government efforts might be better aimed at building infrastructures and institutions supportive of a market economy, working to reduce corruption, and enacting policies that make it easier to start and grow businesses. Additionally, the government should continue its efforts in diversifying the economy to help develop successful companies beyond the natural resource sectors, to ward off the Dutch disease. For instance, in March 2007, President Putin ordered the Industry and Energy ministry to prepare a draft decree establishing a state-controlled shipbuilding company, along with two other sectors – aircraft building and space industries – as part of the government's initiative to diversify the economy away from oil exports (*Moscow Times*, 2007, March 13). And Putin evidently had other insights into diversification when he noted: "It's the information and communication technologies that now in many ways determine the dynamics of economic growth" (cited in Cremer, 2007). Such policy changes will be necessary if Russia's MNEs are ever to be found outside of the natural resource sectors in an important way.

In the area of foreign investment, Russia will have to play by internationally accepted standards, and display a posture of fairness in allowing foreign companies to invest in Russia, if it expects other nations to allow Russian MNEs to invest in their countries as they expand their global reach. Gazprom, for instance, had plans in 2007 to purchase pipelines and gas distribution companies across Europe and possibly take over Centrica, the largest gas retailer in Britain. And in August 2007 Gazprom sought to expand its position in Britain's power generation business by swapping assets with E.On of Germany, which controlled around 10 percent of electricity sales in Britain (*Moscow Times*, 2007, August 10). British officials, however, insisted that there should be reciprocity, with British companies being able to invest upstream in Russian gas fields, which the Russian government had made particularly difficult in recent years (Bergin, 2007). Such reciprocity will likely have to become a focus for Russian policy makers if they are to support the global expansion of the country's MNEs.

Conclusion

This chapter has discussed the rise of Russian MNEs that had their origins in the 1990s privatization era, and came to global prominence by the mid-2000s. The vast majority are natural resource-based firms, particularly energy companies. Of the latter, a number are primarily government owned, but some are privately owned by oligarchs and their partners. Most of the non-energy MNEs are privately owned, but again by oligarchs and their partners. The rise of Russian MNEs has coincided with the increasing prosperity of the Russian economy, which has been driven primarily by energy firms. The increasing role of the Russian government, both in ownership of firms, particularly those in energy, but also in placing government officials in top executive and board positions of other major firms, has tightened the Kremlin's control, and also calls into question the future competitiveness of Russian MNEs.

President Putin's consistent support of Russian MNEs, often as national champions, has been a key element of the government's involvement. Leading Russian MNEs have recently expanded globally, acquiring companies and expanding operations in Eastern and Western Europe, in North America, Latin America, Africa, and Asia, often after consolidating the domestic industry. Many appear to be seeking enhanced market power and control in the natural resource industries in which they operate. Their global activities are clearly aimed at growth through occupying higher value-added positions on their value chains to build sustainability. However, many believe the private MNEs and their oligarch owners might also have defensive goals, such as lessening their dependence on the state and its potential intrusions into their operations, including nationalization.

Russian MNEs have begun to have a marked impact on global market dynamics in natural resource sectors, primarily in the energy arena due to Russia's emergence as a preeminent global energy power. The rise of Russian MNEs to substantial positions in the global economy has implications and provides strategic perspectives for businesses in countries or regions at various stages of development. For their counterparts in other emerging economies, it is the necessity to diversify beyond one activity on the value chain if company growth is to be sustainable, and the consolidation of the domestic market as a precursor to global expansion. For Western and Japanese firms, Russian MNEs have begun to alter the balance of power in natural resource-based industries and potentially the pricing structure of these commodities. For those global competitors that are natural resource firms, this can have immediate and direct implications, while for non-natural resource-based firms, including those that rely heavily on natural resources, the effects would be seen more slowly.

Russia's natural resource-based MNEs have begun to show the potential to influence global commodity industries. In contrast, its non-natural resource-based firms have so far made only limited forays into contiguous international markets, generally in the telecoms, IT, and, to a lesser extent, banking and investment banking sectors.

Russian policy makers should also be influenced by the rise of the country's MNEs. Increasing government involvement could limit their international competitiveness and growth. Instead, the government would be well advised to focus on rebuilding the country's infrastructure, supporting the diversification necessary to produce a more balanced economy, and reducing bureaucratic obstacles to starting and growing companies, including corruption.

Russia's increasing involvement in the world economy is seen by most analysts as a positive development; they will have to be more transparent and to operate according to globally accepted standards. "The Magna investment is a step in the right direction," noted Andrew Kuchins of Washington's Center for Strategic and International Studies, referring to Oleg Deripaska's investment in the Canadian auto parts firm, and adding: "We want the Russian economy more integrated in the world economy … This is a major way that it's going to happen" (cited in McKenna, 2007). Still, the actions of the Russian and other governments, as well as the reputation and business practices of Russian executives (Goodley, 2007), will go far in determining whether Russian MNEs will continue extending their global reach. Russian companies were reported to have lost international deals worth $50 billion in 2006 partly due to "political attitudes" (Bush, 2007a). A key conclusion is that Russian MNEs will have to play by the rules of the global economic community if they are to achieve real acceptance, and they will need the cooperation of the Kremlin in doing so. If the Russian government and the MNEs are able to rise to this challenge, it will most likely result in an increase in transparency and better corporate governance, developments that should lead to greater acceptance globally of Russian MNEs, their owners, and their managers.

References

Adelaja, T. 2007. Graft, red tape are CEOs' main worries. *Moscow Times*, March 16: 6.

Bergin, T. 2007. Britain demands reciprocity. *Moscow Times*, May 15: 5 (Reuters).

Bush, J. 2007a. Rubles across the sea: Russian companies are on a global buying spree. *BusinessWeek*, April 30: 43.

Bush, J. 2007b. Russia's new deal: The Kremlin is pumping money into education, housing, and health care. *BusinessWeek*, April 9: 40–45.

Chazan, G. 2007. Fueled by oil money, Russian economy soars. *Wall Street Journal*, March 13: A1, A21.

Cremer, A. 2007. Russians make high-tech fair debut. *Moscow Times*, March 16: 7 (Bloomberg).

Daniel, R. 2007. Alcan bid prepared by Norsk Hydro: Report: Takeover battle involving Montreal aluminum producer said to widen. www. MarketWatch.com, May 28, 2007.

Delany, M., and Elder, M. 2007. After Putin's speech, foreign executives wait. *Moscow Times*, October 11: 1.

Dempsey, J. 2007. Analysts: Putin's tough talk spurs Europe to unite. *Boston Globe*, May 17: A16 (*International Herald Tribune*).

EBRD. *Transition Report 2007*. London: European Bank for Reconstruction and Development.

Economic Newsletter. 2005. Davis Center for Russian and Eurasian Studies, Harvard University, December 19.

Ekspert 400. 2006. www.gateway2russia.com

Fallico, A. 2007. Russian–Italian economic cooperation. *Moscow Times*, March 27: 12.

Federal Customs Service of the Russian Federation. 2007. www.customs.ru/en

Goodley, S. 2007. Russian firms need directors to clean image. March 12. www.telegraph.co.uk.

Goskomstat. 2006. Moscow: State Committee for Statistics of the Russian Federation.

Goskomstat. 2007. Moscow: State Committee for Statistics of the Russian Federation.

Hoffman, D. 2002. *The oligarchs: Wealth and power in the new Russia*. New York: Public Affairs, Perseus Books.

IMF (International Monetary Fund). 2007. www.imf.org

Khanna, T., and Palepu, K. G. 2006. Emerging giants: Building world-class companies in developing countries. *Harvard Business Review*, October: 1–9.

Lagorce, A. 2007. Is Gazprom Vladimir Putin's retirement haven? *MarketWatch*, May 16. www.marketwatch.com.

Levitov, M., and Korchagina, V. 2006. Putin rebuffs fears of state control. *Moscow Times*, February 1: 5.

Lodge, G., and Wilson, C. 2006. *A corporate solution to global poverty: How multinationals can help the poor and invigorate their own legitimacy*. Princeton: Princeton University Press.

Martinuzzi, E., and Prince, T. 2007. Moscow bankers get $7 million payday, double New York average. *Bloomberg*, May 14.

McCarthy, D. J., Puffer, S. M., and Naumov, A. I. 2000. Russia's retreat to statization and the implications for business. *Journal of World Business*, 35(3): 256–274.

McCarthy, D. J., Puffer, S. M., and Shekshnia, S. V. 2004. *Corporate governance in Russia*. Cheltenham, UK, and Northampton, MA: Edward Elgar.

McCarthy, D. J., Puffer, S. M., Vikhanski, O. S., and Naumov, A. I. 2005. Russian managers in the New Europe: Need for a new management style. *Organizational Dynamics*, 34(3), 231–246.

McKenna, B. 2007. Vladimir Putin wants his country's "champions" to step onto the world stage: The Russian invasion is here. *Globe and Mail*, May 12.

MN-files. 2005. www.mosnews.com/mn-files/siloviki. Siloviki. September 23.

Moscow Times. 2006. Poll says Russians prefer strong leader to democracy. January 10: 3 (*International Herald Tribune*).

Moscow Times. 2006. Novolipetsk, Duferco form $1.6Bln venture. November 28: 5 (Bloomberg).

Moscow Times. 2007. Putin orders the creation of state shipbuilding champion. March 13: 5.

Moscow Times. 2007. Microsoft starts production in Russia. March 14: 6 (Bloomberg).

Moscow Times. 2007. Severstal's Michigan buy. March 16a: 6.

Moscow Times. 2007. VimpelCom in Georgia. March 16b: 6 (Bloomberg).

Moscow Times. 2007. Business briefs. March 19: 1.

Moscow Times. 2007. Business briefs. March 22: 6.

Moscow Times. 2007. GDP rises 8.3% on consumer demand. March 27: 7 (combined reports).

Moscow Times. 2007. Food retail to expand 10% annually. March 30: 6 (Bloomberg).

Moscow Times. 2007. Kudrin puts inflation worries aside. May 2: 5 (Reuters).

Moscow Times. 2007. Evraz takes control of Highveld. May 8: 6.

Moscow Times. 2007. Alrosa is looking to go public soon. May 11a: 5.

Moscow Times. 2007. Deripaska to pay $1.5Bln for Magna Stake. May 11b: 1.

Moscow Times. 2007. Deripaska buys 5% of GM. August 8: 5 (Reuters).

Moscow Times. 2007. Gazprom seeks U. K. power assets. August 10: 5 (Reuters).

Moscow Times. 2007. Rosy outlook prevails for foreign investment. October 17: 9 (*Vedomosti*).

North, D. 1990. *Institutions, institutional change, and economic performance*. New York: Norton.

Pronina, L., and Humber, Y. 2006. Arms dealer wants into titanium. *Moscow Times*, January 23: 5.

Puffer, S. M., and McCarthy, D. J. 2007. Can Russia's state-managed, network capitalism be competitive?: Institutional pull versus institutional push. *Journal of World Business*, 42(1): 1–13.

Puffer, S. M., McCarthy, D. J., and Wilson, J. W. 2007. Emerging capitalism in Russia and China: Implications for Europe. *European Journal of International Management*, 1(1&2): 146–165.

Rodrigues, V. 2007. Gaidar says boom will survive lower oil prices. *Moscow Times*, May 2: 5 (Reuters).

Russia Business Watch. 2006–2007. Annual meeting 2006: Panel: State capitalism, strategic sectors & foreign investment. *Winter*, 14(4): 14–15.

Shuster, S. 2007a. Rosneft cash pushes reserves up $11Bln. *Moscow Times*, March 30: 7.

Shuster, S. 2007b. Troubleshooting starts as energy loses steam. *Moscow Times*, March 19: 8.

Smolchenko, A. 2007a. Chinese banks offer $2Bln in loans. *Moscow Times*, March 27:1.

Smolchenko, A. 2007b. Hu to oversee up to $4Bln in deals. *Moscow* Times, March 22:1.

Smolchenko, A. 2007c. Magna worries about the state's role. *Moscow Times*, August 7: 5.

World Bank, 2007. www.worldbank.org

World Economic Forum. 2006. *Global Competitiveness Report: 2006–2007*. Davos, Switzerland: World Economic Forum. www.weforum.org/gcr

Zubkov, V. 2004. All the president's men: Go forth and spy out the land of big business. *Russia Profile*, 5, November: 16.

8 | Brazilian multinationals: Surfing the waves of internationalization

AFONSO FLEURY AND MARIA TEREZA LEME FLEURY

Recent years have seen a flourishing of interest in the economies of the BRICs and their growing role as producers and intermediate rank powers in the global economy (Goldman Sachs, 2003; Humphrey and Messner, 2006). Although often taken as a single group, they have taken different paths, with China and India on the one hand and Brazil, Russia, and South Africa on the other.

The objective of this chapter is to analyze the emerging Brazilian multinationals, with special reference to how the national context affected the evolution of those firms. Two distinct approaches will be combined to achieve that aim. The first provides historical perspective; the second defines the conceptual framework that will be utilized in the analysis of selected cases.

After WWII, Brazil performed differently in relation to the three main waves of internationalization. In the first wave, in the 1950s and 1960s, Brazil was essentially a receiver of FDI, hosting new subsidiaries of foreign MNEs. During the second wave, in the late 1970s and early 1980s, isolated attempts by native Brazilian firms to move into international markets were observed. "The so-called Third World Multinationals (non-financial) in Brazil," it was noted, "are still at a rather incipient stage where the number of firms is concerned and as a percentage of the total value of exports ... construction and engineering firms predominate. Manufacturing firms are moving at a much slower pace, though one group has recently announced ambitious plans" (Villela, 1983, p. 267). In fact, the firms observed by the author were not successful in their internationalization attempts.

In order to study the emergence of Brazilian MNEs, extensive research of secondary sources was initially conducted. More than forty Brazilian MNEs, from the manufacturing, IT, and engineering services industries which operate in world markets, were identified. From that database, twelve cases were chosen to exemplify the distinct

200

patterns of internationalization in six different industries. The analyses of those cases were based on historical data from the literature as well as recent information gathered from specialized media and corporate websites. The initial outcomes of a survey of the Brazilian MNEs and their subsidiaries were also utilized. In all cases, visits and interviews provided important additional information.

The cases were analyzed through the application of Rugman's (1981) basic concepts of CSAs and FSAs, as has previously been done for other emerging countries, such as China (Rugman and Li, 2007).

The evolution of industry in Brazil during the twentieth century

Industry in Brazil before the first wave: 1900–1950

Brazil was essentially an agricultural economy until 1930. Before that point, the country's industrial activities stemmed either from the entrepreneurship of immigrants – especially those of Italian or German origin (who, for example, founded the two local breweries, – Antarctica in 1885 and Brahma in 1888) – or the subsidiaries of multinationals (Ford in 1919, Rhodia in 1919, and GM in 1925, among others).

In 1930, an internal revolution brought to power a coalition that shifted priorities and put industry at the top of the agenda. For Simonsen (1969, p. 51), "Brazil adopted a policy of import substitution industrialization as of 1930. However, until the end of WWII, this was not associated to a long term development philosophy but consisted of a series of individual reactions to trade balance difficulties. Only after WWII did the notion that industrialization should drive the country's economy become firmly ingrained."

The foundations of Brazilian industry were built during the 1940s. First, as a consequence of WWII, the shortages of imports created the conditions for the growth of the local consumer goods industries (food, shoes, and textiles/apparel) and basic capital goods industries (e.g., conventional machine tools).[1]

---

[1] The textiles/apparel and shoe industries became major exporters by the late 1970s. In the capital goods sector, the only Brazilian enterprise to achieve international status was Romi, a lathe and machining center producer, founded in 1930.

Table 8.1. *The formation of industry in Brazil: Natural resources and basic inputs*

SOE	Foundation date	Industry
CSN (Companhia Siderurgica Nacional)	1941	steel
CVRD (Companhia Vale do Rio Doce)	1942	mining and ore
Petrobras	1953	petroleum

During WWII and soon thereafter, in the midst of a strong nationalist movement, the government took the actions needed to create SOEs to exploit the country's natural resources, thus establishing a local natural resources/basic inputs industry (see Table 8.1). This was done with an eye toward the subsequent steps required for the expansion of the local manufacturing industry. According to Brazilian authors, the government undertook these productive activities due to the lack of interest of private Brazilian industrialists in investments that involved high initial capital costs and long payback periods.

The above firms, privatized in the 1990s, play an important role in the internationalization process of Brazilian industry.

Speeding up the industrialization project: The 1950s

The 1950s was a period of intense growth: "Between 1956 and 1961, the growth of the Brazilian economy achieved the most spectacular levels in fifty years. The GDP expanded at the yearly rate of 7% and the primary sector grew at an annual rate of 5.8%, while the annual rate of industrial growth reached 11.1%. The development formula adopted was industrialization at any cost, based on high import duties and tax incentives, as well as large public projects" (Simonsen, 1969, p. 42).

Indeed, the Kubitschek period (1956–1961) was characterized by fast industrialization ("fifty years in five"). The durable consumer goods industry (especially the automotive and white goods segments) was chosen as the driver of Brazilian economic development. Its formation was supported by a large inflow of FDI: new subsidiaries of multinationals started to operate in the country and the multinationals already operating in the country reorganized their operations.

The decision to rely on foreign multinationals to lead the formation of the local durable consumer goods industry was aligned with the purposes and strategies of the MNEs from the most advanced countries, which were expanding abroad at that time. It was also convenient for Brazilian industrialists, who preferred to be involved as financial partners in the large investments required for the establishment of greenfield plants rather than bearing direct responsibility for the functioning of those enterprises. The main investments came from US firms – GM, Ford, Whirlpool, TRW, and Tecumseh – and German firms – Volkswagen (1953), Mercedes-Benz (1953, trucks), and Bosch (1954). Some Scandinavian firms, especially those of Swedish origin, were already established in Brazil: Ericsson (1924) and Electrolux (1926). In the truck industry, Scania entered the country in 1957 and Volvo in 1979.

The industrial programs that drove the expansion of those industries implicitly assumed that MNEs would transfer their technologies and managerial practices, thus benefiting Brazilian firms. Indeed, a number of Brazilian automotive suppliers became important within local industry: MetalLeve, Varga, Cofap, and Sabo, among others. Moreover, in the white goods industry, certain suppliers were successful: WEG and later Embraco are cases to be analyzed. Thereafter, Brazilian private firms maintained an intense and peculiar interplay with the MNEs, sometimes as suppliers and partners but mostly as fierce competitors.

The 1960s and 1970s: Slowing down and speeding up again

In the 1960s, Brazil went through a period of turbulence, ending in the 1964 military coup. The macroeconomics of the country changed: "As of 1962, growth rates became much less spectacular, leading some pessimistic analysts to propose the peculiar thesis of the structural stagnation of the Brazilian economy" (Simonsen, 1969, p. 43).

Industrial development resurged, linked to National Sovereignty and Security doctrines. Five-year National Development Plans and National Science and Technology Development Programs were established. An inward-looking orientation re-emerged and large investments in infra-structure began, funded by foreign capital and implemented by local firms. Within the scope of this study, four points merit attention.

First, in relation to infrastructure projects such as roads, airports, ports and dams, Brazilian firms had preferential access. This influenced the growth of two types of local enterprises. In the capital goods industry, the existing Brazilian firms became large, diversified con-glomerates manufacturing a broad range of complex products based on mechanical and electromechanical technologies. The main example is the Villares Group, which was the main supplier of the Itaipu dam project (the world's largest dam and power plant before the Three Gorge project in China). Villares produced locomotives, marine motors, lifts, cranes, and many other goods. The second group com-prised engineering services firms (e.g., Odebrecht, Camargo Correa, and Andrade Gutierrez), which were able to develop sophisticated competencies in project development and management.

The majority of the capital goods producers sank in the 1990s when the Brazilian market was opened to foreign competition, not being able to reconfigure their operations; conversely, the engineering ser-vices firms were successful, Odebrecht becoming one of the first Brazilian firms to operate in international markets, in Latin America (1979) and in Africa (1984).

Second, the 1960s also saw the establishment of the petrochemical industry based on a tripartite model: local private capital and state capital joined foreign partners, who were chosen as technology sup-pliers (Evans, 1977; Fleury, 1989). Three petrochemical complexes were established around the three main Petrobras refineries. Again, there was the assumption that the foreign partners would transfer technology, thus upgrading local enterprises in terms of production and process competencies. Several Brazilian groups joined the pro-gram, such as Odebrecht, Ultra, Mariani, and Suzano. Later on, when the associations were undone, the main drawback of the program appeared. The production chain became segmented in respect to governance: Petrobras held the refining monopoly, Brazilian firms were responsible for first transformation, and MNEs for the second transformation processes. This resulted in a lack of synergy between the different players in the transformation chain. Of the firms created at that time, two started their internationalization process in the

2000s: Braskem (Odebrecht Group) and Oxiteno (Ultra Group). Their international expansion, however, is heavily influenced and, to some extent, constrained, by their position in the petrochemical production chain.

The third point that deserves attention is the establishment of the Brazilian aerospace industry and, particularly, the creation of Embraer, in 1969. The other two firms involved in the program were Avibras (a producer of equipment such as surface-to-surface missiles) and Engesa (a producer of land-based military equipment). Different from the latter two companies, Embraer was a product of the nationalistic period that followed WWII: in 1950, the government created the MIT-inspired Aeronautic Technology Institute. The establishment of Embraer as a SOE two decades later, in 1969, was due to the diligent work of institute-educated entrepreneurs and the interest of the military government, which envisaged Embraer as a supplier not only of regional civilian aircraft, capable of integrating the Brazilian territory, but also of military equipment.

At that time, Embraer was also seen as the pivot of an ambitious program to modernize Brazilian industry by creating demand for highly sophisticated and precise mechanical systems and components. That aim was not achieved: local firms had grown accustomed to the automotive industry's high-volume, low-precision regime, and were unsuccessful in making the transition to the low-volume, high-precision standards of the aeronautics industry (Fleury, 1989).

Embraer is one of the most visible Brazilian multinationals. Some scholars attribute its success to the government program in which it was nurtured. However, its path was not as smooth as one might imagine (Fleury, 1989). The mid-1990s privatization process was of paramount importance. This point will be reconsidered below.

Fourth, the efforts undertaken to create a Brazilian IT industry are also worth mentioning. A government program was established in the mid-1970s to "pick winners." However, the discontinuities caused by lobbyist pressures and changes in government institutions drove this program to fail dismally in the late 1980s (Schmitz and Cassiolato, 1992). Currently, the only potentially competitive segment of the Brazilian IT industry is the software segment, more specifically niche type software. Some firms in that branch are currently moving to the international market.

The exhaustion of the import substitution model: 1975–1990

The expansion observed in the late 1960s and early 1970s is often referred to as the "Brazilian miracle." The country grew at annual rates of roughly 7 percent. The problem created by that expansion was foreign debt growth. In addition, worldwide economic turbulence in the 1970s – especially oil price increases – set the stage for the subsequent decades of Brazilian development, characterized by chronic foreign debt problems, trade imbalances, and uncontrolled inflation. Consequently, the preceding subtle and implicit orientation toward industrial development vanished entirely: short-term economic policies prevailed over any long-term development decisions.

In the early 1980s suitable conditions for a new internationalization wave appeared, spurred by changes in the dynamics of products and markets. Japanese industry was increasing its share of international markets, supported by a broad, carefully crafted and implemented program (Fleury and Fleury, 1995). In contrast, Brazilian institutions and enterprises were not prepared to profit from this new window of opportunity.

Contrary to the Japanese approach, there was neither concern with establishing priorities in terms of what should or could be exported, nor standards to certify the quality of what was being exported. As a result, the majority of firms that opportunistically joined the program were ill prepared to meet the quality requirements then being established in international markets.

Actually, the exports promotion program created by the Brazilian government was an attempt to reduce trade deficit, the effectiveness of which was questioned in its basic principles. For example, studying a sample of 210 firms that had access to subsidized capital for exporting in the late 1970s, Rocha, Blundi, and Dias (2002, p. 82) conclude that "firms more committed to exports were less likely to survive … they became more vulnerable, probably due to frequent exchange rate fluctuations that resulted from the reshaping of the government's macroeconomic plans, which made exporting riskier than selling domestically." Therefore, the main outcome was an ephemeral increase in exports, the deception of foreign clients due to the products' quality problems, and the degrading of the "Made in Brazil" trademark.

Industrial restructuring in the 1990s

Overall, the 1980s were considered "Brazil's lost decade." Ferraz, Rush, and Miles (1992) summarize it as follows:

- the institutional context: an inward-oriented approach to growth;
- the economic context: unstable growth;
- the technological context: low investment and concentrated efforts;
- the social context: a lost decade.

Nevertheless, a change in mindset and behavior was triggered; the lessons learned in the 1980s' failures laid the groundwork for a radical restructuring of Brazilian industry in the 1990s.

To begin with, there was a general understanding that "The mechanisms adopted to stimulate industrial development in Brazil since the early stages of the import substitution period were highly efficient in terms of production growth but had two negative effects. The first was the mismanagement of issues such as competitiveness (both internal and external) and efficiency, while the second was an anti-exporting culture that predominated at least up until the mid-1980s" (Bonelli, 1997, p. 42). For Amadeo (1997, p. 266), the 1990s mark the transition from "an interventionist development strategy to a liberal agenda where policies are geared toward a state responsible only for macroeconomic stability and for providing basic social services."

Ferraz, Kupfer, and Haguenauer (1996, p. XVIII) make this point more strongly:

During the 1980s, the pursuit of absolute self-sufficiency, the target of several decades of import substitution policy, lost its relevance as the objective and function of national development and Brazilian entrepreneurs began looking for other directions for their decision processes. As a result, enterprises began to save resources and to replace, in their strategy formulation processes, the local context for the international horizon. Behavioral and performance transformations gained speed in the early 1990s, when productivity records were broken year after year, thanks to the rationalization of production and layoffs.

In the political sphere, the 1980s witnessed the transition from military dictatorship to democracy. That transition was put to the test when the elected president was impeached in 1993, but the

vice-president was smoothly installed, thus consolidating the democratic regime and the institutional apparatus.

However, during his short term, President Collor introduced major
changes that redefined the structure and the competitive system of the
country. His government began by freezing bank accounts, which had
a brutal impact on demand, especially for non-essential goods. Many
industries had to rediscover their markets and establish new strategies.
For example, the automotive industry stood idle for more than three
months. That set the stage for the industrial restructuring that was
completed years later through privatizations.

The government changed the competitive system by introducing a number
of major policy initiatives: the Industrial Competitiveness Program, the
Technological Capability Program and trade reforms. The Industrialization
and Foreign Trade Policy established a timetable for progressive import
duties reductions, designed to gradually expose Brazilian producers to
stronger foreign competition. For example, duties on toys fell from 85% in
1991 to 20% in 1994; on cars, from 60% to 35%; on computers, from 65%
to 40%; and on capital goods, from 50% to 25%. The aims were clear: to
improve international competitiveness, deregulate trade, and achieve marketing selectivity, a transparent industrial policy, and medium- and long-
term improvements in competitiveness, by developing enhanced skills and
product quality. (Fleury and Humphrey, 1993, p. 14)

At the same time, the government created the Brazilian Quality and
Productivity Program to disseminate the quality and productivity philosophy, methods, and tools. The program brought together the knowledge and experience of industry, universities, and research centers.

As for industry, it had learned its lessons from the threats generated
by the opening of local markets and the fiasco of earlier attempts at
entering international markets. Thus, heavy catch-up investments in
the best practices of world-class manufacturing were made.

Four points are important to consider in the turnaround that led
Brazilian firms to become new multinationals: the privatization process,
the consolidation of the consumer goods industry, the denationalization
of the durable goods industry, and the creation of Mercosur, establishing the conditions for the local firms to begin their experiences in the
international markets.

Table 8.2 shows the year in which CSN, CVRD, and Embraer were
privatized. As to Petrobras, even though the Brazilian government has
sold part of its shares, it still maintains control of the company.

Table 8.2. *The privatization of Brazilian SOEs*

Enterprise	Year	Buyers
CSN	1993	Brazilian Industrial Group, Bradesco Bank, pension funds
CVRD	1997	Brazilian Industrial Group, Opportunity Bank, pension funds
Embraer	1994	Brazilian government, Brazilian Financial Group, pension funds

The privatization period also marks the entry of pension funds, mostly associated with the former SOEs (Petrobras and Banco do Brasil, among others). Some financial groups, especially the Garantia and Vicunha, became important players in the industrial scene.

For a large group of Brazilian firms rising competition in the internal markets due to increased participation of subsidiaries of foreign MNEs, and the possibility of international procurement due to newly established trade policies, resulted in what some authors called "the denationalization process." Several leading Brazilian firms, especially in the automotive and other technology-intensive industries, were sold to foreign MNEs.

The most striking case was MetalLeve – previously one of Brazil's most advanced firms, and a first-tier supplier with an R&D lab in Detroit and distribution centers in other parts of the US – which was sold to Mahle. Varga (brake systems), Nakata (suspension systems), and Cofap (shock absorbers), among others, soon followed. On the other hand, the survivors, such as Sabo, Metagal, WEG, and Embraco, emerged in a much stronger competitive position.

In the consumer goods industry, M&As were also frequent. In some segments, such as beverages, this led to the formation of large-scale firms like AmBev. In others, such as textiles/apparel, this was not the case.

To summarize: the abrupt changes that were the main feature of the 1990s drove industry from a protected and subsidized to an open and liberalized environment. The statement that best describes this period is ascribed to an economy minister who said, "The best industrial policy is no industrial policy."

Analysis of Brazil's emerging multinationals

The local institutional environment

The main features of the local institutional environment were not significantly changed after the turn of the twenty-first century. Instability and unpredictability are still present and the structural reforms that would have provided local firms with greater competitiveness vis-à-vis the international environment did not advance. Specifically, tax reform and labor reform have been under discussion but have not yet materialized. Consequently, production taxation and labor charges continue to be among the world's highest.

Additionally, there are growing concerns over the deterioration of the country's infrastructure, which impacts logistics, transportation, and the reliable delivery of electricity. All these factors, combined, have come to be known as the "Brazil cost" or the "Brazil risk."

In relation to external markets and the internationalization of Brazilian enterprises, the positions of local governmental institutions have been ambiguous. Three points can be made. First, although the value of exports has risen in absolute terms, Brazil's relative share of international trade has fallen. Concurrently, an analysis of exports has shown a rising share of commodities and a reduction in the percentage of manufactured goods. Second, where international trade agreements are concerned, the results of Brazilian diplomacy continue to be very limited. Mercosur has been beset by political and ideological wrangling. Negotiations for the FTAA (Free Trade Area of the Americas) have failed to yield results. Third, the specific issue of Brazilian firms' internationalization was initially regarded with suspicion, there being a feeling that this process might lead to a reduction of local investment and to the transfer of jobs to other countries. This perception has softened recently and certain mechanisms to help Brazilian firms launch into an internationalization process have been created. Nonetheless, only a few firms strove to tap into these resources, a modest amount that does not offset the limitations of the local capital market (Grosse, 2005).

The Mercosur experience

An important experience for Brazilian firms' internationalization started in 1991, when Argentina, Brazil, Paraguay, and Uruguay signed the Asunción Treaty, establishing a free trade zone and a shared customs system.

Though the figures are not entirely reliable, it is estimated that some 300 subsidiaries of Brazilian origin were established in Argentina, profiting from Mercosur financial advantages. That figure includes both subsidiaries of Brazilian firms and affiliates of Brazilian subsidiaries of foreign MNEs, especially those operating in the electromechanics industry and automotive industry. However, the aforementioned denationalization of Brazilian industry and Mercosur limitations led to a gradual reduction in the above figure. When the Argentine economy collapsed, in 2001, the number dropped dramatically.

The Brazilian MNEs: An overall view

Brazilian firms initiated export operations to neighboring countries in the 1950s. It was only at the end of the 1990s that the internationalization of Brazilian enterprises gained rhythm and consistency. A 2006 report from the BCG classifies 12 Brazilian enterprises among the 100 global challengers from the BRICs (China has 44, India 21, and Russia 7; Boston Consulting Group, 2006). From the twelve, ten have international presence and two are "heavy agribusiness exporters." There is no database to provide information about the internationalization of Brazilian firms; at the last count there were more than forty Brazilian international firms operating a large number of organizational units all over the world (Table 8.3).

Those firms are from industry, services, and the IT industry. The industrial firms operate in different segments and, normally, are not interrelated among themselves as participants in the same global value chain.

The location pattern of the subsidiaries shows that during the 1990s, Brazilian enterprises started operations mainly in Latin American countries. However, after the turn of the twenty-first century, that changed and many late-movers chose to enter the international arena via developed countries. The commodities producers are geographically concentrated (in Latin America only, or in the US only) while manufacturers are much more scattered. As to ownership structure, acquisitions are the preferred option.

Table 8.3. Brazilian companies with organizational units abroad

Company	Sector	Size: (sales US$ m)	First export	First plant abroad	Units abroad	Countries (sequence)	Mode of entry (sequence)
Manufactured products							
Ambev	beverage	14,400	1979	1993	35	LA, USA, EU	Acq, JV
Artecola	auto parts, shoes	120	-	2000	5	LA, USA, EU	JV, Acq
Busscar	bus assembly	260	-	1999	9	LA	Acq, JV
Braskem	chemicals		-	2006	2	LA	JV
Camargo Corrêa	cement and engineering	4,000	-	2003	-	LA	Acq
Cinex	furniture	15	-	2002	2	LA	GF
Citrosuco	beverage	312	-	1997	1	USA	Acq
Coopinhal	coffee	-	-	2006	1	Russia	JV
Coteminas	textile	550	1997	1997	11	USA	JV, Acq
CSN	steel	5,500	1977	2001	9	USA, EU	Acq
Cutrale	orange juice	1,000	-	1990	1	USA	Acq
CVRD	mining	23,350	1949	1984	52	USA, EU, China	Acq, GF
Duas Rodas	food	-	-	1997	3	LA	GF
Duratex	construction materials	692	1957	1995	10	LA, EU	Acq
Embraco	compressors	590	1980s	1994	6	EU, Asia	Acq

Company	Industry	Employees		Year	#	Regions	Entry mode
Embraer	aircraft	3,906	1975	1979	3	China, EU	JV, Acq, GF
Friboi	food	11,500	1997	2005	6	USA, LA, EU, ME	Acq
Gerdau	steel	14,000	1980	1980	63	LA, USA EU, India	Acq, GF
Guerra	trucks	80	1993	2005	1	LA	GF
H.Stern	jewelry	200	-	1955	80	LA, EU, ME	GF, JV
Ipiranga	oil and gas	10,000	-	1995	4	LA	JV, GF
Klabin	paper	1,500	1970s	1996	1	LA	GF
Marcopolo	bus assembly	843	1961	1991	9	South Africa, LA, EU, China	JV, GF, Acq
Metagal	auto parts	-	-	1996	1	LA	-
Metalcorte	electric engines	180		2005	1	LA	Acq
Metalfrio	refrigeration	300	-	2005	4	EU, USA	Acq
Natura	cosmetics	1,600	-	1981	6	LA, EU	GF
Oxiteno	chemicals	2,205	1990s	2003	6	LA	Acq
Perdigao	food	3000	1976	1990	4	ME, EU, LA	JV, GF
Petrobras	oil	79,120	-	1972	100	LA, Africa, USA	Acq
Random	trucks	1,900	1973	1994	7	LA	GF
Sabó	auto parts	170	1975	1992	9	LA, EU, USA	Acq, GF
Sadia	food	4100	1967	1991	10	EU, LA, ME, Japan	JV, Acq
Santista	textile	365	1994	1995	8	LA, EU	Acq, JV
Smar	industries solutions	80	1989	1988	7	LA, EU	GF
Tigre	construction materials	850	-	1977	6	LA	GF, Acq
Tramontina	tools and house supply	700	-	1986	10	USA, ME	GF

Table 8.3. (cont.)

Company	Sector	Size: (sales US$ m)	First export	First plant abroad	Units abroad	Countries (sequence)	Mode of entry (sequence)
Votorantim	mining	1,750	-	2004	1	LA	Acq
Votorantim	cement	11,500	1970	2001	29	Canada, USA	Acq/JV
WEG	electric engines	1,500	1980s	1995	12	LA, EU, China	Acq
IT and Services							
CI&T	business intelligence	150	-	2006	2	USA, EU	GF
Andrade Gutierrez	engineering and construction	2,150	-	1980	11	LA	GF, Acq
Atech	IT	50	-	1997	1	USA	GF
Datasul	business intelligence	95	1993	2001	4	LA	GF
IBOPE	Telecommunication	-	-	1991	16	LA	JV, GF
Odebrecht	engineering and construction	11,322	1979	1979	14	LA, Africa, EU	Acq, GF
Politec	business intelligence	250	-	-	2	USA, Japan	GF, Acq
YKP	business intelligence	18	-	-	-	LA	JV

Notes: LA = Latin America; ME = Middle East; Acq = acquisition; JV = joint venture; GF = greenfield plant

Brazilian multinationals: Selected case studies

The historical overview described the conditions under which today's Brazilian multinationals grew up and evolved. It was shown that they belong to different industrial segments and are not restricted to the natural resources sector.

To better examine the CSAs and FSAs, cases were selected for study from six different industrial segments: resource-based firms, basic input suppliers, construction suppliers, consumer goods producers, equipment and component suppliers, and systems assemblers. In each category two representative cases of Brazilian multinationals will be described, followed by a brief commentary, explaining the relevant CSAs and FSAs. In the section that follows, an integrated analysis will be made and conclusions presented.

Resource-based Brazilian MNEs

The image of Brazil is usually linked to the climate and to the richness of its natural resources. Therefore, it is expected that the Brazilian emerging multinationals be primarily resource based. The two most representative cases will be analyzed: Petrobras and CVRD (Companhia Vale do Rio Doce, also known as Vale).

Petrobras

The Brazilian government authorized the founding of Petrobras in October 1953. From 1954 to 1997, the company held a monopoly on oil exploration and production operations, as well as other activities linked to the oil, natural gas, and derivatives sector, with the exception of wholesale distribution and retailing by gas stations.

In 1963, Petrobras set up a Research Center, CENPES, on the campus of the Federal University of Rio de Janeiro. Thereafter, CENPES performed a fundamental role in sustaining the company's strategies. For example, in the 1950s, the first petrochemical complex was installed using a turnkey contract. CENPES became involved with the design and implementation of a second complex as a technology receiver, and for the bidding of the third complex Petrobras was able to negotiate open transfer of technology, with CENPES actively participating in the project's development (Fleury, 1989). The operational competencies developed by CENPES allowed the systematic reconfiguration of production processes in such a way that the company has maintained its operational efficiency during the frequent power crises and changes in the energy matrix that have occurred in Brazil and also, when the time came, allowed it to prepare refinery projects implemented in less developed countries.

Two important inflection points in the company's history were its internationalization process in the 1970s and the overthrow of its monopoly in the 1990s. The first oil crisis in 1973 was decisive when it came to changing the strategic direction of Petrobras, which started pursuing a strategy of "producing Brazilian oil in foreign countries" (www.petrobras.com.br). In order to do so, it invested in people for its international expansion.

The first country in the internationalization process was Colombia, where Petrobras entered into an association for exploring an onshore area. Then it obtained concession areas to operate in the Middle East, Iraq, Iran, and North Africa. In the 1970s the drilling of wells on Iraqi soil resulted in the important discovery of the giant Majnoon field – the contract for which was "renegotiated" by the Iraqi government and the investments repaid to the company.

The main objectives of Petrobras' international operations have changed over time. In the 1970s the strategy was to guarantee oil for the domestic market, while in the 1980s, in addition to guaranteeing supply, it also looked to export oil. Finally, at the end of the 1990s, after the Oil Law, a more structured and planned way of operating in international markets was put into place.

In 1997 the Oil Law opened up oil industry activities in Brazil to private initiative, thus marking the end of the company's monopoly. As a consequence, multinationals such as Shell, Exxon, Mobil, Texaco, and British Petroleum began to participate in various oil-related and derivative sectors, thus obliging Petrobras to undergo transformations, among them a restructuring of the company and intensification of the globalization process in order to become more competitive and win markets outside Brazil.

From the point of view of corporate governance the Brazilian government is still the main shareholder, with 56% of the voting shares and 32% of the total number, but the company's shares are now publicly traded. The company's pension fund has a significant share in this figure. In 1999 its corporate bylaws were rewritten according to US Securities and Exchange Commission regulations;

shares were listed on the New York Stock Exchange in 2000, when it adopted a management model allowing it to seek financing and contracts abroad.

Petrobras is also the Brazilian company that has invested most abroad and carried out the greatest number of takeovers. More than US$5.2 billion have been invested in foreign countries, including investments to acquire the concession of 130 oil exploration contracts and seven takeovers, when the debts of the companies purchased were assumed. Exploration contracts are generally done by consortiums and, since Petrobras is a pioneer in, and dominates, the deep water drilling technology that was developed by CENPES, it leads several of them. In 2007, for example, Petrobras, ExxonMobil, and Ecopetrol of Colombia started drilling a well in the Caribbean Sea in Colombian territorial waters. Petrobras is the main operator and owner of 40% of the resources discovered, Exxon has 40%, and Ecopetrol the remaining 20%.

Petrobras' largest international operation was the takeover of the Argentine company Perez Companc. This acquisition was the result of a change in the company's focus that extended its area of operation from oil to energy. Petrobras is currently committed to developing biofuels and extending the scope of its exploration and refining activities, particularly on the African continent.

Companhia Vale do Rio Doce – CVRD

CVRD was set up by the federal government on June 1, 1942, and privatized on May 7, 1997, when the Consorcio Brasil, led by the Vicunha Group, won an auction held at the Rio de Janeiro Stock Exchange. CVRD was listed on Latibex in February 2000, and on the New York Stock Exchange in June of the same year.

CVRD is an integrated company (mines, a railroad, ports, and pelletizing) and since it was set up it has cultivated the image of a highly reliable exporting company: "Its development strategy is closely linked to the expansion of the Brazilian economy, particularly the State production sector ... [However,] as a result of the characteristics of its production activities and its involvement with international markets the company has managed to define its growth strategies with a certain degree of autonomy vis-à-vis Government policy. Its autonomous entrepreneurial character is highly valued internally" (Fleury, M.T., 1986).

In addition to having at its disposal natural resources from the best quality deposits in the world, CVRD holds shares in six hydroelectric power stations, an important factor in reducing its production costs.

CVRD set up its own development and technology department in 1965. Since the company's founding, however, it has enjoyed the support of federal and state universities, particularly the Federal University of Ouro Preto, as well as from technical schools, in preparing its employees.

In 1953 CVRD sent its first shipment to Japan. In 1962 it signed the first long-term supply contracts and inaugurated its fleet of cargo ships. As a result of its product/market characteristics CVRD has developed differentiated competences in the supply chain area. It is the largest logistics operator in Brazil and the second largest in Latin America.

In 1989 its strategic plan was already focusing on internationalization, for reasons related to its capital structure, risk prevention, and, above all, the company's past trajectory (path dependence). Structural factors relative to the competitive dynamics of the industry, economies of scale, new technologies, and oligopolistic interdependence also played a role. Previously, the company had only invested in Brazil and its internationalization had been limited to exports. The only minor exception to this was its investment in the US company California Steel, in 1984.

With privatization the company gained agility. It is currently the world leader in the production and commercialization of iron ore and pellets. It also holds the largest nickel reserves on earth. CVRD is an important global producer of concentrates of copper, coal, bauxite, alumina, aluminum, potassium, calcium, kaolin, manganese, and iron alloys.

For many years the customer-focused strategy of CVRD has borne fruit. For example, because it is the preferential supplier for Japanese steel mills, when Japanese companies started preparing steel projects for other countries (e.g., China) they used the specifications of the inputs supplied by CVRD, which gave the company differentiated access conditions to those new markets.

CVRD has been focusing its objectives on greeenfield projects, which put mineral research at the top of the company's needs. In other words, the company's significant investments in mineral research act as guidelines for future production internationalization, via organic

growth. The result of this is that CVRD is currently more internationalized in its mineral research projects than in mining. The company has fourteen projects outside Brazil, five of which are in mining
and nine in mineral research: 64 percent of the projects of CVRD
abroad are in mineral research and not in mineral production, per se.

With regard to mineral production projects it is important to
emphasize that the company produces in the US (steel), Bahrain
(pelletization), France (iron alloys), Belgium (manganese), and Nor-
way (iron alloy and manganese). It also has global research programs
in mining on three continents and in eight countries (Chile, Peru,
Venezuela, China, Mongolia, South Africa, Mozambique, and Angola),
in addition to commercial offices in New York, Brussels, Tokyo, and
Shanghai.

CVRD's competence in the logistics area has also earned it international recognition. In 2003 the company signed an intermodal
transport partnership agreement with Mitsui.

In 2006, CVRD bought the Canadian company Inco, the largest
purchase of a foreign company ever carried out by a Latin American
company. In taking over Inco, CVRD became the second largest
mining company in the world after BHP Billiton. If one discounts the
fact that BHP also works in the oil and gas areas, CVRD is the world's
largest mining company.

Comments

The success of these two major Brazilian companies is only partially
explained by the quality and quantity of the natural resources to
which they have access. Because they belonged to the state sector, they
also had the support of internationally renowned universities and
public research institutes that were part of the same national project.
However, it is important to point out that the very challenge of efficiently exploiting resources led these companies to develop strategies
and competences that put them in positions of prominence in the
global market. Even though they started life as state-owned companies
and enjoyed their monopoly status for fifty years, their international
presence demonstrates the development of distinctive strategic and
management competences. Today, these companies are competing in
markets in which the scale of operations is increasingly growing
in volume, demanding the development of innovative management
strategies and models. The technological competences they have

developed – more apparent in the case of Petrobras – have created an asset that has driven both their internationalization trajectories as well as the strategic alliances they have entered into with other world-renowned companies. The group of FSAs bears a relationship with the CSAs that has underpinned the evolution of these companies.

The basic input suppliers' Brazilian MNEs

The Brazilian basic input industry was a project developed under the auspices of the state, and lived through two very different moments: the first in the 1940s, with the setting up of CSN, and the second in the 1960s, with the tripartite model that provided the conditions for the emergence of other Brazilian multinationals, among them Braskem and Oxiteno.

Braskem (Odebrecht Group) is becoming an international company in Latin America, with a particular focus on Venezuela. Oxiteno (Ultra Group) has already purchased and consolidated four plants in Mexico, the country from which it is meeting demand from the US, where it is setting up commercial offices. CSN will be analyzed in greater detail later. But another Brazilian multinational to be analyzed in this category is Gerdau, which has trod a very different path. This is a family company that produced nails for the construction industry and that evolved in a different way, becoming a supplier of steel for the construction industry in countries on three continents. Gerdau's trajectory illustrates another type of Brazilian multinational.

Companhia Siderurgica Nacional – CSN

CSN was established as a state-owned company in 1941, in the very early days of Brazil's industrialization process, and was privatized in the early 1990s. As a group, CSN is involved in mining, distribution, port terminals, railroads, and hydroelectric power stations. The export share of its steel products grew considerably after 2000, reaching some 60 percent by 2003.

The steel industry is going through a strong concentration process led by the Indian company ArcelorMittal. Technically, this concentration process is based on the premise that the ideal logistic configuration demands that the mines, mills, and ports be close to each other.

Brazil, even though it is the world's largest raw steel producer, has no steel company ranked among the world's ten largest. ArcelorMittal's capacity, on the other hand, is comparable to Brazil's entire steel production. In the Brazilian market, CSN's main competitors are ArcelorMittal, Gerdau, and Cosipa.

In terms of competitive advantages, one should stress CSN's operating competences. With control of its entire logistical chain, it is one of the firms with the lowest production cost in the world: US$180 per ton versus US$300 among US firms. As of 2000, CSN redefined its strategic positioning from cost advantage to customer solutions, seeking more sustainable competitive advantages and attempting to become a global player.

Its first international acquisition was Heartland Steel, in 2001. This was one of most advanced independent steel processing facilities in the US, but it became insolvent and had to reorganize under Chapter 11 of the US Bankruptcy Code. For CSN, this acquisition provided an excellent opportunity for entering the US market. It is a focused plant that receives raw steel from the Brazilian mills and performs the finishing portion of the production process. This is also known as "postponement."

The acquisition of a steel plant in Portugal, in partnership with Corus Steel (the result of the Dutch Hoogovens and British Steel merger), in 2003, allowed it to get its foot in the door of the European market. In this agreement, CSN has responsibility for operations while Corus primarily deals with commercial activities. Though the cultural distance from Portugal may seem small (since Brazil was a Portuguese colony from 1500 to 1922 and its language is Portuguese), the expat managers faced many cultural issues. Still, the implementation process of new operational procedures was carefully negotiated and they were put into place gradually. In less than five years the productivity of Lusinor, the Portuguese plant, has improved considerably. It currently enjoys a great deal of autonomy and essentially supplies the Spanish construction market.

CSN's main declared reasons for production internationalization were financial (hedging and revenues in strong currencies) and regulatory (technical and sanitary barriers). In late 2006/early 2007, CSN lost a bid for the acquisition of Corus to Tata Steel. Consequently, its global market share continued to rank low.

Gerdau

Established by a family of German immigrants in the south of Brazil, Gerdau started operating in 1901, producing nails. In 1948 the decisive phase in its business expansion occurred when it acquired

Siderúrgica Riograndense (steel mill), thereby setting out on its successful trajectory in the steel industry. It is currently ranked fourteenth on the list of the world's largest steel makers, based on data from the International Iron and Steel Institute for 2005.

In understanding Gerdau's strategy, it is important to keep in mind that it evolved from making nails to supplying the steel used in construction. Gerdau's market, therefore, is construction and has different characteristics from CSN's market.

Nearly 90 percent of the company's production capacity is based on mini-mills, a small-scale production process that uses scrap as its main input, allowing the company to operate in a decentralized way, close to its customers, at competitive costs. It also permits Gerdau to be the leader in recycling in Latin America.

Gerdau grew in the Brazilian market via the acquisition of mills that had management problems; their main investment was management capacity, not capital. Because it dealt with metallic construction, Gerdau was especially interested in the American market, and its internationalization process gave preference to the purchase of companies rather than joint ventures.

In 1980, in its first activity outside the Brazilian market, Gerdau acquired LAISA in Uruguay, but due to its proximity and the particular characteristics of the markets this had no significant impact on the company's operating strategy. The real move toward internationalization happened ten years later. Between 1989 and 1992 the company acquired four steel producers: Courtice Steel (Canada), Indac and Aza (Chile), and Inlasa (Uruguay). With the exception of the Canadian company, which was of medium size, all the others were small steel mills.

In 1999 Gerdau acquired its first large mill: the North American steel manufacturer AmeriSteel, the second largest producer of steel rods and the third largest producer of steel bars and profiles in the US, which was also the owner of four other mills in the country. AmeriSteel's installed capacity was 70 percent greater than that of the eight companies acquired abroad up until that time.

In 2005 Gerdau acquired mills in Argentina and Colombia and in 2006 took its first step toward producing steel outside the Americas and outside the civil construction market when it acquired 40 percent of the corporate capital of Corporación Sidenor S.A., the largest producer of special steels and one of the largest manufacturers of stamp-forged products in Spain. In doing so, Gerdau became part of the automotive global value chain. New purchases were also made in the US in 2006.

The main mechanism used for incorporating the companies purchased is the GBS (Gerdau Business System), an instrument that formalizes the best administrative and operational practices. This system seeks to identify best practices, which the company classifies as the macro-processes considered fundamental when it comes to creating value for the business, and which meet the needs of the markets that are of interest to it and which, therefore, achieve the results expected by shareholders.

Comments

These two cases are interesting to analyze when they are compared with the previous cases.

CSN started life as a state-owned company and had access to the same natural resources as CVRD; in fact there is litigation between the two companies for control of the Casa de Pedra mine. The privatization process that occurred in the 1990s allowed the Vicunha Group, one of the country's largest industrial groups, originally in textiles, to become part of the governance structure both of CSN and CVRD, but in different positions. The group effectively took command of CSN, but remained a shareholder of CVRD, which kept the previous autonomous management style and is headed by a former director of Bradesco, the largest Brazilian bank. Therefore, one of the possible explanations for the differences in their internationalization trajectories has to do with the ease with which a company from an emerging country works in international financial circuits and, implicitly, its strategic orientation and management model: in principle, we can say that industrial culture prevailed in the case of CSN, while financial culture gained more relevance in the case of CVRD.

The Gerdau case illustrates another trajectory. Gerdau chose a different market from CSN to develop its strategy. In fact, the value chains in which the two companies operate have very different characteristics. CSN supplies the basic metal-mechanical value chains, while Gerdau supplies construction companies; the former are extremely integrated and have very well-defined command structures ("governance" in the sense used by Gereffi [1994]). Civil construction, on the other hand, has no integrated chains and supply is done in a fragmented and local pattern. Gerdau, by adopting a strategy of decentralized regional operations, has managed to develop a differentiated business model that places it in a position of prominence on the global stage. Therefore, even if the CSAs might have initially favored CSN, it was the FSAs that made the difference in the evolution of the internationalization process.

In addition, we can see that the recent investments of Gerdau, already relatively well consolidated in the civil construction sector, were of the "moving up the value chain" type. The acquisition of Sidenor puts Gerdau in the automotive global value chain. So far, CSN's investments have not made feasible the same type of strategy: Lusinor is essentially a producer of inputs for civil construction; in Brazil, CSN supplies the automotive and white goods chains.

This underlines the importance of understanding the dynamics of global value chains and the role played by Brazilian companies, both at home and abroad, in relation to the GVCs in their internationalization processes.

To explore this point further, we will analyze two additional cases of companies that supply construction materials.

The construction suppliers' Brazilian MNEs

Every country or geographical region is endowed with certain types of natural resources which influence the local civil construction sector. In Brazil, as in Latin America as a whole, soil conditions have had an influence over the types of construction and the materials used. Commercialization conditions have had an influence on the type of company that is successful in the local markets, which is characterized by enormous fragmentation. In this particular context, two Brazilian companies have become international: Tigre is a producer of PVC tubes and materials; Duratex manufactures materials for hydraulic installations and bathrooms.

Tigre

Tigre started out in 1941 as a producer of combs. At the end of the 1950s, when the company had already made considerable progress, with an extensive range of extruded and injected plastic products, it invested in a project that was innovative for its time: PVC tubes and connections for hydraulic installations. Tigre, therefore, assumed a comfortable leadership position in the local market.

Tigre developed a business model appropriate to the reality of the local market, which was, and remains, extremely fragmented: sales occur in small quantities at more than 100,000 outlets spread throughout a territory where access is difficult.

In 1977, the company made its first move toward internationalization, when it formed an association with Paraguayan businessmen and set up a greenfield plant in Paraguay. Since then Tubopar has had an 80 percent market share in this country.

In Brazil the outlook changed with the arrival of the Swiss company Amanco (today controlled by the Mexican group Mexichem), which, in 1991, took over Fortilit and in 1999, Akros, which was Tigre's biggest competitor. Amanco already had operations in other countries in Latin America. Global competition had set up in the same small city in the south of Brazil, Joinville.

In 1997, Tigre intensified its internationalization efforts. Four companies were acquired in Chile, where Tigre has a market share of 42%. In 1998, the target was Argentina, where, via acquisitions, it took 27% of the local market. In Bolivia acquisitions were made in 2000, taking the company to a market share of 80%.

Subsequently, Tigre invested in increasing exports by opening up fronts in Dubai, in the Middle East, and in the US, where it sells its Schedule brands for connections and DWW for drainage, sewage, and ventilation products.

In 2006, Tigre inaugurated a greenfield plant in Chile, and in 2007 it opened its first plant in the US, where US$5 million was invested.

Duratex

Duratex is a publicly held Brazilian company, traded on the Sao Paulo Stock Exchange since 1951. It is controlled by Itaúsa, the same holding company that controls Itau Bank, one of the two largest banks in the country. It is the leader in the Brazilian market for wooden products and sanitary ware and metal accessories for use in the furniture industry and for civil construction. Duratex has eight industrial units in the country.

In 1995 it took over the Argentine company Piazza Hermanos, which, two years into the relationship, became known as Deca Piazza. But Duratex has not expanded its international operations further.

Comments

These two cases show paths that can be taken by private companies in markets with particular characteristics. As already mentioned, construction techniques and materials for civil construction are particularly specific in the case of Brazil and Latin America. There is no global value chain effect, because there is no clear governance structure: the end market is dispersed and fragmented. These characteristics seem to have made possible the entry of Duratex and Tigre, as well as the subsequent expansion of the latter throughout Latin America, because of its FSAs and more specifically its business model.

However, the different trajectories of the companies allow us to hypothesize that the characteristics of products/markets have an influence on the possibilities for internationalization. Tigre is a producer of standard components that have reduced technological content and specific application in tropical countries only. Furthermore, the transport of plastic tubes over long distances is uneconomical, which makes imports/exports of little interest. Therefore, the product/market conditions for Tigre resemble those faced by Gerdau, and decentralized small operations to supply regional/local markets are recommended.

Duratex, on the other hand, is in a market where products have greater value added, design counts and, since products are compact, transport is not problematic and imports are feasible. Duratex faces competition from imports in other Latin American countries; that might be a reason for its reluctance in expanding to other countries.

Therefore, when the characteristics of products/markets are specific to the Latin or South American region, there is no global value chain effect, and the internationalization processes of Brazilian enterprises might be made easier.

The consumer goods Brazilian MNEs

An analysis of the consumer goods industry, in general, favors three particular segments: textiles/clothing, footwear, and food and drink. In these segments we find some major Brazilian companies, but few that are truly international.

One of the basic characteristics of these industries is that they are "buyer driven value chains" and governance (once more using the concept of Gereffi, 1994) either belongs to the major retail companies or to companies that own global brands. Due to a series of circumstances, Brazilian companies either have not shown an interest in doing so or have found it difficult to penetrate these areas. Two Brazilian multinationals will be analyzed below: AmBev, in the beverage sector; and Coteminas, in textiles/clothing manufacture. There are no Brazilian multinationals in footwear.

InBev/AmBev

As previously noted, as far back as the nineteenth century two Brazilian companies were established to produce beer and soft drinks: Antarctica, which was founded by Portuguese businessmen in 1885, and Brahma, founded by a Swiss immigrant in 1888. During the whole of the twentieth century these two companies fought over the protected Brazilian market, in a type of duopoly.

Change came at the end of the 1980s when Brahma went into financial crisis and its capital stock was acquired by the Garantia Bank, an investment bank with an aggressive profile. Brahma went through a profound reengineering process, adopting a high performance management model, inspired by the bank's managerial model that combined technical delivery aspects with job evaluations and reward for differentiated performance. That model became one of Brahma's assets and trademarks.

Brahma's first international operation was set up in 1994, in Venezuela, via acquisition, which provided a first experience of internationalization; the share of this operation reached 3 percent of its revenues.

In 1999 Brahma and Antarctica merged to create AmBev-American Beverage Company. In this merger process the role played by Brahma's executives was much more significant and Brahma's management model prevailed. In Brazil, AmBev reached a market share of over 60% in beer and 17% in soft drinks.

In 2003 AmBev intensified its internationalization process by taking an initial shareholding of 40.5 percent in Quinsa (Quilmes Industrial), thereby establishing a leading presence in the beer markets in Argentina, Bolivia, Paraguay, and Uruguay. Also in 2003, and in the first quarter of 2004, AmBev expanded its operations to the north of Latin America through a series of acquisitions in Central America, Peru, Ecuador and the Dominican Republic.

On August 27, 2004, AmBev and Interbrew S. A./N. V. from Belgium merged to create InBev-International Beverage:

InBev is the world's leading brewer, realizing 13.3 billion euro in 2006. The company has a strong, balanced portfolio, holding the number one or number two position in over 20 key markets – more than any other brewer. It has a key presence in both developed and developing markets, active in 7 out of 10 of the fastest growing markets worldwide. Headquartered in Leuven, Belgium, InBev employs almost 88,000 people worldwide. With sales in over 130 countries, the company works through six operational zones: North America, Western Europe, Central and Eastern Europe, Asia Pacific, Latin America North, and Latin America South. (www.inbev.com)

Interbrew became the majority shareholder. AmBev became responsible for the Americas' operations, where it took control of Labatt, one of the leading breweries of Canada, formerly part of Interbrew.

The association of AmBev and Interbrew merited special attention in Brazil due to the fact that the company remained in a minority position even though it had a strategy that was previously recognized as being aggressive. It is interesting to observe that the financial performance of the two companies was very different, despite both being of a similar size: AmBev's profitability was more than double that of Interbrew. One possible explanation lies in the management model, which has a direct influence on production and distribution operations.

After the merger AmBev's executives started to occupy positions of prominence in InBev's management and to introduce the "AmBev/Brahma/high performance model" which aims for operational excellence. As of September 2007 the CEO and six of InBev's directors were AmBev veterans. It is also relevant to observe that AmBev's operational know-how is considered the key factor in the expansion of InBev worldwide. The only markets in which demand is expected to grow are in emerging economies, an area in which AmBev has deep experience.

Shareholder control being in the hands of InterBrew raises the question of whether the case still relates to a Brazilian multinational. However, for the purpose of understanding the trajectories of internationalization, the case provides very interesting insights.

Coteminas

Coteminas is a family company that was founded in 1967. Its main site is in the city of Montes Claros, the southernmost city in the area that receives financial incentives reserved for the Northeast region, one of the least developed in the country.

Brazil has exceptional conditions for producing cotton, which favors its supply. The company specialized in the production of products for the home and high-volume clothing at low to medium prices, such as basic white t-shirts.

In the textiles for the home segment its main local competitors are four large, vertically integrated firms that produce finished articles for the end consumer in the south of the country. In the clothing segment the company's main competitors are four other companies that are, however, aiming at greater added value markets that depend on design and branding; this demands different strategies.

Of all those companies, Coteminas is the one that has had a different trajectory, based on very large-scale production using modern, automated equipment. While the vast majority of its Brazilian competitors are major exporters, Coteminas is the only one that has sought to become international.

It developed a strong relationship with SENAI, first through the Regional Center of Textile Technology in Recife, and then through the Technological Center for the Chemical and Textile Industry in Rio de Janeiro, one of the most advanced institutes of textile technology in the world.

In 2001 Coteminas formed a strategic alliance with one of the major American textile companies, Springs Industries Inc., with its headquarters in Fort Mill, South Carolina, US. The agreement is for Coteminas to supply textile products for the home (sheets, bath towels, and other items) that are manufactured in its industrial units, to be sold in the US and Canada by Springs through its extensive distribution network and its commercial proximity to the largest retailers in those markets. In 2003, Coteminas acquired Pillowtex Corporation primarily for its intellectual property portfolio, mainly brands.

In 2004, Coteminas set up in Argentina, in the Province of Santiago del Estero, with a plant whose production capacity is 700 tons of towels and fleecy products a month.

Comments

By focusing on the popular consumer goods industry new CSAs were identified, linked specifically to local demand: this is a large, extremely diversified market, with consumers who have low to medium incomes, where geographical distances are large and access is difficult. Some companies that are successful in meeting this demand have developed distinctive competences and use them in their internationalization processes on a global scale – unlike the case of Tigre, mentioned previously, which pursues a regional strategy.

The internationalization process of AmBev has characteristics that are similar to other global brewers, like South African Breweries: a true monopoly in the local market, but with a different outcome as a result of the merger with Interbrew. However, its entry strategy into the international market seems to be oriented towards economies of scale that allow it to negotiate under more favorable conditions with the huge companies that dominate the retail trade and the global value chains.

When we move the focus to the textiles/clothing manufacture industry the same pattern is observed. There are Brazilian companies bigger than Coteminas that have not bought into the idea of internationalization. For example, Hering, the biggest and most traditional Brazilian company, chose to focus on local niches and local brands. What appears to be different in the case of Coteminas is its business model: the production of standard products on a large scale and, initially, with no brand name. Apparently, after going international, Coteminas is looking for a niche strategy in international markets, via acquisitions.

Both companies had CSAs associated with market protection and subsidies, in the case of Coteminas, and financial support, in the case of AmBev.

The equipment suppliers' Brazilian MNEs

As already mentioned, the industrialization process in Brazil favored foreign multinationals, as the drivers of the durable consumer goods industries. The actions of these multinationals led to the development of private Brazilian companies, the suppliers of equipment and components, some of which survived the process of denationalization in the 1990s and became Brazilian multinationals. Two of them will be analyzed below: Sabo, a supplier in the automotive chain; and WEG, a supplier of electric motors for various applications, including white goods.

Sabo

Sabo is a family-owned business founded in 1939. It develops and produces application-oriented sealing elements and sealing systems, mainly for the automotive industry. Sabo has a 70 percent share of the Brazilian market and its competitors in Brazil are MNEs, Magnetti Marelli in particular. Sabo has been strongly oriented toward international markets since 1977, when it became one of GM's world-class suppliers.

It opened its first factory abroad, in Argentina, in 1992. In 1994, after some seven years of negotiations with Kako, a renowned German producer, Sabo obtained local government authorization to acquire the entire operation, which included three plants in Germany and one in Austria. Sabo maintained the profile of Kako's operations and began using it as a European base and main source of R&D. In 1997, Sabo opened a new factory in Hungary; in 2006, it opened its first factory in the US.

The main point to be highlighted in Sabo's case is its role as a "follow source" in the automotive industry. Its first expansion movement was into a neighboring country (Argentina), at a time when there were fairly open market conditions thanks to the establishment of Mercosur. The long-term involvement with the German producer gives an idea of the learning process whereby Sabo acquired the necessary competences and knowledge to successfully move up to the higher performance standards of international manufacturing and technological development. Additionally, by acquiring a German firm, Sabo gained access to new sources of financing (Sull, 2005).

WEG

Brazil holds a significant position in the world market for machinery and equipment. It is tenth in the ranking of the main manufacturers, behind the US, Japan, Germany, the UK, Italy, China, France, South Korea, and Switzerland. The WEG Group – established in 1961 by a business manager, an electrician, and a mechanic – is the leader in the electric motors segment in Brazil and in Latin America as a whole, in addition to manufacturing equipment for industrial automation, transformers, components, electric starters, and industrial paints and varnishes.

Currently WEG is the second largest manufacturer of electric motors in the world. At the same time, it has been trying to create new markets that are different from the standard motors, which are a type of commodity, by moving into the category of supplier of "technological solutions." Among its competitors are Emerson Electric and Rockwell Automation.

From the outset, the company introduced a differentiated management model, with the participation of the employees and profit sharing. It also introduced sophisticated test and prototype laboratories, but the R&D department's structure was only considered to have been finalized in 2000. Investment in R&D has been around 2.4 percent of net operating revenues. On average the company develops sixty new motor prototypes a month, and at the same time it has technological interchange with the research labs of Brazilian universities, especially the Federal University of Santa Catarina, and with international institutions – among them, the Universities of Hanover and Aachen, in Germany, and the University of Wisconsin, in the US.

In 1971 WEG started exporting to neighboring countries in Latin America. Since it sold standard motors its export strategy involved transactions with agents and distributors in the markets for which the goods were destined. The distribution system then turned toward the US, establishing WEG Electric Motors to deal directly with the manufacturers of machinery and equipment, in addition to keeping up with the technological trends in the world's largest market for electric motors. Taking advantage of NAFTA, this distribution system was subsequently extended to cover Mexico and Canada. In order to consolidate its position in Mercosur, the company moved into Argentina, where it became the market leader. In 1992 a company was set up in Belgium to meet demand across Europe.

In 1999, "WEG had representatives or distributors in 50 countries, covering the five continents. It had its own subsidiaries in Germany, Argentina, Australia, Belgium, Japan, the United Kingdom, the US, Spain, France, and Sweden" (Ghoshal *et al.*, 2002).

The internationalization of production started in Argentina in 1994. In the middle of 2000, WEG bought the electric motors division of ABB, located in Mexico City. Currently WEG has plants in Argentina (three), Mexico (two), Portugal (one), and China (one).

For Latin America WEG has perfected its supply chain and distribution structures. In competitive markets, such as the US and Europe, the plans are also to have its own plants, particularly of motors for household appliances. These are important positions that contribute to increased presence in strategic markets abroad.

Comments

The two cases above concern companies that knew how to take advantage of the opportunities created by national development programs. Sabo and WEG grew within a context of high demand from the automotive chain, white goods, and capital goods areas, but even so were subsidized and protected. When the turbulent events of the 1990s struck they had already accumulated resources and competences that made it possible to overcome them, while simultaneously launching themselves into international markets. Both operate in the sector of electromechanical base industries, which are the ones that developed most in the country (Furtado, 2003).

Their internationalization strategies reflect the nature of their products/markets. The internationalization of WEG prioritized the setting up of international offices to provide support for the export of standard products, so that it could start investing directly by setting up its own manufacturing plants. For Sabo, as a result of its position as a supply-follower the export activity was done in a different way and, interestingly, with its direct investment abroad it sought to "move up the value chain." For WEG this is the challenge that is now presenting itself, as the company is seeking to become a solutions provider.

The Brazilian systems assemblers

Using a term first employed in the automotive industry, but today applied in a more general way, in Brazil there are some companies that, as leaders of value chains, assemble complete products that are delivered direct to customers and consumers. Among these, two in particular stand out: Embraer and Marcopolo.

Embraer

Embraer was founded in 1969 as a SOE, linked to the Brazilian Aeronautics Ministry. Its first product, a regional turbo plane, was made for the internal market only, but the second family of products was designed and manufactured with international markets as its main target. An alliance with Piper (US) in the late 1970s was crucial for the creation of the international services and maintenance network.

In the early 1990s, Embraer went through a crisis caused by poor product and marketing strategies coupled with ambitious technical projects. For the sake of illustration, the number of employees plummeted from 12,000 to 2,500.

After privatization, in 1994, when the new administration took office, there was an injection of marketing and financial knowledge. A new business model was put in place: for the launch of a new product, a 45-seat regional jet, risk partnerships were established with four foreign suppliers from Chile, Spain, Belgium, and the US. This model was innovative not only because it was based on a global supply network, but because of its cooperative character regarding partnerships and risk sharing. In its subsequent product family, a 70- to 110-seat jet, Embraer increased the number of risk partners to eleven, including large traditional MNEs. Therefore, Embraer can be seen as a successful case of internationalization, despite having no plants abroad. Product design, project management, partnering, and supply chain and operations management support this strategy.

In a way, Embraer was international from its very inception, since aircraft are a global product. However, for a long time Embraer sold regional transporters and regional jets that were certified by the US Federal Aviation Administration, but which did not carry the Embraer name. Embraer captured a golden opportunity (Sull, 2005) when the regional transport markets boomed. Currently, the firm leads a complex international supply chain, coordinated by three international offices and logistic centers. Its first foray into international manufacturing, a joint venture in China, was essentially the result of political constraints.

Embraer's plant in China was a prerequisite for delivering jet planes to Chinese airlines, part of an industrial offset agreement. Offset agreements within the aircraft industry have become increasingly complex; major producers such as Boeing and Airbus now operate with globally decentralized supply networks that are shaped by the industrial development priorities of foreign governments that control the purchasing decisions of their domestic airlines and not by cost, quality, or logistic factors. The Chinese operation is a joint venture with a local manufacturer and relies on an assembling system of the completely knocked down type.

It is important to add that Embraer's financial operations receive strong support from the government through the BNDES-Brazilian

Bank for Economic and Social Development. This bank created a specific program and an administrative office to provide support for the financing of Embraer's products.

Marcopolo

Marcopolo is a manufacturer of buses, founded in 1949 in the south of Brazil. Along with other regional companies it competed with Mercedes-Benz, then the major supplier of buses in the local markets. In the mid-1990s Mercedes-Benz changed its product line; at the same time the Brazilian companies embarked on a consolidation process. Marcopolo stood out, at one point controlling more than 50 percent of the Brazilian market.

Its internationalization process started in 1991, thirty years after it had made its first export, in 1961, to Paraguay. Marcopolo currently has plants in six foreign countries (Argentina, Colombia, India – a joint venture with Tata Motors – Mexico, Portugal, and South Africa), and is starting operations in China and Russia. Its products are delivered to 103 countries and its global market share is between 7 percent and 10 percent. Its global competitors are Irizar (Spanish) which has a subsidiary in Brazil, albeit not a very successful one, Vanhool (Belgian), Bova (Dutch), and Orlandi (Italian), in addition to the chassis/engine producers themselves (Mercedes-Benz, Scania, Volvo, Iveco – which is setting up in Brazil – and Toyota).

Marcopolo has developed products suitable for unsophisticated markets and has a globalization strategy guided by a very interesting business model. In the first place, as a producer of bodywork, Marcopolo depends on the manufacturer of the chassis/engine. Its international operations are always carried out jointly with one of the three chassis/engine suppliers: Mercedes-Benz, Scania, or Volvo. In the Argentinean operation, the relationship involved Scania and Volvo; in Mexico the joint venture is with Mercedes-Benz; and in South Africa with Scania. The operation in China started with Iveco (Fiat) but the contract ended in 2007 and currently Marcopolo is deciding how it is going to move forward. The operation in India will be with Tata Motors and in Russia with Ruspromauto.

Marcopolo has developed know-how associated with the production and assembly of buses and it "bundled" this for its internationalization process into four formats: complete bus unit, partially knocked down, completely knocked down, and semi knocked down. It "plays" with these four formats to structure its participation in the different under-takings in which it operates. At the same time Marcopolo has developed competences within a strategy that is customer-oriented and not one of operational excellence – that is, Marcopolo is ready to develop bus projects that meet the specific demands of each country or locality.

Marcopolo is not just another vehicle assembler. In the case of the plants in India and Russia, it is going in as a minority shareholder and, in practice, it is providing guidance in the development of the project, plant, and operations. In the case of Colombia, Marcopolo was invited not only because of its competence in producing bus body-work, but also because of the knowledge it brought to the project for restructuring the transport system in Bogota, called the Millennium Project. Marcopolo started to develop skills in this field when it took part in the urban transport system project in Curitiba, Brazil.

Comments

These two cases illustrate how companies from emerging countries can compete in leading edge industries, as "system integrators." There is a third assembly company, Busscar, which is a direct competitor of Marcopolo, which has also looked to internationalize. It has plants in Cuba, Colombia, and Mexico but since 2001 it has reduced its direct investments abroad.

Embraer competes in a more oligopolized segment and one of greater visibility. Its trajectory was more dependent on CSAs than Marcopolo: initial support from the Aeronautical Ministry, the financial resources that are still injected via the BNDES to make possible the sale of airplanes and, throughout the whole period, the infrastructure needed for training and developing human resources and for developing technological services. But both have developed products and processes that have given them competitive advantages in the international market as a result of local demand and resources.

Both also mobilized new types of FSA. Because they are assembly companies their competence in joint ventures was one of the factors that determined their success. The management model adopted by Embraer may be considered bolder, but it is important to remember that it has enjoyed greater support from the Brazilian government than has Marcopolo.

Final comments and conclusions

Our objective was to analyze the emerging Brazilian MNEs, with special reference to how the national context affected the evolution of those firms.

Early on in this chapter, the historical evolution of industry in Brazil was presented. In each of the historical periods, the structure and competitive regime of the different sectors of local industry and their interface with the international market was briefly described. The trajectory of companies that were successful in their internationalization processes and that today are Brazilian MNEs, as well as those that were not, was highlighted. Later in the chapter, an immersion in the dynamic process of internationalization of twelve Brazilian MNEs provided additional insights.

Summarizing, in the 1950s, during the first wave of internationalization, the bases of the industrialization process were established with the creation of state companies, the arrival and setting up of the subsidiaries of American and European companies, and the growth of private national companies. The closed and protected regime of the Brazilian economy and the ignorance of the functioning of international markets (in part justified by the geographical, cultural, and psychological distance) led the majority of companies to operate only in the domestic market. In the 1980s, during the second wave, there were a few Brazilian companies that sought to go international and survived the process. Nevertheless, this first exposure created a strategic vision, and sparked a learning process, that prepared companies for a new wave.

In the third wave, that of the BRIC countries, the internationalization of Brazilian companies has expanded beyond those segments that can be characterized as based on natural resources; other segments of Brazilian industry have also become international. Services firms, as well as those from the IT industry, are initiating their internationalization processes, although their presence is still somewhat tentative.

The analysis of twelve representative cases from six industrial segments enabled the identification of CSAs and FSAs. Table 8.4 summarizes the results of the analysis. The CSAs were understood as the advantages (as opposed to country-specific disadvantages) that

Table 8.4. CSAs and FSAs in the internationalization processes of Brazilian enterprises

	CSAs					FSAs		
	Resource			Institutional	Markets and products	Production/operations technology	Product technology	Management model
	Nat. (1)	Hu. (2)	Su. (3)					
Resources based	Y	Y	Y	Y	N	Y	N	Y
Basic inputs	Y	Y	Y	N	N	Y	N	Y
Construction inputs	Y	Y	N	N	Y	Y	Y	Y
Consumer goods	N	Y	Y	N	Y	Y	Y	Y
Components/equipment	N	Y	N	N	Y	Y	Y	Y
Systems assemblers	N	Y	Y	Y	Y	Y	Y	Y

Notes: Nat. = natural resources; HU. = human resources; SU. = support activities affected every company in their evolutionary trajectory, that had an influence on the development of their competences and in the formulation of their strategies, internationalization strategies included. In Table 8.4 the CSAs are divided into three categories: resource availability (natural, human, and support activities), institutional (if the industry enjoyed favorable conditions when compared to the international context), and markets and products (if the characteristics of local markets generated competences and strategies in local companies that were used as competitive advantages in their internationalization processes).

An important conclusion is that, despite the fact that Brazil is recognized for the potential of its natural resources, they were of strategic relevance for only two of the companies reported upon in this study.

On the other hand, all of them – some more intensely than others – had at their disposal human resources prepared by the public educational system who had a strong technological and managerial formation; they were, therefore, ready to develop the competences necessary for implementing the competitive strategies that were needed.

The Brazilian MNEs were born and grew within the context of governmental programs at different moments in the industrialization process in Brazil. A large number of these companies, if not the majority, had access to financing programs, used subsidies and, until recently, had a locally protected market. Furthermore, for a period of time, they were able to take advantage of cheap labor costs.

On the other hand, they had to deal with the same country-specific disadvantages, which included instability, lack of continuity, and the unpredictable nature of government actions. They were all affected, to a greater or lesser extent, by the "Brazil Cost," which penalizes companies not only from the point of view of taxes, but also through the costs and uncertainties associated with transportation and logistics. As far as internationalization is concerned, the companies received reduced government support, particularly when compared with other emerging countries, such as China.

In summary, the scale of the importance of the CSAs varied between industrial segments and between companies themselves, as a function of different factors. The factor that, perhaps, was the most important was the position and the commitment of each company in respect to global value chains: the greater the commitment, the lesser the influence of the local context. This corroborates the conclusion of previous studies (Fleury and Fleury, 2001).

From the case studies, four types of internationalization strategy can be identified: global consolidators, local optimizers, global first-movers, and global value chain climbers (see Ramamurti and Singh, Chapter 6).

The global consolidators strategy is illustrated by four cases: CVRD, Petrobras, Ambev, and Gerdau. They operate in mature industries and their internationalization strategies are based on horizontal acquisitions. The stage at which each company finds itself may be different, with CVRD having already consolidated its position as the largest company in the world in certain markets and Petrobras remaining in an intermediate group, depending on the way in which participation in global markets is measured. These companies have in their favor the fact that, in addition to having the distinctive competences already mentioned, they are sitting on huge, good quality natural resource bases and have great financial leverage. The case of AmBev is peculiar but important, as it reveals that InBev's growth in the global markets is dependent on AmBev's management model and its operational know-how because that is the key factor for expansion in the emerging economies, the only ones in which demand is rising. Finally, Gerdau can be considered a regional consolidator more than a global one to the extent that it focuses its activities on American construction markets only. CSN could also be in their category had it succeeded in its later attempts to increase scale and global presence.

Tigre and Duratex illustrate the strategy of the local optimizers. They are companies that look for regional leadership in markets with regional characteristics. Their positions seem to be sustainable despite threats from other Latin American companies.

Embraer and Marcopolo are representative of global first-movers. They are companies that developed products that were appropriate for local markets and then took them to international markets. Their internationalization strategies are based on a significant number of partnerships, although these two cases are distinct when their products/markets and management models are considered. Marcopolo adopts a vertical production system, and then integrates its product into systems supplied by its partners. Embraer manufactures a more complex product and operates a modularized and decentralized production system, making it the leader of a sophisticated international supply chain. To some extent, the role of Marcopolo as a leader, or follower, in the global value chain that supplies buses in international markets is not as clear as it is in the case of Embraer.

Finally, there are various companies that should be considered global value chain climbers. These are companies that actively participate in the dynamic relationships among companies that operate connected to global value chains. Their processes of internationalization aim to guarantee and extend the scope of their participation in these global value chains and they seek to assume activities where there is greater added value. Among the companies mentioned in the case studies are WEG, Coteminas, and Sabo. The Gerdau case, already mentioned among the consolidators, has an additional facet to the extent that this company is also becoming involved with the automotive industry global value chain. This strategy is, to a large extent, justified by the reconfiguration of early-movers, in a process of revising and restructuring their international operations, focusing on highly value-adding activities, and seeking the command of global production networks. This opens space for the late-movers which primarily internationalize to the more developed countries by escalating the value chain.

References

Amadeo, E. (1997). Opening, stabilization, and development prospects for Brazil. In *East Asian development experience: Economic system approach and its applicability.* Symposium held by the Institute of Developing Economies, Tokyo.

Bonelli, R. (1997). Política industrial en Brasil: Intención y resultados. In *Políticas de competitividad industrial: América Latina y el Caribe en los años noventa.* Siglo Veintiuno Editors.

Boston Consulting Group (2006). *The new global challengers.* BCG report, May 2006.

Evans, P. (1977). *Dependent development: The alliance of multinationals, state, and local capital.* Princeton, Princeton University Press.

Ferraz, J. C., Rush, H. and Miles, I. (1992). *Development, technology and flexibility: Brazil faces the industrial divide.* London, Routledge Publishing.

Ferraz, J. C., Kupfer, D. and Haguenauer, L. (1996). *Made in Brazil: desafios competitivos para a indústria.* Rio de Janeiro, Editora Campus.

Fleury, A. (1989). The technological behaviour of state-owned enterprises in Brazil. In Jeffrey James (ed.), *The technological behaviour of public enterprises in developing countries.* London, Routledge.

Fleury, A. and Fleury, M.T. (1995). *Aprendizagem e inovação organizacional: As experiências de Japão, Coréia e Brasil.* Sao Paulo, Editora Atlas.

Fleury, A. and Fleury, M.T. (2001). A competitividade das cadeias produtivas da indústria textil baseadas em fibras quimicas. Report prepared for the BNDES, November 2001, p. 78.

Fleury, A. and Fleury, M.T. (2007). Evolution and reconfiguration of production systems. *Journal of Manufacturing Technology Management*, Vol. 18, No. 8.

Fleury, A. and Humphrey, J. (1993). Human resources and the diffusion and adaptation of new quality methods in Brazilian manufacturing. Institute of Development Studies, Research Report, p. 14.

Fleury, M.T. (1986). O simbolico nas relações de trabalho – um estudo sobre relações de trabalho numa empresa estatal. Sao Paulo, Universidade de Sao Paulo, Tese de Livre Docencia, p. 237.

Furtado, J.E. (2003). Quatro eixos para a politica industrial. In M.T. Fleury and A. Fleury (orgs.), *Política Industrial.* Sao Paulo, Publifolha.

Gereffi, G. (1994). Capitalism, development and global commodity chains. In L. Sclair (ed.), *Capitalism and development.* London, Routledge.

Ghoshal, S., Tanure, B., Sull, D., Santos, H., Escobari, M., and Cardoso, R. (2002). WEG: adaptando o capitalismo familiar ao Mercado global. Belo Horizonte: Fundação Dom Cabral, Casos FDC, CF 0204 – August 2002.

Goldman and Sachs (2003). Dreaming with BRICs: the path to 2050. *Global Economics Paper No. 99.*

Grosse, R. (2005). Can Latin American firms compete? Paper presented at the BALAS Conference, Lima, Peru.

Humphrey, J. and Messner, D. (2006). The impact of the Asian and other drivers on global governance. *IDS Bulletin*, Vol. 37, No. 1, January 2006.

Rocha, A., Blundi, M.D., and Dias, V.T. (2002). O que aconteceu as empreas exportadoras da decada de 1970? In A. Rocha (org.), *A internacionalizacao das empresas brasileiras.* Rio de Janeiro, Ed. Mauad

Rugman, A. (1981). *Inside the multinationals: The economics of internal markets.* New York, Columbia University Press.

Rugman, A. and Li, J. (2007). Can China's multinationals succeed globally? Paper presented at The Internationalization of Indian and Chinese Enterprises Conference, Brunel University, London, April.

Schmitz, H. and Cassiolato, J. (1992). *Hi-tech for industrial development: Lessons from the Brazilian experience in electronics and automation.* London, Routledge.

Simonsen, M. H. (1969). *Brasil 2001*. Rio de Janeiro, APEC Editora.

Sull, D. (2005). Strategy as active waiting. *Harvard Business Review*, August.

Villela, A. (1983). Multinationals from Brazil. In S. Lall (ed.), *The new multinationals: The spread of third world enterprises*. New York, John Wiley & Sons.

9 South African multinationals: Building on a unique legacy[1]

ANDREA GOLDSTEIN AND WILSON PRICHARD

In the complex landscape of MNEs from emerging markets, the case of South Africa is peculiar in many respects. First, the history of apartheid created a historically unique economic structure in which deep poverty and highly advanced industry existed side by side. Second, some South African companies have traditionally maintained strong international connections, even under apartheid when they were by and large prevented from investing overseas. Third, South African MNEs have traditionally invested in other Commonwealth countries, including some high-income Organization for Economic Co-operation and Development (OECD) ones, much more than in fellow developing countries. Fourth, and somewhat paradoxically, the latter feature has not prevented South Africa from becoming a major source of international capital for many African countries.

This chapter provides an introduction to some of the key issues regarding outward FDI from South Africa. What limited literature exists on South African MNEs is mostly restricted to South African investment in the rest of the continent, and thus we hope to expand the understanding of the broader transnationalization strategies of South African firms (Gelb 2005; Goldstein and Prichard 2007). In doing so we seek to draw connections between South Africa's unique history of economic development, and the very particular patterns of transnationalization that have prevailed since the end of apartheid. We review:

- the extent and distribution of investment since the end of apartheid, including the strategies used to build international presence, the

[1] We thank Daniel J. McCarthy, Ravi Ramamurti, Mike Spicer, and participants at the Emerging Multinationals from Emerging Markets Conference for their kind comments on an earlier draft and Business Leadership SA for precious help in gathering background information. The opinions expressed and arguments employed are the authors' sole responsibility and do not necessarily reflect those of the Institute of Development Studies, the OECD, and its members.

countries that have been targeted (rich, poor, or both), the speed of the internationalization process, the modes of entry that have been used, and the underlying reasons;

- the key drivers of South Africa's rise as a major outward investor, including FSAs, advantages of proximity, structural factors that have shaped South African investment patterns, and advantages stemming from the economic and political environment within South Africa;
- the sustainability of their competitive advantages and the implications that the internationalization of big business has for competitive dynamics in South Africa.

Where does South African big business come from?

A proper analysis of South African MNEs requires a short preliminary historical excursus, to explain how they acquired the resources that have proven necessary for their subsequent internationalization. Taking a long-term view is also important to understand the socio-economic and political factors that have dominated the history of big business in South Africa both during and after apartheid.

The history of big business in Southern Africa is inevitably and closely tied with the discovery of precious metals and diamonds (Thompson 1995). By 1888 Cecil Rhodes' De Beers had achieved the amalgamation of diamond production in the region through buying out minority investors in the Kimberley mine. This has remained to this day, by and large, the structure of the industry. In gold mining, by the end of the nineteenth century, control of the 124 gold companies that accounted for more than a quarter of the world's total output was firmly in the hands of fewer than ten British, French, and German groups. In 1917 Ernest Oppenheimer founded Anglo American Corporation with capital from Britain, the US, and South Africa to exploit the gold mining potential of the East Rand. Knighted in 1921, Sir Ernest made Anglo American the largest single shareholder in De Beers in 1924 and formally established the cross-holdings linking the two companies in 1929. The London-based Central Selling Organization was formed one year later to facilitate more orderly marketing and greater stability in the diamond industry.

The (limited) backward linkages created by the mining industry and the demand for consumer goods generated by white wage-earners provided a stimulus for industrial development, driven by the large mining houses which began to diversify into related industries: for example, Anglo American invested (in chronological order) in explosives and mining equipment, banking, industrial commodities (steel, paper, and chemicals), engineering, and consumers goods (including beer and furniture) (Fine and Rustomjee 1997).

But the rapid development of the English-controlled mineral economy did not result in major growth in Afrikaner business. This contributed to the rise of the Nationalist government in 1948, that brought with it two profound changes for the South African economy. First, SOEs became a vehicle for Afrikaner-focused economic development. SOEs had three main policy goals: to offset the economic dominance of the gold mining industry; to provide some autonomy from foreign producers; and to create jobs for Afrikaner workers (Clark 1994). Sasol (originally Suid Afrikaanse Steenkool en Olie – South African Coal and Oil) started using Fischer-Tropsch synthesis to produce petrol and diesel from coal and natural gas in order to reduce reliance on imports. The policy of 'Afrikaner favoritism' also included direct assistance to private Afrikaner companies, while interlocking directorships with state corporations gave many Afrikaner undertakings a crucial inside edge. Government contracts and subsidies benefited particularly Federale Volksbeleggings, the industrial investment subsidiary of Sanlam.

Second, the introduction of full-blown apartheid forcefully removed the non-white population to townships and homelands, where basic economic infrastructure and opportunities were lacking. Two distinct economies developed in South Africa, with the non-white one characterized by deep poverty and legal discrimination while the urban modern economy became increasingly diversified and industrialized. The coexistence of these two starkly different realities has persisted as a major determinant of the unique pattern of South African corporate development.

Under the combined effect of legal discrimination, heavily protected markets and government activism to promote development among Afrikaners, economic concentration and conglomeration became increasingly entrenched features of the economy.

The diversification of South African conglomerates had two main phases. The first was built on mining linkages and included the development of explosives, steel, and engineering. While this required the development of production capabilities, it was also driven by linkages and vertical integration (Fine and Rustomjee 1997). The second followed the divestment of foreign firms and sanctions. Reflecting both the sudden lack of international competition and the difficulty that South African firms faced in investing abroad, diversification included moves into a range of consumer goods and food products.[2]

In both periods conglomerates maintained close links with the colonial, and then apartheid, state. Indeed, notwithstanding Anglo American's steel and chemicals interests, the major investments in these two industries were made by the apartheid state. Moreover, at the end of the 1980s, South Africa had the most dispersed tariff system in the world, with many tariffs being effectively firm-specific, since the number of producers in any one product market was limited (Belli *et al.* 1993).[3]

In late-industrializing countries diversification of conglomerates is an important feature of manufacturing development (Amsden 2001). In order to adopt and adapt imported technologies, late-industrializers required firms to have strong organizational capabilities that could be applied to different industries. Partly because South Africa is not a typical 'catch-up story' – it had a much higher level of development

---

[2] Somewhat surprisingly, given the history of sanctions during the late apartheid era, some firms did manage to maintain significant overseas assets to which they are now adding. Luxembourg-registered Minorco, in which Anglo American, De Beers, and the Oppenheimer family had a combined three-quarters stake, held a range of international minerals and forestry assets valued at US$5.2 billion in 1997 (more than a third of the size of Anglo American), while the Rupert and Hertzog families owned Swiss-registered Richemont. The shares of South African companies, however, tended to trade relatively low due to currency risk and the complex cross-holdings that reduced transparency, making it difficult for shareholders to assess how operations were being managed.

[3] In fact, the issue of the concentration of economy-wide power in the hands of a few conglomerates, much more than the debate about competition policy per se, took centre stage of the policy debate immediately after the end of apartheid. The Freedom Charter of 1955, which can be viewed as the basic policy statement of the African National Congress, included the goal of nationalizing the 'commanding heights' of the economy: underground mineral wealth, banks, and 'monopoly industry'. By the time of its unbanning, however, the African National Congress had not elaborated any thorough ideas concerning economic policy making beyond such general statements, as other goals had been prioritized during the struggle period.

Table 9.1. *Summary of control of Johannesburg Stock Exchange market capitalization (percentage of total)[a]*

	1985	1990	1991– 1995	1996– 2000	2001– 2003	2004
Anglo American Corp.	53.6	44.2	38.9	22.7	23.3	18.7
Sanlam	12.2	13.2	12.7	11.2	6.1	2.7
Stanbic/Liberty Life	2.0	2.6	5.8	9.0	5.2	4.7
Rembrandt/Remgro	3.8	13.6	13.2	10.2	9.2	7.9
SA Mutual/Old Mutual	10.6	10.2	11.2	10.4	9.9	4.5
Anglovaal	2.1	2.5	3.1	1.2	0	0
Black owned groups	-	-	-	7.4	4.2	6.3
Top five groups collectively	82.3	83.9	85.9	70.6	53.6	38.5

Note:
[a] Control is assessed by taking into account the various cross-holdings of shares that exist and may be associated with a relatively small direct shareholding in any given company.
Source: Goldstein (2009), Table 2

than South Korea in the 1950s – the conglomerates' diversification was quite different. Historically, the conglomerate structures were similar to Chandler's 'personal capitalism' – managerial structures were relatively unsophisticated and relationships between the groups were characterized by co-operation and some contestation for position, but only a relatively low level of competition (Chandler *et al.* 1997). As a result, big business facilitated two of Chandler's 'three-pronged' investments – namely, in scale and, partly, in scope – but not the third – investment in managerial capabilities.

With the end of apartheid in 1994, and the rapid opening of the economy, major conglomerates have been unbundled, as reflected in the top five groups' rapidly falling control of shares on the Johannesburg Stock Exchange (down from 83.9% in 1990 to 38.5% in 2004; see Table 9.1). The conglomerates have sold off many non-core activities in an effort to become more focused and replace their personal and family character with a strict managerial focus (Chabane *et al.* 2006). Within the domestic market this has opened the way for new firms to emerge, including a diverse group of black-owned firms, which are growing rapidly but have yet to establish an important international presence. Post-unbundling, listing on international markets provided both the capital and the impetus to look abroad.

Ultimately, the historical context of economic development in South Africa has defined four distinct characteristics of domestic firms which have had implications for the pattern of internationalization since 1994:

- the conglomerate structure, followed by a period of rapid unbundling and reorganization in the recent past;
- unusually strong ties between some South African firms and the European (particularly, though not exclusively, British) business community;
- a level of industrialization and business sophistication uncommon in countries at similar income levels, owing to the combined effect of a wealthy white population and of isolation;
- strong incentives to rapidly expand internationally with the lifting of sanctions at the end of apartheid.

Patterns of internationalization

The particular features of the South Africa economy make it opportune to consider the particular pattern of outward investment since 1994. For a number of reasons, outward FDI statistics for non-OECD countries tend to be incomplete and relatively unreliable (UNCTAD 2005). The South African Reserve Bank (SARB) collects official data on aggregate FDI stocks by region, but data disaggregated by country is only available for a limited group of countries, while data by sector is not publicly available at all (Swart 2005). Exacerbating this issue is the problem of defining a 'national firm'. For example, SABMiller has historic roots in South Africa and is overwhelmingly run by South Africans, but it is registered in Britain, while its top shareholders hail from the US (Altria) and Colombia (the Santo Domingo family). Similar complexity arises with respect to:

- firms registered and listed abroad but owned partially or predominantly by South Africans (e.g., Anglo American, TEAL);
- South African subsidiaries of OECD-based MNEs that in turn invest in other developing countries (e.g., AngloGold Ashanti);
- South African companies that have been recently acquired by OECD investors (e.g., Absa);

- foreign companies with corporate centres in South Africa (BHP Billiton).[4]

As a consequence, considerable caution must be exercised when deciding what can, and cannot, be considered a South African firm. In what follows we mostly rely on balance of payments data, cognizant of the limits of this source but also of its greater reliability.

Aggregate stocks and flows

According to SARB data, the total stock of direct investment stood at R232,925 million (US\$32.5 billion) at the end of 2005 (Table 9.2). The share that corresponds to direct equity investment – as opposed to reinvested earnings, long-term capital, and short-term capital – increased gradually but steadily from 1995 (22.61%) to 2004 (34.73%), before dipping lightly in 2005 (33.51%). Of the direct equity portion of investment, the private non-banking sector accounts for the overwhelming majority (98.91% in 2005), while the banking sector reached a high of 12.12% in 2000, before falling to 0.95% in 2005, only marginally higher than public corporations (0.14% in 2005 vs. 1.24% in 1999).

Geographic distribution

The majority of South African investment goes to OECD countries (Figure 9.1). In 2005, Europe represented 81.24% of the outstanding assets and the OECD area accounted for 87.48%. While Africa represented only 8.19% of the South African FDI stock, investment in

---

[4] BHP Billiton comprises two separate companies (BHP Billiton Limited and BHP Billiton Plc) which operate as a combined group. The headquarters of BHP Billiton Limited, and the global headquarters of the combined BHP Billiton Group, are located in Australia. BHP Billiton Plc is located in London. BHP Billiton maintains pre-existing primary listings on the Australian and London Stock Exchanges, along with a secondary listing on the Johannesburg Stock Exchange and American Depositary Receipts listings on the New York Stock Exchange. It also maintains corporate centres in Johannesburg and Houston. Billiton is the successor of a company created in 1994 when the mining assets of Shell (called Billiton) were bought by South Africa's Gencor. The new head of BHP Billiton is a South African executive who was part of the team that put together the 2001 merger between Billiton and BHP.

Table 9.2. *SARB statistics on outward FDI stock (millions of rand; US$1 = R7)*

	Direct investment by public corporations – equity capital	Direct investment by banking sector – equity capital	Direct investment by private non-banking sector – equity capital	Total direct equity investment
1995	0	473	18,746	84,991
1996	0	1,039	25,809	114,013
1997	23	1,349	33,539	113,170
1998	302	4,946	38,233	157,385
1999	714	6,683	48,419	203,036
2000	870	8,636	61,754	244,653
2001	50	3,588	65,917	213,184
2002	75	2,364	55,331	189,911
2003	81	2,605	58,909	180,507
2004	78	1,972	73,637	217,900
2005	108	745	77,191	232,925

Source: SARB, *Quarterly Bulletin* (various years)

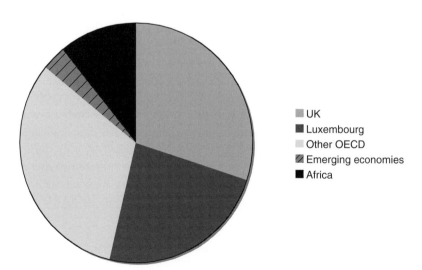

Figure 9.1 Geographic distribution of South Africa's outward FDI stock

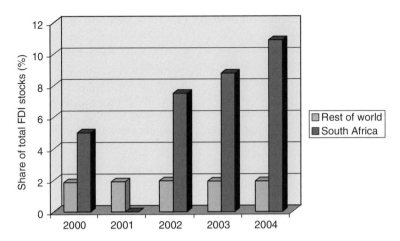

Figure 9.2 Share of FDI stock held in Africa, 2000–2004.
Note: For unknown reasons official data for South Africa in 2001 is not available

Africa has been growing very rapidly, rising from R1,747 million in 1990 to R23,601 million in 2004, before falling to R19,083 million in 2005. Thus, a large majority of South African FDI goes to Europe, while the share of South African investment in Africa is also notable for being dramatically higher than that of other investors who held, on average, only 1.94% of FDI stocks in Africa in 2004 (Figure 9.2).

Despite the attraction of relying heavily on these aggregate statistics, it is important to recall the limitation implied by the fact that firms that moved their listings abroad no longer show up in SARB figures. A prime example of this problem is South African investment in China, which is estimated at nearly US$2 billion by Stellenbosch University's Centre for China Studies, whereas SARB data indicates that South African investment in all of Asia peaked at only about US$600 million (R4,444 million) in 2002, and has fallen since then.[5] While the SARB data likely captures recent activity by firms such as Naspers and Goldfields, it excludes major investments by SABMiller

---

[5] Cited in 'Business groups eye China potential', *Financial Times*, 7 May 2007. According to government figures, South African investments in China amount to about US$400m (see 'SA companies look to China', *Financial Times*, 6 February 2007).

and by Anglo American.[6] SABMiller, for example, has won 15 per cent of the local market in partnership with China Resources Enterprise, its government partner. Perhaps most tellingly, Sasol is in discussions to build two coal-to-liquid fuel plants, and while this would create a major new South African presence in China, the possibility that Sasol may eventually list abroad is indicative of the potential imprecision of official figures.

Mode of entry

M&As in South Africa increased dramatically from 1994 to a peak of R502.4 billion in 2001, reflecting a couple of very large deals – the R223.2 billion merger of Billiton and BHP and the R153.7 billion restructuring and delisting of De Beers. The 1999–2005 cumulative value of mega-deals (above R5 billion) has been R1,125,715 million, of which R203,696 million (18.09 per cent) corresponds to cross-border deals in which South Africa has been the acquirer (Table 9.3). South African M&As have been dominated by specific domestic consider-ations, including conglomerate unbundling and restructuring to ensure stronger focus and better strategic direction. Yet, as this process of restructuring slows, in 2006 South African companies continued to look for expansion opportunities in other parts of the world, amply demonstrated by the MTN Group's R33.5 billion acquisition of tele-coms group Investcom (the year's largest transaction) and Naspers' acquisition of a minority shareholding in Brazilian media group Abril.

South Africa's (outward) mergers have been dominated by the tri-umvirate of Anglo American, SAB (later renamed SABMiller), and Old Mutual (Table 9.4), all of which are now listed outside South Africa. This highlights an important feature of South African firms' internationalization strategies, but also points again to the limitations of the SARB investment data cited earlier. The total value of these firms' outward acquisitions from 1999–2005 is almost equivalent to the total level of foreign assets reported by SARB, highlighting the fact

---

[6] Naspers, South Africa's largest media group, has a sizeable stake in the *Beijing Youth Daily* newspaper and also a 36 per cent shareholding in Hong Kong-listed internet company Tencent, which made up 16 percent of the Naspers valuation in 2006. "Naspers smiling as Chinese stock surges," *Business Day*, 26 May 2006.

Table 9.3. *Number of mergers involving South African firms, by size*

Size of deal	1994–1995	1996–1997	1998	1999	2000	2001	2002	2003	2004	2005	2006
>R5bn ("mega")				13	17	6	8	6	6	8	14
of which outward FDI				1	7	2	3	1	0	1	
>R1bn	9	53	48	42	52	24	36	25	43	45	
>R500m	5	24	34	20	46	33	28	29	27	36	
>R100m	46	141	142	148	112	118	118	117	128	112	
>R50m	45	128	85	61	71	62	51	51	63	59	
>R10m	121	270	186	184	150	149	125	119	144	117	
<R10m	94	145	110	113	131	124	120	86	94	61	
Total number, where value disclosed	310	761	605	568	562	510	478	427	500	430	729
Total value (Rbn)		228.5	314.7	231.6	372.3	502.4	242.4	150.1	177.4	269.1	284
No value disclosed (no. of deals)		340	414	346	440	387	305	363	323	314	
Total number		1101	1019	914	1002	897	783	790	823	744	

Source: Ernst & Young (various years)

Table 9.4. *Largest international acquisitions by South African firms*

Buyer	Target	Country	Sector	Date	Amount (Rm)
SAB	Phillip Morris	US	brewery	2002	53,944
Old Mutual	Skandia	Sweden	life assurance	2005	38,000
MTN Group	Investcom	Lebanon	telecommunications	2006	33,500
Netcare, private equity firms	General Health Group	UK	health services	2006	25,000
Anglo American	Exxon Mobil	US	energy	2002	13,702
Billiton	Rio Algom	UK	mining	2000	12,528
Anglo American	Tarmac	UK	mining	2000	12,313
Billiton	Worsley Alumina	Australia	mining	2000	10,385
Old Mutual	United Asset		life assurance	2000	10,016
Anglogold	Ashanti Goldfields	Ghana	gold mining	2003	9,847
Sasol	Condea		chemicals	2000	8,710
Dimension Data	Comparex		information technology	1999	7,000
Anglo American	Shell Coal		mining	2000	5,969
Sappi	Potlatch		forestry and paper	2002	5,600
SAB	Cerveceria Hondureña	Honduras	beverage	2001	5,295
Old Mutual	Gerrard Group		life assurance	2000	5,250
Old Mutual	Fidelity and Guaranty Life		life assurance	2001	5,137

Source: Ernst & Young (various years)

Table 9.5. *South African firms' acquisitions of African firms undergoing privatization*

Acquiring firm	East Africa	Southern Africa
AngloGold	Ashanti Goldfields Geita project (Tanzania)	
Illovo (sugar)[a]		Sucoma (Malawi)
Nedbank		FINCOM (Malawi)
SAA (air transport)	Air Tanzania	
Stanbic (banking)	National Bank of Commerce (Tanzania), Stanbic Kenya	Commercial Bank of Malawi, Lesotho Bank
Tongaat-Hulett (sugar)		Mafambisse mill (Mozambique)
NetGroup Solutions (utilities)	Tanesco (Tanzania)	
Telkom (telecoms)	Uganda Telecom	

Note: [a]Illovo is now owned by British Food.
Source: Goldstein and Prichard (2007)

that the rate of post-1994 international expansion has been much greater than SARB data would suggest. This rapid pace of expansion has been aided by the fact that (with one exception) South African MNEs have largely been immune to the resistance that other emerging economies' MNEs have experienced in their overseas acquisitions (Goldstein 2008).[7]

The only other data that exists regarding South African firms' modes of entry relates to their African operations. Preliminary data

---

[7] Old Mutual launched a US$6.04 billion takeover bid for Skandia in September 2005, which ABN Amro found to be fair from a financial point of view. Nonetheless, eight of Skandia's eleven directors (but not the chair) rejected the offer; in January 2006, after extending its offer period three times, OM declared its offer unconditional. Swedish managers of Skandia, Scandinavia's largest insurer, contrasted its strategy as a niche player in the unit-linked savings market with Old Mutual's business plan as a financial conglomerate. The Swedish state pension funds also leaned against Old Mutual's offer saying that it entailed unacceptable currency and political risks, even if foreign shareholders deemed the offer for the loss-making operation fair. Old Mutual eventually succeeded.

suggests that South African firms are more likely than international investors to make small investments (i.e., worth less than US$1m) and to partner with local entrepreneurs (Grobbelaar 2004). But whether this reflects distinct characteristics of South African investors, or is simply an artefact of the different sectoral composition of South African investment, is an open question. What is clearer is that privatization has provided a unique opportunity for South African firms to enter into a number of sub-Saharan markets (Table 9.5).

South African firms in the global economy

While aggregate figures provide a snapshot of overall patterns of FDI by South African firms, they provide little insight into the ways that patterns of internationalization may differ across firms from different sectors and of different sizes. In the absence of any existing studies of this question, we have constructed a basic database providing details on sixteen leading South African firms. The database provides information on the distribution of corporate activity and corporate decision-making influence across four regions – namely, South Africa, the rest of Africa, emerging economies, and the OECD. A full description of the methodology employed to select the firms and to assemble the data is provided in the chapter appendix.

Because the database relies on publicly available data from corporate annual reports, many potential indicators are only available for some of the firms in the sample, while several other indicators that have been suggested by other studies of corporate internationalization are not available at all (Dorrenbacher 2000; Veron 2006). Thus the analysis that follows relies most heavily on two universally available indicators: the geographical distribution of revenues and the national distribution of membership of the boards of directors (Figures 9.3 to 9.8).

The data reveal several trends. First, despite the relatively short time since the end of apartheid, the transnationalization of South Africa's largest firms has progressed very rapidly. Second, many of these firms have not only managed to expand into other emerging markets, but have established major operations in OECD countries. Third, while the overall level of outward expansion is significant, it has varied dramatically across firms and sectors. Finally, it is noteworthy that with few exceptions (SABMiller and MTN in particular), the regional

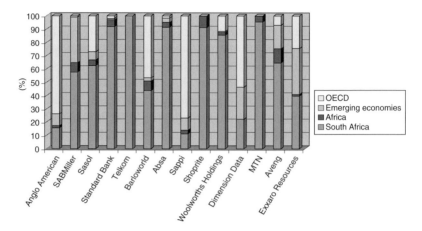

Figure 9.3 Distribution of revenues by customer location, 2001

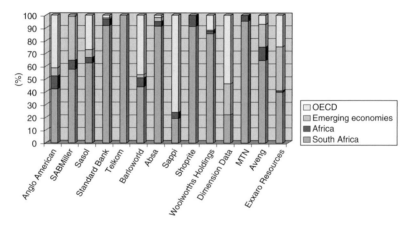

Figure 9.4 Distribution of revenues by production location, 2001

distribution of corporate activity has remained fairly constant from 2001 to 2006. This is surprising, given that most of these firms would have had quite limited international operations under apartheid, and as such their international expansion has overwhelmingly taken place over the past fifteen years. Although older data are not available, the implication seems to be that most of these firms underwent sudden internationalization immediately after 1990, but have now settled into

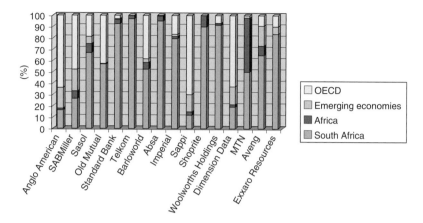

Figure 9.5 Distribution of revenues by customer location, 2006

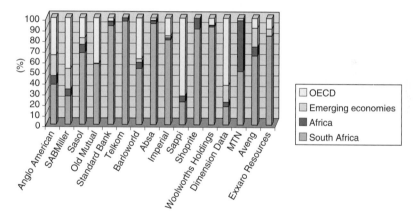

Figure 9.6 Distribution of revenues by production location, 2006

more regular patterns of growth. It is noteworthy that MTN and SABMiller, the two firms that have pursued a more conventional and progressive expansion strategy, are also those showing a pattern of continued rapid change in their international footprint. They first grew into Africa, then into other emerging markets and finally, in the case of SABMiller, into OECD markets.

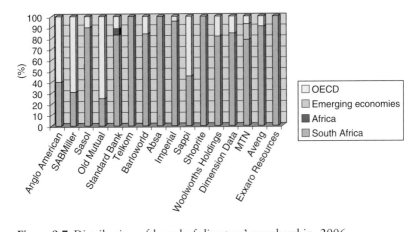

Figure 9.7 Distribution of board of directors' membership, 2006

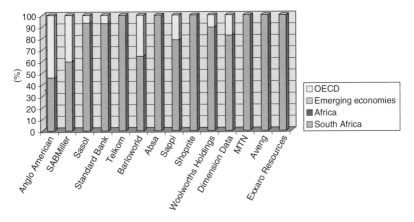

Figure 9.8 Distribution of board of directors' membership, 2001.
Notes: Most firms provide only one set of revenue data, in which case it was assumed that revenues by production and customer location were equivalent. The exception is Exxaro Resources, where data is by production location for the 2006 data, while it is for customer location for the 2001 data, and the two vary significantly. Data for Old Mutual and Imperial are excluded from the 2001 data due to a lack of segmental reporting and the unavailability of annual reports, respectively. Where segmental reporting did not correspond with the geographic regions used here, the authors estimated the appropriate allocation of values. Where directors' nationalities were not provided the authors assigned these values based on available information. Full details on all data collection issues are available on request

Patterns of internationalization

Given the trends in our small sample of firms, the challenge is to account for the patterns that we observe. Two particular questions emerge. First, how have South African firms been able to expand so rapidly into OECD countries? Second, what factors have led to the dramatically different patterns across firms and sectors? In order to address these questions, we test several hypotheses from the literature about the drivers of expansion among EMNEs. The section on transnationalization then investigates the applicability of these various hypotheses to different firms within the sample.

Firm- and country-specific competitive advantages

Theories of foreign investment emphasize that the most prominent determinant of the ability of firms to invest abroad is whether or not they possess unique competitive advantages. Previous research on South African firms suggests that these advantages may be of several kinds (Gelb 2005; Goldstein and Prichard 2007).

Firm-specific ownership advantages
Standard theories of foreign investment assumed that firms would expand on the basis of unique *world-class ownership advantages* (Dunning 1981). These could include, among others, technological knowledge, superior organizational and managerial expertise, privileged access to particular inputs or markets, or extensive access to financial resources. By contrast, research on South–South investment has argued that EMNEs have succeeded on the basis of their superior ability to adapt to developing country conditions, reflecting the context of their evolution and their position within the global economy (Lecraw 1977, 1993; Wells 1983). The basic hypothesis of the literature is that EMNEs investing in developing countries derive some advantages over industrial-country firms from better appreciation and more informed understanding of local conditions, cultural proximity, and the use of 'intermediate', 'small-scale technologies' that directly substitute labour for capital.

A limited group of studies have found that Third World MNEs are more likely to make creative use of local inputs; invest in lower income countries within regional markets; rely on local knowledge and partners, often through kin and ethnic networks; and compete on the basis of low-cost inputs (Lecraw 1997, 1993; Athukorala and Jayasuriya 1988). Yet, empirical evidence of these phenomena, particularly in more recent years, is rather limited (Aykut and Goldstein 2007), making South Africa a valuable case study of the possible existence of such EMNE-specific characteristics.

Country-specific location and political advantages

Nationality (i.e., being from a particular country) may bestow important advantages upon firms. *Location advantages* are those that derive direct from proximity, including geography, common culture and language, and the quality of transportation networks. *Political advantages* refer to those resulting from the explicit or implicit support of home-country governments. This might include direct efforts by governments to support firms seeking to secure contracts or investment opportunities, as well as the actions of SOEs or trade promotion agencies.

Historical and personal relationships

History may provide some firms with unique ownership advantages in certain destination markets. That might imply a longstanding knowledge of market conditions and the idiosyncrasies of doing business, or the existence of personal contacts and social networks to facilitate investment.

Conditions in local and global markets

Competitive conditions within home and global markets provide a second possible explanation for patterns of internationalization. Although management scholars and economists agree that the environment is a key dimension determining the performance and even the survival of firms, very little theoretical and data-based research has been done to measure and to analyse the factors that trigger environmental change (Oliva and Suarez 2007). Porter (1990) and others have stressed the strategic advantage of preserving a strong home-market position in a global environment. It is also argued that an already established domestic relationship often is to be given higher priority and considered more strategically important than an international alliance (Gulati 1995). Domestic ties can be easier to deal with culturally, and transaction costs often are lower.

Given the relative lack of evidence on this topic, intuition can provide the basis for two hypotheses, both of which stress the importance of competitive pressures in driving internationalization. First, insofar as firms prefer, all else being equal, to operate in the home market, the *extent of competition within the home market* will be an important factor pushing internationalization. Second, the *consolidation of the industry on a global scale* may have mixed effects on corporate strategies. Extensive consolidation will put pressure on larger firms to rapidly upscale international operations in order to remain globally competitive; on the other hand, smaller firms, lacking the financial clout to enter developed-country markets, are likely to be forced to look initially to African and other emerging markets where competition and scale are less demanding.

Analytic narratives of transnationalization

To what extent can these variables explain the observed patterns of internationalization? While developing a precise quantitative model is surely too ambitious, these variables can provide the basis for comparative narrative histories of firms that have followed similar trajectories. Accompanying these narratives, Table 9.6 provides an indicative classification for each firm with regard to each variable, though these classifications are admittedly subjective. In order to analyse the experience of different firms, we divide our sample into three groups that seem to exhibit relatively distinct characteristics.

Extensive internationalization and entry into developed-country markets

Within our sample, seven firms secured at least 40 per cent of their revenues outside South Africa in 2006. Of this group, only MTN received less than 38.4 per cent of its revenues from OECD markets, indicating that as a general rule it is the ability to enter OECD markets that distinguishes the South African firms that have become thoroughly multinational. This view is reinforced by the fact that Anglo American, SABMiller, Old Mutual, and Sappi all have only a minority

Table 9.6. *Key competitive features of selected South African firms*

	World-class technological and financial advantages	Locally adapted comparative advantages	Political advantages	Location advantages	Historical links to Europe	Domestic competition	Global industry consolidation
Extensive OECD-focused internationalization							
Anglo American	yes	some	some	no	yes	moderate	high
SABMiller	yes	yes	no	no	no	low	high
Dimension Data	yes	some	no	no	no	low	low
Old Mutual	some	no	no	no	some	moderate	high
Sappi	yes	no	no	some	yes	low	moderate
Barloworld	yes	some	no	some	yes	moderate	moderate
Regionalization							
Standard Bank	no	some	some	some	no	moderate	high
Telkom	no	some	yes	some	no	moderate	moderate
Absa	no	some	some	some	no	moderate	high
Shoprite	no	some	no	yes	no	high	moderate
Woolworths	no	some	no	some	no	high	moderate
Mixed							
Sasol	yes	some	some	some	no	low	moderate
Imperial Holdings	some	some	no	no	no	moderate	moderate
MTN	no	yes	no	some	no	moderate	moderate
Aveng	some	yes	yes	yes	no	high	moderate
Exxaro Resources	no	some	yes	some	no	moderate	moderate

Source: Authors' evaluation based on interviews, academic resources, statistical data, and annual reports

of South Africans on their boards of directors. In the case of Anglo American, the transformation culminated in the appointment of Cynthia Carroll as its new CEO in October 2006 – the first woman, outsider, and non-South African to occupy the position in what has traditionally been a male-dominated industry.

Focusing on the six firms other than MTN, the common denominator is that they possess *world-class technological and financial advantages* which have allowed them to penetrate the world's largest markets. Whereas theory predicts that EMNEs will rely on locally adapted advantages to undertake initial regional expansion, and then progressively gain the technical and financial clout to reach more developed markets, a number of South African firms possessed world-leading comparative advantages at the end of apartheid and have been able to rapidly enter developed-country markets on that basis. Some of them, most notably Anglo American, have further benefited from having long-standing connections to Europe that predate apartheid, and which have provided bases from which to pursue further expansion. While the group's South African pedigree is second to none, the Oppenheimers have maintained a very close relationship with the UK. As the *Financial Times* wrote in Harry's obituary: 'Anglo's top executives were seen as smooth Rhodes scholars educated at Oxford (Cambridge men, it was said, somehow did not fit in), who belonged to a discreet inner circle and ran much of the South African economy.'[8] In similar fashion, his son, Nicky Oppenheimer, was 'educated in the right way for an aspiring Anglo executive, at Harrow and Christ Church, Oxford. [He] retains old world manners, calling journalists "gentlemen of the press" and using Latin phrases such as *mirabile dictu*.'[9] This urbane, liberal, intellectual, and consensual corporate culture, reinforced by individual membership in some of the high places of the British establishment, clearly helped Anglo American in its move to London.

---

[8] '"Randlord" who opposed the system', *Financial Times*, 21 August 2000. On the same occasion, *The New York Times* wrote that Sir Harry 'was particularly fond of a Renoir he bought in London for £40 while a student at Oxford, where he developed a reputation as a generous host when he took friends on Champagne picnics. He collected manuscripts of English poets and had a special regard for Lord Byron' ('Harry Oppenheimer, 91, South African Industrialist, Dies', 21 August 2000).

[9] 'Rock hard beneath the old charm', *Financial Times*, 19 October 1999.

Why have leading South African firms displayed competitive advantages more reminiscent of developed-country firms than of traditional EMNEs? The answer seems to lie in the combination of three features of the South African economy – an extremely lucrative minerals industry, a highly dualistic economy, and a recent history of international isolation.

First, the vast extent of mineral wealth in South Africa laid the foundation for the emergence of world-class mining firms, and, to a lesser extent, significant development of upstream and downstream industries. Second, despite the poverty that prevailed in most of the country – in the context of tremendous, legally mandated inequalities between whites and non-whites – a highly sophisticated economy developed, which catered to a sizeable population of white South Africans. Thus the level of technical and managerial excellence was well above the level predicted by the country's average income. Third, the relative isolation of the South African economy, at first due to import substitution and later due to international sanctions, opened up enormous opportunities to producers of high-end services and products. The case of Dimension Data is perhaps the most illustrative, as the emergence of such a high-technology firm in a middle-income country would seem intuitively unlikely. Yet, high demand from white businesses, coupled with high levels of protection, allowed it to flourish.

The one case that conforms closely to the classic model of EMNE expansion is SABMiller. Brewing is a global oligopoly, with a few firms competing largely on the basis of high advertising investments. At the end of apartheid, SABMiller (then known as South African Breweries – SAB) showed world-class brewing and logistics efficiency, but lacked the financial strength and management experience to enter the largest and fastest-growing foreign markets. The global beer industry then entered a phase of rapid consolidation, which put pressure on SAB to expand internationally if it was to remain an independent player. Responding to this pressure, SAB undertook a rapid program of acquisitions in Africa, as well as entering selectively into other emerging markets such as China, the Czech Republic, and Poland. This allowed it to build the financial strength to ultimately purchase Miller Brewing in the US, thus entering decisively into developed-country markets, diminishing its operational and financial dependency on the home market, and providing a base for further expansion, including the recent purchase of Bavaria in Colombia. The rapid evolution of SAB's international footprint is reflected in the fact that from 2001 to 2006 the South African share in turnover declined from 57% to 26.5%, while the OECD share increased from 1% to 47.8%.

Old Mutual presents a slightly different case, having expanded significantly in developed-country markets despite not having clear technical competitive advantages comparable to those of the other firms in this group. At the end of apartheid it was among the five large South African conglomerates and controlled over 10 per cent of total Johannesburrg Stock Exchange capitalization. The following years saw Old Mutual take advantage of its financial strength, as well as the availability of capital during a period of conglomerate unbundling, to enter developed-country markets through acquisitions. Yet unlike the other firms in this group, Old Mutual's investments in OECD markets initially failed to achieve profitability, likely owing to its reliance on financial strength, rather than unique technical capabilities, to drive expansion. Over time, Old Mutual has managed to diversify away from low-margin insurance policies and towards more sophisticated financial instruments. Expectations that it could achieve the same results in Scandinavia led to the decision to acquire Scandia in 2006.

Finally, Sasol possesses world-leading technical capabilities, related to its mastery of gas-to-liquid refining technology, but unlike the other firms in this group has so far experienced more moderate internationalization. In a case of the exception proving the rule, this inconsistency simply seems to reflect a time lag; formerly a SOE, Sasol did not have a single international sales office until the relaxing of sanctions in 1990. Sasol is now involved in two major gas-to-liquid projects: Oryx was inaugurated in Qatar in July 2006, while Escravos is to open in 2009 in Nigeria.[10] Arya Sasol Polymer Company, a 50-50 joint venture with Iran's National Petrochemical Company, has recently completed construction of a new ethane cracker. Thus, Sasol's world-class capabilities seem set to transform the company into a major international firm in the years to come.

[10] For more details on Sasol's strategy to use synthetic fuel technology, see 'Right place, right time', *Financial Mail*, 26 May 2006.

Regional multinationalization

In contrast, a significant group of large South African firms have experienced a much smaller absolute level of internationalization focused primarily on regional markets. Here we include those firms that continued to receive at least 90 per cent of their revenues from South Africa in 2006: Standard Bank, Telkom, Absa, Shoprite, and Woolworths Holdings. Of these five, all but Woolworths Holdings receive the largest share of their non-South African revenues from other African markets, and while in each case the African share is small in absolute terms (2.6–9.9 per cent of total revenues), each firm places significant emphasis on the African market in their long-term strategic plans.

Why have these firms focused on Africa rather than pursuing a more general expansion strategy? The first part of the answer is that they lack the technical advantages and financial might necessary to penetrate large developed-country markets. None of these firms could be said to have world-class technical competence, nor the financial resources to force their way into developed-country markets through acquisitions. While Woolworths successfully acquired a subsidiary (Country Road) in Australia, it was forced to discontinue modest efforts to enter the US market.

The second part of the answer is that these firms nonetheless face strong pressures for expansion, at the same time as they enjoy distinct advantages when competing within the African market. The dominant push factor was the increasingly intense *competitive pressure in the domestic market* brought about by the end of apartheid. The retail, banking, and telecoms markets in South Africa are all characterized by very intense competition among a small number of large firms which came to dominate the market under apartheid, and this has manifested itself in declining margins within South Africa. The profitability of African operations, on the other hand, is relatively much larger – in telecoms, revenue is increasing by 20–50% annually and margins are around 40%.[11] The strength of this push factor is made clear in the mobile telecoms market: MTN was initially dwarfed by Vodacom (a joint venture of Telkom and British Vodafone) in the

---

[11] 'Out of Africa', *The Economist*, 7 December 2006.

domestic market and this prompted it to invest aggressively in continental expansion.

Complementing the push of increasing competition has been the pull provided by the existence of distinct firm- and country-specific ownership advantages. Although these firms have, at times, exhibited a unique ability to operate in low-income settings, they were until recently accustomed to serving only the wealthier white market within South Africa. For this reason, these advantages have been more limited than might be expected, owing to the fact that they have had little exposure to low-income markets, the so-called bottom of the pyramid. More important to their successful expansion in Africa seems to have been a combination of location and political advantages. The retail firms have relied particularly strongly on locational advantages. They have coordinated their supply chains from a South African base and relied heavily on imports from South Africa and established sourcing networks to expand outwards into new markets.

The case of the banks is somewhat more complex. At the end of apartheid the banks had significant technical expertise, but were neither world leaders, nor did they have special expertise in working in African markets given their historic focus on the white South African market. Unlike Old Mutual, they also lacked the independent financial strength to acquire a presence in OECD markets. Thus it was largely out of a lack of alternatives that the banks looked to the African market, where competition was less demanding and where they enjoyed the added benefit of implicit political support from South Africa. Interestingly, this initial expansion into Africa in both retail and corporate banking resulted in these banks subsequently developing locally specific competitive advantages, more consistent with the classic EMNE model. For example, many banks entered into corporate banking on the continent by structuring financial arrangements for mining firms. This was at first facilitated by the availability of risk insurance from the South African government, but in time the firms have become world leaders in their ability to tailor risk instruments to an African context. An equally interesting driver of the expansion of South African banks on the continent is the evolution of policy within South Africa. While the banks historically did not serve the non-white population, recent government policy mandating the expansion of banking services to low-income groups is now expected to carry over to other African operations, albeit gradually.

Having all pursued some initial expansion into African markets in an effort to establish an international presence, banks have been faced with the question of what to do next. Standard Bank has sought to leverage its strength in Africa to progressively push its way into other emerging markets. In the 1990s, Standard Bank bought ANZ Grinlays' operations in Africa and also established representative offices in about twenty countries outside Africa. Although the bank's international presence outside Africa was not highly visible, it served to build a corporate and investment banking and commodities trading empire across many of the world's top emerging markets. In the late 1990s Standard Bank was censured for the large dollar exposure it had in Russia after some Russian banks defaulted on financing that it had provided. But while other banks abandoned Russia, Standard Bank stood firm. It is now aiming for a larger international retail presence (upgrading many of its representative offices outside Africa to branches), a foothold in the burgeoning Indian market, and finalizing the integration of BankBoston in Argentina, Standard Bank's first foray into retail banking outside Africa. In the CEO's words, 'Standard Bank's expansion strategy beyond South Africa is all about Africa and international emerging markets. We want to position ourselves as a key emerging-market player and uniquely as a key emerging market-player that comes from an emerging market.'[12]

Absa provides an alternative model. By virtue of the development of unique competences for working in Africa, Absa began to be increasingly discussed as a potential acquisition target for international banks looking to expand their African operations. Lacking the financial clout of the major international banks, it was taken over by Barclays in 2005 for US$5.5 billion.

Mixed internationalization

This final group of firms includes those that have expanded beyond Africa, but have yet to make decisive inroads into the OECD. They include those firms that received 60–90 per cent of their revenues in South Africa in 2006, along with MTN, which has expanded dramatically in emerging markets but has not entered the OECD.

---

[12] 'Stanbic's Expansion', *Africa Research Bulletin: Economic, Financial and Technical Series*, Vol. 44, No. 1, p. 17262, March 2007.

While this is a more diverse group, the companies that compose it are in some ways the most interesting, as they highlight the diverse circumstances and opportunities that simultaneously coexist within South Africa. In terms of FSAs, they conform most closely to the traditional image of EMNEs, as they have, in general, relied on competitive advantages that are particularly well adapted to developing-country conditions. Thus, they have not exhibited the type of world-class technical and financial capacity exhibited by the largest national firms, but have also not relied as heavily on political and locational advantages as those firms that have only expanded within Africa. Consistent with the view that their competitive advantages remain rooted in South Africa, board of directors membership in each of these firms is at least 78.6% South African, while none have more than 10% of their board based in OECD countries.

MTN is the most prominent example of a firm that has succeeded on the basis of exploiting competitive advantages that are specifically tailored to developing-country markets. Facing intense competition in the domestic mobile telephone market, MTN began investing in smaller Africa markets such as Uganda, Rwanda, and Swaziland in 1997 to 1999, before embarking on a bold, and at the time widely criticized, decision to invest heavily in Nigeria in 2001. These ventures proved to be hugely successful, with MTN now deriving far and away the largest share of revenues from Africa of any large South African firm, after deriving only 4.5 per cent of revenues in Africa as recently as 2001. MTN achieved this result by developing innovative solutions – pre-paid cards to overcome problems of credit risk, plan structures that were better adapted to local needs, and privately installed mobile telephone infrastructure where no previous fixed-line infrastructure had existed. In the wake of their success in Africa, MTN has recently made aggressive efforts to move into the Middle Eastern market, first by entering the Iranian market, and then by purchasing Lebanon-based Investcom.

Aveng (previously Anglovaal Engineering) has similarly relied on locally adapted knowledge to support expansion, though it has encountered more mixed results. Originally part of the Anglovaal group, Aveng has since been established as an independent entity focused on construction, steel, and cement. The 1999 unbundling of Anglovaal into Avmin (mining), AVI (consumer products), and Aveng (engineering services) was accompanied by the acquisition of a minority stake in Grinaker Construction in November 1999, the acquisition of 100 per cent of LTA, its delisting and merging with Grinaker, and the creation of Grinaker-LTA in November 2000. LTA also possessed significant assets in Australia and New Zealand.

Aveng's South African units possessed significant technical expertise, owing to their long involvement with the South African mining and construction industries. Unlike the situation of many South African firms these skills were well adapted to emerging-market conditions, as construction and engineering projects in South Africa and the region had often involved working in moderately isolated areas with limited infrastructure and relatively high risk. Thus, the end of apartheid saw Aveng expand not only in Africa but also in emerging markets in the Middle East and Southeast Asia, based on a combination of world class and locally adapted competitive advantages. Aveng has now substantially diversified internationally, though it is worth noting that the level of internationalization remains essentially unchanged since 2001. While not in our sample, Murray and Roberts is another South African corporation that has internationalized on the basis of strong corporate competencies. At home it is building the world's first pebble bed modular nuclear reactor, while overseas it is responsible for Bahrain's World Trade Centre and the new Dubai air terminal. Yet, while both Aveng and Murray and Roberts have successfully expanded to non-African emerging markets based on well-adapted competitive advantages, both have encountered increasing challenges as they have gone further afield from South Africa. This suggests the possibility that locational proximity and the political support of the South African government may have also played a role in their success in the region.

Imperial Holdings illustrates a unique pattern of international-ization, as it has maintained South Africa as the centre of its oper-ations, while the vast majority of its international expansion has occurred in developed markets, rather than emerging markets. A relatively new firm, Imperial has based its success on pioneering innovative business models in South Africa (such as motor dealerships and leasing, fleet management and related value-added services for passenger and commercial vehicles, and materials handling and earth-moving equipment) before expanding those operations to developed countries. This is an expansion model more reminiscent of a successful developed-country firm than of a classic EMNE, and again illustrates the diversity of South African experience owing to its unique economic and political history.

The final two firms in the group seem to represent outliers, rather than alternative trajectories of internationalization. As noted earlier, Sasol seems poised to follow the pattern of rapid internationalization on the basis of world-leading technical and financial competence. By contrast, the apparent major transformation in Exxaro Resources' business reflects the nature of the data and the unbundling of certain assets, rather than a particular change in actual activities.[13]

The firm was included in the sample largely to investigate whether there was evidence of Black Economic Empowerment firms in South Africa taking advantage of a privileged political position to expand elsewhere in Africa. For the case of Exxaro, at least, there is no evidence of such a pattern to date, as it has remained heavily focused on domestic operations, reflecting the very real benefits to Black Economic Empowerment firms operating within South Africa.

Conclusions

The growing presence and activism of EMNEs within global, and particularly regional, markets is one of the distinguishing features of the current redrawing of the geography of world business. South African firms have featured centrally in this process, establishing themselves as major investors across a range of sectors. While the bulk of investment has gone to OECD countries, by some measures South Africa has also emerged as the largest single foreign investor in Africa over the past decade (Rumney 2006).

---

[13] First, the firm only provides data on revenues by customer location, which disguises the fact that the vast majority of mining has been in South Africa throughout the study period, with some slow growth in other Southern African countries. Second, Exxaro was formed by the merger of Kumba Resources and Eyesizwe mining in a 2005 Black Economic Empowerment transaction. When the merger was completed, the South African competition authorities forced the new entity to unbundle its iron ore assets into a new firm, Kumba Iron Ore. Within our sample, the data for 2001 refers to Kumba Resources, while the 2005 data refers to Exxaro Resources, which includes Kumba Resources' non-iron ore holdings along with coal resources previously held by Eyesizwe. The removal of the iron ore resources from the data would seem to be primarily responsible for the reduction in international turnover, as the iron ore business was particularly internationalized.

We have sought to analyse in some depth the internationalization strategies pursued by South African MNEs. To this end we presented a dataset of sixteen representative and large South African MNEs, based upon which we identified three broad trajectories of internationalization: extensive, regional, and mixed internationalization. Our core insight is that differing FSAs, CSAs, and competitive conditions in local and global markets result in different corporate trajectories. Firms that have primarily expanded regionally have tended to rely on CSAs linked to location (proximity), and to the direct and indirect political support of the South African government. Their advantages are locally bred and hence only transferable to countries that have a low 'psychic' distance from South Africa. This is the case in particular for services companies, possibly including those retailers that have expanded to Australia, only to discover that income-level differentials are more important determinants of success than Commonwealth membership.

By contrast, firms that have internationalized more widely have tended to possess more specialized advantages. Some of these firms, such as MTN and Aveng, have relied on skills such as locally adapted technology and an ability to manage risk which are well adapted to conditions in developing countries, and thus consistent with received wisdom about the drivers of expansion of EMNEs. On the other hand, several of the largest South African firms, led by Anglo American, have expanded on the basis of world-class technical and managerial skills, as well as extensive financial resources and strong historical ties to Europe.

These cases represent a clear divergence from the findings of most studies of EMNEs, and are a reflection of South Africa's unique history: enormous mineral wealth, a history of protectionism, and the development of two parallel, but utterly unequal, economies under the racist policies of apartheid. This unique history also highlights the importance of a further explanatory factor: the impact of competitive factors on the decision to internationalize. Most of the firms developed their competitive advantages in a highly protected environment, and often as part of the massive conglomerates that dominated the South African economy prior to the end of apartheid. This was the case, for instance, in engineering (Murray and Roberts) and in consumer non-durables (SABMiller). Yet, the impetus for successfully expanding outwards has often been the introduction of new competitive pressure. Many of the firms that have expanded regionally have done so in response to shrinking margins in the South African market, owing both to the introduction of international competition and the growth of domestic competitors. Likewise, the challenge posed by the global consolidation of certain industries has motivated larger firms to expand sufficiently rapidly to keep pace. Given the effect of competition policy on both the development of competitive advantages and the decision to internationalize, this appears to be an area worthy of further study.[14]

The research presented here raises interesting questions, beyond those related to competition, about the role of public policy in shaping outcomes. The internationalization of big business in South Africa is not isolated from a broader range of other structural transformations, such as Black Economic Empowerment, privatization, and overseas listing. In some cases internationalization may have been a response by corporate managers to increased policy volatility in South Africa (Chabane *et al.* 2006), and to the increased demands of Black Economic Empowerment regulations. Likewise, we have noted elsewhere the ways in which South African legislation to encourage the extension of services to traditionally disenfranchised groups has opened the door to similar pro-poor innovations abroad (Goldstein and Prichard 2007).

Finally, we have raised the question of whether the promotion of Black Economic Empowerment businesses within South Africa may eventually lead them to play an important role on the African continent. While there is little evidence of this so far, the question of how continued changes within South Africa will affect the behaviour of its corporations remains an important one.

---

[14] South Africa provides at least anecdotal evidence to support each of the prevailing hypotheses. Those who argue that a subdued pro-market attitude is necessary for the formation of national champions will find confirmation in the experience of South Africa's financial and telecoms service companies, that operate in a largely protected environment. Those who, on the contrary, argue that competition policy must be aggressive in protecting consumers' rights, as this stance also help firms become more international, will feel vindicated by the experience of Sasol, and other firms that invested overseas when they saw domestic enlargement curtailed by the relevant authorities.

References

Amsden, Alice 2001. *The Rise of the Rest*. Oxford: Oxford University Press.

Athukorala, Premachandra and Jayasuriya, S. K. 1988. 'Parentage and Factor Proportions: A Comparative Study of Third-World Multinationals in Sri Lankan Manufacturing', *Oxford Bulletin of Economics and Statistics* 50, 4: 409–423.

Aykut, Dilek and Goldstein, Andrea 2007. 'Developing Country Multinationals: South–South Investment Comes of Age', in *Industrial Development for the 21st Century: Sustainable Development Perspectives*. New York: United Nations.

Belli, Pedro, Finger, Michael and Ballivian, Amparo 1993. 'South Africa: Review of Trade Policy Issues', *Informal Discussion Papers on Aspects of the South African Economy* 4. World Bank, Southern Africa Department.

Chabane, Neo, Goldstein, Andrea and Roberts, Simon 2006. 'The Changing Face and Strategies of Big Business in South Africa: More Than a Decade of Political Democracy', *Industrial and Corporate Change* 15, 3: 549–577.

Chandler, Alfred Jr., Amatori, Franco and Hikino, Takashi (eds.) 1997. *Big Business and the Wealth of Nations*. Cambridge: Cambridge University Press.

Clark, Nancy L. 1994. *Manufacturing Apartheid. State Corporations in South Africa*. New Haven: Yale University Press.

Dorrenbacher, Christoph 2000. 'Measuring Corporate Internationalisation: A Review of Measurement Concepts and Their Use', *Intereconomics* 35, 3: 119–126.

Dunning, John H. 1981. *International Production and the Multinational Enterprise*. London: Allen and Unwin.

Ernst & Young (various years), *Mergers & Acquisitions: A Review of Activity for the Year*. Johannesburg.

Fine, Ben and Rustomjee, Z. 1997. *The Political Economy of South Africa: From Minerals-Energy Complex to Industrialisation*. Johannesburg: Witwatersrand University Press.

Gelb, Stephen 2005. 'South–South Investment: The Case of Africa', in J. J. Teunissen and A. Akkerman (eds.), *Africa in the World Economy – The National, Regional and International Challenges*. The Hague: FONDAD.

Goldstein, Andrea 2007. *Multinational Companies from Emerging Economies: Composition, Conceptualization and Direction in the Global Economy*. Basingstoke, UK: Palgrave.

Goldstein, Andrea 2008. 'Who's Afraid of Emerging Multinationals?', in K. Savant (ed.), *The Rise of Transnational Corporations from Emerging Markets: Threat or Opportunity?* Cheltenham, UK: Edward Elgar.

Goldstein, Andrea 2009. 'South Africa', in A. Coplan, T. Hikino, and J. Lincoln (eds.), *The Handbook of Business Groups in Emerging Economies.* Oxford: Oxford University Press.

Goldstein, Andrea and Prichard, Wilson 2007. 'South African Multinationals: South–South Co-Operation At Its Best?', in N. Grobbelaar (ed.), *Growing Africa's Private Sector: A Role for Corporate South Africa.* Johannesburg: South African Institute of International Affairs.

Grobbelaar, Neuma 2004. ' "Every Continent Needs an America": The Experience of South African Firms Doing Business in Mozambique', *Business in Africa Research Project.* Johannesburg: South African Institute of International Affairs.

Gulati, Ranjay 1995. 'Does Familiarity Breed Trust? The Implications of Repeated Ties for Contractual Choice of Alliances', *Academy of Management Journal* 38, 85–112.

Lecraw, Donald 1977. 'Direct Investment by Firms from Less Developed Countries', *Oxford Economic Papers* 29, 442–457.

Lecraw, Donald 1993. 'Outward Direct Investment by Indonesian Firms: Motivation and Effects', *Journal of International Business Studies*, 24, 589–600.

Oliva, Rogelio and Suarez, Fernando F. 2007. 'Economic Reforms and the Competitive Environment of Firms', *Industrial and Corporate Change*, 16, 131–154.

Porter, M. 1990. *The Competitive Advantage of Nations.* New York: Free Press.

Rogerson, C. M. 1990. 'Sun International: The Making of a South African Tourism Multinational', *GeoJournal*, 22, 345–354.

Rumney, Reg 2006. 'South Africa's FDI Flows into Africa', presented at the National Treasury Interdepartmental Workshop on *South Africa's Economic Presence in Africa*, Pretoria, 15 February.

Swart, Pieter 2005. 'Wrong Data, Wrong Policies: The South African Data Collection Experience', presented at the United Nations Conference on Trade and Development Expert Meeting on *Capacity Building in the Area of FDI: Data Compilation and Policy Formulation in Developing Countries*, Geneva, 12–14 December.

Thompson, L. 1995. *A History of South Africa.* New Haven: Yale University Press.

UNCTAD 2005. 'FDI Statistics: Data Compilation and Policy Issues', presented at the United Nations Conference on Trade and Development Expert Meeting on *Capacity Building in the Area of FDI: Data*

Compilation and Policy Formulation in Developing Countries, Geneva, 12–14 December.

Veron, Nicolas 2006. 'Farewell National Champions', *Bruegel Policy Brief*, No. 2006/04.

Wells, Louis Jr. 1983. *Third World Multinationals: The Rise of Foreign Investment from Developing Countries*. Cambridge, MA: The MIT Press.

Appendix: Case selection and data compilation

The goal of the case selection was to select the largest and most international South African firms, subject to an effort to include a wide range of sectoral diversity. With an initial target of fifteen firms, ten of the fifteen largest South African firms by turnover were selected. The five remaining firms in the top fifteen were excluded on the following grounds:

- BHP Billiton: weak South African ties make its national identity questionable;
- Bidvest: there was insufficient data availability in annual reports;
- Sanlam, Nedcor, First Rand: the list already included three financial services firms.

In place of the excluded firms, six additional firms were included in order to increase sample diversity, with the added goal of including certain firms that have acquired attention for their international expansion:

- Shoprite (retail – supermarkets, seventeenth largest South African firm)
- Woolworths Holdings (retail – general, thirty-seventh)
- Dimension Data (IT, twenty-eighth)
- MTN (mobile telecommunications, twentieth)
- Aveng (construction and engineering, thirty-fifth)
- Exxaro Resources (formerly Kumba Resources, mining, forty-sixth).

Data was compiled on the basis of publicly available annual reports. While the presentation of the data here is based on four geographic segments, many annual reports were based on slightly different segmental breakdowns. Transforming the data involved estimating the appropriate allocation of value across different segments (e.g., distributing values for an 'Australia and Asia' segment between 'OECD' and 'Emerging economies'). This estimation was based on available information and should be treated as a rough approximation, though on a small enough scale that general patterns should not be affected.

In allocating board of directors members to particular regions, educated guesses were required on the basis of information provided about individuals' education and past employment. In the few cases where an informed judgement was impossible, the board member was dropped from the calculation. Similarly, a board member was 'split' between two regions in the few cases in which the member had been based in both regions for significant periods.

Additional data related to the distribution of assets, profits, and employment were only available for a minority of firms and thus could not be used in the analysis.

10 | Mexican multinationals: Insights from CEMEX

DONALD R. LESSARD AND RAFEL LUCEA

Since Vernon's seminal work (Vernon 1966; Vernon 1971), international firm expansion has been predominantly portrayed as a phenomenon led by firms located in economically and technologically developed countries in search of new markets, natural resources, knowledge leverage, and/or risk diversification. While venturing abroad is not devoid of obstacles (Hymer 1960; Zaheer 1995; Zaheer and Mosakowski 1997), the general view has been that developed-country multinational enterprises (MNEs) were able to overcome these hurdles as a result of possessing better technologies, superior organizational processes, more financial power, or sounder home-country institutions than their host-country counterparts.

The emergence of emerging-market multinationals (EMNEs) challenges classic theories of the international firm that attempt to explain *why* multinational enterprises actually exist. In response to this puzzle, a number of studies, including those in this book, have pointed at a combination of environmental and organizational factors that help us understand why EMNEs might enjoy a competitive advantage over developed-country MNEs even when competing with these firms in developed markets – labeled "up-market FDI" by Ramamurti and Singh (Figure 1.1 in this volume). Nevertheless, most of these competitive advantages appear to be temporary in nature and only provide plausible explanations as to how these EMNEs are able to take their *first* steps into the international competitive arena. However, they are significantly silent when it comes to explaining if and how they can sustain their competitive edge. And, yet, a small but growing number of EMNEs have been able not only to sustain their initial competitive position vis-à-vis developed-country MNEs but to significantly improve it over time. *How* this has happened and what implications this phenomenon has for current theories of international business is the subject of this chapter.

In this chapter, we propose a co-evolutionary model of international firm expansion and learning that explains why EMNEs are able to achieve and sustain their global competitive position even in the face of limited or waning home-country specific advantages. Our model posits that the idiosyncratic institutional and competitive conditions faced by emerging-market firms strongly influence the shape and nature of the initial capability-set developed by these organizations. Under certain conditions, these capabilities may result in a source of international competitive advantage, making geographic expansion into more developed countries a possibility. In other words, they need to pass what we call the RATs (Relevance, Appropriability, Transferability) test – that is, their capabilities need to be *relevant* to customers in the foreign market, they need to be *transferable* internationally, and the rents they generate need to be *appropriable* by the firm.

Once EMNEs start to operate in more developed countries, they will need to continue to develop new, locally relevant capabilities if they are to maintain their competitiveness in these markets. If, and to the extent that, these new capabilities are integrated with those forming the initial core set, the EMNE may find itself in a better position to further its international expansion than other firms. Crucial to this model are four elements. First, the recognition that idiosyncratic local conditions in emerging markets may constitute initial sources of international competitive advantage (Narayanan and Fahey 2005). Second, and contrary to classic theories of international business, we emphasize that the development of new capabilities that are crucial for the sustainability of the EMNE may derive from operating in *foreign* markets and not only from long-lasting home-country specific advantages. Third, that both sets of firm capabilities, the ones derived from being born in an emerging-market environment and the ones derived from operating in developed economies, need to be continuously evaluated, adapted, integrated, and diffused throughout the organization. It will be the capacity to renew its capabilities that will make it possible for EMNEs to sustain and improve their competitive standing in the global arena. Finally, we point out that strong imprinting effects and some inherent EMNE characteristics, ranging from their late entrant status to idiosyncratic governance forms, will continue to differentiate the bases on which EMNEs and developed-country MNEs compete.

While the main thrust of this chapter is to propose an extension of the current body of theories concerning the existence of the MNE, we will draw heavily on the corporate story of the Mexican cement, concrete, and aggregates company CEMEX, to illustrate our perspective. CEMEX is a prototypical "global consolidator" in Ramamurti and Singh's typology (Table 6.4 in this volume), expanding by acquisition and competing on operational excellence in a mature industry in both emerging and developed economies. CEMEX is a "middle out" MNE in two senses of the word: it has expanded both "up-market" and "down-market" from a middle country in terms of income levels, technological development, and institutional development, and much of its sustained competiveness lies in middle management processes, characterized as "middle out" by Nonaka (1988).

We do not claim that the contextual and organizational circumstances that this firm encountered are fully representative of those faced by other potential EMNEs, or that the specific responses it undertook are an example to follow. Indeed, the challenges faced by CEMEX in the late 1980s and early 1990s are unlikely to be faced today by any other company in Mexico or elsewhere, and, as we will see, this firm's history has not been devoid of setbacks. However, we believe that the nature of the institutional, competitive, technological, and organizational challenges that CEMEX faced and the outcomes resulting from its actions will help to give texture to our arguments. Further, we believe that the *learning organization* that CEMEX has become is a relevant example for other MNEs from both developing countries and advanced economies.

The rest of this chapter is organized as follows. First, we succinctly contrast classic theories of the multinational that justify MNEs expanding down-market from developed to developing markets, with more recent theories that explain how the reverse phenomenon, expanding up-market from developing to developed countries, can occur. We highlight that currently accepted EMNE sources of international competitive advantage are temporary at best and that a theory that explains their sustainability is wanting. We continue by offering an overview of the internationalization story of CEMEX that helps us present the main elements of our proposed framework. A somewhat more formal description of the model follows.

Why do MNEs (and EMNEs) exist?

Two questions have preoccupied international business (IB) scholars since the beginnings of the field: What are the benefits for local firms that go international? And, what makes it possible for MNEs to exist?

On the first question, scholars have developed a more or less consensual categorization of the benefits that domestic firms reap by venturing beyond the borders of their countries of origin. These benefits, summarized by Dunning (1998), include access to new markets, and new pools of scarce resources, the possibility to more efficiently exploit the firm's tangible and intangible assets, and the acquisition of strategic assets. Later, financially minded academics (Agmon and Lessard 1981; Lessard 1982) pointed out that by operating in multiple countries firms could significantly reduce the impact of economic, financial, operational, and political risk relative to the diversification benefits available to purely financial investors.

Expanding internationally, however, comes at a cost. Foreign firms are, at least initially, less familiar with the peculiarities of the new environment and face higher coordination costs in operating across greater geographic, institutional, and cultural distances than their domestic counterparts (Buckley and Casson 1976; Dunning 1977; Johanson and Vahlne 1977; Caves 1982; Zaheer 1995). As a result, a firm's foreign subsidiary needs to enjoy some particular advantage over its indigenous competitors to successfully compete against them. Theorizing and empirically testing the sources of these advantages has been one of the core themes in the field of international management from its inception. IB scholars have emphasized multiple sources of international competitive advantage and these can be categorized in two big groups: those that are common to all firms located in a given country, and those that are specific to a particular firm as a result of its history and (in broad terms) its asset configuration. The relevance of these sources of competitive advantage at any given point in time strongly depends on the predominant social, economic, political, and technological conditions in the global arena. Hence, the international macro context, country-level factors, and firm-specific characteristics have to be taken into consideration to explain why some firms, and not others, are able to operate and thrive in foreign countries.

In the remaining part of this section we produce a highly stylized characterization of these three dimensions at two different points in time and the main theories of the multinational that emerged in each period. We are well aware that changes in each of these dimensions took place gradually and unevenly across countries, and we by no means imply that earlier theories have lost their value. However, to look at the body of work on international management from this perspective helps to emphasize our central points. Namely, that operating across borders was seen as the prerogative of developed-countries' firms, and that EMNEs were predominantly portrayed as competing on the basis of country-specific advantages (CSAs) that are available to all firms based there, and typically short-lived.

The macro context of the 1960s and 1970s in which the "classic" IB theories were developed was characterized by a number of elements. First, barriers to both trade and FDI were significantly higher than those prevailing in the later period. Second, the cost of transportation of goods and, particularly, information was also significantly lower in the second period. A third factor was that basic technological development was geographically concentrated in the US, Europe, and, later, in Japan. As a consequence, international trade and investment became the domain of large, vertically integrated, and product-, not services-, oriented corporations.

Scholars attributed the predominant source of competitive advantage of these companies to a set of home-country factors (Vernon 1966; Dunning 1998). In particular, direct access to sources of new technology and knowledge, large and mature home markets, and well-developed and stable legal and financial institutions were regarded as the necessary elements on which to base the international expansion of firms. Interestingly, enjoying large endowments in natural resources or a large pool of unskilled and cheap labor, was seen at the time as neither a necessary nor a sufficient condition for firms in a particular country to engage in international activity. Indeed, the companies that internationalized the most during this period were from countries that were at a relative disadvantage in this regard. Tapping foreign pools of scarce resources to serve the host market was frequently the reason for venturing abroad rather than the factor that made international expansion possible.

At the firm level, operating successfully across borders also involved the exploitation of what came to be referred to as firm-specific advantages (FSAs) (Rugman 1981). The nature of these firm-level advantages was thought to be, mainly, of two kinds: proprietary assets and common governance. The most common proprietary assets cited by IB scholars in this first period were firm-specific technologies and brand. Some scholars (e.g. Kogut 1989) also stressed the network advantages that MNEs could reap through common governance. Importantly, the origin and renewal of these FSAs was seen as residing in the headquarters of the organization; rarely in the foreign subsidiaries.

In sum, this first period was characterized by a highly fragmented international system whereby the key sources of international competitive advantage were geographically bound at the country level and organizationally concentrated at the level of firm headquarters. In trying to explain the MNE phenomenon, IB scholars developed an array of theories (see Part I of Rugman and Brewer, 2001, for a review of the key literature on IB) that were a reflection of the circumstances of this era. Of central importance for this chapter, these early theories suggest that the emergence and persistence of EMNEs – in particular up-market developed-country MNEs – is an unlikely event. Among other things, the lack of effective institutions in most developing countries made it extremely difficult for multinationals-to-be to access the necessary sources of finance, knowledge, or technology needed to overcome the liability of operating in a foreign country. Moreover, the political and economic fragmentation of the international system made it extremely difficult for potential EMNEs to "borrow" foreign institutions (Siegel, forthcoming) in order to access foreign markets for capital and technology (Arora *et al.* 2001). As a result, the predominant view in this earlier period was that EMNEs could only exist to the extent that they had control of valuable and internationally scarce resources in their home country. In practice, this meant that EMNEs would concentrate in natural resource sectors or in industries where it was cost effective to substitute cheap labor for capital and technology.

Starting in the late 1980s and particularly after the mid-1990s, significant changes at the macro, country and firm levels dramatically transformed the global competitive landscape. Concomitantly, the classic theories of the MNE were revised and expanded upon.

At the macro level, this new scenario is characterized by lower barriers to trade and investment, the liberalization of the telecommunications and financial services industries, dramatic improvements in the digitalization and transmission of data, and the consolidation of a number of supra-national institutions and global markets. As a consequence of these developments, a significant number of industries experienced a process of vertical disintegration and international dispersion that was at shocking variance with the precepts of the previous period. It was also at this time that a growing number of firms from developing economies started to emerge. Two aspects of these early EMNEs were particularly difficult to explain using the classic theories of the MNE. The first was that these EMNES were not only developing "horizontally" into other countries of similar levels of economic development but also "upwards" into more developed countries. Second, and perhaps more problematic, was the fact that a significant amount of this expansion was *not* founded on the existence of privileged access to home-country natural resources. As a result, a growing number of IB scholars started to pay closer attention to elements at the country and organizational level that made the emergence of these EMNEs possible.

The picture emerging from these efforts, this book being a good example, is one of significant diversity depending on the country and industry under study. Some emerging countries' multinationals such as those from China or Russia (see Chapters 5 and 7) clearly respond to the classic model of international expansion based on the privileged access to cheap or scarce resources in the home country. In other cases, such as India or Israel (Chapters 6 and 12), most of the companies venturing abroad have done so in sectors where natural resources or unskilled labor were irrelevant or non-existent. Finally, countries such as Brazil, South Africa, and Thailand (Chapters 8, 9, and 11) represent intermediate cases on this spectrum.

From a theoretical standpoint, the first type of EMNEs did not pose a significant problem. That is, to the extent that firms had access to internationally scarce but domestically abundant resources they would be able to compensate for the disadvantage of competing with foreign firms in their own markets mainly based on cost differentials. Significantly more puzzling were cases where these sources of competitive advantage were irrelevant. In order to provide plausible explanations for the emergence of these latter kinds of EMNEs, a number of theories were advanced. These early theories of the EMNE pointed at the gradual process of technological accumulation that developing-country based companies enjoyed from interacting with developed-country MNEs operating in their countries. Learning from these companies, it was argued, gave developing-country firms the capacity to eventually venture abroad (Lall 1983; Wells 1983). However, these theories are hard pressed to explain how firms from emerging markets would be able to compete with their "masters" in sectors where cost differentials are not the key driver for competitiveness. Later authors have pointed out that idiosyncratic governance structures such as corporate family groups can fill the institutional voids existing in some developing countries (Khanna and Rivkin 2001; Luo 2003). In a similar vein, skillful use of individual social networks has been described as a substitute for poorly functioning institutions (Boisot and Child 1996; Ahlstrom and Bruton 2006; Yiu *et al.* 2007). To the extent that the architecture and use of these networks is culturally rooted, they help explain the emergence of EMNEs. Still another important explanation for the emergence of EMNEs turns around the argument of poor institutions as a constraint on the international expansion of firms. Authors such as Narayanan and Khanna have argued that it is precisely because institutions are weak that firms in developing markets need to develop a particular set of capabilities to successfully operate in their *domestic* market. To the extent that these capabilities happen to be relevant in other developing countries (i.e. pass the RATs test), horizontal or down-market EMNEs may emerge. However, they are unlikely to explain how EMNEs can successfully expand into countries with stronger and more complete institutions. At the organizational level of analysis, EMNEs are explained by some authors as the result of technological and organizational leapfrogs. This is a central thesis in Amsden's work (1989, 2001), for example. As latecomers, EMNEs are not constrained by past investment decisions or by outdated mental maps of the competitive environment (Barr *et al.* 1992; Tripsas and Gavetti 2000). In so far as developing-market firms could access key technologies and knowledge by purchasing them in the open markets, through their suppliers, or through other firm acquisitions (Vermeulen and Barkema 2001), they might find themselves in a better competitive position than rival developed-country MNEs. Finally, at the individual level of analysis, EMNEs are portrayed as being strongly dependent on leaders that, having grown up in the home country, have studied or worked in more developed markets. Their experience as boundary spanners, it is argued, makes them better able to spot opportunities in foreign countries that can successfully be satisfied by emerging-market firms operating abroad.

Most of the theories providing an explanation for the emergence of EMNEs are still in the process of being tested empirically and, as a result, it is difficult to evaluate their potency and scope conditions. Nevertheless, we find that the factors enumerated above provide EMNEs, at best, a temporary advantage and, as a result, may explain the emergence but not the sustainability of EMNEs. For example, EMNEs that base their international competitive advantage on the basis of privileged access to natural resources or cheap unskilled labor are, almost by definition, non-sustainable: natural resources are finite and wage differentials with more advanced markets may narrow quickly as emerging markets develop. The second group of explanations provided above is similarly limited in its capacity to explain how EMNEs may maintain, let alone improve, their initial competitive edge. For example, relying on an individual's social networks severely limits the growth potential of a firm. Similarly, advantages stemming from being latecomers to a particular industry start to disappear the moment a firm makes its first investment or commits to a particular strategy. The disappearance of this type of advantage may be particularly dramatic in sectors characterized by fast technological change.

Given the fleeting nature of the factors that have been used to explain the emergence of EMNEs, we think it is necessary to account also for the mechanisms that explicate the renewal of these companies' initial competitive advantage. The study of these mechanisms – largely related to the creation, integration, and diffusion of knowledge within the organization – is not new to the IB field (Barkema *et al.* 1997; Barkema and Vermeulen 1998; Vermeulen and Barkema 2001). In fact, these topics have represented the core of the research agenda of the IB community in the past decade. What we think *is* new and valuable is the integration of both strands of research in a way that acknowledges the differential traits of firms born in emerging markets.

In the following section we present the case of CEMEX, the Mexican cement and concrete producer. Through this example, we want to make two main propositions. First, that EMNEs' initial competitive advantage may be based on elements other than privileged access to scarce or cheap resources. Second, and most important, that in order to explain how EMNEs are capable of sustaining and improving their international competitive position, current theories of the EMNE need to explain how these companies are able to renew the capabilities that allowed them to venture into foreign markets. The CEMEX example places emphasis on the fact that these sources of capability renewal are as likely to originate in the foreign markets where the firm operates as in its home market, and on the firm's ability to capture and incorporate this learning throughout the system.

Our model is one of exploration, exploitation, and enhancement in a continuous learning cycle, in many ways harking back to Penrose's (1995) vision of the MNE, enhanced by March's (1991) insight.

The CEMEX case[1]

On June 7, 2007, Mexico-based CEMEX won a majority stake in Australia's Rinker Group. The $15.3 billion takeover, which came on top of the major acquisition in 2005 of the RMC Corporation – then the world's largest ready-made concrete company and the single largest purchaser of cement – made CEMEX the world's largest supplier of building materials. This growth also rewarded CEMEX's shareholders handsomely. In the three-year period beginning June 2004, CEMEX's share price shot up from $13.50 to $37, resulting in a compound annual growth rate of 40 percent and a total annual shareholder return since CEMEX's debut on the New York Stock Exchange in 1999 through 2007 of 24 percent – which would have been substantially higher from a starting point in the 1980s or early 1990s.

CEMEX's success was not only noteworthy for a company based in an emerging economy, but also in an industry where the emergence of an EMNE as a global leader cannot be explained by cost arbitrage. Given cement's low value-to-weight ratio, little output moves across national boundaries.

---

[1] This section draws on Lessard and Reavis (2007), an MIT Sloan case written by Don Lessard and Cate Reavis with the collaboration of Rafel Lucea and Rodrigo Canales. We are grateful for CEMEX's willingness to collaborate in the development of this case, and particularly to Ricardo Naya, MIT SF 2007, who had been PMI manager for CEMEX, for providing key insights regarding CEMEX's journey. We have also benefitted substantially from the cases on CEMEX written by Lee and Hoyt (2005); Ghemawat and Matthews (1999); Podolny and Roberts (1999); and, Spulber (2007).

In this section, we review the development of CEMEX's growing international footprint, and the associated learning process, in four stages as identified in the timeline in Table 10.1. Particular emphasis is placed on how CEMEX has exploited its core competencies, initially generated at home, and enhanced them, learning from new countries, to begin the cycle again.

Laying the groundwork for internationalization

In the twenty-five years leading up to the Rinker deal, CEMEX had evolved from a small, privately owned, cement-focused Mexican company of 6,500 employees with $275 million in revenue to a publicly traded global leader, with 67,000 employees, a presence in fifty countries, and $21.7 billion in annual revenue in 2007.

Well before its first significant step toward international expansion in 1992, CEMEX had developed a set of core competencies that would shape its later trajectory, including strong operational capabilities based on engineering and IT, and a culture of transparency. It also had mastered the art of acquisition and integration within Mexico, having grown through acquisitions over the years.[2] Between 1987 and 1989 alone, it spent $1 billion in order to solidify its position at home.

The 1982 crash undercut the state-led and nationally focused economic model that had been predominant in Mexico, prompting the process of entering GATT (General Agreement on Tariffs and Trade), the precursor of the WTO. When current CEO Lorenzo Zambrano assumed this post in 1985, Mexico had already begun the process of opening up its economy, culminating with its entry into NAFTA. Recognizing that these events would significantly change the Mexican cement industry from a national to a global game, Zambrano began preparing the firm for the global fight. This first step would involve

---

[2] CEMEX was formed in 1931 from a merger between Cementos Hidalgo and Cementos Portland Monterrey. Later acquisitions and domestic expansion activity included: 1966–1967 acquisition of Cemento Maya's plants in Merida, Yucatan (Southeast Mexico) and construction of new plants in Torreon, Coahuila, and Ciudad Valles, San Luis Potosi (Central Eastern); 1976, acquisition of Cementos Guadalajaras' three plants (Central Western); 1987, acquisition of Cementos Anahuac; and 1989, acquisition of Cementos Tolteca (Distrito Federal).

Table 10.1. *CEMEX internationalization timeline*

Year	Stage	Key events	Key steps in internationalization process (italics indicate acquisition)
	Laying the groundwork		
1982		Mexican crash	
1985		Zambrano named president	
1989		Consolidates Mexican market position with acquisition of *Tolteca*	
1989		Anti-dumping penalties imposed on exports to US	
	Stepping out		
1992			Spain
1994			Venezuela
1995		Mexican recession	
	Growing up		
1996			Colombia
1996		Death of chief financial officer	"PMI Mexico"
1997–1999			Philippines, Indonesia, Egypt, Chile, Panama, Costa Rica
1999		New York Stock Exchange listing	
	Stepping up		
2000			*Southdown* (US)
2005			*RMC* (UK-based global ready-mix)
2007			*Rinker* (Australian/US-based global concrete, aggregates)

divestiture of non-related business and disposal of non-core assets. CEMEX also began "exploring" opportunities in foreign markets through exports, which required a fairly aggressive program of building or buying terminal facilities in other markets. Finally, the company began laying the groundwork for global expansion by investing in a satellite communication system, CEMEXNET, in order to avoid Mexico's erratic, insufficient, and expensive phone service, and to allow all of CEMEX's eleven cement factories in Mexico to communicate in a more coordinated and fluid way (Lee and Hoyt 2005). Along with the communication system, an Executive Information System was implemented in 1990. All managers were required to input manufacturing data – including production, sales and administration, inventory and delivery – that could be viewed by other managers. The system enabled CEO Zambrano to conduct "virtual inspections" of CEMEX's operations, including the operating performance of individual factories, from his laptop computer.

Stepping out

In 1989, CEMEX completed a major step in consolidating its position in the Mexican cement market by acquiring Mexican cement producer Tolteca, making it the second largest Mexican cement producer and putting it on the top ten list of world cement producers. At the time of the acquisition, CEMEX was facing mounting competition in Mexico. Just three months before the deal with Tolteca was finalized, Swiss-based Holderbank (Holcim), which held 49% of Mexico's third largest cement producer Apasco (19% market share), announced its intention to increase its cement capacity by 2 million tons (*Neue Zürcher Zeitung* 1989). This, along with easing foreign investment regulations that would allow Holderbank to acquire a majority stake in Apasco, threatened CEMEX's position in Mexico (Barham 2002). At the time, CEMEX accounted for only 33% of the Mexican market while 91% of its sales were domestic.

In addition to these mounting threats in its home market, CEMEX was confronted with trade sanctions in the US, its largest market outside of Mexico. Exports to the US market began in the early 1970s, but by the late 1980s, as the US economy and construction industry were experiencing a downturn, the US International Trade Commission slapped CEMEX with a 58% countervailing duty on exports from

Mexico to the US, later reduced to 31% (Ghemawat and Matthews 1999).

In 1992, CEMEX acquired a majority stake in two Spanish cement companies, Valenciana and Sanson, for $1.8 billion, giving it a majority market share (28 percent) in one of Europe's largest cement markets (Ghemawat and Matthews 1999). The primary motivation for entering Spain was a strategic response to Holcim's growing market share in Mexico. As Hector Medina, CEMEX Executive Vice President of Planning and Finance, explained, "Major European competitors had a very strong position in Spain and the market had become important for them" (Podolny and Roberts 1999).

A further important reason for the acquisition was that Spain during this time was an investment-grade country, having just entered the European Monetary Union, while domestic interest rates in Mexico were hovering at 40 percent, and Mexican issuers faced a country risk premium of at least 6 percent for offshore dollar financing (Hossie 1990). Operating in Spain enabled CEMEX to tap this cheaper source of capital not only to finance the acquisition of Valenciana and Sanson, but also to fund its growth elsewhere at affordable rates. While this benefit could have been obtained in any European Community country, Spain offered considerable opportunities for growth and was relatively affordable. In addition, the linguistic and cultural ties between the two countries made it a sensible strategic move.

In order to pay off the debt taken on to fund the acquisition, CEMEX set ambitious targets for cost recovery. However, it soon discovered that by introducing its current Mexican-based best practices to the Spanish operation, it was able to reduce costs and increase plant efficiency to a much greater extent, with annual savings/benefits of $120 million (Duncan 1993) and an increase in operating margins from 7% to 24% (Podolny and Roberts 1999).

Thus, while the primary motive for the Spanish acquisition was to respond to a competitive European entry in its home market, a major source of value resulting from the acquisition was the improvement in operating results due to the transfer of best practices from a supposedly less advanced country to a supposedly more advanced one. CEMEX discovered that its home-grown operating capabilities passed the RATs test and generated considerable value.

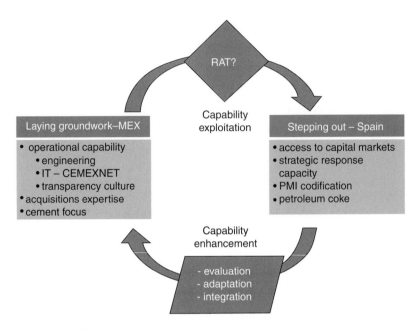

Figure 10.1 Stepping out

Further, although it had acquired and integrated many firms within Mexico, this acquisition, because of its size and the fact that it was in a foreign country, forced CEMEX to formalize and codify its Post-Merger Integration (PMI) process. CEMEX also enhanced is capabilities through direct learning from Spain. The company discovered, for example, that the two Spanish companies were unusually efficient due to the use of petroleum coke as their main source of fuel. Within two years, the vast majority of CEMEX plants began using petroleum coke as a part of the company's energy-efficiency program (Chavez 2006).

Figure 10.1 depicts the improvement in Spanish operations resulting from the adoption of Mexican best practices as a single "forward" learning loop (exploiting existing capabilities), the resource enhancement to all of CEMEX from Spain's lower cost of capital as a single "reverse" enhancement loop, and the improvement of the PMI process as double loop learning regarding the PMI process.

Accelerating internationalization and consolidating the CEMEX Way

CEMEX's move into Spain was followed soon after by acquisitions in Venezuela, Colombia, and the Caribbean in the mid-1990s, and the Philippines and Indonesia in the late 1990s. These acquisitions, by and large, could be seen as exploiting CEMEX's core capabilities, which now combined learning from the company's operations in Mexico and Spain.

The PMI process also underwent a significant change during this period. Attempts to impose the same management processes and systems used in Mexico on the newly acquired Colombian firms resulted in an exodus of local talent. As a result of the difficult integration process that ensued, CEMEX learned that alongside transferring best practices that had been standardized throughout the company, it needed to make a concerted effort to learn best practices from acquired companies, implementing them when appropriate. This process became known as the CEMEX Way.

The CEMEX Way, also known as internal benchmarking, was the core set of best business practices with which CEMEX conducted business throughout its operations. More a corporate philosophy than a tangible process, the CEMEX Way was driven by five guidelines:

- Efficiently manage the global knowledge base.
- Identify and disseminate best practices.
- Standardize business processes.
- Implement key information and Internet-based technologies.
- Foster innovation.

As part of the integration phase of the PMI, the CEMEX Way process involved the dispatch of a number of multinational standardization teams made up of experts in specific functional areas (Planning Finance, IT, Human Resources), in addition to a group leader, and IT and Human Resources support. Each team was overseen by a CEMEX executive at the vice president level (Whitaker and Catalano 2001).

The CEMEX Way process was arguably what made CEMEX's PMI process so unique. While typically 20% of an acquired company's practices were retained, instead of eliminating the remaining 80% in one swift motion, CEMEX Way teams cataloged and stored those practices in a centralized database. Those processes were then benchmarked against internal and external practices. Processes that were deemed "superior" (typically two to three per standardization group or fifteen to thirty new practices per acquisition) became enterprise standards and, therefore, a part of the CEMEX Way. As one industry observer noted, CEMEX's strategy sent an important message: "We are overriding your business processes to get you quickly on board, but within the year we are likely to take some part of your process, adapt it to the CEMEX system and roll it out across operations in [multiple] countries" (Austin 2004). The cumulative effect of this process has been substantial. By some estimates, 70 percent of CEMEX's practices have been adopted from previous acquisitions (Whitaker and Catalano 2001).

A key feature of the PMI process is the strong reliance that CEMEX places on middle-level managers both to diffuse CEMEX's standard practices and to identify existing capabilities in the acquired firms that might contribute to the improvement of CEMEX's capability platform. PMI teams are formed ad hoc for each acquisition. Functional experts in each area (finance, marketing, production, logistics, etc.) are selected from the operations that CEMEX has across the world. These managers are then relieved of their day-to-day responsibilities and sent, for periods varying from a few weeks to several months, to the country/ies where the newly acquired company operates.

Because these managers are the ones who *do* at home what they are teaching the newly acquired firm's managers, they are the best teachers as well as the most likely CEMEX employees to identify which of the standard practices of the acquired firm might make a positive contribution if adapted and integrated into the CEMEX way. On the other hand, because they are seen as the best and the brightest within CEMEX, these managers have the legitimacy to propose and advocate for changes in the firm's operation standards in a way that no other managers could. Hence, as in Nonaka's (1988) middle-up-down management, PMI team members are low enough in the organization that they are in a unique position to identify and evaluate different ways of doing things. At the same time, however, these managers are high enough in the organization that they can effectively "sell" to corporate-level managers the value of changing a particular practice.

Drawing key people from multiple countries to form these teams represents a significant challenge for what CEMEX calls "legacy operations". Since these positions are not covered with new hires, and lowering performance is – definitely – not in the realm of possibility, ongoing operations have to find ways to do the same work with fewer people. This is the cost of assembling these teams with managers who are key to the daily functioning of CEMEX operations.

A significant step in consolidating the CEMEX Way and making "One CEMEX" a global reality occurred as the result of the tragic death in 1996 of CEMEX's chief financial officer, Gustavo Caballero. Hector Medina, then general manager of Mexican operations, took over the role, and Francisco Garza, who had been general manager in Venezuela, was named to head Mexican operations. When Garza took charge of the Mexican operations he decided to "PMI Mexico", to apply the PMI process to Mexico as if it had just been acquired. Roughly forty people broken down into ten functional teams spent between two and three months dedicated to improving the Mexican operation. Savings of $85 million were identified (Podolny and Roberts 1999). More importantly, it clearly established the principle of learning and continuous improvement through the punctuated PMI process and the continuous implantation of the CEMEX Way.

Improvements resulting from the CEMEX Way were not limited to operational processes. During the 1990s, CEMEX also developed a branded cement strategy in Mexico that addressed the specific needs of customers for bag cement. While bulk cement accounted for roughly 80 percent of CEMEX's cement sales in developed countries, bagged cement represented the same percentage in developing countries like Mexico, reflecting the fact that many householders built their own houses (Lee and Hoyt 2005). These customers were willing to pay a premium for known quality and convenient distribution, and CEMEX steadily introduced value-added features for these customers. While this unique business model was developed primarily in response to the characteristics of Mexican buyers, it clearly passed the RATs test with respect to other emerging markets where CEMEX was expanding, and drew in relevant innovations from a number of other countries.

Finally, with a growing number of plants and markets on the Caribbean rim, CEMEX began to actively exploit the capacity for cement trading to smoothen and pool demand, economizing on capacity and raising average utilization rates in an industry notorious

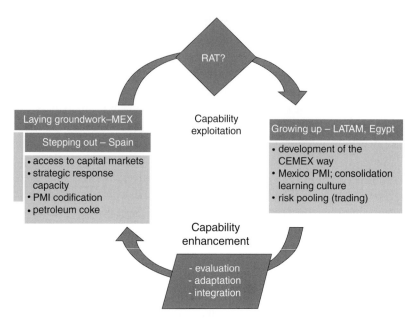

Figure 10.2 Growing up

for large swings in output in line with macroeconomic fluctuations.[3] Figure 10.2 summarizes the exploit-enhance cycle over this period.

Stepping up

Toward the end of the 1990s, CEMEX found that there were few acquisition targets that met its criteria of market attractiveness and "closeness" to CEMEX in terms of institutional stability and culture at a reasonable price, and began to consider diversification into other activities. However, in order to "shake up" its strategic thinking, it made a series of changes in the way it explored potential acquisitions, including asking BCG, its long-time strategic advisor, to assign a new set of partners. One important resulting change was to redefine large markets, such as the US, into regions. Once this was done, the US, which CEMEX planners had viewed as a slow-growing market with

---

[3] For a description of how CEMEX was able to turn an environmental disadvantage – the macroeconomic volatility that has characterized the Mexican economy and many of the emerging markets in which it has invested – into a source of competitive advantage see Lessard and Lucea (2007).

little fit with CEMEX, was transformed into a set of regions, some with growth and other characteristics more aligned with the rapidly growing markets CEMEX was used to. This set the foundation for the acquisition of Texas-based Southdown, making CEMEX North America's largest cement producer.

Another change was to shift the emphasis in the way that performance was measured from margins, which had made cement appear much more attractive than concrete or aggregates, to return on investment, which in many cases reversed the apparent attractiveness of different businesses. With this reframing, other targets were identified – most prominently RMC, a UK-based, ready-mixed concrete global leader.

On March 1, 2005, CEMEX finalized its $5.8 billion acquisition of RMC. This acquisition, which surprised many in the industry who assumed that RMC would be acquired by a European firm, was CEMEX's first acquisition of another internationally diversified, as opposed to single-country, firm.

To prevail, CEMEX had to pay a 39 percent premium (Grancher 2005), and the financial markets did not respond favorably. CEMEX's share price dropped 10 percent within hours of the announcement, and Moody's indicated that it was putting CEMEX on credit watch for a possible downgrade, voicing concern that the size of the RMC acquisition would distract management from its goal of cutting the company's debt (Derham 2004).

The acquisition of RMC significantly changed CEMEX's business landscape. The deal gave the company a much wider geographic presence in developed and developing countries alike – most notably France, Germany, and a number of Eastern European countries. Analysts predicted that as a percentage of product revenue, cement would fall from 72% to 54% and aggregates and ready-mixed concrete would nearly double from 23% to 42% (Akram *et al.* 2004). Meanwhile, revenue from CEMEX's Mexican operations would fall from 36% prior to the deal to just 17%. (Ironically, during the company's annual meeting in July 2004, Zambrano told a group of analysts that, "CEMEX does not have to diversify to grow; we are an integrated cement company today and we will be a more integrated cement company tomorrow. Only bigger, more profitable, and more valuable.")

Financially, RMC was suffering. The company recorded a net income loss of over $200 million in 2003, and was trading at six times

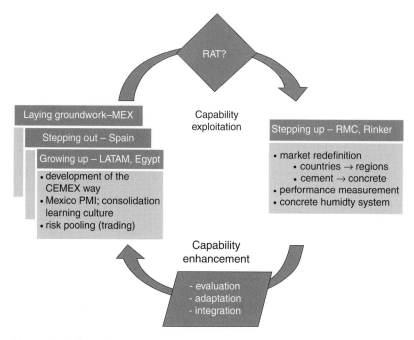

Figure 10.3 Stepping up

EBITDA (Earnings Before Interest, Taxes, Depreciation, and Amort-ization), compared to the industry average of 8.5–9 times (Derham 2004). RMC's profit margin of 3.6% was far below the ready-made concrete average of 6% to 8%.

Culturally, RMC was the polar opposite of CEMEX. RMC was a highly decentralized company with significant differences in business model across countries, organizational structure, operating processes, and corporate culture. CEMEX, in contrast, brought the CEMEX Way and a single operating/engineering culture that connected much more readily at the plant and operation level than RMC.

And yet, despite all of RMC's challenges, CEMEX was able to work its PMI "magic" in a very short period of time. Within one year, CEMEX had delivered more than the $200 million in synergy savings that it had initially promised, and it expected to produce more than $380 million of savings in 2007 (Prokopy 2006). CEMEX had clearly joined the big league, yet the imprint of its early years remained very strong.

In 2007, CEMEX took another major step, acquiring control of the Rinker Corporation. Rinker did not suffer the same lack of learning processes and cultural integration as RMC and thus at least some analysts questioned whether CEMEX would be able to work the same magic once again. Only time will tell. Figure 10.3 summarizes CEMEX's development during this final period.

Extending the theory of EMNEs

In the first section we briefly reviewed the current theories of the EMNE. We argued that they provide a plausible story of how these firms are able to take their first steps in the international arena but that they are deficient in explaining how sustained success is achieved. In the section titled "The CEMEX case," we have traced the corporate history of CEMEX and highlighted the specific mechanisms that have made this company one of the most successful EMNEs in the world. We consider this case to be of particular interest because in the cement and concrete industry privileged access to natural resources is *not* a determining factor for market success. As a consequence, the CEMEX case brings to the fore the mechanisms by which intangible and organizational capabilities are systemically exploited and enhanced. In this section we take a step back from the particularities of the case and propose a more general framework to explain the emergence and sustainability of EMNEs.

The starting point of the model – see Figure 10.4 – is no different, in the abstract, from classic theories of the MNE: the interaction of CSAs and FSAs determines the original set of capabilities, or capability platform, on which firms compete in their domestic market. What differs significantly from earlier theoretical approaches is that because of the changes in the macro context reviewed in the section titled "Why do MNEs (and EMNEs) exist?", the nature of what may constitute a CSA or FSA has significantly changed. In the case of developing economies, lack of large domestic markets, limited indigenous technological development or weak institutions are no longer impossible hurdles to overcome.

What seems indisputable, though, is that domestic country conditions will have a significant effect on the shape of the initial capability platform developed by a firm. This original capability platform will allow emerging-market firms to initially compete in their domestic markets. In addition, and to the extent that this capability platform travels well internationally, it will allow firms to expand beyond their home-country borders. Three conditions are necessary for this to

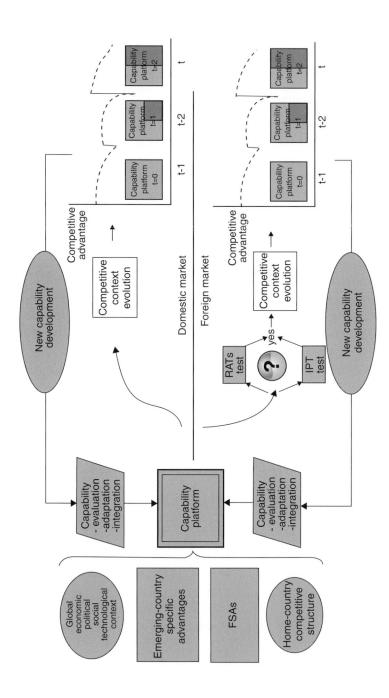

Figure 10.4 Sustainable advantage through capability development and recombination.
Notes: RATs = (Capabilities) Relevant, Appropriable, Transferable; IPT = (Internationalization) Imperative, Possibility, Trap

happen. First, this domestically developed set of capabilities needs to be relevant to customers in other countries. That is, the value proposition that the firm is able to offer to customers in other countries has to be superior, in the aggregate, to other alternatives available to these customers. Second, these capabilities need to be transferable across borders. This is not a trivial point since some operational processes, technologies, and business practices may face strong political, regulatory, or cultural barriers that severely constrain their adoption in other countries. Finally, the rents resulting from the exploitation of these capabilities in the foreign country need to be appropriable by the firm. Barriers to appropriability are also extremely varied, ranging from different regulatory regimes (e.g. regarding patent or trademark protection), to deeply ingrained social values (think of the popular revolts against water privatization in several parts of the world), to problems such as corruption or open conflict.

These three conditions, which make up the RATs test, will determine whether the original capability platform of an emerging-market firm can travel well internationally. It is important to note that they are country specific. That is, the capability platform of a particular company may pass the RATs test for one country but not for another.

In addition to passing the RATs test, EMNEs soon discover whether internationalization for them is an imperative, a possibility, or a trap. The typical case of internationalization being an imperative is that of companies with small domestic markets. In this book, for example, we see how Israeli software companies were born global or had to, very quickly, find more sizable markets abroad. Similarly, business models of telecommunications companies in Nordic countries incorporated, almost from the beginning, a strong international perspective. However, internationalization can also be a trap in those cases where foreign markets require extreme localization. More often, though, the course to follow is more ambiguous, and internationalization may not be a clear option to follow. One of the most obvious sources of ambiguity stems from the uncertainty in properly evaluating foreign market opportunities and the relevance of one's own capabilities abroad.

Firms operating in competitive markets, in the neoclassical sense of the word, see their competitive advantage eroded over time due to a variety of competitive forces. In order to sustain or improve their competitive position, firms need to adapt and renew their capability platform. This process usually takes place in a punctuated, rather than gradual, manner. While this argument is at the core of the dynamic capabilities literature, what is important in the case of EMNEs is that this capability renewal is as likely to originate in the home market as in the host markets where the firm operates. Indeed, classic theories of the multinational assumed that capabilities originated at the core of the organization, which resided in the home country, and were transferred to the foreign subsidiaries where they were exploited. As argued above, more recent research has strongly challenged this view by demonstrating the crucial role played by the periphery of the firm in the renewal of key capabilities. This capability renewal may come from two main sources. The first one, in line with the resource-seeking motives for venturing abroad, is achieved by accessing resources through the subsidiary that are not available in the home market. In the CEMEX case, this is clearly illustrated by the access to European capital markets that the firm gained through the acquisitions of the Spanish companies Valenciana and Sanson in 1992. A second source of capability renewal stems from the responses developed by foreign subsidiaries to the domestic challenges and opportunities they face. Particularly relevant in this respect is the literature that studies the emergence of "centers of excellence" at the subsidiary level (Fratocchi and Holm 1998; Nobel and Birkinshaw 1998; Kuemmerle 1999; Frost *et al.* 2002), the changing roles of subsidiaries as a consequence of sequential investments abroad (Kogut 1993; Chang 1995; Birkinshaw and Hood 1998), transfers of best practices among units (Szulanski 1996), and how subsidiaries draw from and contribute to the knowledge pool of their local industry cluster (Almeida 1996; Almeida and Kogut 1996). It is quite striking that in spite of this broad body of recent research, most of the literature on EMNEs strongly focuses on the elements that allow emerging-market firms to take their first steps in the global arena but is notably silent with regard to the benefits that these companies derive from operating abroad.

The last element of our framework involves the transference of these locally developed new capabilities to the rest of the organization. In order to do so, it is necessary to establish formal and informal processes to evaluate the relevance, transferability, and appropriability of the new capabilities to other markets – and, indeed, to shape these emerging capabilities so that they will be relevant, appropriable, and transferable (the RATs test in reverse). Next, it is necessary to integrate these new capabilities in a coherent manner within the original capability platform. And finally, it is necessary to establish the mechanisms to diffuse these practices to the rest of the organization. It is on this continuous process of capability platform exploitation-enhancement-exploitation that the sustainability of the MNE is built. CEMEX is perhaps an extreme case of institutionalization of this co-evolutionary process. Indeed, its extremely centralized structure and emphasis on documentation, evaluation, and standardization of new practices across countries makes this company something of a Weberian ideal case. Nevertheless, research on the transfer of practices among subsidiaries (Szulanski 1996) and from subsidiaries to headquarters (Gupta and Govindarajan 1991; Gupta and Govindarajan 1999), certainly supports our argument that new capabilities do, in fact, originate in places other than the home country and that they selectively blend with the original capability platform of the firm. It is through this process of capability renewal that MNEs are able to sustain their competitive advantage at home and abroad.

What is then special about EMNEs? As argued above, the original domestic conditions that an emerging-market firm encounters strongly determine the original capability platform on which its international competitive advantage will be based. Research on organizational imprinting (Stinchcombe 1965; Swaminathan 1996; Marquis 2003) and managerial cognition (Barr *et al.* 1992; Tripsas and Gavetti 2000) has convincingly shown that early events in the history of an organization – including the conditions that determined the configuration of the original capability platform – have a long-lasting effect on its structure, predominant practices, and the dominant mindset of executives. As a consequence, what is different about EMNEs is that even as their capability platforms evolve, they are likely to continue to reflect some of the key features that made them internationally competitive in the first place. In CEMEX's case, for example, the obsession with standardized operational excellence can be traced back to the early days of the company. In a country characterized by poor infrastructure, weak institutions, loose business practices, and urban traffic chaos, product and processes standardization was the strategy that allowed CEMEX to differentiate itself from other local competitors and achieve dominance in its home market. Similarly, the emphasis on controlling the operations from the center and a rigid vertical structure reflects the weight that family control and social status still carry in Mexican society. These are traits that will surely not go away any time soon and that will keep differentiating CEMEX from its competitors from developed countries.

While this framework tries to explain and to generalize the processes through which EMNEs gain and sustain internationally relevant sources of competitive advantage, there are a number of scope conditions that we think apply. The first one is that we would expect this framework to be most relevant for EMNEs from countries at middle levels of development. A second element of note in successful EMNEs is that the development of new capabilities and the initiation of the feedback loop described above is a phenomenon that tends to take place at intermediate levels of the organization. Consistent with Nonaka (1988), we find that it is usually managers sitting between the corporate and the purely operational level of the organization that are better suited to identify opportunities for new capability development and to evaluate their potential value in other markets where the company operates.

Conclusions

This chapter tries to achieve three main goals that we think contribute to a better understanding of the EMNE phenomenon. The first objective has been to briefly review the current explanations for the existence of emerging-market multinationals and position them within the broader international management literature. We note that current theories of the EMNE provide plausible explanations of how these companies are able to initiate their international journey. However, they are of less help in understanding how they are able to sustain or even improve their international performance. This is particularly troublesome when the competitive advantage of EMNEs is not based on privileged control of internationally valuable resources in the domestic market.

Our second objective was to provide a factual story of one EMNE that has been able to successfully compete with MNEs from developed countries in their own home markets. While CEMEX's evolution is clearly unique, it helps us identify a number of processes that seem to be relevant in explaining how EMNEs may compete in the world market on factors other than cheap domestic labor or control of internationally scarce natural resources.

This CEMEX case also helped us to flesh out an expanded conception of the sources of competitiveness of EMNEs – our third objective. The framework we proposed in the section titled "Extending the theory of EMNEs" generalizes the insights gained from the CEMEX case and emphasizes the relevance of the co-evolutionary process by which EMNEs renew and upgrade their original capability platform. Initially, EMNEs gain access to international markets by exploiting their domestically generated but internationally relevant capability platforms. To the extent that they have to respond to competitive challenges or gain access to new resources in these foreign markets, their original capability platform will be enhanced. It is only through this co-evolutionary process of capability exploitation-enhancement-exploitation, where the sources of capability enhancement are both foreign and domestic, that it is possible to explain the persistent competitiveness of EMNEs in the global arena.

References

Agmon, T. and D. Lessard (1981). "Investor Recognition of Corporate International Diversification – Reply." *Journal of Finance* 36(1): 191–192.

Ahlstrom, D. and G. D. Bruton (2006). "Venture Capital in Emerging Economies: Networks and Institutional Change." *Entrepreneurship Theory and Practice* 30(2): 299–320.

Akram, I., P. Roger, and D. McGoey (2004). "Global Cement Update: Mexican Wave," Deutsche Bank, November 26, 2004.

Almeida, P. (1996). "Knowledge Sourcing by Foreign Multinationals: Patent Citation Analysis in the U.S. Semiconductor Industry." *Strategic Management Journal* 17 (Winter Special Issue): 155–165.

Almeida, P. and B. Kogut (1996). "Localization of Knowledge and the Mobility of Engineers in Regional Networks." *Management Science* 45(7): 905–917.

Amsden, A. (1989). *Asia's Next Giant: South Korea and Late Industrialization.* Oxford: Oxford University Press.

Amsden, A. (2001). *The Rise of the "Rest": Challenge to West from Late Industrializing Economies.* Oxford: Oxford University Press.

Arora, A., A. Fosfuri, and A. Gambardella (2001). *Markets for Technology: The Economics of Innovation and Corporate Strategy.* Cambridge, MA, The MIT Press.

Austin, M. (2004). "Global Integration the CEMEX Way," *Corporate Dealmaker*, February 2004.

Barham, J. (2002). "An Intercontinental Mix," *Latin Finance*, April 1, 2002.

Barkema, H.G., O. Shenkar, F. Vermeulen, and J.H.J. Bell (1997). "Working Abroad, Working with Others: How Firms Learn to Operate International Joint Ventures." *Academy of Management Journal* 40(2): 426–442.

Barkema, H.G. and F. Vermeulen (1998). "International Expansion through Start-up or Acquisition: A Learning Perspective." *Academy of Management Journal* 41(1): 7–26.

Barr, P., J.L. Stimpert, and A.S. Huff (1992). "Cognitive Change, Strategic Action and Organizational Renewal." *Strategic Management Journal* 13 (Special Issue): 15–36.

Birkinshaw, J.M. and N. Hood (1998). "Multinational Subsidiary Development: Capability Evolution and Charter Change in Foreign-owned Subsidiary Companies." *Academy of Management Review* 23(4): 729–754.

Boisot, M. and J. Child (1996). "From Fiefs to Clans and Network Capitalism: Explaining China's Emerging Economic Order." *Administrative Science Quarterly* 41(4): 600–628.

Buckley, P. and M. Casson (1976). *The Future of the Multinational Enterprise*. London, MacMillan.

Caves, R. (1982). *Multinational Enterprises and Economic Analysis*. Cambridge and New York, Cambridge University Press.

Chang, S.J. (1995). "International Expansion Strategy of Japanese Firms: Capability Building through Sequential Entry." *Academy of Management Journal* 38(2): 383–407.

Chavez, F., (2006). "CEMEX Takes the High Road," *NYSE Magazine*, October/November.

Derham, M.T. (2004). "The CEMEX Surprise," *Latin Finance*, November 1.

Duncan, J. (1993). "CEMEX Wrings Savings from Spanish Purchases," *Reuters*, March 19.

Dunning, J. (1977)."Trade, Location of Economic Activity and the MNE: A Search for an Eclectic Approach." *The International Allocation of Economic Activity*. B. Ohlin, P. Hesselborn, and P. Wijkman (eds.). London, MacMillan: 395–418.

Dunning, J.H. (1998). "Location and the Multinational Enterprise: A Neglected Factor?" *Journal of International Business Studies* 29(1): 45–66.

Fratocchi, L. and U. Holm (1998). "Centers of Excellence in the International Firm." *Multinational Corporate Evolution and Subsidiary*

Development. J. M. Birkinshaw and N. Hood (eds.). London, Mac-Millan: 189–212.

Frost, T. S., J. M. Birkinshaw, and P. C. Ensign (2002). "Centers of Excellence in Multinational Corporations." *Strategic Management Journal* 23(11): 997–1018.

Ghemawat, P. and J. L. Matthews (1999). "The Globalization of CEMEX." *Harvard Business School Publishing*, Harvard Business School Case No. 701–017.

Grancher, R. A. (2005). "U.S. Cement: Development of an Integrated Business." *Cement Americas*, September 1.

Gupta, A. and V. Govindarajan (1991). "Knowledge Flows and the Structure of Control within Multinational Corporations." *Academy of Management Review* 16(4): 768–792.

Gupta, A. and V. Govindarajan (1999). "Feedback-seeking Behavior within Multinational Corporations." *Strategic Management Journal* 20(3): 205–225.

Hossie, L. (1990). "Remaking Mexico." *The Globe and Mail*, February 7.

Hymer, S. (1960)."The International Operations of National Firms: A Study of Direct Investments." Unpublished Ph.D. thesis, MIT.

Johanson, J. and J. E. Vahlne (1977). "Internationalization Process of Firm – Model of Knowledge Development and Increasing Foreign Market Commitments." *Journal of International Business Studies* 8(1): 23–32.

Khanna, T. and J. W. Rivkin (2001). "Estimating the Performance Effects of Business Groups in Emerging Markets." *Strategic Management Journal* 22(1): 45–74.

Kogut, B. (1989). "A Note on Global Strategies." *Strategic Management Journal* 10(4) (July–August): 383–389.

Kogut, B. (1993). "Foreign Direct Investment as a Sequential Process." *The Multinational Corporations in the 1980s*. C. P. Kindleberger and D. Audretsch (eds.). Cambridge, MA, The MIT Press.

Kuemmerle, W. (1999). "The Drivers of Foreign Direct Investment into Research and Development: An Empirical Investigation." *Journal of International Business Studies* 30(1): 1–24.

Lall, S. (1983). *The New Multinationals: The Spread of Third World Enterprises*. New York, John Wiley and Sons.

Lee, H. and D. Hoyt (2005). "CEMEX: Transforming a Basic Industry." *Harvard Business School Publishing*, Stanford Graduate School of Business Case No. GS-33.

Lessard, D. (1982). "Multinational Diversification and Direct Foreign Investment." *Multinational Business Finance*. D. K. Eiteman and A. Stonehill (eds.). Reading, MA, Addison Wesley.

Lessard, D. R. and R. Lucea (2007). "Embracing Risk as a Core Competence: The Case of CEMEX." Unpublished working paper, MIT Sloan School.

Lessard, D. R. and C. Reavis (2007). "Globalization the CEMEX Way." MIT Sloan Courseware 07-039.

Luo, Y. D. (2003). "Industrial Dynamics and Managerial Networking in an Emerging Market: The Case of China." *Strategic Management Journal* 24(13): 1315–1327.

March, J. G. (1991). "Exploration and Exploitation in Organizational Learning." *Organization Science* 2(1)(February): 71–87.

Marquis, C. (2003). "The Pressure of the Past: Network Imprinting in Intercorporate Communities." *Administrative Science Quarterly* 48: 655–689.

Narayanan, V. K. and L. Fahey (2005). "The Relevance of the Institutional Underpinnings of Porter's Five Forces Framework to Emerging Economies: An Epistemological Analysis." *Journal of Management Studies* 42(1): 207–223.

Neue Zürcher Zeitung (1989). "Holderbank of Switzerland Announces Major Investment Plans." October 13, 1989.

Nobel, R. and J. M. Birkinshaw (1998). "Patterns of Control and Communication in International Research and Development Units." *Strategic Management Journal* 19(5): 479–498.

Nonaka, I. (1988). "Toward Middle-Up-Down Management: Accelerating Information Creation." *Sloan Management Review*, Spring 1988.

Penrose, E. T. (1995). *The Theory of the Growth of the Firm*. Oxford: Oxford University Press.

Podolny, J. and J. Roberts (1999). "CEMEX S.A. de C.V.: Global Competition in a Local Business." *Harvard Business School Publishing*, Stanford Graduate School of Business Case No. S-IB-17.

Prokopy, S. (2006). "Merging the CEMEX Way." *Concrete Products*, May 1, 2006.

Rugman, A. (1981). *Inside the Multinationals*. New York, Columbia University Press.

Rugman, A. and T. L. Brewer (eds.) (2001). *The Oxford Handbook of International Business*. New York, Oxford University Press.

Siegel, J. (forthcoming). "Is There a Better Commitment Mechanism than Cross-Listings for Emerging Economy Firms? Evidence from Mexico." *Journal of International Business Studies*.

Spulber, D. F. (2007). *Global Competitive Strategy*. Cambridge, Cambridge University Press.

Stinchcombe, A. L. (1965). "Social Structure and Organizations." *Handbook of Organizations*. J. G. March (ed.). Chicago, Rand-McNally: 142–193.

Swaminathan, A. (1996). "Environmental Conditions at Founding and Organizational Mortality: A Trial-by-fire Model." *Academy of Management Journal* 39: 1350–1377.

Szulanski, G. (1996). "Exploring Internal Stickiness: Impediments to the Transfer of Best Practices Within the Firm." *Strategic Management Journal* 17 (Special Issue): 27–44.

Tripsas, M. and G. Gavetti (2000). "Capabilities, Cognition and Inertia: Evidence from Digital Imaging." *Strategic Management Journal* 21 (10–11): 1147–1161.

Vermeulen, F. and H. Barkema (2001). "Learning through Acquisitions." *Academy of Management Journal* 44(3): 457–476.

Vernon, R. (1966). "International Investment and International Trade in the Product Cycle." *Quarterly Journal of Economics* 80: 90–207.

Vernon, R. (1971). *Sovereignty at Bay, the Multinational Spread of U.S. Enterprises*. New York, Basic Books, Inc.

Wells, L. (1983). *Third World Multinationals*. Cambridge, MA, The MIT Press.

Whitaker, J. and R. Catalano (2001). "Growth Across Borders." *Corporate Strategy Board*, October 2001.

Yiu, D. W., C. M. Lau, and G. D. Bruton (2007). "International Venturing by Emerging Economy Firms: The Effects of Firm Capabilities, Home Country Networks, and Corporate Entrepreneurship." *Journal of International Business Studies* 38(4): 519–540.

Zaheer, S. (1995). "Overcoming the Liability of Foreignness." *Academy of Management Journal* 38(2): 341–363.

Zaheer, S. and E. Mosakowski (1997). "The Dynamics of the Liability of Foreignness: A Global Study of Survival in Financial Services." *Strategic Management Journal* 18(6): 439–463.

11 | *Thai multinationals: Entering the big league*

PAVIDA PANANOND[1]

The international expansion of companies from emerging markets is increasingly seen as a new defining feature of the global investment landscape. Southeast Asia is one region that has emerged as an important source of FDI. The region accounted for 14 per cent of the total outward FDI stock from developing countries in 2005 (UNCTAD 2007). Within Southeast Asia, Thailand came fourth, following Singapore, Malaysia, and Indonesia, in the 2005 ranking of outward FDI stock. Although Thailand's numbers appear modest when compared with its neighbours,[2] Thailand nonetheless is home to some large regional MNEs, including the CP (Charoen Pokphand) group which has long been one of the largest foreign investors in China. At the same time, the characteristics of Thai outward FDI are markedly different from those of their southern neighbours. While Singapore and Malaysia's outward FDI has been predominantly led by SOEs (so-called government-linked companies, GLCs, in the case of Singapore), Thai outward FDI has mainly been driven by the private sector. The development of Thai multinationals should therefore shed some light on the emergence of other multinationals from developing economies, whose home governments are not directly involved as active players in outward FDI.

This chapter explores the current status of Thailand's emerging multinationals and the challenges facing them in their international expansion through two levels of analysis: country and firm. First, we

---

[1] I would like to thank the organizers for the invitation and all the conference participants for their input. My special gratitude goes to Paul Beamish, Yair Aharoni, Ravi Ramamurti, Jitendra Singh, and Andrea Goldstein for their insightful comments on earlier drafts. The research assistance of Kanda Jaruwatanaskul is highly appreciated.

[2] OFDI stock in 2005 for Singapore, Malaysia, Indonesia, and Thailand were US$ 111 billion, US$ 44.5 billion, US$ 14 billion, and US$ 4 billion respectively (UNCTAD 2006, Table B.2)

seek to understand the emergence of Thai multinationals through an analysis of the country's outward FDI. Questions addressed include: where does Thai outward FDI go? and in which industries is it concentrated? We then explore the experience of Thai multinationals that have ventured abroad through four firm-level case studies. The case studies explore key aspects of these firms' international expansion, including their geographical spread, motives, and the nature of their competitive advantages. The firm-level case studies should reveal the dynamics of Thai multinationals' international expansion to supplement the broad aggregate view gained from the country-level analysis of outward FDI statistics.

The chapter is divided into six sections. After this introduction and the review of the literature, outward FDI statistics are examined to explain some discernible patterns and trends. Then we discuss and compare the four case studies, and conclude by taking stock of the past and present patterns of the emergence of Thai multinationals, and consider the challenges facing these firms in the future.

Review of the literature

The literature on the emergence of emerging-economy multinationals, although still limited compared with studies on multinationals from developed economies, is vast enough to stimulate debate on the rise of this new group of multinationals. Two main topics addressed in this part are the nature of outward FDI from developing countries and the nature of competitive advantages of their firms.

Outward FDI from developing countries: When, where, and how

Once a firm makes a decision to invest overseas, choices involving 'when, where, and how' bring about much debate on the best ways to implement an international expansion strategy. At the macro-, country-level analysis, one model that has received much interest for its explanation of a country's involvement in FDI is the IDP, first formulated by Dunning (1981), then later extended by Narula (1996), Dunning (1988, 1993), and Dunning and Narula (1997, 2004).[3]

---

[3] The IDP concept is in fact an application of the eclectic paradigm advanced by John Dunning since the late 1970s (Dunning 1981, 1988, 1993, 1995, 2001).

Cantwell and Tolentino (1990) and Tolentino (1993) extended the IDP concept to explain outward FDI from developing countries. They suggested that outward FDI initially takes place in less technology-intensive or resource-based industries and extends to high value-added activities later. They also found that MNEs from developing economies, particularly richer ones, tended to engage in outward FDI at a much earlier stage compared to the conventional MNEs from developed economies.

Dunning (1993, 1998) differentiated FDI into four types based on the key location advantages of host countries: natural resource-seeking, market-seeking, efficiency-seeking, and strategic asset-seeking (Dunning 1993, 1998). Applying this framework to outward FDI from developing countries, UNCTAD (2006) suggested that market-seeking FDI was by far the most common type of strategy for developing-country multinationals, followed by efficiency-seeking (more commonly interpreted as lower cost-seeking than synergy-seeking FDI), resource-seeking FDI, and created asset-seeking FDI. The patterns suggested here will be used to analyse Thailand's outward FDI in the section on 'Patterns and trends'.

Competitive advantages of multinationals from developing economies

In the analysis of competitive advantages of MNEs from developing countries, the conventional view that has been advanced since the beginning of the literature pointed to the importance of capabilities that are acquired through the process of technological accumulation. This view is common for both the first group of literature that emerged in the late 1970s and the early 1980s (see Wells 1977, 1981, 1983, Lecraw 1977, 1981, O'Brien 1980, Kumar 1982, Aggarwal 1984), and the second group that came forth in the late 1980s and the 1990s (Lall 1983a, 1983b, Vernon-Wortzel and Wortzel 1988, Cantwell and Tolentino 1990, Tolentino 1993, Lecraw 1993, Ulgado, Yu, and Negandhi 1994, Dunning, van Hoesel, and Narula 1997, van Hoesel 1999).

With the sole emphasis on proprietary technological capabilities, the above literature has been criticized on two counts. First, the existing literature implied that emerging multinationals had to accumulate sufficient industry-specific technological skills prior to their international expansion. This implication left out other types of advantages that could contribute to the emergence of multinationals from developing economies. With an emphasis that competitive advantages are derived mainly from technological skills, the literature's second drawback is that it is 'under-socialized' – viewing firms as detached from other social institutions and therefore perceiving a firm's competitive advantage as resulting only from its own resources, within its own boundaries. This view is contrary to empirical evidence of MNEs from late-industrializing countries, especially those from Asia, which showed that network relationships and networking capabilities were significant advantages of Asian multinationals in their domestic and international expansion.

The view that network relationships contributed to the competitive advantages of multinationals from developing countries, especially those from Asia, has been widely acknowledged (see, for example, Yeung 1998, Pananond and Zeithaml 1998, Pananond 2001, 2006, 2007, Peng 2003, Peng and Zhou 2005, UNCTAD 2006). Sociologists considered it a cultural trait in Asian societies, especially among the Chinese. Proponents of this view argued that personal relationships formed the basic mechanisms of business contacts in these societies. These networks could benefit Chinese or ethnic Chinese firms when they expanded in the region because personal relationships promoted trust and reduced transaction costs (see Limlingan 1986, Redding 1990, 1995, Kao 1993, East Asia Analytical Unit 1995, Weidenbaum and Hughes 1996).

Institutionalists, on the other hand, viewed the reliance on networks as a response to weak institutional frameworks in developing countries (see, for example, Khanna and Palepu 1997, 2000). Among the variety of institutional explanations on the emergence of Asian countries, the 'late industrialization' view stood out (see Amsden 1989, 1995, 2001, Amsden and Hikino 1993, 1994, Hikino and Amsden 1994, Wade 1990, van Hoesel 1999). Proponents of this view argued that firms from late-industrializing countries were obliged to develop an additional set of 'generic' skills that could be transferred across industries to compensate for their lack of proprietary technological skills. Following this view, I have argued (Pananond 2001, 2004) that networking capabilities, or the firm's ability to draw on complementary resources of partners and turn them to the firm's benefits, formed an equally critical part of Thai multinationals' competitive advantages by serving as 'generic' strategies that allowed them to grow in domestic and regional markets. Four types of network relationships that were key to the emergence of Thai multinationals were: close ties with domestic and international financial institutions; political relationships with both home- and host-country governments; alliances with foreign technology partners; and relationships based on social ties. Although each firm may give different emphasis to each type of network, the overall ability to draw necessary resources from these four types of networks contributed to their emergence. This chapter elaborates on the dynamic of how Thai firms relied on networking capabilities through four case studies. The above review of the literature provides conceptual frameworks that could be used to analyse the evolution of outward FDI from Thailand and the emergence of Thai multinationals.

Thailand's outward FDI: Patterns and trends

Two observations can be noted from Figures 11.1 and 11.2. First, outward FDI flows from Thailand are still rather small. In 2006, outward FDI flows from Thailand reached Bt 27,400 million (US$ 727 million), a modest amount compared to Singapore's US$ 5.5 billion in 2005 (UNCTAD 2006, Table B.1). The importance of outward FDI to the Thai economy is also limited, with outward FDI flows in 2005 accounting for only 0.5 per cent of gross fixed capital formation, a miniscule level given the Southeast Asian average rate of 6 per cent (UNCTAD 2006, Table B.3). The stock[4] of outward FDI from Thailand also pales in comparison to what the country receives. The accumulated size of Thai outward FDI as percentage of GDP is approximately ten times less than that of inward FDI (see Figure 11.2). Second, Thailand's experience with outward FDI is still in its early development, starting to be notable only in the late 1980s. As seen from Figure 11.1, outward FDI from Thailand only became

---

[4] The Bank of Thailand provided stock data only after 2000 (see Bank of Thailand 2006). To present a longitudinal evolution of Thai outward FDI stock from 1980 to 2006, this paper follows the World Investment Report method of calculating outward FDI stock by adding up Thai equity flows (see more discussion on World Investment Report methodology in UNCTAD 2006, p. 295).

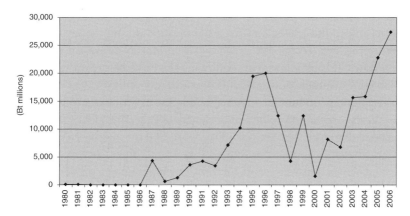

Figure 11.1 Outward FDI flows, 1980–2006

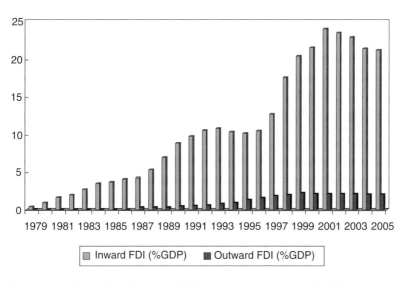

Figure 11.2 Inward and outward FDI stock as percentage of GDP, 1979–2005

significant after 1986, partly as a result of the country's economic prosperity in the latter half of the 1980s.

Despite its limited degree and the early stage of its development, it is clear that Thailand has already witnessed three discernible phases of outward FDI: the early beginning in the 1980s; the sharp rise during the 1990s, and the post-1997 period. Thailand's outward FDI became noticeable in the 1980s, increased significantly during the early 1990s, before the 1997 economic crisis put a temporary brake on outward FDI flows. It took a few years following the crisis before outward FDI showed a resurgence, from 2000 onward.

The limited amount of outward FDI in the 1980s was a result of the country's restriction on foreign exchange (Vachratith 1992). It was no surprise therefore that the rise of outward FDI during the 1990s came after Thailand adopted a series of financial liberalization policies. Two schemes that were most relevant to encouraging capital outflows were the removal of exchange controls following the adoption of the International Monetary Fund's Article 8 in 1990 and the creation of Bangkok International Banking Facilities in 1992 (see Unger 1998). The latter was intended to develop Bangkok into a regional financial centre by allowing local and foreign banks to engage in offshore banking activities. The suddenly easy access to cheaper loans on international markets lured many Thai firms into rapid expansions both at home and abroad. The outward FDI flows increased almost six fold in the four-year period from 1992 to 1996.

This rising trend took a sharp downturn after the economic crisis struck Thailand in 1997. The Baht flotation and its subsequent depreciation increased the cost of foreign operations and almost doubled the amount of foreign-currency debts of most Thai firms that had been borrowing heavily to finance both their domestic and international expansions. The slowdown in the economies of many countries in the region following the crisis aggravated the problems of domestic entrepreneurs. Most Thai firms that had been enjoying international expansion decided instead to focus on domestic survival. Starting in 2001, however, many Thai firms regained their strength and gained the confidence to re-embark on outward FDI. The increase in outward FDI was also consistent with the global trends of increased FDI outflows from developing economies (see UNCTAD 2006).

In order to get a better understanding of how outward FDI has evolved, Figures 11.3, 11.4, and 11.5 present geographical and sectoral distributions of outward FDI stock in different periods, starting from the very beginning of outward FDI in the 1980s to the present. As seen in Figure 11.3, the destinations of Thai outward FDI in the 1980s were countries more developed than Thailand, namely the US,

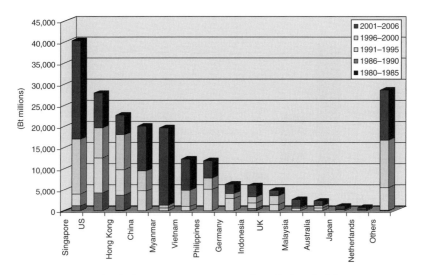

Figure 11.3 Stock of Thai equity investment abroad classified by country, different periods

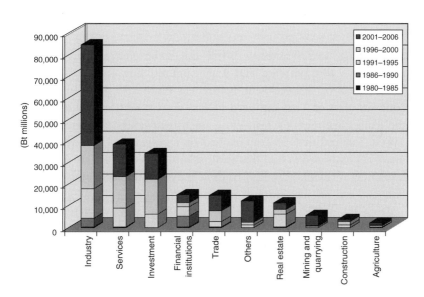

Figure 11.4 Stock of Thai equity investment abroad classified by sector, different periods

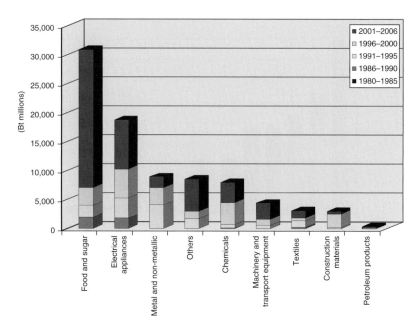

Figure 11.5 Industrial distribution of outward FDI from Thailand, different periods

Hong Kong, and Singapore. While this trend contradicted the IDP prediction – that outward FDI would initially flow to countries with lower levels of development before the more advanced ones – the concentration of Thai outward FDI in these countries resulted from the Thai government's restriction on foreign exchange prior to the 1990s. Vachratith (1992) explained that outward FDI in the 1980s mainly comprised Thai financial institutions setting up overseas branches in Thailand's key trading partner (the US) and regional financial centres (i.e. Hong Kong and Singapore).

From the 1990s, however, Thai outward FDI flows were increasingly directed at developing countries in the region, particularly ASEAN[5] countries and China, conforming more to the IDP view. The Chinese share in Thailand's total outward FDI stock increased

[5] Membership of the Association of Southeast Asian Nations (ASEAN) comprises ten countries in the region. The founding members in 1967 were Indonesia, Malaysia, the Philippines, Singapore, and Thailand. Brunei joined in 1983, Vietnam and Laos in 1994, and lastly Myanmar and Cambodia in 1997.

noticeably from a negligible 0.37 % in 1990 to 10% in 2006. The rise of Thai FDI outflows to developing countries in the region has been especially noticeable in the post-crisis period (see Figure 11.3).

The sectoral distribution of outward FDI stock in Figures 11.4 and 11.5 also confirms that there have been changing patterns throughout the development of Thai outward FDI. While financial institutions made up the majority of outward FDI in the beginning phase of the 1980s, industrial sectors became more significant in the 1990s and 2000s. Key industrial sectors of Thai outward FDI have been food, particularly sugar, and electrical appliances. Other than food and sugar, growth in service sectors, particularly trading, construction, mining and quarrying, has also been noticeable in the 2000s. I have previously suggested (Pananond 2004) that these were the sectors that benefited from Thailand's weakened currency after the crisis (i.e. food), a rebound of the regional economy (i.e. construction and real estate), and strong government support (i.e. restaurants).[6]

In sum, Thai outward FDI complies, by and large, with the IDP predictions that outward FDI evolves from the less technology-intensive industries to the more advanced ones and is initially located in countries with a lower level of development compared to that of the home country. However, the geographical destination of pre-1997 outward FDI was more diversified, compared with the post-crisis

---

[6] Although the Board of Investment has established the Department of Thai Overseas Investment to help promote and facilitate Thai firms' expansions overseas since 1996, the efforts were dampened in the post-crisis period when most businesses were more concerned with domestic survival. It was not until late 2003 that the promotion scheme was resumed. The Board of Investment then targeted three groups of industries: 1. those that could promote Thailand as a regional centre and would be beneficial to Thailand's economic development (e.g. petrochemicals/natural gas/energy; auto parts; agribusiness; and electrical parts); 2. those that encountered limitations in their domestic market expansion (e.g. fishery, textiles and garments, animal farming, and jewelry); 3. those in which Thai operators possessed global potential (e.g. industrial estate, construction, animal feeds, sugar, plastic, leather products, tourism, Thai restaurants, hotels, health and fitness, and retailing of Thai products). Thai outward FDI received more support in 2007 when the Board of Investment approved an overseas investment policy as a national policy. The Board urged investors to invest overseas as alternative sources for resources, cheaper production locations, and new markets for Thai products and services. The Board of Investment also targeted countries in the region, including Cambodia, Laos, Vietnam, Myanmar, China, India, Indonesia, and the Philippines (see Board of Investment 2007).

period. Investment during the pre-crisis period was targeted not only to countries with similar or lower levels of development, but also to more advanced economies. The post-crisis investment, on the other hand, showed a much stronger emphasis on developing countries in the region.

Second, there have been rises and falls of different industries in the pre- and post-crisis periods. Sectors that were booming before 1997, including real estate and metal and non-metal, experienced much slower growth after the crisis. On the contrary, other sectors whose growth rates were average before the crisis – for example, the food and sugar industries – have enjoyed rapid growth in recent years. These rises and falls could be interpreted as an indication of the sustainability of Thai firms' competitive advantages in various industries. It is difficult, however, to extract explanations on firm behaviours from an aggregate set of statistics.

Case studies

Four case studies – the Charoen Pokphand (CP) group, Siam Cement Group (SCG), the S&P group, and PTT – are chosen for the following reasons. First, these four firms are representative of two sets of Thai multinationals – the pioneers who began their international expansion prior to the 1997 economic crisis (i.e. CP and SCG), and the new-comers whose overseas expansions are more evident in the post-crisis period. Comparing these two groups should provide insight into the evolution of Thai multinationals that are at different stages in their development. Second, with the exception of S&P, the three other groups are among the largest firms in the country. PTT and SCG were included in *Forbes* magazine's Global 2000 list of the world's largest firms in 2007, at numbers 354 and 863 respectively, while CP ranked 38th in *World Investment Report 2004*'s top 50 largest non-financial multinationals from developing economies, although the group has fallen outside the top 100 rank in recent years.[7] Their positions in these globally ranked lists imply that they have now

---

[7] The *World Investment Report* ranking was based on foreign assets of 2002 (see UNCTAD 2004). For the list of the world's 2,000 largest firms, see Forbes.com (2007).

entered into global competition in their respective industries. Third, the industries represented by these firms are among the most significant sectors for Thailand's outward FDI, or the most rapidly growing sectors in global FDI flows. As seen from the discussion in the previous section, Thai outward FDI flows in food sectors and restaurant services have shown fast and steady growth since 2000. The CP group and S&P are among the country's most active firms that have undertaken overseas investments in these sectors. Outward flows in chemicals and petrochemicals, represented by Siam Cement and PTT, have also been on the rise, albeit at a slower rate. Similarly, UNCTAD (2006) identified oil and gas, PTT's field, as one of the leading industries for global FDI flows.

The CP group

Of all the firms in Thailand, the CP group is probably the foremost example of a Thai multinational. Best known for its long-time investment in China, the group claimed to be the 'first major foreign investor in China in 1979'. Beginning in 1921, the group has grown into a multinational conglomerate with subsidiaries in twenty countries, employing more than 250,000 people, and generating an estimated total group turnover of more than US$ 14 billion in 2006 (see www.cpthailand.com).

With a modest start as a small shop selling vegetable seeds and other agricultural products, CP has expanded to become a fully integrated agribusiness firm whose operations range from animal feed production, livestock farming, and meat processing, to retail distribution in the broiler industry. A major milestone in CP's agribusiness activities was its 1970 joint venture with Arbor Acres, a leading poultry-breeding firm from the US. The joint venture not only provided CP with breeding technology but also allowed it to learn more about vertical integration – a key strategy in the broiler industry. This successful pattern of vertical integration was later extended to swine, and shrimp production, turning CP into the largest and most completely integrated agribusiness firm in Thailand. In addition to agribusiness, CP also diversified into other sectors unrelated to agriculture. CP's activities are organized under ten business groups: agro-industry and food; marketing and distribution (retailing); telecommunications; seeds, fertilizer, and plant protection; international trading; crop integration; automotive and other industrial products; real estate and land development; plastic; and pet food.

CP's international expansion was pioneered by animal feed production in Indonesia (1972), Hong Kong (1974), Singapore (1976), and Taiwan (1977). After China opened its door in 1979, CP's international activities were mainly concentrated in China, with activities ranging from agribusiness, motorcycle manufacturing, aquaculture, downstream petrochemical and real-estate development to beer brewing, and telecommunications. CP's investment in China followed a formula that had proven successful in Thailand and Indonesia. Agribusiness was used as a pioneering industry before diversification into other industries. It should be noted that it is only in China that CP's international activities are broadly diversified. CP's investments elsewhere are mainly concentrated on its core activity – the agribusiness industry. Revenues from the overseas subsidiaries of CPF (Charoen Pokphand Foods PCL) accounted for 12 per cent of CPF's total revenues in 2006 (CPF 2006).

CP's rapid and highly leveraged expansion in the years before the crisis became a serious financial burden when the Thai currency was devalued in July 1997. The difficulty forced the group to undertake many crucial restructuring steps. Among the most significant changes were a clearer focus and emphasis on agribusiness and the food industry, and an attempt to improve its corporate image. CP concentrated more on increasing the value of its food sectors through brand building and producing higher value-added products, such as processed and semi-cooked food items. In addition, the group increased its emphasis on downstream activities, especially retailing and distribution, both at home and in China. Although in Thailand the group sold its hypermarket chain, Lotus, to Tesco from the UK, CP still maintained Lotus Supercenter operations in China on top of its 7-Eleven convenience store chain. CP's retailing activities were also reinforced through the creation of its own outlet, CP Fresh Mart, to exclusively carry a broad range of the group's food products. The group also tried to increase its overall efficiency in agribusiness production through tighter integration of its domestic and overseas production bases. Rather than producing for each domestic market, CP started to designate specific roles for each production unit. For example, Thailand was set to be the production centre of cooked and processed meats for export, while China served as a poultry production base for exports to

Japan, and Turkey for the EU. Despite CP's emphasis on agribusiness and food, the group still maintained its activities in many unrelated sectors, such as plastics, automotive part production, and real estate development. It should be noted, however, that these activities were mostly concentrated in Thailand and China. CP's activities in other countries were mainly limited to agribusiness and the production and processing of food, and to international trading. Table 11.1 summarizes CP's pre- and post-crisis overseas activities.

Another significant change from the pre-crisis period was CP's attempt to improve its corporate image from that of a shady, family-owned conglomerate to a more professionally managed multinational. A major reason for this strategic redirection was to shift its financing strategy from debt to equity through the use of capital markets. In order to attract more international institutional investors, CP needed to become more open and transparent, leading to some organizational restructuring and increased information disclosure. Before the crisis, CP's activities were hard to trace, due to its myriad subsidiaries at home and abroad. For agribusiness activities in Thailand alone, CP had four subsidiaries listed on the Stock Exchange of Thailand (Pananond 2001). After the crisis, however, three listed subsidiaries were delisted and its operations concentrated under CPF, which became the group's main subsidiary in agribusiness and food both at home and abroad. Despite this attempt, it is still difficult to trace the group's entire range of activities as CP does not provide any group-wide consolidated accounts, nor individual business group's consolidated ones. Therefore, most of the information that the group provides comes from its key publicly listed subsidiaries.

Despite its agribusiness presence in many countries, CP is well known for its diverse range of activities in China. Given its founder's Chinese origin, CP has become one of Southeast Asia's best-known representatives of the 'overseas Chinese' business groups. How these 'bamboo networks' may have contributed to CP's growth will be addressed below, in the section 'Nature of competitive advantages', when we discuss Thai multinationals' competitive advantages.

The Siam Cement Group (SCG)

Since its foundation in 1913, SCG has grown to be among the largest industrial conglomerates not only in Thailand, but also in Southeast

Table 11.1. *CP's pre- and post-crisis overseas activities*

| Pre-crisis | | Post-crisis | | |
Type of business	Country	Type of business	Country	Changes
trading company	Japan, Korea, Hong Kong, Malaysia, Singapore, India, Myanmar, Chile, China, Belgium, US, UAE, South Africa, Vietnam	trading company	Japan, Korea, Hong Kong, Malaysia, Singapore, India, Myanmar, Chile, China, Belgium, US, UAE, South Africa, Vietnam, Turkey, Germany, Switzerland, UK, France, Italy	more expansion to Europe
agribusiness	Indonesia, Hong Kong, Taiwan, Malaysia, Singapore, China, Turkey, US, Vietnam, Myanmar, Cambodia, India	agribusiness	Indonesia, Hong Kong, Taiwan, Malaysia, Singapore, China, Turkey, Vietnam, Myanmar, Cambodia, India	withdrawal from US
aquaculture	India, Taiwan, China	aquaculture	India, Taiwan, China, Malaysia, Vietnam	expansion
retailing	China	retailing	China, Taiwan	expansion
automotive	China	automotive	China	expansion of plants and activities
telecommunications	China, US	telecommunications	China	withdrawal from USA
real estate	China	real estate	China, Hong Kong	reduced activities
petrochemicals		petrochemicals	China	expansion

Source: Pananond (2007)

Asia. Before its major post-crisis restructuring in 1998, SCG was the parent company of more than 130 subsidiaries, employing more than 35,000 people in various industries spread across nine business groups: cement and trading; construction materials; iron and steel; ceramics; electrical and metal products; machinery, tyre and auto accessories; petrochemicals; paper and containers; and corporate finance and administration (SCG 1997). The post-crisis restructuring made it leaner, with approximately 100 major companies in five major business groups: chemicals, paper, cement, building materials, and distribution which included international trading. The group's consolidated turnover in 2006 was US\$ 7.75 billion (see www.siamcement. com). What is most notable about SCG is its majority shareholder – the Crown Property Bureau, which used to own up to 50 per cent of SCG until the 1997 crisis forced SCG to issue more shares to cope with financial losses, diluting the Crown Property Bureau's ownership stake. Nonetheless, the Bureau continued to be SCG's largest single shareholder, with a 30 per cent stake as of March 2007. The Crown Property Bureau's status is unique as it is neither public nor private. Although its objectives are in the public domain, the Bureau enjoys flexibility similar to, but not on a par with, a private enterprise.[8] Despite the Bureau's ownership stake in SCG, the group's status is that of a private-sector company.

SCG had its beginnings in cement production, an industry in which it enjoyed monopolistic control from the very beginning until 1956, when the government finally allowed the establishment of a second

---

[8] During Thailand's absolute monarchy, which lasted from the thirteenth century to 1932, the royal wealth was supervised by the Privy Purse. In 1890, it became the Privy Purse Bureau, acting as the main investment arm for the monarchy. In 1936, four years after the coup that ended the absolute monarchy, the Royal Assets Restructuring Act established the Crown Property Bureau as a separate unit from the Privy Purse, which continued to manage the monarchy's personal property. The same Act also exempted the Crown Property Bureau income from tax, although the king must still pay tax on his personal income. The Bureau is under the management of a special committee, personally appointed by the king and chaired by the finance minister. Its revenues come mainly from dividends from the Siam Commercial Bank and SCG, although the group is increasingly benefiting from real estate investment. The Bureau's status and many of its activities have long been a topic of debate, but the continued existence of *lèse-majesté* law in Thailand may have hampered truly open criticism of the Bureau. For more discussions on the Crown Property Bureau, see Jiamteerasakul (2006) and Ouyyanont (2006).

cement manufacturer. Its initial diversification concentrated on the construction material industries which used cement as raw materials. Diversification to non-cement sectors started in the 1970s, including iron and steel (1966), plastic and fibre glass (1970), pulp and paper (1976), auto accessories (1977), international trading (1978), ceramic tiles (1979), electrical products (1984), sanitary ware (1985), and petrochemicals (1986). These industries featured some common characteristics, including low competition levels and generous government support.

SCG had always been domestically oriented until the early 1990s when the group's major export market for ceramic tiles – the US – was challenged by the termination of the Generalised System of Preferences. This investment taught SCG expensive lessons regarding international investments. Most importantly, the group realized that it was not yet ready for highly competitive markets like that of the US. Since then, SCG has shifted its focus to Southeast Asia. Priority was given especially to Indonesia, Philippines, China, Vietnam, Laos, and Cambodia. From 1993 to 1997, SCG announced a total of twenty-seven projects in those countries, covering a wide variety of industries, including ceramics, cement and trading, construction materials, petrochemicals, pulp and paper, and machinery. The actual implementation of these projects was rather limited, however, with only twelve projects actually realized when the economic crisis broke out in 1997. Table 11.2 summarizes SCG's pre- and post-crisis overseas activities.

In the post-crisis period, the group undertook three important changes. First, the group took a bold step in restructuring its overall operations to focus only on core industries. This strategy resulted in the group reducing its activities at home and abroad to five core business groups: chemicals, paper, cement, building materials, and distribution. The restructuring also reflected a change in the group's priority. From a growth-led orientation, the group became more concerned with profitability. Value-adding activities such as product innovation and design were undertaken to increase product marketability and attractiveness, while organic expansions along with M&As were carried out to expand its scale economies and to extend vertical integration in its core industries. Third, SCG integrated international activities into its overall strategy. Prior to 1997, SCG's international expansion strategy was driven by growth opportunities in various markets, resulting in a lack of integration of international activities

Table 11.2. *SCG's pre- and post-crisis overseas activities*

Pre-crisis		Post-crisis		Changes
Type of business	Country	Type of business	Country	
ceramics	US, Mexico, Indonesia, Philippines, China	ceramics	Indonesia, Philippines	reduced activities
construction materials	Indonesia, China	construction materials	Indonesia, Philippines, Cambodia, Laos, Vietnam, Myanmar, Malaysia	withdrawal from China and expansions in other countries
trading company	Indonesia, Vietnam, Philippines, Myanmar, Cambodia	trading company	Philippines, Laos, Singapore, Hong Kong, India, UAE, Bangladesh, Australia, China, Taiwan, US	expansion
petrochemicals	Indonesia	petrochemicals	Indonesia, Iran	reduced activities in Indonesia and expansion in Iran
pulp and paper machinery	Philippines	pulp and paper machinery	Philippines, Vietnam	expansion
	Philippines, China		Philippines	withdrawal from China

Source: Pananond (2007)

and the group's overall inefficiency. With the group's reduction in core industries, SCG's post-crisis overseas ventures were much more focused on cost reduction and efficiency creation. Examples included investment in upstream activities in pulp production in the Philippines and upstream petrochemical activities in Iran. SCG has grown from being the country's only cement producer to being Thailand's largest industrial conglomerate. Its current vision is to become a leading regional player in selected core areas.

The S&P group

With a modest start as an ice-cream and bakery shop in 1973, S&P has developed into a group of integrated restaurant and bakery businesses with over 200 outlets in Thailand and 25 overseas, under ten different brand names. Its total sales in 2006 were Bt 3,706 million (US$ 107 million), 19 per cent of which came from overseas operations (see www.sandp.co.th). S&P's operations are organized under four business units: domestic restaurants and bakeries, overseas restaurants, retailing of food and bakery products, and home delivery and catering services.

The group's first international expansion took place in 1990 in London. Overseas branches have since been added in Europe as well as in Asia. In addition to the restaurant and bakery business, S&P has also expanded into the manufacturing of baked products and frozen food. Although the group's manufactured foods have traditionally been geared toward the local market, the group plans to increase its frozen food exports to large overseas markets in the US, Australia, and Europe. Unlike other leading restaurant groups whose rapid overseas expansions have relied on franchising, S&P prefers to invest in its own overseas branches, with local joint venture partners with relevant industry experience and local market knowledge. Despite its small size compared to the other three cases, S&P is among the limited number of Thai restaurant groups that have continuously expanded their presence abroad, thanks to the increasing popularity of Thai cuisine.

With its conservative style of family business management,[9] S&P opted for incremental expansion based on the group's own financing

---

[9] Although S&P is a publicly listed company, the two founding families continue to be the largest shareholders, controlling 44.39 per cent together (S&P group 2006).

Table 11.3. *S&P's pre- and post-crisis overseas activities*

Pre-crisis		Post-crisis		
Type of business	Country	Type of business	Country	Changes
restaurant	Singapore, UK	restaurant	Singapore, UK, Switzerland, Taiwan, Malaysia	expansion

Source: S&P group, information disclosure reports (Form 56–1) and annual reports (see www.sandp.co.th)

in the pre-crisis years, saving it from the financial losses that many Thai firms encountered as a result of rapid, highly leveraged expansions. S&P continued to rely on strengthening its brands and expanding its retail outlets, along with finding appropriate partners in overseas markets, as its main expansion strategies. S&P serves as an interesting lesson of a small family firm that has been slowly making inroads into the global markets. Table 11.3 compares the group's pre- and post-crisis activities.

PTT

PTT Public Company Limited, henceforth PTT, was incorporated as a public company in 2001, on corporatization of the state-owned Petroleum Authority of Thailand, under the 1999 Corporatization Act. As of June 2007, PTT's shares are 52.3% owned by the Ministry of Finance, 15.5% by state funds, and the rest traded on the Stock Exchange of Thailand (PTT 2006). This shareholding structure makes PTT Thailand's de facto national oil company.

The early stage of PTT was heavily domestically oriented, with most activities focusing on exploration and production of natural gas in the Gulf of Thailand, and diversification into downstream petrochemical activities. It was only in the mid-1980s that PTT began to diversify its energy resources to cover other sources, particularly petroleum. PTTEP (PTT Exploration and Production) was therefore established with the goal of exploring, developing, and producing oil and gas products from reserves in Thailand and around the world.

PTTEP therefore became a major subsidiary that undertakes most of the group's exploration and production activities. Revenue from PTTEP's overseas operations accounted for 17.37 per cent of its total revenue (PTTEP 2006).

The oil price hikes in the past decade and the increasing demand from large developing countries such as China and India have prompted many national oil companies to secure their energy supplies by tapping into new resources in the region and around the world. PTT is no exception, as it began its global expansion in both upstream and downstream activities in the mid-1990s. The group's activities are divided into three major business groups: gas, oil, and petrochemicals and refining. In the gas business, PTT operates a fully integrated chain of activities that include exploration and production, procurement, transmission, and distribution. In the oil business, the group leaves the exploration and production activities to PTTEP, while PTT's two main activities are retailing and marketing, as well as international trading. In petrochemicals, the group has invested in both olefins and aromatic projects.

With its global focus starting in the 1990s, PTT's international activities are still concentrated in the Southeast Asian region, although its exploration subsidiary has started to venture into the Middle East and Africa in search of new and untapped reserves. Apart from those exploration projects, PTT's international activities are centred around natural gas projects, particularly the ambitious project to lay a future trans-ASEAN gas pipeline for countries in the ASEAN (Crispin 2004). PTT, through its subsidiary PTTEP, is also a keen investor in the military-ruled Myanmar. Thailand is among the few countries that are competing for new offshore gas supplies in Myanmar. Other countries that are actively seeking opportunities there are China, India, and Malaysia. PTTEP and Petronas are the largest investors in the military-ruled country, snubbing sanctions on Myanmar from the US and Europe.[10] Thailand invests there to secure supplies. Thailand

---

[10] Despite calls from activists for oil companies with operations in Myanmar to pull out of the country to protest the bloody crackdown on demonstrators in Rangoon during the last week of September 2007, most oil companies, including PTT, continued business operations in Myanmar. PTTEP said in a statement that production of natural gas was at the normal rate, and should not be affected by the unrest (Hogue 2007).

Table 11.4. *PTT's pre- and post-crisis overseas activities*

Pre-crisis		Post-crisis		
Type of business	Country	Type of business	Country	Changes
gas pipeline system	Malaysia	gas pipeline system	Malaysia	
gas exploration and production	Malaysia	gas exploration and production	Malaysia	
		oil/gas exploration and production	Algeria, Cambodia, Egypt, Oman, Vietnam, Indonesia, Iran, Myanmar, New Zealand	expansions and new activities
LPG trading	Malaysia	oil/LPG trading	Philippines, Singapore, Vietnam, Malaysia	more activities and expansion in South East Asia
		oil marketing	Cambodia, Laos, Philippines	new activity
		aircraft refuelling service	Hong Kong	new activity

Source: PTT, information disclosure reports (Form 56–1) and annual reports (see www.pttplc.com; www.pttep.com)

accounted for 23 per cent of Myanmar's total export revenues in 2004 (*International Gas Report* 2006). Table 11.4 gives more details on PTT's overseas activities.

Case comparison

Three key characteristics of the cases – geographical spread, motivations, and competitive advantages – are discussed here in relation to the literature reviewed earlier. Table 11.5 provides an overall summary of the cases.

Geographical spread

From Table 11.5, it is quite clear that the geographical spread of Thai multinationals remains focused on nearby Asian countries, whose levels of development are similar to or less than that of Thailand. The majority of investment activities, as shown in Table 11.5, were directed to developing countries in Southeast Asia, with Indonesia and the Philippines among the most popular host countries. However, marketing facilities, especially sales offices, are much more spread out compared to production units.

Destinations are also determined by the nature of each industry. The international expansion of PTT and its exploration subsidiary, PTTEP, is concentrated in oil- and gas-rich countries. SCG's overseas activities in petrochemicals are similarly concentrated in resource-rich countries such as Iran. CP's activities in agribusiness, on the other hand, are less limited by the availability of natural resources. CP's choices of location are therefore determined by a combination of factors, including lower operation costs (e.g. shrimp farms in Vietnam and India), and potential market opportunities (e.g. China, India, and the EU). CP's keen interest in China, especially in non-agribusiness sectors, is often attributed to its 'overseas Chinese' origin. Nonetheless, it would be dangerously simplistic to characterize CP's investment in China simply as arising out of ethnic ties and ancestral loyalty. Common cultural background and language may have made it easier for CP to invest in China; but China offered a host of locational advantages other than cultural sentiment. China's gigantic domestic market could more than absorb CP's agribusiness and food products, not to mention numerous growth opportunities in many

Table 11.5. *Summary table of the case studies' overseas activities*

Company (consolidated sale, 2006)	Revenues from overseas operations (2006)	Activities	Country	Key motives
Charoen Pokphand (CP) (US$ 14 billion)	12% of CPF total revenues	trading companies	Japan, Korea, Hong Kong, Malaysia, Singapore, India, Myanmar, Chile, China, Belgium, US, UAE, South Africa, Vietnam, Turkey, Germany, Switzerland, UK, France, Italy	market-seeking
		agribusiness	Indonesia, Hong Kong, Taiwan, Malaysia, Singapore, China, Turkey, Vietnam, Myanmar, Cambodia, India	market-seeking, efficiency-seeking
		aquaculture	India, Taiwan, China, Malaysia, Vietnam	market-seeking, efficiency-seeking
		crop integration	China, Indonesia, Vietnam, Laos, Cambodia, Myanmar, India	market-seeking, efficiency-seeking
		retailing	China, Taiwan	market-seeking
		automotive	China	market-seeking
		real estate	China, Hong Kong	market-seeking
		telecommunications	China	market-seeking
		plastic	China	market-seeking

Table 11.5. (*cont.*)

Company (consolidated sale, 2006)	Revenues from overseas operations (2006)	Activities	Country	Key motives
Siam Cement Group (SCG) (US$ 7.75 billion)	Export sales = 30% of total sales	trading companies	Philippines, Laos, Singapore, Hong Kong, India, UAE, Australia, China, Taiwan, US, Jordan, Myanmar, Malaysia, Cambodia	market-seeking
		paper	Philippines	market-seeking, resource-seeking
		building materials	Indonesia, Cambodia, Vietnam, Philippines, Singapore, Laos	market-seeking, efficiency-seeking
		cement	Cambodia, Bangladesh, Singapore	market-seeking
S&P (US$ 107 million)	19% of total group revenues	restaurants	England, Switzerland, Taiwan, Singapore, Malaysia	market-seeking, some efficiency-seeking
PTT (US$ 22.63 billion)	17.37% of PTTEP total revenues	upstream	Algeria, Cambodia, Egypt, Oman, Indonesia, Iran, Malaysia, Myanmar, Vietnam	resource-seeking
		downtream	Cambodia, Hong Kong, Laos, Malaysia, Philippines, Singapore, Vietnam	market-seeking

industrial and service sectors, including retailing, motorcycle assembly, and telecommunications.

Thai multinationals' strong regional focus is consistent with the strategy of other multinationals in ASEAN countries (Hiratsuka 2006) and other developing host economies (UNCTAD 2006). The existing literature suggested that without strong proprietary ownership advantages, multinationals from developing countries were likely to exploit their advantages in countries with similar or lower levels of economic development. Only the more established firms have shown an inclination to venture beyond Asia. Nonetheless, it should not be concluded that most emerging multinationals have an exclusive preference for investing in other developing economies. Industry-specific as well as firm-specific factors also contribute to the location choices of these multinationals. As seen from the experiences of our cases, their geographical spread increased as they accumulated international experience.

Motives

Market-seeking FDI is by far the most obvious strategy for the selected Thai multinationals. This pattern was even more evident in the initial internationalization before the 1997 economic crisis. I have previously suggested (Pananond 2001) that the rapid international expansion of Thai firms in the early 1990s was driven mainly by rising opportunities in the booming regional market. For example, in a short period in the early 1990s, CP expanded its activities in China from mainly agribusiness to aquaculture, downstream petrochemical projects, real estate development, banking, brewing, and retailing (see Pananond and Zeithaml 1998). Similarly, SCG announced a total of twenty-seven overseas expansion projects to be undertaken in Southeast Asia and China between 1993 and 1997. Only a few of those projects were actually realized. Although the market-seeking motive still applies in the post-crisis international expansion, it is not to the same extent and degree of opportunistic expansion compared to pre-crisis expansions.

Thai multinationals have increasingly embarked on efficiency-seeking FDI, although most attempts are mainly to lower production costs rather than to increase synergies from integration. Examples include CP's investment in shrimp farming in Vietnam, Malaysia, and

India, where lower costs of operations led CP to expand their production bases in those countries. However, there are some signs that
the more advanced Thai multinationals are beginning to put greater
emphasis on creating efficiencies and synergies within their overseas
subsidiaries. Rather than focusing on separately producing for each
domestic market, CP started to integrate its production bases by
designating appropriate roles for each one, making its global production activities more coordinated. For example, Thailand was set to
be the production centre of cooked and processed meats, while China
served as poultry production base for exports to Japan, and Turkey to
the EU (see Pananond 2007). Similarly for SCG, post-crisis international expansion was increasingly led by efficiency-seeking objectives, to reduce costs and to increase the group's overall efficiency
and profitability. Examples included the group's recent emphasis on
logistics management to help support its domestic and international
activities. Although international expansion in the restaurant industry
is mainly market-seeking in nature, S&P has been trying to increase
its overall efficiency by integrating some functions of its operations
in Europe under its London base to create economies of scale.

Resource-seeking FDI has become quite evident for Thai multinationals in the primary sectors, such as PTT and SCG (for its paper
and petrochemical businesses). Examples include SCG overseas
expansions in upstream activities of pulp production in the Philippines
and petrochemical activities in Iran (see Table 11.2). Similarly, PTT's
overseas exploration projects are undertaken in countries with rich
resources in oil and gas, most notably in the Middle East and North
Africa (see Table 11.4). In addition to the case studies in this paper,
other Thai multinationals in extractive industries, such as Banpu
in mining, have similarly embarked on international expansion to
secure raw materials in resource-rich countries (see Pananond and
Kanchoochat 2006).

Strategic asset-seeking FDI is likely to be the least common motivation among Thai multinationals, given their early stage of development. None of the four cases in this chapter has yet demonstrated this
type of FDI. There are, however, some examples of Thai firms that
have used international expansion as a strategy to enhance their competitive advantages in overseas markets. In 2001, Thai Union Frozen
Products, the country's largest canned tuna exporter, took a bold step
by acquiring Tri-Union Seafoods, the second largest canned tuna

manufacturer in the US and the owner of the well-known brand 'Chicken of the Sea', to make its entry into the US retail market. Later in 2003, Thai Union Frozen Products acquired Empress International, a leading US-based importer and distributor of seafood products, to strengthen its distribution networks in the US (see Pananond 2004). Although asset-seeking FDI through cross-border mergers and acquisitions is still new to many Thai investors, the value and the number of such deals have been on the increase over the past few years (see UNCTAD 2006, Tables B.4 and B.5).

Nature of competitive advantages

Unlike multinationals from developed economies whose competitive advantages are mainly derived from technological superiority, the competitive advantages of Thai multinationals have been based on supplementing their industry-specific technological skills with networking capabilities. The former are generally derived from economies of scale and scope in their production and production process capabilities, as well as skills in that particular industry. CP's complete vertical integration in agribusiness and other food industries enabled the group to achieve scale and scope economies not only in Thailand, but also in other developing countries where there were few modern, big, fully integrated enterprises in agribusiness. Similarly, SCG's vertical integration in construction materials and other industries allowed the group to build up its scale and scope in the domestic market. Given its long history, SCG was also able to hone its production process capabilities in many industrial sectors in which the group partnered with foreign technology partners. With Southeast Asia's industrial sectors still a few steps behind Thailand's, SCG was able to transfer these production capabilities to the group's initial investments in Southeast Asia.

Scale, scope, and skills were also evident advantages in S&P's domestic and international expansion. Scope economies were derived from the group's extensive range of restaurant and bakery outlets. The group's domestic restaurant and bakery operations were provided under six different brands, two of which were also used in overseas markets. The variety of brands and services allowed the group to target different customer groups and enhanced its position as one of the country's largest restaurant groups. S&P also integrated vertically into the production of ready-to-eat meals, other food items (e.g. ham and sausages, and pasta) and bakery products.

It would be incomplete, however, to explain the nature of Thai multinationals' competitive advantages as deriving simply from industry-specific technological skills. As earlier discussed in the review of the literature, the other source of Thai multinationals' competitive advantages was based on generic networking capabilities. Skills of these Thai firms in drawing resources from four types of network relationships – close ties with financial institutions, relationships with home- and host-country government, alliances with foreign technology partners, and social and ethnic ties – equally contributed to the initial internationalization of Thai multinationals. These networking skills, combined with relevant industry-specific technological expertise, allowed Thai firms to rapidly expand abroad in the pre-crisis period (Pananond 2001).

SCG is a good example of how close relationships with domestic and international financial institutions contribute to international expansion. SCG is closely linked to the Siam Commercial Bank, the country's third largest bank, through the Crown Property Bureau, which owned 30% of SCG and 23.72% of SCB, as of March 2007.[11] In addition to the Bureau's direct ownership in these two firms, relationships between SCG and the Siam Commercial Bank were also based on cross-shareholding[12] and interlocking directorates (see Ouyyanont 2006). Having both the Crown Property Bureau and the Siam Commercial Bank on its side not only strengthened SCG's credibility, but also endowed the group with valuable information, and expansion opportunities in the domestic and international markets.

Close political ties in home and host countries were also crucial for Thai firms that have long been established. The Crown Property Bureau's links to SCG certainly contributed to the group's favourable standing among the Thai elite and top-level technocrats. CP has long been known for its connections with different political parties as well as the military, an institution that remained significant in Thailand's political economy. These ties took different forms, ranging from direct

---

[11] Information on shareholder structure is based on company reports to the Stock Exchange of Thailand (www.set.or.th).

[12] Siam Commercial Bank held 0.76 per cent of equity in SCG, as of March 2007.

donations, invitations to sit on company boards and employment of high-level retired government officials. For PTT, state ownership came in handy as it could guarantee lower-cost financing, provide opportunities following the government's privatization policy, and shield PTT from competition as national oil companies normally benefited from monopolistic control of the domestic market.

Domestic political ties were not of much use in these firms' international expansion. Thai multinationals solved this problem by either finding the right local partners with strong local networks or cultivating political networks in host countries. SCG's early joint venture partners in Southeast Asia included the region's largest conglomerates, such as the Astra group in Indonesia and the Ayala group in the Philippines (see Pananond 2001). S&P may have relied less on political connections, thanks partly to the nature of the restaurant industry, but one of the group's key competitive advantages was to find strong local partners that could share responsibilities in restaurant management.

In addition to local alliances, the other type of foreign partner that played a crucial role in the international expansion of these firms was the technology partner. Learning from foreign multinationals allowed these Thai firms to speed up their technological accumulation process and helped provide them with sufficient skills for regional expansions. With their strong domestic position, CP, SCG, and PTT had few problems attracting leading foreign multinationals that were looking to expand in Thailand and Southeast Asia.

The fourth type of relationship – social networks based on ethnic ties – was more evident for CP compared to the other three cases. While CP's ethnic Chinese origin may have played favourably in the beginning stage of China's open door policy, when not many foreign investors other than the overseas Chinese from the region were interested in entering China, CP's continued interest in China resulted from other industry- and China-specific factors as previously discussed in the 'Geographical spread' section.

Over a brief period during the early 1990s, some emerging Thai multinationals were able to enhance their competitive advantages based on technological skills with these networking capabilities in their initial international expansion. Such practice was feasible under a favourable environment when Southeast Asia was growing, with opportunities abundant. But the economic difficulty that ensued after

1997 and the increased competition from foreign multinationals[13] led to major changes in the business environment and in the international expansion behaviour of emerging Thai multinationals. No longer could they rely on the resources of others without strengthening their own capacity. Perhaps one positive outcome of the 1997 crisis was that it forced Thai firms, big and small alike, to be on their toes and really enhance their competitive advantages in order to survive. The welcome result is that Thai multinationals are enhancing their industry-specific technological skills through value-adding activities and transforming their networking relationships from personal ones to more formal and transparent ones (Pananond 2007).

On technological capabilities, all of our four cases confirm that value-adding activities, such as innovation (SCG), brand building (CP, SCG, and S&P), operation integration (CP, SCG, S&P, and PTT), and service provision (CP and SCG), are crucial for their future survival. Likewise, they appear to strengthen their networking capabilities by reducing their dependence on social and political ties and cultivating more formal and transparent ties with technology partners. CP was a case in point. From a company that was ready to form joint ventures and alliances with many types of partners through both formal and informal channels, CP has, in the post-crisis period, placed more emphasis on creating formal links with foreign multinationals that could provide the group with necessary technology. A recent example was the joint venture agreement in 2005 between CPF, the group's main subsidiary in agribusiness, with Japan's Yonekyu Corporation, a leading producer and exporter of high-quality pork products (see www.cpfworldwide.com). With the continuing problem of bird flu, the CP group has been trying to reduce its reliance on chicken products and expand its markets to cover other types of meat, particularly pork and shrimp.

It is clear that the nature of competitive advantage of Thai firms has gone through some changes in the pre- and post-1997 periods. In their initial stage of international expansion, Thai multinationals supplemented their weak industry-specific skills with generic networking capabilities to speed up their international expansion, mainly

---

[13] Thailand's inward FDI stock almost doubled in value in a short period of five years. From US$ 27.0 billion in 2000, inward FDI stock shot up to US$ 52.9 billion in 2005 (Bank of Thailand 2006).

directed toward neighbouring Southeast Asian countries. Relying on the resources of others may have worked for a short period, when growth in the region tempted emerging multinationals to quickly seize growing opportunities. But when competition intensified in the aftermath of the 1997 crisis, Thai multinationals came to realize that, in order to survive in the long run, they had to place a much stronger emphasis on developing competitive advantages that were based more on conventional industry-specific factors as well as on their own firm-specific conditions.

Conclusion: Past, present, and future of Thai multinationals

Although the rise of Thai multinationals is still in an early stage of development, as outward FDI flows took off with a modest amount only in the late 1980s, it appears that Thailand has already witnessed two discernible phases of this phenomenon. The pre-crisis emergence took shape in the early 1990s, before the 1997 economic crisis that affected much of Asia put a temporary pause on outward FDI flows from Thailand. The post-crisis phase of Thai multinationals' emergence became more apparent only in the early 2000s, as most Thai firms had a more urgent agenda at home in the immediate aftermath of the crisis.

The pre-crisis emergence was largely characterized by market-seeking FDI directed at countries in the region that were experiencing rapid economic development. Evidence can be drawn both from the aggregate outward FDI statistics and from the direct experience of the pioneering Thai multinationals. From the statistics, outward FDI flows in this phase showed a rather mixed pattern in geographical spread and sectoral distribution. Thai investors seemed to enter countries with higher levels of economic development at the same time as those with lesser levels. Sectoral distribution similarly showed a mixture, with investment in capital- and technology-intensive sectors, such as telecommunications, as well as in labour-intensive ones, such as food and textiles. Likewise, a closer look at the cases showed that international expansion was undertaken in a rather hasty manner to benefit from growing opportunities that were rapidly opening up in the region. How did these Thai multinationals do that, given that their rather brief experience should imply weak competitive advantages in overseas markets? Early trendsetters compensated for their weak technological expertise by networking with a variety of partners, including financial institutions, governments, multinational technology partners, local host-country firms, and allied Thai firms. Resources drawn from this set of partners allowed Thai multinationals to rapidly expand abroad to seek new markets where opportunities arose. Then came July 1997 when the Thai currency was floated and deeply depreciated in value, setting off domino-like effects in other Asian countries that had previously enjoyed a similar growth pattern. The economic difficulty that ensued, along with the hefty financial burden of rapid expansion, practically put an end to this pre-crisis phase of the emergence of Thai multinationals.

The post-crisis phase appeared to be quite different both at the aggregate country and the firm levels. The outward FDI statistics displayed a clearer pattern both in geographical spread and sectoral distribution. While market-seeking FDI remained the dominant motivation for overseas expansion, efficiency-seeking and resource-seeking purposes received more attention from Thai investors. As a consequence, FDI outflows were clearly directed to developing countries in the region, especially ASEAN and China. The more integrated regional market and rapid expansion in China offered Thai multinationals opportunities to enlarge their market reach as well as increase the overall efficiency of their operations through closer integration. For those Thai multinationals in the primary sectors, the limited range of resources that Thailand could offer prompted them to look elsewhere for their required materials. Accordingly, Thai outward FDI flows were geared toward industrial sectors that would answer to the emerging needs of Thai multinationals. A changing dynamic of Thai firms' international expansion was also observed from the case studies. From a heavy dependence on a variety of partners, Thai firms became much more committed to developing their own industry-specific technological capabilities. Strategies that had been adopted in the post-crisis period included the selection of core industries and the reduction of non-related activities, the increased emphasis on profitability over growth, and the introduction of value-adding activities such as brand creation and service provision. In addition, the increasing focus on creating industry-specific technological skills is accompanied by the changing nature of their network relationships. The interpersonal relationships that were the feature of the pre-crisis networking capabilities gave way to more formal and transparent ties.

According to Ramamurti and Singh (Chapter 6 in this volume), strategies of developing-country multinationals can be categorized into four types. The 'local optimizer' derives ownership advantages from optimizing products and processes to suit the markets of developing countries before they exploit these advantages in other emerging markets. The 'low-cost partner' leverages the low-cost advantages of developing countries to serve partner firms and customers in rich countries, often through OEM contracts at some stages of the value chain. Third, the 'global (or regional) consolidator' consolidates an industry on a global or a regional basis and may culminate in making acquisitions in developed-country markets. Last, the 'global first-mover' spots a new business opportunity in an existing industry and pursues it on a global scale.

The four cases in this chapter followed different types of generic strategies. PTT's internationalization shared similarities with oil and gas companies in other countries in that it focused on vertical integration across borders to secure resources under conditions of resource scarcity and uncertainty. This strategy led PTT to invest mostly in oil- and gas-rich countries. To a certain extent, S&P can be considered a global first-mover for its attempt to expand Thai food and the Thai restaurant business to other parts of the world, although the group is still far from being a global player in the Thai restaurant industry.

CP and SCG appeared closest to the local optimizer strategy, as they both developed their firm-specific advantages based on Thailand's country-specific advantages before they took these capabilities to other developing countries in the region. While CP built on Thailand's comparative advantages in agribusiness, SCG honed its industrial production process capabilities during Thailand's import substitution period. However, both CP and SCG realized the limitations of the local optimizer strategy, and have tried to move away from this strategy to join the ranks of the global (or regional) consolidators through increased integration of their global activities and an extension of activities to industrialized countries.

A variety of challenges remain for Thai multinationals in their future growth. Among the most important are the need to develop capacity and capabilities to compete at the regional and global levels. The continuous increase in global FDI flows in recent years involved not only conventional MNEs from developed economies, but also the rising new players from developing economies. The depth of players is a sign that global competition is becoming more intensified and is getting closer to home. With this level of competition knocking on the door, Thai firms in general and Thai multinationals in particular can no longer be complacent in their comfortable domestic status quo. International expansion has moved from an alternative to, perhaps, a key survival strategy. To successfully implement the internationalization strategy, Thai firms are urged to seriously consider where their competitive strength lies. This chapter points out that the nature of competitive advantages of Thai multinationals has been transformed as these firms evolve. From reliance on drawing resources from network partners in the early stage of international expansion, Thai multinationals are now faced with the challenge to sustain their competitive advantages in the long run. The sustainability of networks-based competitive advantages will depend on their ability to change, as well as their complementary role toward industry-specific technological capabilities.

In the future, the responsibility to make Thai multinationals more competitive will also lie in the hands of the Thai state. The existing policy regime toward outward FDI could be called 'reactive' at best and 'futile' at worst. The Thai government considers overseas investment simply as a response to the increased competition in the global economy, rather than a key part of a broader strategy to develop Thai firms' competitive advantages. As a result, policies on outward FDI have been made to encourage Thai firms to expand abroad in order to seek lower-cost resources or to seek new markets for their existing products and services, without a thorough understanding of where Thai firms stand in the global value chain. Policies on outward FDI should therefore be viewed from a proactive and integrated point of view that involves policies favouring capacity building and capability development in the domestic private sector, in addition to policies that aim to give incentives for outward FDI. Lessons learned from the emergence of Thai multinationals should therefore benefit multinationals from other developing countries that are trying to make their presence felt on the vast and rough sea of global competition.

References

Aggarwal, Raj (1984) 'The strategic challenge of third world multinationals: A new stage of the product life cycle of multinationals?' In

R. N. Farmer (ed.) *Advances in international comparative management: A research annual*. Greenwich, CT and London: JAI Press, pp. 103–22.

Amsden, Alice (1989) *Asia's next giant: South Korea and late industrialization*. Oxford and New York: Oxford University Press.

Amsden, Alice (1995) 'Like the rest: South-east Asia's "late" industrialization'. *Journal of International Development*, 7(5): 791–99.

Amsden, Alice H. (2001) *The rise of "The rest": Challenges to the west from late-industrialising economies*. Oxford: Oxford University Press.

Amsden, Alice H. and Hikino, Takashi (1993) 'Borrowing technology or innovating: An exploration of the two paths to industrial development'. In R. Thompson (ed.) *Learning and Technological Change*. New York: St Martin's Press, pp. 243–66.

Amsden, Alice H. and Hikino, Takashi (1994) 'Project execution capability, organisational know-how and conglomerate corporate growth in late industrialisation'. *Industrial and Corporate Change*, 3(1): 111–47.

Bank of Thailand (2006) *Survey results: International investment position of private non-bank sector, as-end December 2005*. Bank of Thailand.

Board of Investment (2007) Press Release No. 56/2550, www.boi.go.th/english/download/hot_topic/91/Press_Release No. 56_07.pdf

Cantwell, John and Tolentino, Paz Estrella (1990) 'Technological accumulation and third world multinationals'. *Discussion Papers in International Investment and Business. No. 139*. Reading, UK: University of Reading.

CPF (Charoen Pokphand Foods PCL) (2006) *Annual Report*.

Crispin, Shawn W. (2004) 'Thai energy concern plans investments'. *Wall Street Journal (Eastern Edition)*. 15 September, p. 1.

Dunning, John H. (1981) 'Explaining outward direct investment of developing countries: In support of the eclectic theory of international production'. In K. Kumar and M. C. McLeod (eds.) *Multinationals from developing countries*. Lexington, MA: D.C. Heath, pp. 1–22.

Dunning, John H. (1988) *Explaining international production*. London: Unwin Hyman.

Dunning, John H. (1993) *Multinational enterprise and the global economy*. Wokingham, UK: Addison-Wesley.

Dunning, John H. (1995) 'Reappraising the eclectic paradigm in an age of alliance capitalism'. *Journal of International Business Studies*, 26(3): 461–91.

Dunning, John H. (1998) 'Location and the multinational enterprise: A neglected factor?' *Journal of International Business Studies*, 29(1): 45–66.

Dunning, John H. (2001) 'The eclectic paradigm (OLI) of international production: Past, present, and future'. *International Journal of the Economics of Business*, 8(2): 173–90.

Dunning, John H., van Hoesel, Roger and Narula, Rajneesh (1997) 'Third world multinationals revisited: New developments and theoretical implications'. *Discussion Papers in International Investment and Management, Series B, No. 227*. Reading, UK: University of Reading.

Dunning, John H. and Narula, Rajneesh (1997) 'The investment development path revisited: Some emerging issues'. In J. H. Dunning and R. Narula (eds.) *Foreign direct investment and government catalysts for economic restructuring*. London: Routledge, pp. 1–41.

Dunning, John H. and Narula, Rajneesh (eds.) (2004) *Multinationals and industrial competitiveness: A new agenda*. Chelthenham, UK: Edward Elgar.

East Asia Analytical Unit (1995) *Overseas Chinese business networks in Asia*. Canberra: Department of Foreign Affairs and Trade, Australia.

Forbes.com (2007) 'The Global 2000'. www.forbes.com/2007/03/29/forbes-global-2000-biz-07forbes2000-cz_sd_0329global_land.html

Hikino, Takashi and Amsden, Alice H. (1994) 'Staying behind, stumbling back, sneaking up, soaring ahead: Late industrialization in historical perspectives'. In W. J. Baumol, R. R. Nelson, and E. N. Wolff (eds.) *Convergence of productivity: Cross-national studies and historical evidence*. Oxford: Oxford University Press, pp. 285–315.

Hiratsuka, Daisuke (2006) *Outward FDI from and intraregional FDI in Asean: Trends and drivers*. Discussion Paper. Institute of Developing Economies.

Hogue, Thomas (2007) Firms seek access to Burma oil fields despite bloody crackdown. *The Irrawaddy*, www.irrawaddy.org, 27 September.

International Gas Report (2006) 'Myanmar junta benefits from rising gas sales to Thailand'. *International Gas Report*. October 2006, p. 21.

Jiamteerasakul, Somsak (2006) 'What is the Crown Property Bureau?' *Fah Diew Kan*, 4(1): 67–93 (Original in Thai).

Kao, J. (1993) 'The worldwide web of Chinese business'. *Harvard Business Review* (March–April): 24–36.

Khanna, Tarun and Palepu, Krishna (1997) 'Why focused strategies may be wrong for emerging markets'. *Harvard Business Review* (July–August): 41–51.

Khanna, Tarun and Palepu, Krishna (2000) 'The future of business groups in emerging markets: Long-run evidence from Chile'. *Academy of Management Journal*, 43(3): 268–85.

Kumar, Krishna (1982) 'Third world multinationals: A growing force in international relations'. *International Studies Quarterly*, 26: 397–424.

Lall, Sanjaya (1983a) 'The rise of multinationals from the third world'. *Third World Quarterly*, 5(3): 618–26.

Lall, Sanjaya (1983b) *The new multinationals: The spread of third world enterprises*. New York: John Wiley & Sons.

Lecraw, Donald (1977) 'Direct investment by firms from less developed countries'. *Oxford Economic Papers*, 29(3): 442–57.

Lecraw, Donald J. (1981) 'Internationalization of firms from LDCs: Evidence from the Asean region'. In Kumar and Mcleod (eds.) *Multinationals from developing countries*. Lexington, MA: D.C.Heath, pp. 37–51.

Lecraw, Donald (1993) 'Outward direct investment by Indonesian firms: Motivations and effects'. *Journal of International Business Studies* (Third Quarter): 589–600.

Limlingan, Victor S. (1986) *The overseas Chinese in Asean: Business strategies and management practices*. Manila: Vita Development Corporation.

Narula, Rajneesh (1996) *Multinational investment and economic structure*. London: Routledge.

O'Brien, Peter (1980) 'The new multinationals: Developing-country firms in international markets'. *Futures*, pp. 303–16.

Ouyyanont, Porphant (2006) 'The crown property bureau and its role in business'. In P. Phongpaichit (ed.) *Thai capital's battle: Changes and dynamism*. Bangkok: Matichon Publishing, pp. 41–150 (Original in Thai).

Pananond, Pavida (2001) The making of Thai multinationals: The internationalisation process of Thai firms. *Department of Economics*. Reading, UK: University of Reading.

Pananond, Pavida (2004) 'Thai multinationals after the crisis: Trends and prospects'. *ASEAN Economic Bulletin*, 21(1): 106–26.

Pananond, Pavida (2006) 'The changing dynamics of Thailand CP group's international expansion'. In L. Suryadinata (ed.) *Southeast Asia's Chinese businesses in an era of globalization: Coping with the rise of China*. Singapore: Institute of Southeast Asian Studies (ISEAS), pp. 321–63.

Pananond, Pavida (2007) 'The changing dynamics of Thai multinationals after the Asian economic crisis'. *Journal of International Management*, 13(3): 356–75.

Pananond, Pavida and Kanchoochat, Veerayooth (2006) 'Thai capital gone abroad'. In P. Phongpaichit (ed.) *Thai capital's battle: Changes and dynamism*. Bangkok: Matichon Publishing, pp. 293–372 (Original in Thai).

Pananond, Pavida and Zeithaml, Carl P. (1998) 'The international expansion process of MNES from developing countries: A case study of Thailand's CP group'. *Asia Pacific Journal of Management*, 15(2): 163–84.

Peng, Mike W. (2003) 'Institutional transitions and strategic choices'. *Academy of Management Review*, 28(2): 275–90.

Peng, Mike W. and Zhou, Jessie Qi (2005) 'How network strategies and institutional transitions evolve in Asia'. *Asia Pacific Journal of Management*, 22: 321–36.

PTT (2006) *Information Disclosure Report (Form 56–1)*

PTTEP (2006) *Information Disclosure Report (Form 56–1)*

Redding, Gordon (1990) *The spirit of Chinese capitalism*, New York: Walter de Gruyter.

Redding, Gordon (1995) 'Overseas chinese networks: Understanding the enigma'. *Long Range Planning*, 28(1): 61–69.

S&P group (2006) *Information Disclosure Report (Form 56–1)*.

SCG (Siam Cement Group) (1997) *Siam Cement: Fact Book*. Bangkok: Siam Cement Group.

Tolentino, Paz Estrella (1993) *Technological innovation and third world multinationals*. London and New York: Routledge.

Ulgado, Francis M., Yu, Chow-Ming J., and Negandhi, Anant R. (1994) 'Multinational enterprises from Asian developing countries: Management and organisational characteristics'. *International Business Review*, 3(2): 123–33.

UNCTAD (2004) *World investment report 2006. The shift toward services: Overview*. New York and Geneva: United Nations.

UNCTAD (2006) *World investment report 2006. FDI from developing and transition economies: Implications for development*. New York and Geneva: United Nations.

UNCTAD (2007) *Asian foreign direct investment in Africa: Towards a new era of cooperation among developing countries*. New York and Geneva: United Nations.

Unger, Danny (1998) *Building social capital in Thailand: Fibers, finance and infrastructure*. Cambridge: Cambridge University Press.

Vachratith, Viraphong (1992) 'Thai investment abroad'. *Bangkok Bank Monthly Review*, 33 (April): 10–21.

van Hoesel, Roger, (1999) *New multinational enterprises from Korea and Taiwan: Beyond export-led growth*. London: Routledge.

Vernon-Wortzel, Heidi and Wortzel, Lawrence H. (1988) 'Globalizing strategies for multinationals from developing countries'. *Columbia Journal of World Business*, (Spring 1988): 27–35.

Wade, Robert (1990) *Governing the market: Economic theory and the role of government in east Asian industrialization*. Princeton, NJ: Princeton University Press.

Weidenbaum, Murray and Hughes, Samuel (1996) *The bamboo network: How expatriate Chinese entrepreneurs are creating a new economic superpower in Asia*. New York: The Free Press.

Wells, Louis T. Jr. (1977) 'The internationalization of firms from developing countries'. In Agmon and Kindleberger (eds.) *Multinationals from small countries*. Cambridge, MA: MIT Press, pp. 133–56.

Wells, Louis T. Jr. (1981) 'Foreign investors from the Third world'. In K. Kumar and M. C. McLeod (eds.) *Multinationals from developing countries*. Lexington, MA: D. C. Heath, pp. 23–36.

Wells, Louis T. Jr. (1983) *Third world multinationals: The rise of foreign investment from developing countries*. Cambridge, MA: MIT Press.

Yeung, Henry Wai-Chung (1998) *Transnational corporations and business networks*. London and New York: Routledge.

Websites

www.boi.go.th
www.bot.or.th
www.cpfworldwide.com
www.cpthailand.com
www.forbes.com
www.irrawaddy.org
www.pttep.com
www.pttplc.com
www.sandp.co.th
www.set.or.th
www.siamcement.com

12 Israeli multinationals: Competing from a small open economy

YAIR AHARONI[1]

Orthodox IB theory initially depicted MNEs as giant firms based in large, developed home markets. The headquarters of these MNEs transfer technology, management know-how, and capital from the home country to their various subsidiaries. Only much later did some researchers recognize that an MNE could be a knowledge seeker in addition to being a knowledge creator. Established MNEs endeavor to augment their knowledge by getting access to foreign-created knowledge, for example by acquisition of foreign firms. The MNE participates in various kinds of localized knowledge simultaneously (Rugman and Verbeke, 2001). The acquired knowledge is then transferred from one subsidiary to another or even to headquarters.

Today, established MNEs actively search outside the firm for technologies, ideas, and products. Procter and Gamble, for example, expects half of its future products to be based on technologies and concepts it will acquire from third parties (on the process see, for example, Huston and Sakkab, 2006). They acquire new technology rather than transferring existing technologies.

Porter's (1990a, 1990b, 1998) "demand conditions" are a major part of his "diamond." Firms must have a large home base in order to develop the skills to operate an MNE and to prosper. MNEs possess FSAs that are transferred to a network of subsidiaries in other locations. FDIs, therefore, are assumed to flow from large, developed economies to other developed economies as well as to less developed ones. Recognizing the benefits of FDI to the domestic economy,

[1] I am very grateful to Pavida Pananond and Peter Williamson for their very constructive comments on an earlier draft of the chapter. The figures were updated when the chapter was submitted in 2007. In 2008 Teva announced its intention to acquire Barr Pharamaceuticals in the US. In September 2008 Iscar acquired Tungaloy Corporation of Japan, a manufacturer of drilling and milling tools, for $1 billion.

nations compete intensely with each other to get MNEs to locate value-added activities within their borders.

Far less attention has been paid – at least until recently – to the possibility of encouraging domestic firms in emerging economies to transform into MNEs. In fact, in many economies, foreign exchange controls and other governmental restrictions made the creation of home-based MNEs difficult if not impossible.

Based on Canadian experience, Rugman and Verbeke (1993) pointed out that firms may draw on the strengths of the "diamond" of more than one nation, leading to the development of "double diamond" or even "multiple diamond" perspectives. Such perspectives appear useful mainly when firms from a small, open economy are analyzed (Van den Bulcke and Verbeke, 2001). Israel clearly demonstrates that a large home market is not a prerequisite for creating MNEs. On the contrary, the tiny size of the home market is a major incentive for Israeli firms to become multinationals by catering to much larger foreign markets. In some cases, the move abroad came after the possibilities available in the domestic market were exhausted, but in other cases, the firms sold 100 percent of their output outside Israel. All in all, by 2007, a few hundred Israeli firms had become successful MNEs, with several emerging as global, Israel-based powerhouses.

These outliers can serve as role models for other Israeli firms as well as for managers in other small countries. At the same time, these cases challenge mainstream IB theories, which are mostly based on studies of the world's largest MNEs. While it is true that the largest MNEs account for 90 percent of the world's FDI stock, IB theory must also be able to explain the internationalization of firms from small, open economies, which present different challenges than large economies.

Globalization is often cast as a vehicle by which large firms crush hapless small firms – and small countries. In discussing the case of Israel, this chapter seeks to show that seamless global operations enhance rather than negate the options available to prosperous small nations. As long as the policies of the government in the small country create the proper environment for local entrepreneurs, firms may thrive in global markets if they make the right strategic choices and are managed well. They may not possess the capabilities to build global consumer brands, but they can thrive by dominating well-differentiated niches.

To be sure, neither competing in large foreign markets nor integrating globally is easy. Indeed, many Israeli firms failed in their attempts to become MNEs, even when they had innovative technologies, because they lacked expertise in marketing, or in managing growth processes. Others succumbed to acquisitions by large European or US-based MNEs. Our focus here is on those that overcame these odds to become Israel-based MNEs.

We identify two types of Israeli MNES: those going abroad only after exploiting the possibilities of the domestic market and those "born global," that started out as multinationals. The first type can be found in most economic sectors, with the exception of public utilities. The second is limited to a few high-tech sectors, such as electronics, telecommunications, and software.

This chapter starts with a brief background on Israel, emphasizing the changes in its economic policies since 1985. The next section describes key changes in the country's business elite. The new macroeconomic environment and the new attitudes of managers were necessary but not sufficient for the creation of Israeli multinationals. The following section demonstrates the key drivers for the success of Israeli MNEs through a detailed case study of the largest of these firms, Teva Pharmaceutical Industries Ltd. A more comprehensive picture of all outward FDIs, comparing their magnitude to other small countries, is then presented. The next section presents a case study of Check Point Software Technologies Ltd, one of Israel's most interesting "born global" MNEs. Based on the above, the following section proposes some hypotheses about the ingredients of a successful strategy for the creation of Israeli MNEs. The section that follows raises some public policy issues. The chapter concludes with possible lessons, generalizations, and suggestions for further research.

Israel – the country and its economy[2]

Israel is a tiny economy with very few natural resources within its borders. Like other small countries, it attempts to define and maintain for itself a place in a world that is becoming increasingly globally integrated. It is one of the few modern states founded by a migration

---

[2] A part of this section is condensed from Aharoni (1991) and Aharoni (1992).

of settlers, forging new institutions in territories perceived to be uninhabited.

The return of Jews to their homeland started in 1882, when 20,000 Jews lived in Eretz Israel (Palestine). At that time, the area was rife with swamps and eroded by generations of neglect; there was no electricity; roads were extremely poor. In less than a generation, a group of dreamers worked diligently to form a new nation, to restore a virtually dead language, to create some of the finest universities in the world, and to establish a network of political and economic institutions.

Israel has encouraged Jews to return to their homeland and assisted them in doing so. An "ingathering of the exiles" was one of the highest priorities. In 1948, when the state was proclaimed after Eretz Israel was partitioned, there was a Jewish population of 650,000. From 1948 to 1951 686,739 new immigrants, 76.4 percent of them from Asia and Africa, doubled that population. The burden of absorbing them resulted in the rationing of food and other essentials.

In 2007 the Jewish population was about 6 million out of a total population of 7.2 million. In the 1990s, the influx of about 1 million Jews from the former Soviet Union included over 10,000 scientists and engineers, augmenting Israel's educational and technical advantages.

The founding fathers of Israel preached a return to agricultural work as a counterpart to the occupational structure of Jews in the Diaspora. These dreams were expected to be achievable by the sheer willpower of the pioneers. Economic laws, it was believed, could be ignored as irrelevant. Instead, reality was mystified and sacrifices were expected. The obstinate devotion of hard-working pioneers, combined with a massive capital flow, turned the land to a mosaic of green; world records were set for milk production; economic growth was rapid.

In the first decade of Israel's existence, GNP tripled; it doubled in the second decade. Until 1972 GNP per capita growth averaged 5.2 percent annually. The first development plan for agriculture (presented in 1950) saw agriculture as a source of employment to 26 percent of all employed. The number of employees in agriculture steadily dwindled – and a large percentage of them are now foreign workers. The weight of agriculture in the business sector in 2006 was a mere 2.6 percent.

Israel is unique among new societies in that it developed on the basis of socialist principles and was created by immigrants from Eastern Europe, not by settlers from Britain or Western Europe. Later, Israel was to be unique because it moved from the dominance of socialist thinking to a strategic alliance with the United States. Its institutions keep modifying their shape as society undergoes metamorphoses.

Israel is also unique in the magnitude of foreign unilateral transfers it received, allowing a high rate of capital formation. The government tapped large sources of capital and therefore could decide on the allocation of that capital. Another unique factor has been the heavy burden of defense expenditures on the economy (peaking at 27.4 percent of GNP in the period 1974–1980). Israel has been vulnerable to military and terrorist attacks. As a result, it has found it necessary to devote a high proportion of resources to defense, to maintain a qualitative military edge over its potential enemies. Another result of the "hostile neighborhood" was that almost all large MNEs refused to defy the Arab boycott and to invest in Israel.

Defense needs created major leverage for developing science-based industries, to ensure a reliable supply of military-related goods. The government established (and owned) Israel Military Industries, Israel Aircraft Industries (1953)[3] and Rafael[4] – the Hebrew acronym of the Armaments Development Authority. The Ministry of Defense traded only with its own firms.[5] In 1967, France imposed an embargo on military-related supplies to Israel. One result was an expansion of the budgets for military research and development. Another result was that these funds were no longer granted only to SOEs.

The need for security was coupled with two other requirements, dictated by the basic values of the state's leaders. The first was the super importance of mutual aid both to existing citizens and to new immigrants, which resulted in the forging of a welfare state. The second need stemmed from a utopian view of the superiority of

---

[3] It provides maintenance and rebuilding services for aircraft, and produces military and executive planes, weapons and missile systems, satellites, and electronic and radar-based combat systems. It is Israel's largest enterprise and its biggest exporter.

[4] It also developed and manufactured air-to-air missiles, sea-based missiles and other weapon systems.

[5] One exception was a communications and batteries firm, Tadiran, of which it sold 50 percent to General Telephone and Electronics. In 1966 the Ministry agreed to acquire a 50 percent share in Elbit (military electronics).

collective decision making, versus what was perceived as the wild pursuit of private gains.

The combination of these three factors with the gloomy realities of a less developed country reinforced the belief that the state alone could achieve security, social goals, and accelerated economic growth. These beliefs led to a very high level of involvement of government as well as of Histadrut (the General Federation of Labor) and the Jewish Agency in ownership of economic units.

They established – sometimes separately, often jointly – many relatively large enterprises financed heavily from public sources. In the 1960s, the government or the Histadrut owned 45 percent of all large industrial plants. Virtually all economic activities were controlled, regulated, and directed by the various authorities. A national authority owned almost all land, leasing such lands for limited periods. Water was allocated by another authority. Importers needed a license. So did those wishing to buy foreign exchange. Bank credit was regulated and the government granted subsidized rates of interest to preferred recipients.

The government protected domestic production, restricting imports through quotas or sky-high tariffs. Most output was subject to price controls. It also subsidized exports. All sources of funds, including pensions, as well as the allocation of these funds, were tightly controlled and were distributed at the discretion of civil servants and politicians.

Since the government fully controlled the capital market, a public offering of shares was not feasible. New entrepreneurs had to present their business plans to the government and/or financial institutions – most of which were also controlled by the government or the Histadrut. Finally, perhaps because of the long reign of ideology, Israelis were told they should be ashamed for wanting to consume more, and that preferring cheaper imports to locally made goods was irresponsible. Outward FDI was certainly not encouraged. Very few firms received foreign exchange allocations for this purpose.

In 1973, Israel was caught by surprise, attacked by Egypt and Syria. Further, the high growth rate in economic activity that had characterized Israel until 1972 came to a halt. One reason was the rise of oil prices. Another was that many Israeli firms were not yet ready to face competition in the world market and achieve export-led growth.

By the 1970s the majority of Israelis were of Asian and African origin. They perceived themselves as deprived persons. They saw the Labor Party elite as an arrogant, intolerant, and paternalistic establishment. The Labor government was toppled in 1977 after several decades of Israel living under the rule of a single, socialist party.

A coalition of right-wing parties formed the government, declared a full liberalization of the economy, and abolished some of the controls on foreign exchange. The country suffered at the time from rampant inflation that at its height reached a level of more than 400 percent per annum. The net external debt reached 80 percent of GDP. It was widely agreed that drastic steps were called for and that the economy had to be reformed.

In 1985, a unity government accepted a stabilization plan proposed by several senior Israeli economists. These economists, trained in Chicago School theory, moved the economy toward liberalization. The plan has been very successful. Since then politicians have been much more willing to accept economists' proposals.

Between 1985 and 1994, major reforms were carried out in the capital markets, the money markets, the foreign exchange markets, the labor market, and in the role of the public sector. Average annual public spending was reduced from 1980–1984 to 1994–1998 by not less than 21 percent of GDP, money transferred from the public to the private sector. The government also increased purchases from the private sector, abolishing its own operations. Foreign exchange controls were totally abolished in 1988 and today there are no restrictions even on institutional investors. Import restrictions were abolished. Tax laws were changed, equalizing the tax consequences of various activities at home and abroad. Corporate taxes were reduced from 61% in 1987 to 45%, then to 36% in 1990 and to 31% in 2006.

The government significantly reduced its control of all sources of funds, the allocation of capital, and the determination of yields. Thus, the allocation of so-called directed credit went down from 65% of total credit in 1983 to 3% in 1998.

A series of reforms reduced the hold of monopolies. In 2005 the ports and the refineries were divided into several firms and were privatized, the telephone company was privatized, and a partial pension reform was implemented. Free trade agreements were signed with both the EU (1989) and the United States (1995) and imports from low-cost countries such as China, Turkey, Mexico, and Poland were allowed with no need for an import license and with much-reduced tariffs.

Another result of the 1985 plan was that many firms – used to protection from imports, a strictly regulated environment, and focused more on good relations with the government rather than efficiency in the marketplace – went bankrupt. A wave of acquisitions consolidated many industries. SOEs were privatized. Privatizations reduced the share of the SOE sector in manufacturing from 27% in 1985 to 10% in 1993. Histadrut-owned enterprises, most of which were characterized by bloated labor forces, were sold to private investors. The share of Histadrut in net product that had gone up from 10% in 1948 to 17.9% in 1953 and 23.0% in 1960 dwindled to 14% in 1993 and to almost zero by 2004.

Entrepreneurs who could achieve results in the marketplace replaced many of the older generation of businesspeople. The Law for the Encouragement of Industrial Research and Development was passed in 1985. Since then, the Office of the Chief Scientist at the Ministry of Industry and Trade has helped to fund innovative projects. Also in 1985, the first Israeli venture capital firm was established. Today, over 100 venture capital firms operate in Israel.

Between 1985 and 2007, a revolution took place in terms of the openness of the economy, foreign currency supervision, budgetary policy, and competition policy. On March 16, 2007, the OECD's Ministerial Council meeting approved a decision to open accession discussions with Israel. Israel's GNP per capita in 2006 was $19,900. The OECD average was $33,400, that of the Euro countries $33,500 and the United States $43,000. Inflation was −0.1% in Israel compared with 2.1% in the United States and 2.3% in the EU.

Israel is still classified by the Institute of International Finance and by Morgan Stanley as an emerging economy. UNCTAD, on the other hand, classifies Israel as a developed economy. Today, Israel's high-tech industry promotes itself to investors as an alternative to Silicon Valley. The industry is carefully watched by venture capitalists, and dozens of Israeli technology companies have been sold to overseas buyers.

By 1982, Israel counted 300 high-tech firms, of which 122 employed 49 employees or fewer, 67 had 50–99 employees, and 111 employed 100 or more. All in all, these were very small firms. It was estimated at that time that about two thirds of the development engineers in Israel, directly or indirectly, served defense-related needs.

In 1987, the government decided to stop the development of an Israeli jet fighter, the Lavi. Israel Aviation had to fire a large number of skilled engineers with experience in cutting-edge technologies, who were then absorbed into the civilian marketplace. Advanced technologies that were originally developed for military purposes were later used to develop commercial products for civilian use. Thousands of visionaries formed start-up companies, some of which later became successful high-tech MNEs.

By 2004, 33% of Israeli manufacturing exports were in electronics and only 3.6% in textiles (Bank of Israel, Annual report for 2006, p. 60). Information, Communication, and Technology firms (ICT) are classified as trade and services; ICT product was 16.8% of business product in 2006 while the OECD average was 9% (Bank of Israel, 2006, p. 74). Because of the limited size of the domestic market, the share of exports in the output is very large: 57% in 2006, 72% in information technology alone (p. 74).

By 2000, Israel's share of the US and European high-tech market was 1.4%. That share went down as a result of a recession but by February 2007 was up again to about 1.3%. Israeli companies are developers of advanced technologies, enjoying top-notch human resources and government support for corporate R&D and manufacturing facilities. Since 1991, the Technological Incubators Program has provided comprehensive support to new ventures.

Israel still suffers threats to its very existence, resulting in a high level of uncertainty and many swings – for example, in the number of incoming tourists. The country is also far from its markets, unable to sell to its immediate neighbors. This problem is alleviated somewhat by the widespread use of the Internet as a means of quick communication and, more recently, the use of video conferencing. It is still not easily solved.

The new managers

Another change that came gradually was in the recruitment, education, and tendencies of Israeli managers. In the 1960s managers in the state sector were political appointees, as were managers in the

Histadrut sector. There was a strong belief in the superiority of egalitarian society. To avoid a class system, managerial jobs in the Histadrut were rotated. The private sector consisted of a large number of small enterprises, managed by several families of the owners. Those who attempted to grow faced the constraint of the small size of the market. Once competing firms were acquired, the only way to grow internally was to expand into other economic activities. Indeed, holding companies or conglomerates controlled jobs in many parts of the Israeli economy. Each one of these holding companies had a financial institution that allowed it to finance the operations of the various firms related to it. With time, the founders retired. Civil servants and former Army officers were major sources of recruitment of managers in addition to the children or the sons-in-law of the owners.

During the sixties, almost all Israeli entrepreneurs were institutional rather than individualistic, working for the increased power and the glory of their sector and for the expansion of the size of the firms they managed. The managers of these firms also had very cordial relations with government officials and politicians. Personal contacts were deemed essential for business success: the success of the firms they headed depended more on governmental decisions than on their success in managing the firm or finding the right strategy in the marketplace. Firms were shielded from competition. Private entrepreneurs found it extremely difficult to establish new ventures.

A few renegades were encouraged and aided by a major private conglomerate in Israel: DBIC (Discount Bank Investment Company). Its manager was Dr. Augusto Levi, who recruited Dan Tolkowski after he retired in 1958 from his position as Commanding Officer of the Israeli Air Force. Mr. Tolkowsky recognized the need to modernize Israeli industry. The firm he managed helped in the financing and management of several visionaries who demonstrated tenacity and fortitude in getting things done against the odds.

One such company was Iscar, a producer of precision carbide cutting tools, founded in 1952; DBIC became a partner in 1961. Another – Elron (1962) – was the first Israeli start-up in electronics devices. In 1966, Elbit was established to utilize the accumulated know-how of Rafael and Elron in computers. Another joint venture of Elron was Elscint (1969), specializing in CAT scan, and later MRI, technology.

DBIC also established Scientific Technology, which became Scitex (1968), focusing on computerized preprinting (Sherman,1988, Levav, 1998).[6]

These firms were the buds of the high-tech industry of Israel and a few of them were its first "born globals." They focused on knowledge creation rather than knowledge acquisition. They targeted the competitive international markets, not the protected domestic one. They believed they could invent better products and overcome any problem.

As Stef Wertheimer said: "an Israeli can succeed in anything he does. He has to succeed because there is no way back to Hitler" (Levav, 1998, p. 151). These pioneers were often naïve but also full of enthusiasm. They were innovators but were cutting milk teeth on production and lacked any marketing proficiency. In quite a few cases, the innovators did not even make the most cursory market survey before they spent time and money on their inventions.

A few of these pioneers were employed by US firms and started the new businesses as a means to return home. Arazi, for one, was able to convince the US firm he worked for to start a subsidiary in Israel for him. In 1974, Intel agreed to open its first development center outside the United States to retain the services of Dov Froman who decided to return to Israel (Breznitz, 2007, p. 195). Benny Landa, the founder of

---

[6] Iscar was founded in 1952 by Stef Wertheimer. DBIC acquired the shares of a partner of the small knives producer in 1961. Since then the firm has grown. It also established a separate firm to produce jet engine blades. Elron was founded by Uzia Galil to manufacture electronic devices. Initial funding of $160,000 was received from DBIC and from a venture capital fund owned by Laurence and David Rockefeller. The Rockefellers sold their shares to DBIC in 1966 because they decided to pull out of Europe. Efi Arazi returned to Israel after the 1967 war. His first firm provided computerized printing solutions to the textile industry. He then moved to preprinting. The founders were also the managers of these firms. In 1966 Elbit became a joint venture of Elron and the Ministry of Defense. In 1970, the ministry sold its share to Control Data Corporation. In 1969 Avraham Suhami, with Elron, founded Elscint. Initially the firm sold nuclear physics lab equipment but moved to nuclear scanners with medical applications. Other firms were not part of DBIC. ECI Telecom was established in 1957. It produced military products. It moved to civilian products only in the 1980s. In 1968 Morris Kahan, who immigrated from South Africa, formed the Aurek group with ITT, after the partners won a tender from the Ministry of Communications to publish a *Yellow Pages* telephone directory. Kahan acquired ITT's shares in Aurek in 1973. In 1970 Aurek won a tender to publish telephone directories and formed a subsidiary to set up the computing system for the project. This became Amdocs.

Indigo and an innovator in ink-cased electric photography, came from Canada. To date, Israeli expatriates who worked for global US-based MNEs have tended to form bridges between Israeli firms and firms in Silicon Valley. Many managers in the high-tech firms rotate between Israel and the United States.

The vast majority of Israeli managers today hold an MBA from one of dozens of business schools operating in the country. Many of these managers are engineers; some are economists. These managers were trained to appreciate well-thought-out business plans and clear strategic vision, to think strategically, to value marketing and – above all – profits.

A significant percentage of Israel's business elite may accurately be called part of the "global elite," independent of the government and regulations. They did not inherit their wealth; they created it, tapping venture capital funds, offering IPOs on NASDAQ or in Europe. In the process of getting the funds, they did not need to ask for permissions, licenses, or foreign exchange allocations.

I have studied for decades the structure and conduct of Israeli business firms. These studies show a major revolution (Aharoni 1976, 2007) in the composition of the business elite, the sources of their recruitment, and their relationships with the political elite. A major reason for the change seems to have been that entrepreneurs today are not dependent on government or on holding companies or Israeli banks. Managers in high-tech firms today are judged by their ability to achieve business results, not by contacts in government or with the old business elite.

Even in regulated enterprises, the level of dependency seems much lower than it was several decades ago. All in all, the business elite are no longer composed of managers relying on the government for help. The new managers look for success by competing in the global market. They value personal success, but at the same time are very much committed to creating a successful country, and to the values of that country.

These managers, scientists, and engineers could easily find lucrative jobs in other countries. They are, however, firmly committed to living in Israel and building the state. One reason, perhaps, is memories of the holocaust: after the loss of a third of the world's Jewish population, Israelis value the security of having their own country to protect them.

The new breed of Israeli business leaders learned that if they wanted the firms they led to grow they had to go abroad, designing and implementing strategies that made them competitive MNEs in world markets.[7] All in all, perhaps the greatest CSA of Israel today is the culture of its residents. It places a premium on entrepreneurship and risk taking. This is manifested in the thousands of start-ups, created by Israelis who left more stable jobs.

Compulsory military service, moreover, creates comradeships that carry over into teamwork in business and informal networks, enhancing mutual learning. Many managers of born globals were pilots, or served in the intelligence corps.

In addition, close-knit communities are created as a result of the small size of the country. There is in the national culture an innate stubbornness, resilience, a strong ability to improvise, the creative drive of a polyglot people, but also impatience with, and a lack of respect for, other cultures. Within this culture it was possible to develop FSAs but also clusters of firms that helped each other and learned from each other's experiences.

One successful example – Teva Pharmaceutical Industries

The most successful Israeli multinational has been Teva Pharmaceutical Industries Ltd. Its story is a fine example of success but also of the problems and tribulations of establishing and operating a multinational enterprise from a tiny country such as Israel.

Teva's roots can be traced back to 1901, when three businessmen – Chaim Salomon, Moshe Gutel Levin, and Yitschak Asher Elstein – established in Jerusalem a wholesale drug distributor named after them (SLE) that imported drugs and sold them in the local market.

One result of the Nazi's ascent to power in Germany was that many Jews fled; some emigrated to Palestine. Many of the new immigrants were highly educated and a few of them had experience in the pharmaceutical industry. They established several small cottage plants

---

[7] Several decades ago, I observed that "small countries like Israel produce an exportable surplus of educated, middle-class members of the work force who cannot be absorbed at home. One means of allowing them to keep their national identity and to work abroad is to use them in multinational corporations based in the small country" (Agmon and Kindleberger, 1977, p. xiii).

to produce drugs under license. One of these plants was named Teva ("nature" in Hebrew). These plants flourished during World War II because they became suppliers to the British army. Immediately after the war, the newly created Arab League initiated a boycott against any business operating in the Jewish part of Palestine (and, since 1948, any business dealing with Israel). Large pharmaceutical firms, reluctant to invest in Israel, licensed domestic firms to produce their drugs for the local market.

About twenty small family-owned firms served this domestic market, each with annual sales of about $1 million. In the 1950s, SLE acquired one of these firms (Assia). Eli Hurvitz, who married Dalia Solomon, started working at Assia while pursuing evening studies for a bachelor's degree in economics. By 1962 Hurvitz was CEO. His early strategic vision was to become the market leader in Israel by consolidating the industry. He thus acquired Zori in 1963. Teva, which has been publicly listed on the Tel Aviv Stock Exchange since 1951, was acquired in 1968. The three firms merged in 1976 into Teva Pharmaceutical Industries Ltd., with Hurvitz as the CEO.

Teva became the largest pharmaceutical firm in Israel, producing under license drugs and fine chemicals for the domestic market, with annual sales of $28 million. In 1980 Teva acquired the second largest pharmaceutical firm, Ikapharm, which ran a US Food and Drug Administration (FDA) approved plant, and Plantex, a leading producer of active pharmaceutical ingredients.

Koor Industries, the largest Israeli conglomerate controlled by the Histadrut's Hevrat Ovdim, owned both these firms. Both lost money, and Koor proposed to sell them to Teva for 20 percent of Teva's shares. In addition, Koor loaned Teva IL60 million for ten years. Migada, a manufacturer of disposable medical equipment, was acquired in 1984 and Abic, a major drug manufacturer, in September 1988.

Teva became dominant in the small home market. Clearly, however, the opportunity for further domestic growth was extremely limited. Teva started to export to Africa, but this market was also quite small.

In the early 1980s Hurvitz hired Dr. Joseph Aleksandrowicz to start a strategic planning process, an unheard-of move in Israel at the time. Aleksandrowicz organized a program of seminars for the top executives of the firm to which he invited professors of business administration from Israel and abroad. In one of these sessions,

Hurvitz noted that Teva with its diversity of products, technologies, know-how and management should become a billion dollar company.

The reason it was not was that it operated in Israel. The limited size of the Israeli market was a barrier to further expansion, so it would have to enter a large Western market. Entering Europe meant registering each drug seventeen times compared to one time in the United States (Stauber, 2001, p. 33).

In 1982 Teva registered American Depository Receipts on NAS-DAQ. By 1985, sales revenues were $88 million. In 1985, together with W. R. Grace, a major US conglomerate, Teva acquired Lemon, a small $20 million US arm of a German company, to access the then-embryonic US generic drug market. Once a foothold was established, the company's market share and sales steadily grew. Teva became a bi-national company.

In 1989 the firm and two banks bought out Koor's ownership stake in Teva. In 1990 W. R. Grace sold its Lemon shares to Teva. Hurvitz built an internal team to evaluate acquisitions and the firm gained a reputation for its success in targeting candidates for acquisition, and integrating them quickly and successfully.

By 2007, Teva had become the number one pharmaceutical company in the US in terms of the number of prescriptions written for all drugs, as well as for generics in particular (Teva Pharmaceutical Industries Ltd., 2007, p. 9). Since 1985, Teva has executed fourteen transactions for over $12 billion. By 1993, Teva's sales were $502 million. It passed the billion dollar mark in 2000. By 2002, when Hurvitz retired as CEO and became Chairman of the Board, sales were $2.519 billion and Teva was one of the three top providers of generic drugs in the United States, Canada, the Netherlands, Hungary, France, and the UK. The company continues to grow at an annual growth rate of sales of 20 percent (and more than that on the profit side) both organically and through acquisitions, doubling its sales volume every four years.

Sicor was acquired for $3.4 billion in 2003, not only expanding the company's geographic sphere, but also moving into selling injectable liquid products direct to hospitals. In 2005 Ivax was acquired for $7.4 billion, giving access to a very strong first-to-file Paragraph IV[8]

---

[8] A certification standard of the FDA.

pipeline in the United States and to markets in Eastern Europe and Latin America.

By 2006, 60 percent of the company was owned by mutual funds and institutions. Teva's sales in 2006 were $8.4 billion. Its headquarters is in Israel with subsidiaries in over fifty countries. Its by-laws dictate that the CEO must reside in Israel. By now it is a global leader in generic drugs and an active pharmaceutical ingredients manufacturer in Europe and North America.

Hurvitz also aspired to leverage Israeli science. The huge investment required for in-house R&D and regulatory approval of a new drug (estimated at $1 billion) was beyond Teva's reach. It did develop, register, produce, and market molecules discovered by Israeli researchers – for example, at the Weizman Institute of Science. (Compaxone for multiple sclerosis, for example, registered in the US in 1996. In 2005, Compaxone's sales were $1.2 billion, 12% of Teva's global sales. Compaxone continued to grow by about 22% in 2006.)

Given the limited population of prescribing physicians, the marketing costs are relatively low. Teva had partnered with Sanofi-Aventis to manage the marketing of the drug. Teva also developed Azilect for treating Parkinson's disease, approved by the EU (2005) and the United States (2006). Teva has in the pipeline several other innovative drugs, and some analysts are concerned that this might be too much for Teva's research budget and its limited experience in bringing drugs to market.

Teva is perhaps the best example of a very successful global firm with a home base in Israel. It eschewed the traditional conglomerate model, choosing instead a highly focused approach embraced by later generations of successful Israeli companies. It was able to keep a low-cost mentality and to integrate acquired firms into its culture, creating and maintaining synergies.

The company bred a class of professional managers and scientists never before seen in the country. It served as a bridge from Israeli science to the market and has been an important source of talent and capital for the growing biotechnology sector. With an increasing portfolio of innovative drugs, Teva has to manage quite diverse operations under one roof. It also faces increased competition from new low-cost players – for example, from India – eager to follow Teva's success and increase their own market share.

Outward FDI from Israel: Facts and figures

Outward FDI from Israel is a relatively new phenomenon. A few MNEs emerged in the 1960s; the majority did not survive. A few more started in the 1980s[9] and in the past two decades their numbers have increased. MNEs became possible as a result of major reforms in government policies leading to structural changes, a key change in the composition of the Israeli business elite, major changes in global conditions – detailed by Williamson and Zeng in Chapter 5 in this volume – and of course the strategies and management processes of the firms themselves.

Teva is the largest of the Israeli multinationals, but only one of more than 150 such firms. Teva is also one example of a firm that internationalized only after it could not continue to grow in the local market, behaving as one would expect based on theory. Other firms in traditional fields went abroad only after they faced limits to growth in the domestic market. Some examples of relatively large Israeli traditional multinationals, in addition to Teva, are:

> *Israel Chemicals*, a producer of potash, phosphate rock, magnesium and bromide, raw materials available in or near the Dead Sea. The firm was state owned and at that time its managers had a hard time convincing government bureaucrats that foreign exchange should be allocated to it to purchase a subsidiary to jump tariffs in its exports to Europe.[10] It has been privatized and is now operating in Europe, North America, Latin America, and China. It also maintains global marketing and logistics facilities.

---

[9] In 1981 brothers Zohar and Yehuda Zisappel formed the RAD group which became one of Israel's high-tech leaders. Many start-ups were formed under RAD's auspices, several of which became MNEs. In 1983 Efrat was founded to develop computerized voice mail. The partners concurrently registered Comverse as the US parent. After a decade of difficulties the firm became a world leader in its niche. In the same year, Indigo developed its digital printer. In 1985, Amdocs was founded to provide billing services to an American firm. In 2006, its revenues were $2.48 billion. It has development centers in Israel, India, the United States, Cyprus, and Brazil.

[10] In one case in the 1960s the firm asked for a foreign exchange allocation to acquire an Italian manufacturing firm for $10 million. Management believed this acquisition would allow a major expansion. The Minister of Finance refused.

It is the only resource-based Israeli MNE. Its global sales from July 2006 to June 2007 were about $4 billion.

Makhteshim-Agan Industries Ltd. (MAI), the result of a merger of the two Israeli producers of crop protection products. Today, MAI is the world's leading manufacturer and distributor of off-patent crop and non-crop protection products. MAI ranks among a handful of the world's largest manufacturers of crop protection chemicals, with subsidiaries in Latin America and Europe. Its global sales from July 2006 to June 2007 were $2.25 billion.

Iscar, a producer of precision carbide cutting tools for hard metal cutting and engine blades. It owns manufacturing facilities in France, Germany, Italy, the Netherlands (established in 1962 to service the German market), Spain, Switzerland, Turkey, and the UK, as well as in the United States, South Korea, Brazil, and Argentina. Being privately owned, the firm does not publish financial information. Globally, it is the second largest producer in its industry, up from number ten twenty years ago. In 2006, Berkshire Hathaway acquired 80 percent of Iscar's shares (but not of the blades firm).[11]

Delta Galil, a global provider of private label apparel, with factories in Jordan, Egypt, Turkey, Thailand, Romania, and Central America, producing ladies' intimate apparel, socks, men's underwear and leisure apparel for the UK and US markets, with global sales of $706.7 million in 2006.

Netafim, an example of a firm that turned Israel's disadvantage into a FSA. Israel suffers from a chronic shortage of water. Netafim invented drip irrigation to preserve scarce water resources and increase crop yields. Today, Netafim leverages cutting-edge core drip irrigation technologies to provide end-to-end solutions for biofuel energy, turnkey greenhouse projects, wastewater management, and advanced crop management and monitoring systems. With over 2,000 employees, 14 manufacturing facilities in 11 countries, more than 30 subsidiaries and a distribution presence in 110 countries Netafim's global sales are more than $400 million.

Other firms were able to exploit FSAs developed in the domestic market in foreign operations. Thus, Bank Hapoalim, the largest Israeli

---

[11] See Letter to Shareholders, 2006, Berkshire Hathaway, p. 4.

bank, acquired banks in Turkey and in the United States; Bank Leumi established a bank in Romania.

Other examples are Ormat, an innovator and producer of solar, geothermic, and other alternative energy equipment (with twenty-two plants abroad), Elite in coffee, Electra in white appliances, Elbit in military electronics, Israel Aerospace Industries (which in September 2007 opened a wholly owned subsidiary of its international subsidiary to produce unmanned aerial vehicles in Mississippi), and 'Dor Alon and Delek in gasoline distribution.

By 2007, most large firms in Israel in most economic sectors, acutely aware of the limited growth opportunities in the domestic market, had attempted to expand through foreign operations. An insurance company (Phoenix) acquired a Romanian insurance firm, and many real estate developers and construction firms expanded to Eastern Europe, Russia, India, and the United States.

Among the largest twenty-five firms traded on the Tel Aviv Stock Exchange 58 percent of the revenues in 2006 came from operations outside Israel. The highest percentage of foreign operations was in the chemical industry (93%), followed by electronics (81%), holding companies (80%), real estate (67%), and food (40%). At the bottom were banks (11%), insurance (4%), and communications (0%) (*Globes*, 2007 May, p. 30).

Needless to say, firms must develop the proper strategy and avail themselves of the proper managerial talent, creating the capabilities to compete in foreign countries. Israel Chemicals bases its competitive advantage on the availability of raw materials in Israel. Others rely on unique knowledge – in agricultural products, for example – or on the availability of human resources with deep knowledge of the language and the culture of target countries. Because of immigration, one can find in Israel a bank manager who speaks Romanian, a construction engineer fluent in Hungarian, and so on.[12]

Since the 1960s, the internationalization processes of firms have been the topic of widespread research. Several researchers (e.g. Johanson and

---

[12] As one example, Ossem, one of the largest food manufacturers in Israel, chose to partner with the giant Nestlé. In 2007, it built its first plant abroad. It produced an Israeli innovation, vegetarian frozen entrees, in the Czech Republic, in the same city from which the grandfather of Ossem's owners had operated a pasta factory.

Vahlne, 1977, 1990, Bilkey, 1978, Cavusgil, 1980) have emphasized the gradual and sequential nature of the decision making process. A firm is assumed to build a stable domestic position before starting international activities.

Since the 1990s, these views have been challenged. Zander and Zander (1997) followed a hundred years of Alfa Laval. They criticized the idea of evolutionary determinism, pointing out that Alfa Laval's growth shows an oscillating rather than a linear pattern of development.

Others have demonstrated that many firms now do *not* develop their international activities in incremental stages. Rather, they start international activities, entering very distant markets, right from their birth. Such firms have been labeled "international new ventures" (Oviatt and McDougall, 1994), "high-technology start-ups" (Jolly *et al.*, 1992), and "born global" (McKinsey & Co., 1993, Rennie, 1993, Knight and Cavusgil, 1996, Madsen and Servais, 1997). The explanation for this new sequence of internationalization of firms is claimed to be more global market conditions, new developments in transportation and communications technologies, and the rising number of people with international experience (Oviatt and McDougall, 1994, 1997).

Indeed, many high-tech Israeli firms are born global (Almor, 2000). Israel is widely acknowledged to be a technological innovator (Breznitz, 2006). Israeli entrepreneurs have been successful in creating and managing science-based firms in IT, Internet applications, and telecommunications, as well as in medically related areas (e.g. Medinol, founded in 1992).[13] They develop products solely for international markets, based on niches that have not been developed by larger firms in other countries.

A combination of an ample reservoir of trained personnel, advanced research and development facilities, government incentives, and access to the US and European markets has made Israel a good base for science-based industry (Avnimelech and Tuebal, 2004, de Fontenay

---

[13] Medinol is expert in the field of stenting and the inventor of the flexible closed cell stent design. Medinol owns patents relating to both stent design and stent manufacturing. Medinol invented breakthrough technology based on etching as opposed to the traditional laser cut method. Stents for both coronary and peripheral applications were exclusively distributed by Boston Scientific Corporation between 1995 and 2002.

and Carmel, 2004). R&D in areas such as plant and animal propagation helped create a large farm-export industry.

By the 1970s, Israel's R&D prowess had rapidly expanded out of the agricultural and military spheres into expertise in software, semiconductors, medical equipment electronics and communications, and then into biotechnology and advanced materials.

Moreover, as the result of a report from a public commission of scientists (submitted in 1968) the government created an Office of the Chief Scientist (OCS) in the Ministry of Trade and Industry to help finance R&D programs in manufacturing industries, albeit on a small scale (Breznitz, 2007: pp. 50–57). Today grants by the OCS cover between 30% and 66% of total development costs. The OCS also aids start-ups via its Technological Incubators Program, providing institutional support in infrastructure, financing, and business networking.

OCS receives royalties from successful alumni. It also coordinates several bilateral R&D programs. The first of these, established in 1977, is the Israel–US Bi-National Industrial Research and Development Foundation (BIRD F). It was designed to enable Israeli start-ups to form strategic partnerships with large American firms. Others are foundations with Canada, Singapore, Great Britain, and Europe. Currently, with the increase in scope of venture capital firms and the ability to link with global financial markets (Avnimelech and Teubal, 2005) these foundations are relatively less important.

As already pointed out, Elron was the first Israeli start-up, established already in 1961. At that time high tech in Israel was carried out within the state-owned defense enterprises that did not want to compromise their monopoly position on defense orders. Some Israeli firms produced under foreign license but very little interaction existed between research carried out in universities and the operations of manufacturing industries.

Without access to defense orders, the fledgling new ventures did not have any market within Israel. They had to sell all of their production in foreign markets. But they did not have any knowledge of marketing. One way to get an international marketing base was through tie-ins with foreign partners, but this route left the most important ingredients of survival in the hands of others.

Firms that tried this route faced many problems, from clashes of interest to clashes of culture, to strategy shifts on the part of foreign partners.[14] Even a small change in direction of a giant partner could create an untenable situation for the smaller Israeli partner, inhibiting its growth and leaving it exposed and vulnerable.

Further, markets and customers were changing very fast and these rapid changes challenged many assumptions. A major lesson was that one must be near the market, and therefore essential marketing should not be predicated solely on arrangements with foreign partners.

Scitex was the first to establish a marketing subsidiary in the United States and then a European subsidiary headquarters in 1974 in Brussels. Uzia Galil advocated the "two-legged industrial animal." To be successful, a firm should have operations based in Israel but also maintain a subsidiary or sometimes a parent in the United States, thus becoming bi-national.[15] The firms should develop their own expertise in R&D, production, and marketing. Clearly, it would be futile to develop products of the "me too" category since the tiny Israeli firms could not compete head on with industrial giants. Instead, the firms had to develop products with unique advantages, looking for applications that others either could not address or had overlooked.

In the 1970s, Scitex and Elscint were the two flagships of Israeli high tech, and both were early born globals. Scitex stunned the printing industry in 1979 by introducing the computer-based turnkey Response color prepress system. It served a labor intensive and costly niche. By 1984 its sales were $104 million. It also developed a sister product line to be used in the mapping industry. It then moved to other niches in the preprinting industry. Some products were successful. Others were not.

---

[14] Thus, Scitex started as Scientific Technology by building a computer-based design system for the textile industry. The marketing was to be done by a textile firm in North Carolina that invested $250,000 in seed money. Alas, the firm was more interested in owning the only working machine than in selling more machines. Arazi had to renegotiate and to pay dearly (Levav, 1998, pp. 119–121). Thereafter, he vowed to have his own marketing subsidiary. Monsanto was forced to retrench and pulled out of a joint venture; Xerox took over SDS, inhibiting the growth of the joint venture SDS had carved out with Elbit. (Elbit developed and produced the first mini computer.)

[15] Thus, when Fibronics International was created in 1978 to exploit the new field of fiber optics, the firm was established as a US firm functioning through an Israeli subsidiary. Many other examples of bi-national firms followed.

By February 1992, Scitex's share of the worldwide color prepress market was estimated to be 45 percent. In 1995, with the advent of desktop publishing on PCs, Scitex's costly machines became too expensive for most publishers. In 2000, Creo acquired Scitex graphic arts operations. In 2004, Eastman Kodak acquired Creo. Efi Arazi left Scitex in 1988, creating a new firm called EFI (Electronic for Imaging) in California.

Elscint, managed by Avraham Suhani, introduced its CAT scanner in 1974. Each scanner was sold for around $500,000. It gambled on new products such as MRI and ultrasound. The world market for computer tomography was estimated at $660 million in the early 1980s with an annual growth rate of 15 percent. Elscint established marketing centers in the United States, Canada, Belgium, France, Germany, Holland, Italy, Sweden, Switzerland, the UK, Brazil, Mexico, South America, and Australia. It had to maintain adequate, comprehensive, and timely after-sales service centers. Its sales were $140 million. In MRI, Elscint produced its own magnets at a wholly owned subsidiary in Oxford, UK. In December 1983 it acquired certain parts of Xonics Medical System, but in February 1984 Xonics filed for Chapter 11 reorganization. Further, changes in health policy in the United States resulted in heavy losses in 1984. Suhami left and the firm went through a difficult restructuring.

Frederick P. Adler, a New York investment banker and venture capitalist, demonstrated that it was possible to raise capital on NASDAQ. Israeli firms could go public in the United States to solve the chronic need for more capital. In 1972 he launched an IPO with Elscint,[16] underwritten by Hambrecht & Quist, and Bache & Co. He later floated the shares of other firms, too, among them Scitex and Elron.

The new generation of Israeli high-tech firms tapped capital from venture capital funds, from NASDAQ, and from Europe. The firms are often incorporated in the United States, they maintain marketing and sales offices outside Israel, produce components in Asia, but maintain some core R&D and managerial decision making in Israel.

Between 1990 and 1996 fifty-six Israeli firms issued stock on NASDAQ, raising $18,155 million. Since then the number has more

---

[16] Elscint was also the first firm to be allowed to issue its own common stock and get tax concessions. Other firms followed.

than doubled. In 2005, with the registration of Ituran, Israel became the second country after the United States in terms of the number of firms registered on NASDAQ (seventy-one firms). Canada moved to third place with sixty-eight firms. NASDAQ created a listing of seventy-three Israeli companies called ISRQ with combined capitalization of $50 billion. The daily quote in the Israeli press of Israeli shares in New York includes 116 firms, and 60 more firms appear on European stock exchanges: London, (AIM) Amsterdam, Brussels, Zurich, and Frankfurt.

One reason for the gap in figures is that a relatively large number of Israeli-based firms are incorporated in the United States and therefore are officially US – not Israeli – firms. Others were incorporated in Holland (e.g. Indigo, a major producer of digital printing machines). Many of these born globals grew quite substantially.[17] In addition to Israeli firms officially incorporated in the United States, there were Israelis less interested in maintaining ties to the motherland. They moved to other countries (mainly the United States) and founded firms there. Some of them built quite an empire, but, of course, those are not considered Israeli multinationals.

Table 12.1 provides some statistics from the *World Investment Report* (UNCTAD, 2006) on Israeli overseas FDIs for the years 2002–2005. In 2006, outward FDIs from Israel surged. Balance of payments figures show an increase in the investments of Israeli residents abroad (including portfolio investments) from $4.3 billion in 2001 to $4.6 billion in 2002, $7.8 billion in 2003, $13.5 billion in 2004, $18.5 billion in 2005, and $32.1 billion in 2006 (Bank of Israel 2006, p. 248). These figures are underestimates since they do not include firms registered outside Israel.

Giant multinationals such as Hewlett Packard, Cisco, Lucent Technologies, and San Disk acquired many of the very successful firms. The number of these acquisitions and the dollar value of the

---

[17] Some examples are: Check Point Software Technologies with annual sales of $605.5 million; Nice, which offered comprehensive performance management and interaction analytics solutions, with annual sales of $437.7 million; Amdocs, a billing and customer care provider, with annual sales of $2.48 billion; Orbotech, a supplier of automated optical inspection systems, with annual sales of $416.5 million; and Comverse, a software company, with annual sales of $1.12 billion (all data pertain to calendar year 2006 or fiscal year 2006–07).

Table 12.1. *Statistics on Israeli outward FDIs*

	2002	2003	2004	2005
Greenfield investments abroad–number	39	39	58	54
Number of MNEs for which parent is an Israeli firm			154	
Bilateral Investment Treaties (BIT)				36
Double Taxation Agreements (DDT)				44
Cross border investments purchases (millions of dollars)		1,357	4,003	1,446
Cross border M&A – number of deals		13	29	29
FDI outflows ($ millions)		2,064	4,543	2,492

Source: UNCTAD (2006)

Table 12.2. *Acquisitions of Israeli high-tech firms by foreign multinationals*

Year	Number of transactions	Value ($ thousands)
2000	64	6,882
2001	29	483
2002	63	21,452
2003	59	1,083
2004	61	1,811
2005	70	2,678
2006	76	10,584

Source: Israel Venture Capital (www.ivc-online.com)

transactions for the years 2000–2006 are shown in Table 12.2. Such acquisitions continued into 2007. [18]

---

[18] Thus, Spansion Inc. acquired Saifun Semiconductors Ltd., a producer of non-volatile memory, for $370 million in cash and shares; Spansion was the only customer of Saifun. ICAP, the largest inter-bank broker, acquired Triana (maker of software for banks), for $247 million. And Goldman Sachs acquired a block of shares in Mobileye, which made control systems for vehicles, based on an enterprise value of $600 million.

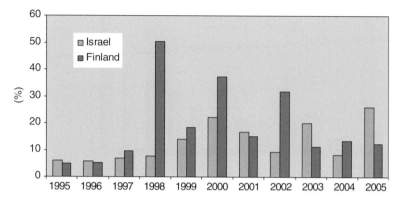

Figure 12.1 FDI share in total capital stock, Israel vs. Finland

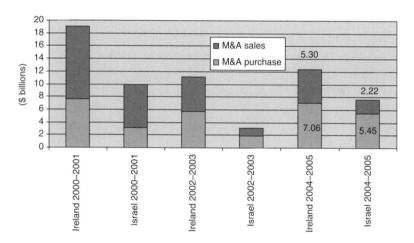

Figure 12.2 M&As, Israel vs. Ireland, various years

It is useful to compare Israel to other small countries. Finland is of interest: its economy is also based to a large extent on high-tech firms. Figure 12.1 demonstrates that as of 2005 the share of inward FDI to the total capital stock in the economy peaked at 26% for Israel but was only 12.3% for Finland.

World M&As surged in 2000 to $1.1 trillion and sank to a mere $296 million in 2003, jumping again to $716 billion in 2005. Figure 12.2 presents data comparing cross border M&As in Israel and

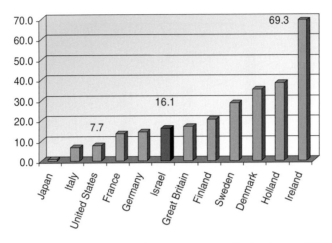

Figure 12.3 Percentage of GDP accounted for by foreign MNEs

in Ireland. In the figure, M&A sales refer to M&As by foreign firms in the respective economies. M&A purchases are M&As by Israeli/ Irish firms. The impact of the bubble can be seen to be much stronger in Israel: the figures for 2002–2003 show a sharp decline compared to 2000–2001. However, the improvement in 2004–2005 is also much faster in Israel compared to Ireland. Ireland was able to attract many MNEs. As a result, most of its economy (almost 70% of GDP) is accounted for by operations of MNEs, compared to 16.1% in Israel (Figure 12.3).

The Bank of Israel compared Israel to nations with a comparable level of technology and per capita GNP: Poland, Slovenia, Hungary, the Czech Republic, Singapore, South Korea, Portugal, and Spain (the "comparison group"). The long-range average (1998–2005) of inward FDI in Israel is 3% of GNP compared to 5.2% in the comparison group. Clearly Israel lagged behind in this respect. The reasons may be distance, the lack of natural resources, or the geopolitical situation. In 2006 inward FDIs were 10.8% of GNP and the percentage of inward FDI in Israel from all developing nations increased to 6% from a long-term average of 3% (Bank of Israel, 2006, p. 270). Of course these figures may be a result of one or two large investments. The inward FDIs in start-up firms have been much more consistent, with investment of about $0.8 billion per annum. Outward FDI as a percentage of GNP for the period 1998–2005 was 1.6% in Israel but 2.5% in the "comparison group." However, Israeli shares have been growing fast since 2001 and in 2006 were 8.5% (Bank of Israel, 2006, p. 274).

In 2006 Israel's population represented 0.1% of world population. It produced 0.25% of world gross product, but was responsible for 1.02% of world M&As and its share in the US and European high-tech markets was about 1.3% (UNCTAD, 2006; Bank of Israel, 2007, p. 10). Several firms achieved very interesting innovations that could lead to another Teva. Unfortunately, many entrepreneurs are tempted to be acquired by a giant MNE instead of following the torturous road leading to becoming a large MNE themselves. Certainly, the long road from a start-up to an IPO to becoming at least a billion dollar company is full of hazards, obstacles, and stumbling blocks; it is quite tempting to take "the bird in hand."[19]

The initial success of a start-up means domination of a well-defined niche, but the limited size of the niche may constrain further growth. The firm is also often dependent on a very small customer base – sometimes only one (e.g. a retailer). If the firm moves to larger niches or more diversified geographic markets it increases the risk of failure. Quite often, success necessitates heavy investments in an after-sales service network. Again, the firm may decide to give up its independence and be acquired by a giant that can supply such crucial resources. Thus, Indigo, a producer of digital printing machines, was sold to Hewlett Packard when faced with spending large sums to create and maintain an after-sales service network. Both managers and venture capitalists have strong incentives to exit.

---

[19] Mirabilis is one example; the four young entrepreneurs who created ICQ, the first online instant messaging service, sold the firm quite early to AOL, receiving among themselves $406 million. Another example is that of Orni Petrushka and Rafi Gidron, who founded Scorpio Communications and sold it to US Robotics in 1996. In 1998, they founded Chromatis Networks and sold it two years later to Lucent Technologies for Lucent stock valued at $4.8 billion. Chromatis' flagship product, Metropolis MSX, integrated data, voice, and video services on metropolitan networks. In August 2001, after the dot-com bubble burst in the United States, Lucent dropped Chromatis' product line and fired all its employees. As Lucent's share price plunged, the value of the Chromatis sale to its Israeli owners also plunged: to $590 million.

A case study of a successful born global

Check Point Software Technologies Ltd. is a leader in global network security software. Gil Schwed, Shlomo Kramer, and Marius Nacht, three young programmers, who met in the Israeli army, founded the company in 1993. They recognized the growth of the Internet and saw that a major impediment to this growth would be the fear of hackers. Thus, they focused on Internet security, inventing technology that enabled the creation of Internet firewalls, thereby creating a new market. On June 28, 1996, Check Point launched an initial public offering on NASDAQ. At that time, the firm employed about forty people and its annual revenues were $34.6 million. By 2000 sales had grown to $425.3 million, and a year later the workforce had grown to 1,568, half of whom were employed outside Israel. Its revenues thus grew at an average rate of 50 percent per annum and the company leveraged its leadership position in Internet security. See Figure 12.4 for financial results. From 1998 to 2000, the firm adapted its organization to global operations. Check Point's focus is on IT security with an extensive portfolio of security solutions. In 2007, the company enjoys dominant market share in these markets. Extending the power of the Check Point solution is its Open Platform for Security, the industry's framework. Check Point solutions are sold, integrated, and serviced by a network of OEM partners, distributors, VARs, systems and network integrators, and Internet Service Providers. Its customers include 100 percent of Fortune 100 companies.

Check Point's development centers are located in Israel and in Belarus. It has offices in Redwood City, California, and in the Dallas, Texas, area. Gil Shwed has been CEO since the firm started. He was inducted into the highly respected CRN Industry Hall of Fame, honored for his work as an early firewall pioneer and for diversifying Check Point into data security. The company has received numerous industry recognitions and awards.

An integral ingredient of the firm's strategy has been reliance on internal growth, avoiding acquisitions, even though the firm had a mountain of cash at its disposal ($900 million by the end of 2006).

The firm's few acquisitions included SofaWare Technologies, founded in 1999 in Ramat-Gan, Israel. SofaWare's embedded software powers Internet security appliances, DSL and Wi-Fi routers, as

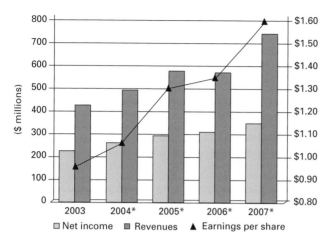

Figure 12.4 Check Point: Annual financial results, 2003–2007.
Note: *Presented in non-GAAP format. Financials exclude amortization of intangible assets, acquisition-related expenses, and stock-based compensation

well as broadband modems. It also bought Zone Labs, a security software company, in 2004.

In October, 2005, Check Point announced an agreement to acquire Sourcefire, the developers of Snort, for $225 million. The deal was expected to close by the first quarter, 2006, but Check Point notified the Securities and Exchange Commission in February that the deal was on hold pending approval under the 1988 Exon-Florio provision of the (US) Defense Production Act of 1950, which gives the president the ability to suspend or prohibit a foreign acquisition, merger, or takeover of a US corporation that threatens national security.

It turned out that both the FBI and the Department of Defense objected to the acquisition on security grounds. The deal had been under scrutiny by the CFIUS (Committee on Foreign Investment in the United States), a panel made up of representatives from a dozen government agencies tasked with investigating foreign investments in US companies that could affect national security. According to SecurityFocus, "the process fell afoul of international politics following the public outcry over the failure of CFIUS to further investigate a proposed deal that would have given a Middle Eastern company (United Arab Emirates-based Dubai World Ports) control over six major US ports" (IEMOS, 2006).

The Dubai World Ports deal eventually fell to political pressure. Further investigation by CFIUS into Check Point's proposed purchase of Sourcefire was announced the following day. The decision on Check Point's acquisition of Sourcefire would have been due by March 30. Check Point's decision to pull out of the process was considered an acknowledgment that CFIUS would deny permission for the acquisition. Companies commonly pull out of a pending acquisition before CFIUS renders its judgment.

Of the fourteen cases that have not had approval after further investigation, only one has actually been denied. The companies that had proposed the merger, according to the report published by Congressional Research Service, withdrew the thirteen other deals.[20]

Check Point is facing increasing competition from Sisco, Juniper, and Microsoft's Vista operating system. In early 2007, Check Point announced that it had acquired Protect Data AB (PROT.ST) and Pointsec Mobile Technologies AB of Sweden. Pointsec is a provider of mobile device security. Check Point also announced in early 2007 that it had acquired NFR Security, a threat prevention and intrusion prevention company, creators of the Network Flight Recorder, touted as a tamper-proof architecture and tool kit for building network traffic analysis and statistical event records.

According to Mr. Schwed, an Israel-based global firm must capitalize on indigenous advantages: the initiative, fast adaptation to changing conditions, efficiency, and dedication that are Israeli traits (*Globes*, 2004, December). The major challenge, according to him, is to bridge between the Israeli culture and other cultures. Seeing the world as having the same culture is wrong and would not work. It is imperative to mold a uniform organizational culture for the firm despite the different national cultures. According to Schwed, Israel has an advantage in the development of excellent new products (*Globes*, 2005, May 18). It must find ways to market the products and to install

---

[20] The failure of Check Point to get approval to acquire Sourcefire for security reasons was seen as an indication that defense-related firms would not be able to acquire firms in the United States. Yair Shamir, Chairman of the Board of Israel Aerospace Industries (IAI), had a vision of increasing military-related items from 20% of IAI's sales in the US to 40% or 50%. He noted, "We shall not acquire any firm in the US until we shall be sure the Administration would not oppose" (*Globes*, 2007, October 9–10, p. 10).

them. It is also important to satisfy existing cusomers' demands while at the same time making better and improved products.

Some lessons from the Israeli experience

What are some of the lessons from the experience of Israeli firms? First and foremost, in a global arena a firm from a small country does not need to cater to the domestic market. For almost any firm, world markets are wide open and these firms can sell in the large countries. Moreover, a firm from a small country can (and perhaps should) develop a global supply chain, allowing each country to specialize in the part of the product or service for which it enjoys a comparative advantage. There are still many exceptions – for example, in security-related business or in airlines.

Second, the capability of a tiny country such as Israel to produce wealth depends on the extent to which it can create new resources or assets based on technological capacity, management knowledge, and organizational competence. Unlike Russia or South Africa, the advantage of almost all Israeli-based MNEs is the creation of new assets, not the use of God-given natural resources. These created assets are intangible, mobile, and acknowledge no national borders.

In the 1960s, products were sold for very high prices to a small number of customers. Miniaturization allowed much smaller products and lower transportation costs. Since the 1990s, some products are sold on a tiny compact disk. Note also that it takes several decades before a full transformation of the firms, attitudes, and learning processes take place.

In the global economy there is a new division of labor in which income-generating assets are conceived and designed in developed countries but different parts of them are produced in different locations, creating a global supply chain. This global integration is powered by shrinking costs of transportation and communication and by the widespread use of the World Wide Web. In this world, the quality, energy, resourcefulness, and enterprise of people allow competitive advantage.

Israel has a major advantage in having a relatively large number of scientists. Indeed, Israel is a country of 7 million but has more scientific publications per capita than any other nation, including the United States. Israel has 135 engineers per 10,000 people compared to

85 per 10,000 in the United States. It also enjoys the highest number of medical doctors per capita in the world. Most important, there is a free market for new ideas and also for their financing. The highly educated work force is a major asset in the development of new ideas.

In the 1960s, an entrepreneur with a business plan had to convince the bureaucracy of an industrial development bank, or that of a large conglomerate, of the virtues of an idea to gain access to funds. Today, such an entrepreneur can opt for an IPO on NASDAQ or other equity markets. All in all, a nation can create for itself dynamic competitive advantages in the world markets by a high level of investment in human capital.

Availability of raw materials or cheap labor is not the only means of achieving economic growth or creating home-based MNEs. MNEs can prosper if a nation invests in the creation of new knowledge and skills and if firms are innovative in designing strategies, which introduce to the world economy new products and new processes, differentiated from commodity-like products. To be sure, superior technology is essential but without market knowledge, expertise in distribution, logistics, and management the firm is doomed. It is also possible that Israel will face a short supply of both engineers and managers.

Third, firms from small countries do not enjoy the luxury of growth in the domestic market. In any small country, a firm may first grow by acquiring its competitors. To reach a relatively large size, it must by definition dominate the domestic market. Further growth can only be achieved by diversification – either to other products in the same country or to new geographic areas. If geographic diversification is chosen, the firm may export, but more often it has to take the route of outward FDI. Each of these routes involves certain risks; neither is easy to implement. These firms may try to grow by entering the huge and lucrative US market even before US firms would expand globally or even regionally.

Fourth, almost all Israeli firms are small by world standards. None is among the Fortune 500. Had some firms been huge, they might have had too much political clout and too much impact on the small economy. In this sense, hundreds of small and medium-sized multi-nationals are preferable to a few giant ones. In a small home market, one firm can easily supply the whole market, thus enjoying monopoly power.

Fifth, the best way to force firms to face competition is to open the economy to foreign competitors and foreign-based MNEs. An Israeli firm faces one of three strategic choices: (1) It can be acquired by a foreign MNE. (2) It can lobby the government to be protected because of national interest, security considerations, or some other political reason. (3) It can become a multinational itself. These characteristics are very common in small countries but are very different in large economies.

Sixth, the firm must enjoy a clear competitive advantage. The advantage must be dynamic, since whatever advantage one has could be copied by other firms in other countries. In Israel, again, such an advantage is based on created assets mainly as a result of having a better-educated labor force, not by relying on cheap labor or natural resources. The created assets have been forged in specific areas in which Israelis had a competitive advantage because of a stock of accumulated knowledge (e.g. data security). The presence of many firms led to positive cluster effects. These cluster effects included professional networks with other Israeli firms as well as with firms founded by Israelis abroad. These effects have been particularly useful in overcoming difficulties of access to markets because of distance from markets and inexperience (de Fontenay and Carmel, 2004).

Achieving sustainable competitive advantage or creating FSAs requires a deep understanding of the environment but also of the strengths and weaknesses of the firm. In this sense, it is important to avoid the dogma of "generic strategies." The environment of the firm shapes performance but does not fully determine results (Aharoni, 1993, p. 31). Industry analysis is crucial, but a firm can also create a new industry or define a well-differentiated segment within an industry. Thus, producing generic drugs is not the same as producing a pharmaceutical industry, and attempts to gain the 180 day US exclusivity advantage is not the same as R&D for a new ethical drug. Most Israeli MNEs created a new industry or carefully carved a well-defined niche within the existing industry. Given Imaging developed the first ingestible video camera that fits inside a pill. Providing a view of the small intestines from the inside, it helps diagnose digestive disorders. Check Point created the market for network security. Amdocs is a leader in integrated customer management of IT. Retalics specializes in retailing applications: Mercury in enterprise testing and performance management solutions. Radvision is the leading provider of products and technologies for unified visual communications over intellectual property and 3G networks. M-Systems created a new market for USB flash disks but did not attempt to create a global brand. They all dominate a well-defined niche.

The conditions for success are very different at different stages of the firm's life. A firm must continuously adapt to a complex set of shifts. In many cases, unique strategic innovations are crucial to attain advantages. Crucial also is the ability to avoid reliance on areas of weaknesses for the specific firm. Israeli firms are generally more creative and more flexible, but they rarely have strengths in mass marketing to the final customer, nor do they possess the scale and the resources to establish a global brand or to erect a global system of after-sales service for equipment. Israeli firms have been extremely successful when focused on a very clear segment, starting with a small segment and growing to a larger one. Even today, some start-ups develop valuable technologies only to discover that their target market is unaware of them.

Several ingredients of the success of Israeli MNEs (not only in high tech) seem to have been the following:

- focus on a well-defined market segment;
- specialization in innovative ways to meet specific customers needs;
- high degree of flexibility allowing fast reaction to changes in economic, political, and technological conditions;
- optimized use of a global value chain;
- fast response to changing market needs;
- offering a superior service or customized products to those willing to pay a premium;
- reduced marketing costs through large transactions to a limited number of well-defined customers;
- ability to identify targets for acquisition and capabilities of integrating the acquired firm to gain synergies.

A more macro lesson of the Israeli experience is that transformation of large communities to new ideals does not seem to hold in the third generation. Israel's pioneers believed community life could and should transform the basic nature of human beings by creating new economic and social arrangements. For these arrangements to work effectively, individuals must sacrifice private interests, placing themselves at the disposal of the community and suppressing their greed.

Israel's experience shows that such a commitment is possible for special reasons and for a limited time. The commitment to live only for nationalistic ideals has waned three generations after the declaration of statehood. To be sure, many Israelis still will not consider living in another country – although for some moving to the United States is a possible alternative to managing an Israeli firm.

Since a very large percentage of Israeli MNEs are born globals, it is possible to offer a few generalizations regarding the characteristics of this new type of multinational. First, the major competence of these firms is in R&D and knowledge, not in production. In fact, production is often outsourced. "Globality from inception is possible because of intangibility of [the] most critical resource – i.e. technological knowledge as well as market knowledge, which does not necessarily require much capital and is not dependent upon scale economies" (Almor, 2000, p. 139).

Second, managers of born globals enjoy an intimate knowledge of foreign markets or at least can rely on a network of persons with such knowledge. Third, the industry and the firms within it enjoy the fruits of a learning curve. As one example, when the first prospectus was prepared to float Elscint, the lawyers had difficulty reconciling the legal and regulatory requirements of both Israel and the United States. Today, after hundreds of IPOs, these lawyers are very knowledgeable regarding legal requirements. Further, other law firms learned too and became proficient in the art of prospectus writing. Learning has been important in many aspects of the creation of a born global.

Fourth, new firms inherit the culture of a founding firm and face fewer difficulties in their early stages. Fifth, one shortcut to growth is acquisitions. Born globals seem to acquire firms for several reasons. One is to reduce competition. Another is to learn, to gain competitive knowledge; another is getting access to related technologies, to new geographical markets, or to related niches.

By definition, a niche is limited in its size. To grow, a firm has to expand to larger niches even though it is likely to encounter fierce competition from giant firms. Unfortunately, in many cases the born globals are acquired before they reach a large size. Indeed, the jury is still out as to the ability of a few dozens Israeli firms to reach the size of Teva. Too many of them are acquired, and venture capital funds tend to prefer exit. Quite a few Israelis think this is normal: the sharks always eat the sardines, not the other way round. Further, the venture capitalists press for exit and the founders of the firm are always tempted to receive the large sums available to them personally in such an exit. From a public policy point of view, it would be much better if the firms continued to grow as Israeli-based multinationals. Perhaps ways should be found to make such a path more attractive to the original entrepreneurs.

A few public policy issues

Rapid globalization has led to many political concerns. It evokes many issues related to the choices that nations have in pursuing economic development. When domestic firms relocate value-creating activities abroad, many are concerned that the economy loses employment opportunities. This, of course, is a worldwide problem. Managers would claim that they maintain more lucrative jobs by exporting the low skilled ones. Thus the previous manager of Delta Galil argued: "The plants in Jordan and Egypt make it possible to work on management in Israel as well as development, design, and marketing, all the capital intensive activities" (*Ha'Aretz*, 1999, August 8).

Several US-based MNEs – IBM, Intel, Motorola, Google, and Microsoft, among them – maintain R&D facilities in Israel.[21] It may not matter to a young Israeli engineer if one of these firms or an Israeli-owned firm employs him or her. Yet others claim that these firms gain resources by using the rarest resource: the ingenuity of the local "brain power," but do not funnel much more into the local economy. Manufacturing facilities, the more massive employers, are built in other, lower-cost, countries, thus not allowing Israel to leverage its major resource (Levav, 1998, p. 168).

Perhaps Israel's policy makers made the wrong choice in vigorously trying to attract such research centers. More generally, studies of the benefits of FDI tend to ignore the possibility that a home-based MNE can confer more benefits than a foreign MNE. The question revolves around both the benefits of the FDI but also the potential alternative

---

[21] In fact, in 1981 the Israelis developed a cheaper version of the 8086 processor, renamed the 8088. In 2003, an Israeli-designed chip named Banias got a break with Intel's push into the notebook computers and was a part of the Centrino package (Lerner, 2008).

uses of scarce human resources such as scientists, innovators, or engineers.

A more specific issue is that Israel (or any small country) is less able than a large country to diversify risks. Indeed, many small countries are dependent on one firm for a majority of the foreign exchange earnings. This is true for countries whose major earnings come from a natural resource such as oil or tin. Moreover, if the country gains a competitive advantage in a certain global industry, this advantage would mean high dependence on one large firm. Such a firm becomes by definition a dominant force in the economy. It may also enjoy a great deal of political power and in some cases it may make the government subservient to its power. This may be true even if the government owns the firm (Aharoni, 1982). Further, the state cannot afford to allow such a firm to go under because of the impact of such a bankruptcy on the whole economy.

The less a country is dependent on one or even a few firms, the better off it is in terms of spreading risk. It is also better off in terms of avoiding or at least reducing the high cost of economic power stemming from concentration of economic activities in the hands of a few firms. Global integration, driven by the advance of electronic commerce, coupled with the shrinking cost of transportation and communications, has enabled even tiny firms to become multinationals. Yet another necessary condition is that these firms should be able to tap capital from foreign stock exchanges or from venture capitalists. In the 1960s, these firms could not have taken off unless the government or an owner of one of a few conglomerates had financed their initial operations. If public policy creates conditions favorable for many firms to seize opportunities available in the global market place, a large number of firms in different industries may produce the country's GNP, avoiding reliance on a handful of firms.

Security is also an important issue. The case of Check Point not being allowed to acquire a US firm for security reasons is one example. Israel, being in a constant state of war, must find policy answers to security considerations related to foreign investments in strategic sectors. Of course, as Robert Reich[22] was the first to point out, there is a world of difference between ownership, management, day-to-day

---

[22] US Secretary of Labor (1993–1997) under President Bill Clinton.

operations, and control. Clearly (whoever owns the firm), local workers would be hired to perform the day-to-day operations. Israelis may even manage the firm.

What matters to Reich is the creation of employment. He claims that Honda in the US is more important to the US than Ford in Asia (Reich, 1990, 1991). Yet, control has its ramifications not only because security-related secrets might be leaked but also because the firm may abruptly decide to cease operations. Even if it continues the R&D, it may not produce in Israel, thus not leveraging the major advantage of innovative engineers and creating less employment than desirable.

In a large, developed country, the question of ownership may seem moot. Ownership is extremely diffuse and top management – who may or may not be citizens or even residents of the country in which the firm is incorporated – make the decisions. A firm may be seen as a depository and a creator of knowledge; its major asset is the accumulated knowledge. Therefore, as long as the knowledge is stored in the minds (and computers) of citizens of the country, ownership may be insignificant, in particular when ownership is distributed among many shareholders from different countries. In Israel, ownership is not yet separated from control.

In a globally integrated world, *what is an Israeli multinational enterprise?* As shown above, for tax and other reasons, quite a few Israelis register their firms in the United States or in some tax haven country. Israelis found the firm and manage it but it is not incorporated in Israel. Such a firm would not appear in the official statistics as an Israeli outward FDI, but in many ways may be considered an Israeli MNE. Indeed, the press depicts many of these firms as Israeli firms. As already pointed out, the number of Israeli firms traded on NASDAQ as quoted in the Israeli press is 116, not 73. The difference stems from the large number of Israeli-owned firms incorporated outside Israel. Legally, and therefore for statistical purposes, they are not Israeli.[23]

---

[23] Thus, Verint was the world leader in networked video management. It was the provider of choice for fifty-five airports, twenty-five seaports, seven out of every ten US banks, two of the world's five largest retailers, and government organizations around the globe. This leadership was built on an integrated portfolio of networked video solutions for enhancing security and enterprise efficiency. It was started and is still managed by Israelis. World headquarters is in Melville, NY, but the R&D and strategic direction came from Tel Aviv,

The popular press sometimes gets carried away, counting firms owned by Israelis who long ago left the country and are now US citizens.[24] Perhaps what matters is also the enhanced value added. Strategic decisions made by an Israeli MNE may be more inclined toward enhancing the welfare of the country, or at least allowing Israel right of first refusal.

Conclusions

Israel went through a revolution. In the first three or four decades of its existence it was a state with a strong communal orientation, believing that the individual must serve the public needs, subordinating any individual goals. Economic policies were centered on import substitution and detailed controls of almost all economic activities. The Israeli government protected domestic firms by creating tariff and non-tariff barriers. Successive socialist governments believed in the development of domestically owned industrial infrastructure.

Under these circumstances, it was virtually impossible to create an Israel-based MNE. By 2008, Israel was open to a global world and was much more influenced by American individualism and by liberal economic ideas. The vast welfare state was reduced in scope, SOEs were privatized, and major reforms were carried out in many areas of economic activity. One major result was that business was not dependent any more on the state's resources for its existence. There was a total shift in the leadership of business enterprises. Many firms were acquired or failed. The Histadrut enterprises were sold, the government enterprises were privatized, and the Israeli currency was fully convertible. The government lifted all restrictions even on institutional investors, ended exchange control, enabled free movement of capital, and signed free-trade agreements with Europe and the

---

Israel. The same was true for Comverse, the parent of Verint, and for Amdocs, both Israeli founded and managed.

[24] A case in point is SanDisk, a major producer of flash memory. This US-incorporated firm was founded in 1988 by Dr. Eli Harari, who came from Israel. It had operations in many countries, including a joint venture with Toshiba, and a development center in Israel. In 2006, it acquired a major Israel-based competitor, M-Systems, the inventor of the USB flash drive known as Disk-on-Key, for about $1.55 billion. This acquisition of an Israeli company was registered as inward FDI into Israel despite the acquiring CEO's ties to Israel.

United States, opening up its market to imports from any country in the world.

Business schools educated a new generation of managers, who saw new strategic options for Israeli firms. Deregulation and free imports meant heightened competition from foreign MNEs. Business managers awakened to the inevitability of multinational operations. The Bank of Israel noted: "[T]he direct investments are needed to be able to compete in the global market, since they increase the contact to essential resources for global competition such as production systems, financial markets and foreign capital as well as technology and labor force" (Bank of Israel 2006, p. 274).

When the macroeconomic policy changed, virtually every large firm had to become multinational or be acquired by a foreign MNE. Israel's strength in high tech was bolstered by government support, stemming from the realization that the country lacked much in the way of natural resources and would not want to base competitive advantage on low-cost labor. The government helped by providing funds for R&D, for technological innovation, and for the creation of a local venture capital industry.

By the end of 2006, hundreds of Israeli firms grew by becoming MNEs. Reduced demand in Israel – for example, in construction – combined with the opening of Eastern Europe, helped to encourage outward FDI. At the same time, technology entrepreneurs were lured to the vast US market, starting born global MNEs. These firms used the Internet as a marketing tool. The need to cut costs led to the moving of production to low-labor-cost countries. Many of these firms took the road of greenfield investments, carving their way into the international competitive markets by dominating a niche. They later expanded through M&As. Indeed, it was not easy to attain critical mass by relying only on internal growth. Their major FSAs seem to have been innovation and the flexibility of their management.

The Israeli economy is noted for an increased concentration of capital in the hands of a few individuals and multinationals. Yet many firms blossomed, unrelated to established business elites. Some were very successful and others stumbled. All realized that to grow one had to invest outside the small domestic market. Later, firms faced a choice of a different nature: trying to become a giant or being acquired by giant foreign MNEs. Several firms attempted to become giants but finally succumbed to the lure of being acquired.

Another strategic choice was the degree to which firms should concentrate their investments in Israel or move operations, including possibly headquarters, to other countries. Some firms chose to maintain Israeli headquarters, while others did not. Israeli MNEs also faced the dilemma of whether to create jobs at home or to follow dispassionately the dictates of global market forces. Decisions on these issues seem to have been dependent at least as much on the ideological proclivities and allegiance to Israel of the companies' top management as on economic rationales.

The history of Israel clearly demonstrates that the government of a small country should encourage free trade, investment, and flows of capital, and concentrate on the maintenance of law and order, and on investments in human capital through education. Politically, such a government may opt for distribution policies that enhance social cohesion, prohibit the conversion of natural habitats to urban areas, or achieve any other of a number of cultural and social goals. As long as the country adheres to liberal economic policies, it can prosper, because wealth-creating individuals, who are highly mobile in today's global economy, will relocate elsewhere if the home-country's policies become unfriendly to businesses.

Firms from such a country can become global players. They can remove the shackles of small market size, and finance their operations by access to large global capital markets. Last but not least, much depends on leadership, strategic vision, and the managerial abilities of a very small number of visionaries who lead firms to great success in the global competitive arena. A small country often suffers from a short supply of these individuals.

Researchers can help policy makers from small countries by further examining some of the issues raised above. Thus, what is specific to Israel and what can be generalized to other small countries? Israel is widely acknowledged to be a technological innovator (Breznitz, 2006). Can other countries follow the same route, and if so, how? Further, what should be the policy on security-related enterprises? Should a firm from a small country start as a bi-national, maintaining marketing and pre- and post-sales services facilities in the United States, and R&D at home? How can benefits to the domestic economy be maximized? How are clusters formed, and what are their significant contributions? What are the costs of distance? What is the role of expatriates in allowing access to firms from the homeland?

Decision making in MNEs involves high levels of uncertainty and is based on incomplete information. Unfortunately, many studies assume perfect information and full rationality, thus missing the problems that decision makers face in the real world. These studies also miss the impact of corporate culture. Incorporating behavioral theory, bounded rationality, effects of clusters, cultural impact, and the role of expatriates and their willingness to help their country of origin may allow a better, fuller explanation of the Israeli story, and perhaps thus enhance IB theory.

References

Agmon, Tamir and Charles P. Kindleberger (1977) *Multinationals from Small Countries*. MIT Press.

Aharoni, Yair (1976) *Structure and Conduct in Israeli Economy*. Tel Aviv: Gomeh (Hebrew).

Aharoni, Yair (1982) "State-Owned Enterprise: An Agent Without a Principal" in Leroy Jones *et al.* (eds.), *Public Enterprise in Developing Countries*. New York: Cambridge University Press, pp. 67–78.

Aharoni, Yair (1991) *The Israeli Economy Dreams and Realities*. London: Routledge.

Aharoni, Yair (1992) *The Political Economy of Israel*. Tel Aviv: Am Oved (Hebrew).

Aharoni, Yair (1993) "From Adam Smith to Schumpeterian Global Firms" *Research in Global Strategic Management*, Vol. 4, pp. 17–39.

Aharoni, Yair (2007) "New Business Elites" in Eliezer Ben Rafael and Yitzhak Steinberg (eds.), *New Elites in Israel*. Jerusalem: Bialik Institute (Hebrew).

Almor, Tamar (2000) "Born Global: The Case of Small and Medium Sized, Knowledge-Intensive Israeli Firms" in Tamar Almor and Nir Hashai (eds.), *FDI, International Trade and the Economics of Peacemaking*. College of Management of Rishon LeZion, Israel, pp. 119–139.

Avnimelech, Gil and Morris Teubal (2004) "Venture Capital-Startup Coevolution and the Emergence and Development of Israel's New High Technology Cluster" *Economics of Innovation and New Technology*, Vol. 13, pp. 33–60.

Avnimelech, Gil and Morris Teubal (2005) "Evolutionary Innovation and High Tech Policy: What Can We Learn from Israel's Targeting of Venture Capital?" STE-WP-25, March.

Bank of Israel (2006) *Annual Report*.

Bank of Israel (2007) *Recent Developments in the Economy*, May, p. 10.

Bilkey, Warren J. (1978) "An Attempted Integration of the Literature on the Export Behavior of firms" *Journal of International Business Studies*, Vol. 9, No. 1, pp. 33–46.

Breznitz, Dan (2006) "Innovation-Based Industrial Policy in Emerging Economy? The Case of the Israeli IT Sector" *Business and Politics*, Vol. 8, pp. 1–38.

Breznitz, Dan (2007) *Innovation and the State Political Choice and Strategies for Growth in Israel, Taiwan, and Ireland*. New Haven: Yale University Press.

Cavusgil, S. T. (1980) "On the Internationalization Process of Firms" *European Research*, Vol. 8 (November), pp. 273–281.

de Fontenay, Catherine and Carmel, Erran (2004) "Israel's Silicon Wadi: The Forces Behind Cluster Formation" in T. Bresnahan, A. Gambardella, and A. Saxenian (eds.), *Building High Tech Clusters*. Cambridge: Cambridge University Press.

Globes (2004, December) G Magazine (Hebrew).

Globes (2005, May 18) G Magazine.

Globes (2007, May) Financial Consumerism supplement, p. 30.

Globes (2007, October 9–10) p. 10 (Hebrew).

Ha'Aretz (1999, August 8) (Hebrew).

Huston, Larry and Nabil Sakkab (2006) "Connect and Develop: Inside Procter and Gamble's New Model for Innovation" *Harvard Business Review*, Vol. 84, No. 3, March, pp. 58–69.

Johanson, Jan and Jan-Erik Vahlne (1977) "The Internationalization Process of the Firm: A Model of Knowledge Development and Increasing Foreign Market Commitments" *Journal of International Business Studies*, Vol. 8, pp. 23–32.

Johanson, Jan and Jan-Erik Vahlne (1990) "The Mechanism of Internationalization" *International Marketing Review*, Vol. 7, No. 4, pp. 11–24.

Jolly, Vijayk, Matti Alahuta and Jean-Pierre Jeannet (1992) "Challenging the Incumbents: How High Technology Start-Ups Compete Globally" *Journal of Strategic Change*, Vol. 1, pp. 71–82.

Knight, Garya and S. T. Cavusgil (1996) "The Born Global Firm: A Challenge to Traditional Internationalization Theory" *Advances in International Marketing*, Vol. 8, pp. 11–26.

Lemos, Robert (2006) "Check Point Calls Off Sourcefire Buy" March 24, www.securityfocus.com/print/news/11382

Lerner, Susan (2008) "Intel Opens Israeli Plant for Next Generation Chips" July 1, Bloomberg.com

Levav, Amos (1998) *The Birth of Israel's High-Tech*. Tel-Aviv: Zmora-Bitan (Hebrew).

Madsen, Tagek and Per Servais (1997) "The Internationalization of Born Globals: An Evolutionary Process?" *International Business Review*, Vol. 6, No. 6, pp. 561–583.

McKinsey & Co. (1993) *Emerging Exporters. Australia's High Value-Added Manufacturing Exporters*. Melbourne: McKinsey & Co. and the Australian Manufacturing Council.

Oviatt, Benjamin M. and Patricia P. McDougall (1994) "Toward a Theory of International New Ventures" *Journal of International Business Studies*, Vol. 25, pp. 45–64.

Oviatt, Benjamin M. and Patricia P. McDougall (1997) "Challenges for Internationalization Process Theory: The Case of International New Ventures" *Management International Review*, Vol. 37, No. 2, pp. 85–99.

Porter, Michael (1990a) *The Competitive Advantage of Nations*. New York: Free Press

Porter, Michael (1990b) "The Competitive Advantage of Nations" *Harvard Business Review*, Vol. 68, No. 2, March/April.

Porter, Michael (1998) *On Competition*. New York: Free Press.

Reich, Robert B. (1990) "Who is Us" *Harvard Business Review*, Vol. 68, No. 1, January–February, pp. 53–65.

Reich, Robert B. (1991) *The Work of Nations Preparing Ourselves to 21st Century Capitalism*. New York: Vintage Books.

Rennie, M. W. (1993) "Global Competitiveness: Born Global" *McKinsey Quarterly*, Vol. 4, pp. 45–52.

Rugman, Alan M. and Alain Verbeke (1993) "Foreign Subsidiaries and Multinational Strategic Management: An Extension and Correction of Porter's Single Diamond Framework" *Management International Review*, Vol. 33, No. 2, pp. 71–84.

Rugman, Alan. M. and Alain Verbeke (2001) "Subsidiary Specific Advantages in Multinational Enterprises" *Strategic Management Journal*, Vol. 22, No. 3, pp. 237–250.

Sherman, Arnold (1988) "A Dream Realized" *Israel Economist*.

Stauber, Joshua (2001) *From Teva to Check Point*. Tel Aviv: Yedioth Acharonot (Hebrew).

Teva Pharmaceutical Industries Ltd. (2007) Investor Lunch Presentation, Tel Aviv, Israel (August). Available at www.tevapharm.com/pdf/CapitalMarketQ2.pdf

UNCTAD 2006 *World Investment Report*.

Van Den Bulcke, Daniel and Alain Verbeke (2001) *Globalization and the Small Open Economy*. Aldershot, UK: Elgar.

Zander, I. and Zander U. (1997) "The Oscillating Multinational Firm – Alfa Laval in the Period 1890–1990" in I. Björkman and M. Forsgren (eds.), *The Nature of the International Firm*. Copenhagen Business School Press.

PART III

Conclusions

13 | *What have we learned about emerging-market MNEs?*

RAVI RAMAMURTI

We began this project with three research questions: What competitive advantages do EMNEs leverage as they internationalize, and how are those advantages shaped by the home-country context? How do EMNEs internationalize, and why? And, how is the rise of EMNEs affecting global industry dynamics? Underlying those questions was the theoretical question of whether existing IB frameworks are adequate to explain EMNE behavior, and if not, how they should be modified or extended.

The studies in Part II show clearly that EMNEs are not a homogeneous group by any means. The countries from which they hail, the industries in which they operate, the competitive advantages they exploit, the markets they target, and the internationalization paths they follow vary quite widely. The evidence does not permit sweeping generalizations about EMNEs nor about how they are different from MNEs that came before, because the latter is also a heterogeneous group.

Equally important, EMNEs have internationalized in a different international context than MNEs that came before, including even Japanese and Korean MNEs, and this makes inter-temporal comparisons even more difficult. Since the 1990s, the international policy environment and the technological environment have changed profoundly. Domestic and foreign markets were more open in this period than in earlier decades, following the collapse of Communism, the conclusion of the Uruguay Round trade deal, and the creation of the WTO. The deregulation and privatization of telecommunications in many countries, along with radical changes in computing technology and the rise of the Internet, dramatically altered the boundaries of the firm and the costs of doing business across borders. These developments fuelled the outsourcing and offshoring trends, resulting in the vertical disintegration of firms and the lowering of entry barriers for EMNEs (Evans and Wurster, 2000). At the same time, the digitization revolution allowed for trade in services that were previously non-tradable. As the transaction costs of coordination and international-ization fell, the value chain was "sliced and diced" and dispersed globally, including to emerging markets. Capital markets also became more open and integrated than ever before, making it easier for EMNEs to raise foreign equity capital and debt or to list their shares on foreign stock exchanges (Farrell, Folster, and Lund, 2008). Glob-alization of the investment banking, private equity, and venture capital industries, as well as accounting, law, and management con-sultancy firms, brought world-class services right to the doorstep of many EMNEs. The emergence of a global labor market for senior management also allowed EMNEs to staff their upper ranks with internationally savvy executives if they wished (Michaels, Handfield-Jones, and Axelrod, 2001). A further temporary advantage was enjoyed by emerging economies such as Brazil and Russia, whose foreign exchange reserves swelled, thanks to booming exports, high commodity prices, and large trade surpluses. Developments of this sort created "global gateways" (Williamson and Zeng, Chapter 5) through which EMNEs could internationalize – gateways that were not available in the 1960s and 1970s. Ghemawat (2007a) may be right that the world is not as flat as Friedman (2005) claimed in his best-selling book, but it was certainly flatter in the 2000s than at any time before.

The heterogeneity of multinational firms and profound changes in the international macro context make it hazardous to generalize about how EMNEs are like, or unlike, MNEs that came before. Studies making such generalizations are often vague about their points of reference – that is, about what is being compared with what – and therefore it is not clear how to interpret their findings (e.g., Luo and Tung, 2007; Mathews, 2002). In what follows, we try not to gloss over differences among EMNEs, or to attribute everything about them to their emerging-market roots when some aspects of their conduct might arguably be the result of internationalizing in a "flatter world."

However, most EMNEs studied in this project shared one incon-trovertible feature: Compared to Western MNEs, they were late glo-balizers, because their countries were late to embrace globalization. This created a common set of challenges in fending off competition from foreign MNEs in the home market, catching up with them on technology and best practices, and expanding into foreign markets. Firms that overcame these challenges often did so by turning their

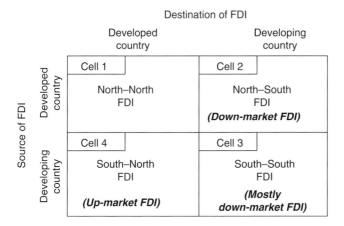

Figure 13.1 Source and destination of FDI.
Note: Down-market FDI refers to investment from a more developed country to a less developed one, and up-market FDI refers to the opposite

late-mover status into a net advantage rather a disadvantage, not only in other emerging economies but sometimes even in developed economies – which explains the significant amounts of "up-market" FDI by EMNEs (Cell 4 in Figure 13.1). It may be no accident that many EMNEs belonged to mid-tech industries that were mature or declining in the West but booming in emerging economies – a setting in which late-movers arguably have an edge over first-movers.

The rest of this chapter is organized as follows. The next section discusses the competitive advantages on which EMNEs based their internationalization, and how those advantages were shaped by the idiosyncratic conditions of emerging economies. After that, we turn to the internationalization process of these firms. We present our findings as a menu of alternative internationalization strategies pursued by EMNEs, each of which leveraged different location- and firm-specific advantages and took them in different geographic directions. Some paths took the EMNE "up-market" to developed countries, others took it "down-market" to less developed countries, and still others took it to both kinds of countries (see Figure 13.1). We turn then to the impact of EMNEs on global industries and incumbent Western MNEs. We conclude with implications for international business theory.

The competitive advantages of EMNEs

A widely accepted view in the IB literature is that a firm operating abroad faces disadvantages compared to local competitors in those countries, because of its liabilities as a foreigner, and the costs of operating in distant markets and cultures (Hymer, 1976; Zaheer, 1995). Therefore, to succeed abroad, such a firm must have compensating firm-specific advantages (FSAs) that are valuable and inimitable. A second important idea is that firms competing abroad can leverage not only their FSAs but also their home-country advantages, or country-specific advantages (CSAs). Rugman (Chapter 3) combines FSAs and CSAs into a two-by-two matrix that can be used to analyze and explain the competitive advantages of internationalizing firms. What do the studies in this volume reveal about the CSAs and FSAs of EMNEs?

Country-specific advantages

The studies in this volume provide many examples of CSAs that EMNEs leverage internationally: In Russia, South Africa, and Brazil EMNEs took advantage of the country's vast natural resources; in China and India, EMNEs took advantage of the large home market and the availability of low-cost skilled and unskilled labor; in Thailand, Chinese entrepreneurs took advantage of their social network to expand into other countries with ethnic Chinese communities, including mainland China; in Israel, firms took advantage of the large pool of highly skilled engineers and scientists, many of whom had migrated from Europe and brought with them advanced skills as well as foreign social networks.

These examples show that each country had idiosyncratic features that in turn created idiosyncratic CSAs. The apartheid era created unanticipated advantages for South African firms in the post-apartheid period. The English language skills of Indian workers, and the large numbers of overseas Indians, created unanticipated advantages for Indian firms looking to export knowledge-based services to high-cost countries. China benefited from an authoritarian political system in which decisions could be made expeditiously, and Mexico benefited from its proximity and privileged access to the US market.

One of the few features shared by all countries in our sample, including Israel, is that they pursued protectionist or import-substituting industrialization policies for many years before embracing globalization in the 1980s or 1990s. Policies during the closed era may not have promoted efficiency or international competitiveness but they helped to incubate indigenous firms in technology-based industries, some of which went on to become EMNEs in the 2000s. Even in China and Russia, most of the leading EMNEs had roots going back to the Communist days, long before they were partially or wholly privatized.

Two emerging economies, China and India, brought into the global economy CSAs that were particularly disruptive, because of the size of their home markets and the size of their unskilled and skilled labor pools. In addition, the low average income of their populations spurred innovations to serve people at the middle or bottom of the economic pyramid. In 2007, China was the third largest market in the world but its per-capita income was one-twentieth that of the US (at official exchange rates). India was the seventh or eighth largest economy and its per-capita income was one-fortieth or one-fiftieth that of the US. For the first time, two of the largest and fastest growing economies in the world were also among the world's poorest countries. The weak institutions in these and other emerging economies forced local companies to be innovative in circumventing institutional voids (Khanna and Palepu, 2006). For instance, in India, entrepreneurial firms used mobile banking and smart cards to serve small borrowers outside the reach of traditional banks. The capabilities that firms built to cope with these country-specific *disadvantages* became FSAs that could be exploited in other emerging markets.

In Chapter 3, Rugman argues that EMNEs expand abroad largely on the strength of home-country CSAs, such as access to natural resources and cheap labor, rather than knowledge-based FSAs of the kind exploited by the world's largest MNEs.[1] Like Lessard and Lucea (Chapter 10), he questions the sustainability of competitive advantages based on CSAs, which, unlike FSAs, are presumably copied more easily by rivals and therefore short-lived. While this may be true, it merits a few qualifications. First, a firm in the early stages of internationalization is likely to rely on home-country CSAs more

---

[1] Rugman has countries like China, India, and Russia in mind when making this observation, rather than a country like Israel, which, as Aharoni points out in Chapter 12, produced many MNEs in knowledge-intensive industries, given that it was so poorly endowed with CSAs such as land or natural resources.

than it would in later stages, when its operations span many countries and it has acquired more FSAs (Kogut, 1985). In other words, the importance of home-country CSAs may decline as an MNE evolves, regardless of nationality. Rugman's observation may thus reflect the current evolutionary stage of EMNEs – as nascent globalizers – rather than a fundamental difference with Western MNEs. Second, it is not clear that CSAs are as ephemeral as they are sometimes made out to be. For instance, thinking of CSAs as advantages that "are common to all firms located in a country" (Lessard and Lucea, Chapter 10) should not be taken to mean that all firms in a country, including foreign firms, can readily access every CSA at will.

For example, a country may be rich in natural resources, but only some of its firms may have access to those resources – witness the Russian experience in oil and gas discussed in Chapter 7. A country may have abundant capital, but the government or state-owned banks may allocate it only to some firms, as in China (Buckley *et al.*, 2007). A country may have plenty of cheap labor, but tapping into that pool may pose insurmountable operational challenges to Western firms, as in India. The broader point here is that firms might need certain FSAs – such as good relations with the local government or deep local knowledge and embeddedness – before they can exploit a country's CSAs. To be sure, the requisite FSAs can be learned over time, or obtained through alliances with local players, or acquired through M&A deals, but it is an oversimplification to assume that a country's CSAs are simply there for all firms to exploit at will. It took IBM and Accenture the better part of fifteen years to move large parts of their software development work to low-cost India, despite unambiguous evidence that India had CSAs in performing such tasks. That relatively long window was sufficient for some Indian firms to build significant FSAs to complement the CSAs with which they began. And even when foreign firms learned the ropes to operate in India, their costs were reportedly 30 percent higher than those of local counterparts, forcing some firms to divest such operations when the Indian rupee strengthened in 2007–2008.

Firm-specific advantages

The notion of FSAs is a useful concept but hard to apply in practice, especially when the firm in question does not possess an obviously valuable and inimitable asset, such as a patented blockbuster drug. A close look at successful firms usually suggests many big and small advantages that come together in complex ways to give the firm an edge in the marketplace (Rivkin, 2000). It is often unclear how much each FSA contributes to the firm's overall success, sometimes even to the firm's owners and managers. Such analysis is also subject to *post hoc, ergo propter hoc* type of reasoning. That said, the most common FSAs attributed to Western MNEs include proprietary technology, powerful brands, marketing prowess, and other managerial capabilities. Intangible assets, including the capacity to create, process, and apply knowledge, are widely considered to be among their core competencies.

But what about EMNEs? They do not usually possess cutting-edge technologies or strong global brands, but this does not mean they possess *no* FSAs. Mathews (2002), for instance, argues unpersuasively that EMNEs internationalize to *acquire* capabilities and advantages rather than to *exploit* pre-existing capabilities – which begs the question of how these firms offset their disadvantages and costs of competing in foreign markets. Luo and Tung (2007) take a similar view in their "springboard model" of EMNE internationalization, where the argument is that EMNEs internationalize to obtain new advantages rather than use initial advantages as a springboard for internationalization.

It took many years of research to identify and empirically confirm the FSAs of Western MNEs, and an equally diligent effort is necessary to uncover the FSAs of EMNEs. A few FSAs suggested by the cases in the earlier chapters are discussed below. These are illustrative, and should be viewed as hypotheses rather than definitive conclusions.

Products suited to emerging markets

One common FSA of many EMNEs is their ability to adapt imported technology to develop products suited to the special needs of local customers – for instance, by making products cheaper and more affordable. Another kind of adaptation was making products that were rugged and easy to maintain in the harsher conditions found in emerging markets, such as poor-quality infrastructure or the absence of after-sales service. Earlier studies of Third World MNEs also identified this as one of their key FSAs (Wells, 1983; Lecraw, 1977).

Making such product adaptations requires technical skills as well as intimate customer knowledge. Local adaptations of this sort provided EMNEs defense against foreign competitors in the home market, but equally important, they provided a basis for internationalizing into other low-income emerging economies.[2]

Examples of EMNEs possessing this kind of FSA include Chinese MNEs, such as Haier, whose washing machines were not only smaller and better suited to small loads but could also be used to wash vegetables. India's Mahindra & Mahindra's produced an indigenously designed, rugged SUV that was later exported to African and Latin American markets. India's Tata Group made trucks that were famous for their ruggedness and ease of maintenance, and in January 2008 Tata launched the world's lowest priced car, the $2,500 Nano. Brazil's Marcopolo, which made high-quality buses suited to emerging markets, sold its products in 103 countries and enjoyed a global market share of 7–10 percent (see Fleury & Fleury, Chapter 8).

In Chapter 2, Wells argues that some of the capabilities developed by firms in the 1960s and 1970s, when developing countries pursued import-substituting industrialization policies, may have become obsolete in the open economy of the 2000s – for example, the ability to substitute imported raw materials with local raw materials. However, many other capabilities and skills built in the earlier era, such as the ability to design products without unnecessary bells and whistles were still relevant and could be exploited internationally through exports and FDI. As Amsden points out in Chapter 4, the import-substitution period prevented foreign firms from "crowding out" local firms and gave the latter the opportunity to master technologies, learn how to set up and run manufacturing plants, and build distribution networks and brands at home. These investments came in handy when the economy was liberalized subsequently.

---

[2] Foreign MNEs are certainly technically capable of making similar adaptations if they have acquired the same level of customer intimacy and embeddedness in the local environment. But as Lall (1983) argued, Western MNEs are less likely to make the necessary investment in learning and adaptation, especially to target lower-income consumers. However, when they do so, as in the case of Unilever in India or Nokia in China, they can match or beat local firms at making products suited to emerging markets.

Production and operational excellence

A second kind of FSA exploited by firms described in the earlier chapters was superior production efficiency and process excellence, particularly in the context of emerging markets. That superiority had a technical component, such as the ability to optimize production processes by using more labor and less capital, using inputs more efficiently, or having lower overheads than Western counterparts. It also arose from late-mover advantages, such as having plants with the newest technology or largest scale available, compared to Western incumbents. Along the same lines, some firms benefited from starting with a clean slate – that is, not having to reengineer old practices and systems but adopting best practices from the very start.

Williamson and Zeng (Chapter 5) provide many examples of Chinese manufacturers that, like Japanese and Korean firms in an earlier time, absorbed foreign production methods and improved upon them. Indian firms such as Hindalco (aluminum) and Tata Steel improved production processes and upgraded capacity and technologies to become two of the world's lowest-cost producers (Chapter 6). Similarly, Indian software firms fared remarkably well in ratings awarded by Carnegie Mellon University's Software Engineering Institute, partly because they set up the right processes from the start. In mid-tech industries, Indian companies reportedly had as much as a 30–40 percent "capex" advantage relative to Western firms, because of engineering skills that enabled them to economize on capital investment, and a comparable "opex" advantage, because of lower wages and overheads.[3]

Privileged access to resources and markets

Another FSA for some firms was the support from the home government in the form of preferred access to markets, preferential regulations, or preferred access to capital. In the post-WTO environment, it was difficult for governments to subsidize national champions overtly,

---

[3] This is based on a conversation with Ranjit Pandit, former chairman of McKinsey & Co., India, as part of Jitendra Singh's Wharton course, Inside Indian Business, April 11, 2007.

but it was still possible to divert capital or other resources to preferred firms, such as SOEs. This was an important factor in China, where some of the largest EMNEs were at least partly state-owned and controlled (Huang, 2003).[4]

State support is usually regarded as an unfair advantage in international competition. As an FSA, it lacks the legitimacy of proprietary technology or brands. But if state support is only extended to some national firms, such as state-owned firms (e.g., in China) or business groups with close ties to the government (e.g., the Siam Cement Group, which was partly owned by the Thai royal family through the Crown Property Bureau), then – legitimate or not – it was an FSA for those firms. Thus, a high savings rate was one of China's CSAs, but it translated into an FSA (i.e., access to cheap capital) for only some firms.

Another category of firms that benefited from a history of state support was private firms that were previously state-owned. In Brazil, the largest MNE was state-owned Petrobras, but several of the other leading private firms were formerly state-owned firms, such as Embraer, Vale (mining), and CSN (steel). Their successful internationalization in the 1990s and 2000s rested on foundations laid during decades of state ownership (see Fleury & Fleury, Chapter 8).

Finally, in the 2000s, several EMNEs in Brazil, Russia, and South Africa enjoyed large positive cash flows because of record-high prices for many raw materials. This gave them a large war chest for acquisitions, which companies such as Lukoil of Russia, CVRD of Brazil, and South African Breweries used to acquire Western firms, such as Getty, Inco, and Miller beer, respectively. In early 2008, CVRD was rumored to be in talks to acquire the Swiss company Xstrata for a staggering $90 billion. Acquisitions of this sort made Brazil one of the emerging economies with substantial up-market FDI in 2007, but such investments may not be sustainable if raw material prices decline, as they did in 2008.

---

[4] State ownership also had its disadvantages – for example, it slowed down or politicized decision making, or invited extra scrutiny when the EMNE targeted Western firms for acquisition (e.g., CNOOC of China's failed bid for Unocal in 2005, or Huawei's failed bid for 3Com in partnership with Bain Capital in 2008).

Adversity advantage

EMNEs also enjoyed an advantage relative to foreign firms in their ability to function effectively in the difficult conditions of emerging markets, where both the "hard" and "soft" infrastructures were underdeveloped. Firms had to operate with unreliable power, congested ports and roads, corrupt bureaucracies, political and regulatory uncertainties, weak educational institutions, and a range of other "institutional voids" (Khanna and Palepu, 2005). As discussed earlier, Western firms were usually stymied by these challenges, but local firms evolved coping strategies, having dealt with such constraints from birth. Local firms were more likely to possess this FSA than foreign firms, and EMNEs were able to transfer this FSA in varying degrees to other emerging markets. However, this FSA was subject to erosion over time, as conditions improved in emerging markets and as foreign firms gained experience operating there. But for a decade or more after economic liberalization, this was an important FSA for many emerging-market firms.

Traditional intangible assets

The image of the typical EMNE is that of a late-globalizing firm possessing few intangible assets, such as cutting-edge technology or strong brands. While largely true, our studies found some interesting exceptions. For instance, a handful of EMNEs seemed to be close to their industry's technology frontier, especially in the larger BRIC economies. Brazil's Embraer, for instance, was the world's third largest aircraft maker and the leader in regional jets. Starting in the 1960s as a state enterprise that made 19-seat turboprops for Brazil, it evolved into a leading maker of 100-seater regional jets, with more than 50 percent of the world market. Another Brazilian firm, Petrobras, had a technical edge in deep-sea oil drilling (see Chapter 8). In China, Huawei seemed to have come close to the frontiers of telecommunications technology, as it strove for leadership in 3G technology (Chapter 5). In 2005, the company spent 10 percent of its annual revenues on R&D, but given China's cheap engineering talent, this reportedly allowed the firm to deploy 48 percent of its 24,000 employees in R&D (Farhoomand and Ho, 2006: 6). In India, Suzlon Energy emerged among the top five global players in wind energy, with access to some of the best technologies, through acquisitions in Germany and the Netherlands, along with engineering and research support in India. In the large-population emerging markets, such as the BRICs, home demand in new industries can sometimes be as big as that in developed countries, despite their lower per-capita income – for example, in telecommunications equipment or wind energy equipment. In a flat world, one should not be surprised if emerging markets periodically spawn companies like Embraer, Huawei, and Suzlon.

Similarly, although few EMNEs had strong global brands to begin with, many of them owned strong local brands that they were developing into international brands. Lukoil of Russia was converting the Getty gas stations it acquired in the US to the Lukoil brand; Lenovo, which bought IBM's PC business and had rights to use the IBM logo for five years, lost no time in building its own brand worldwide; in 2006, Haier's brand already ranked 86th among the world's top 500 brands (Chapter 5). India's Tata Group gained international visibility with its large acquisitions in the UK (Corus Steel, Jaguar, Land Rover, and Tetley Tea) and the launching of the Nano. Over time, many EMNEs are likely to develop global brands, given that in a flat world they have the financial resources and access to the same world-class marketing expertise that Western MNEs employed to build their global brands.

In thinking about the FSAs of EMNEs it is important to keep in mind the possibility that at least some of them will operate at the global technology frontier, enter new industries as global first-movers rather than junior late-movers, and possess globally recognized brands. The "global gateways" discussed earlier make this more likely than in earlier times.

Generic internationalization strategies

Despite the variety of firms and strategies described in Part II, EMNEs seemed to pursue one of five generic internationalization strategies. Each of these strategies leveraged different CSAs and FSAs, and resulted in distinct internationalization paths (see Table 13.1). We describe them briefly here, but more detailed illustrations are contained in the country studies in Part II.

Table 13.1. *Generic internationalization strategies of EMNEs*

Generic Strategy	CSAs	FSAs	Internationalization path	Examples
(1) Natural-resource vertical integrator	• natural resource endowment and/or • large home demand for natural resources	• privileged access to natural resources and/or • privileged access to home markets	• forward integration to downstream markets and/or • backward integration upstream to secure natural resources	• Gazprom, Lukoil, Norilsk, Vale, Anglogold, PTT • Petrobras, Oil and Natural Gas Corporation, Indian Oil, CNOOC, Chinalco
(2) Local optimizer	• low-income consumers • underdeveloped "hard" and "soft" infrastructures	• ability to optimize imported products and processes to home market • local-customer intimacy and local embeddedness	• target market: other emerging markets	• HiSense, Mahindra & Mahindra, Tata Motors, Shoprite, Marcopolo
(3) Low-cost partner	• low-cost labor • size of skilled labor pool, including engineers/scientists, etc.	• process excellence • project management • ability to operate successfully in the adverse conditions of emerging markets	• target market: developed countries • up-market FDI to move up value curve • down-market FDI to diversify supply locations	• Wipro, Infosys, TCS, Dr. Reddy's, WEG, Sabo

Table 13.1. (*cont.*)

Generic Strategy	CSAs	FSAs	Internationalization path	Examples
(4) Global consolidator	• large and rapidly growing home market • price-sensitive customers	• production and project execution excellence • late-mover advantages in scale, organizational processes, technology • strong position in home market, with strong cash flows	• target market: global • up-market FDI to acquire poorly performing companies	• Tata Steel, Hindalco, South African Breweries, Lenovo, Wanxiang, Cemex
(5) Global first-mover	• large and rapidly growing demand in a new industry • low-cost country for design, engineering, and production	• close to global frontiers of technology • strong position in home market, including, possibly, state support	• target market: global • up-market FDI to acquire key technologies or capabilities, and customer access • down-market FDI to gain market access and/or to diversify production bases	• Embraer, Huawei, Suzlon Energy, Check Point, Teva

The *natural-resource vertical integrator* hails either from a country richly endowed with natural resources or one with a large domestic appetite for natural resources. In the former case, the EMNE engages in cross-border forward integration to secure downstream markets (e.g. Gazprom, Lukoil, and Norilsk of Russia, or Vale of Brazil). In the latter case, the EMNE engages in cross-border backward integration to secure upstream natural resources for conversion into end products for the home market (e.g., Oil and Natural Gas Corporation or Bharat Petroleum of India and CNOOC or Chinalco of China). Despite the trend of vertical disintegration in many industries, natural-resource firms continue to place value on being vertically integrated – from resource extraction all the way to processing, distribution, and marketing. Outright state ownership, or heavy state regulation by home and host governments, is still the norm in these industries for both Western MNEs and EMNEs. Although these firms were among the largest EMNEs and had made some of the largest overseas investments, not much was new or novel about how they internationalized, compared to Western or Japanese MNEs in these industries (Vernon, 1983).

The *local optimizer*, on the other hand, follows an internationalization strategy that is probably distinctive to emerging-market firms. Its FSAs are derived from optimizing products and production processes for the distinctive conditions of the home market – that is, serving low-income consumers in countries with underdeveloped "hard" and "soft" infrastructures (Khanna and Palepu, 2005). As discussed earlier, the resulting products and processes may be well suited to other emerging markets as well, thereby providing a basis for internationalization. Thus, a rugged, low-cost vehicle designed for India's middle-class consumers and its bad roads may have a ready market in other emerging markets. Such firms are likely to find that products optimized for emerging markets are sub-optimal for high-income countries; therefore, they may be stymied in their efforts to break into developed-country markets.

The *low-cost partner* strategy is likely to be pursued by firms that arbitrage the low wages of emerging markets to become supplier-partners of companies in high-wage countries. In our sample, this strategy was particularly powerful in China and India, which have large pools of low-wage, skilled and unskilled workers. The arbitrage strategy works less powerfully for middle-income developing countries, such as Brazil, Mexico, and Thailand, and was non-existent in high-income Israel. The target market for the exports of these EMNEs is developed countries, and up-market FDI may follow as the firms attempt to move up the value curve by establishing a presence close to customers in these. Chinese firms pursuing this strategy were more likely to be in manufacturing (e.g., Wanxiang, an auto parts supplier), and Indian firms pursuing this strategy were more likely to be in services (e.g., Infosys or Wipro in software services), but this distinction is likely to blur over time. The low-cost partner is likely to expand into other emerging markets to diversify the supply locations from which it serves customers in high-wage countries. Thus, its competitive foundations and internationalization paths are quite different from those of the local optimizer.

The *global consolidator* strategy is likely to be pursued by firms that build global scale in mature mid-tech industries, such as cement, steel, aluminum, auto parts, personal computers, and beverages. Many (though not all) of these industries use globally standardized products and processes, which makes it easier for EMNEs to expand internationally. In all such cases in Part II, the industries involved had matured in the developed world but were just taking off in the developing world. As a result, firms in emerging economies were adding new capacity, upgrading old capacity, hiring workers, and growing sales and profits. The more aggressive players from emerging markets consolidated their position in the home market through acquisitions and greenfield investments to become dominant suppliers with strong cash flows. In the 2000s, some of these firms then set their sights on counterparts in other emerging economies and/or in developed countries, launching a program of cross-border acquisitions. Examples from our studies include: Lenovo's takeover of IBM's PC business; Tata Steel's takeover of Anglo-Dutch Corus; Hindalco's takeover of Canada's Novelis; South African Breweries' takeover of several beer makers in Africa, Europe, China, and the US; Haier's expansion into many emerging markets as well as the US; Cemex's takeover of large cement companies in Australia, the UK, and the US; Wanxiang's takeover of several Western auto parts suppliers; and so on. Although Western firms in these industries were usually larger than EMNEs and had greater technical expertise, their plants were often technologically outdated and undersized, compared to new-vintage plants in emerging economies; they were saddled with

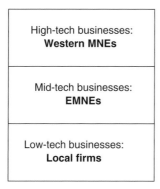

Figure 13.2 Strategic space occupied by many EMNEs

uncompetitive labor contracts, and their sales and profits were often in a downward spiral – making them targets for takeover by EMNEs. Some of the largest up-market investments by EMNEs were undertaken by global consolidators. Not surprisingly, global consolidators typically originated in the larger emerging economies, such as the BRICs, Mexico, and South Africa.

The final strategy type is the *global first-mover*, which involves an emerging-market firm operating at the global technology frontier, or one that is a trailblazer in a new emerging industry, rather than a late-follower in a mature industry. We alluded earlier to examples such as Embraer of Brazil in regional aircraft, Huawei of China in 3G tele-communications equipment, and Suzlon Energy of India in wind power. Other examples include pharmaceutical firms, such as Ran-baxy and Dr. Reddy's of India or Teva of Israel, that had the capability to develop new drugs or new delivery methods for existing drugs. Aharoni (Chapter 12) provides numerous examples of Israeli companies that developed pioneering technologies, usually in high-technology niche businesses, some of which grew into Israeli MNEs, while others were gobbled up by Western MNEs. The target market of the global first-mover is both emerging economies and developed countries, and it is likely to grow through a combination of greenfield investments in emerging markets and M&As in developed countries.

With the exception of the global first-mover, the other strategies typically involve EMNEs in mid-tech and mature industries. This seems to be the strategic sweet-spot occupied by many EMNEs, a space in which they are differentiated from other emerging-market firms as well as developed-country MNEs (see Figure 13.2). The local optimizer and the global consolidator, as already discussed, are typically in industries that have matured in developed countries. The low-cost partner may work for customers in the full range of technologies, but its own activities are likely to be low- or mid-tech in nature.

Impact on global competition

The emergence of EMNEs added to the competitive intensity of many industries, because these firms hailed from a new group of countries and leveraged competitive advantages that Western firms had not seen before (see Table 13.2). EMNEs shook up many a stagnant, mature industry in developed countries. The only exception was the natural-resource vertical integrator, whose forward or backward integration across borders also heightened global competition, in this instance for natural resources, but whose strategy was otherwise traditional and familiar. On the other hand, the local optimizer created new business models aimed at making products ultra-affordable to low-income consumers. It was a tough competitor in its home market and a potentially strong competitor to Western MNEs in other emerging markets. EMNEs pursuing the other three strategies had the potential to be particularly disruptive. Although the low-cost partner helped some Western firms to lower costs, improve quality, reduce time-to-market, and speed up innovation, it threatened the business models of other MNEs, as IBM's CEO, Sam Palmisano, explained in a famous speech (Palmisano, 2006). The global consolidator attacked incumbent MNEs using low-cost locations and facilities, and leapfrogged Western rivals by investing in modern plants and technologies. The global first-mover often took Western rivals by surprise, because Western firms in emerging industries were not expecting to compete with firms from developing countries. Yet when such competitors did emerge, they combined global reach with a strong footprint in low-cost countries, which forced their Western rivals to rethink how their own value chains were configured globally.

Western firms sometimes allied with EMNEs, but at other times fought them head-on. They sometimes sought to neutralize the home-country CSAs of EMNEs by creating their own production bases in those low-cost countries, even as EMNEs tried to match the FSAs of

Table 13.2. *How EMNEs affect global competition*

	Generic strategy	Implications for incumbent (Western) MNEs
(1)	Natural-resource vertical integrator	• heightened competition for natural resources • rising commodity prices
(2)	Local optimizer	• heightened competition in EMNEs' home market and in third-country emerging markets • disruptive competition from low-cost innovations
(3)	Low-cost partner	• strategic partner for lowering costs, improving quality, mobilizing talent, reducing time-to-market, and promoting innovation • potential future rivals, if EMNE successfully moves up value curve and across value chain • forces Western MNEs to neutralize EMNE's CSAs before it catches up with Western firm's FSAs through up-market M&A
(4)	Global consolidator	• may result in the globalization of previously fragmented industries • forces incumbent Western MNEs to merge and consolidate to offset EMNE's low-cost advantage
(5)	Global first-mover	• surprise attack from EMNE with low-cost footprint and global reach • forces Western MNEs to reconfigure value chain from high-cost to low-cost countries

Western MNEs through acquisitions in developed countries. Western MNEs that took seriously the opportunities and threats posed by EMNEs found ways to retain global leadership in their industries – witness the experience of companies such as Unilever in India or Nokia in China. But those that ignored EMNEs or were dismissive of them risked a serious loss of stature, as Ericsson, Lucent, and Motorola discovered in the telecommunications equipment industry.

Implications for IB theory

What does the evidence presented in this volume reveal about the adequacy or inadequacy of existing IB theory? Are EMNEs really a unique breed of MNEs that can only be understood with *de novo* theory, as Mathews (2002) seems to suggest, or was Raymond Vernon right in arguing many years ago that "the multinationalizing trend [is] widely recognized as similar in nature irrespective of the nationality of the parent company" (quoted in Wilkins, 1986: 202)? The answer depends on what questions one asks.

If one asks why EMNEs internationalize, or what challenges they face in host countries, or when they prefer hierarchies over markets, then existing IB theory is quite adequate. But if one asks what the competitive advantages of EMNEs are and where those advantages come from, or why some of them make substantial up-market investments (Cell 4 in Figure 13.1), or why some of them successfully compete head-on against Western MNEs, then existing IB theory falls short. We have drawn on the case studies in this volume to advance answers to some of the not-so-well-understood issues. For instance, we have identified distinctive FSAs that EMNEs leverage when they internationalize, and found them to be rooted in the distinctive CSAs of their home countries. We have argued that up-market FDI occurs because EMNEs, as late-movers, sometimes enjoy an edge over first-mover developed-country firms in mature mid-tech industries. We have also argued that some EMNEs are first-movers or technology pioneers in their industries, despite hailing from developing economies, and that this allows them to expand both up-market and down-market.

The larger point is that we can use EMNEs to buttress mainstream IB theory – or, if we prefer, to challenge and debunk it. But the right goal is to use them to enrich and extend mainstream IB theory. As Narula (2006: 145) rightly argues, "*there are no theories to refute* that offer to explain how and why firms internationalize in today's global economy" (italics in original). Research on EMNEs provides an opportunity to develop such a theory.

First of all, studying EMNEs provides the opportunity to rethink and deepen our understanding of how firms internationalize. As noted in Chapter 1, mainstream IB theory was developed by studying Western multinationals that were already quite internationalized when the IB field was born in the late 1950s.[5] Naturally, therefore, IB scholars focused much of their attention on the challenges of managing the mature MNE rather than the fledgling MNE that was still building its international presence. Only business historians paid close attention to how Western firms got to be multinational in the first place. To be sure, some important ideas were added to mainstream theory by studying the internationalization of Scandinavian firms in the 1970s, but on the whole our understanding of early-stage internationalization is limited, and IB scholars have had to turn repeatedly to a limited number of old ideas.

Table 13.3 shows MNEs at three stages of internationalization: the *infant MNE* is a firm taking the first steps towards internationalization, with a heavy reliance on exports, modest overseas production in a few countries, and unknown brands; it is sometimes referred to as the "international firm" to distinguish it from the multinational firm, which is assumed to have several foreign subsidiaries. The *adolescent MNE* has overseas investment and production in several countries, possibly concentrated in the home region, and owns up-and-coming brands. And the *mature MNE* operates in most major markets and regions, with extensive overseas production and research, and strong global brands. The EMNEs studied in this volume are typically in the infant stage; Korean MNEs such as Samsung, LG, or Hyundai may be examples of adolescent MNEs; and well-known Western or Japanese MNEs, such as IBM, Siemens, Toyota, and Sony, illustrate the "adult" or mature MNE.

In comparing EMNEs with Western MNEs, one must keep in mind that some of the observed differences may arise from differences in their stage of evolution rather than their country of origin. For instance, EMNEs generally do not possess strong brands, whereas Western MNEs do; but this difference simply reflects the fact that Western MNEs are at Stage 3 and have invested in brands for decades, whereas EMNEs are at Stage 1 and have only begun to do so. When Coca-Cola internationalized during World War II to serve overseas US servicemen, its brand was unknown outside the US, but within two decades it owned one of the world's most precious brands. Likewise,

---

[5] The Academy of International Business was founded only in 1959, and its main organ, the *Journal of International Business Studies*, was first published only in 1970.

Table 13.3. *Stages of MNE evolution*

	Stage 1: infant MNE	Stage 2: adolescent MNE	Stage 3: mature MNE
Importance of home-country CSAs	high	high to medium, and falling	medium to low, and falling
Ratio of exports to overseas production	exports exceed overseas production	exports and overseas production in balance	overseas production exceeds exports
Geographic footprint	few countries in home region, unless EMNE is pursuing the low-cost partner strategy	several countries, with emphasis on home region	dozens of countries, in all major regions
Brand	strong at home, unknown abroad	strong at home, up-and-coming abroad	strong global brand
Examples	most EMNEs	Korean MNEs, such as LG or Hyundai	Western and Japanese MNEs, such as IBM, Siemens, Sony, or Toyota

few EMNEs own global brands today but many of them will do so in two or three decades. In other words, after correcting for differences in stage of evolution, EMNEs may be as reliant on brands as Western MNEs.

A second reason for studying EMNEs is to bring context more explicitly and comprehensively into IB theory, as recommended by Cheng (2007), Meyer (2006), Tsui (2007), and others. In addition to the firm's own circumstances, there are at least three aspects of context that need to be brought into the analysis. These are home-country context, industry context, and the macro international context, each of which we have discussed earlier and which collectively shape the internationalization strategy of EMNEs (see Figure 13.3).

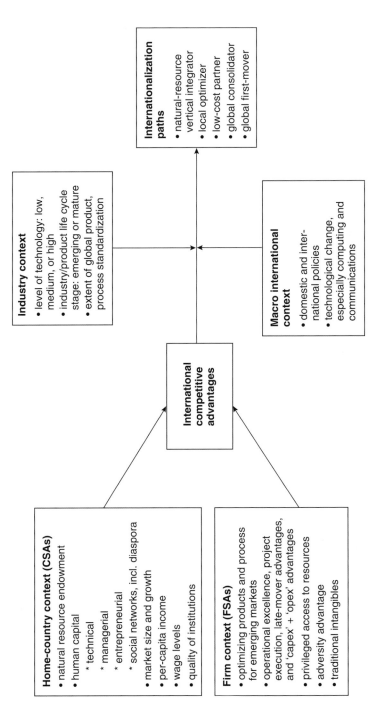

Figure 13.3 The role of context in the internationalization process of EMNEs (Stage-1 MNEs)

We have already noted how emerging economies, with their distinctive and idiosyncratic characteristics, shape the CSAs and FSAs of EMNEs. They contribute new CSAs such as low-wage workers, low-income consumers, and underdeveloped institutions, while countries like China and India also contribute very large labor pools and home markets. In addition, our studies suggest that human capital in the form of entrepreneurial skills and international social networks, such as links with the diaspora, were also important CSAs that shaped the emergence of EMNEs. Although no CSA is common to all emerging markets, and some of their CSAs are similar to those of developed countries (e.g., endowment of natural resources), as a group, emerging markets bring into the global economy many distinctive CSAs. IB scholars need to investigate these CSAs more deeply to understand how and why they translate into FSAs for some emerging-market firms. As discussed earlier, CSAs and FSAs seem to have a more complex relationship than is recognized in IB theory and digging deeper here should yield rich theoretical dividends.

We have also noted that many EMNEs are in mid-tech industries that are neither so simple that any emerging market firm could master them nor so sophisticated that Western MNEs have a clear technological edge in them (see, for instance, Amsden and Chu, 2003). To the extent that technology figures in mainstream IB research on MNEs, it is assumed to be frontier technology of the kind leveraged by Western MNEs, and is measured by indicators such as the R&D-to-sales ratio. On the other hand, EMNEs in mid-tech industries generally have low R&D-to-sales ratios and derive their FSAs from being late-movers rather than first-movers. Another important industry factor seems to be the degree to which products and processes are standardized across countries, which may be correlated with industry maturity. Many of the industries in which EMNEs have emerged as global consolidators use standardized processes to make relatively standardized products, such as cement, steel, paper, or even PCs. Clearly the ideas raised by our research need to be investigated more carefully to understand how technology and other industry characteristics affect internationalization. Vernon's product cycle hypothesis predicted that in the final stages of an industry's evolution,US MNEs would shift most of their production to developing countries, but it did not anticipate that local firms would be the ones to consolidate such industries globally.

A third contextual factor that needs to be brought into IB theory is the macro international environment, which, as we have repeatedly noted, was quite different in the flatter world of the 1990s and early 2000s, compared to prior decades. Shifts in the macro international context have no clear place in IB theory even though they profoundly affect the ease with which firms can internationalize. Mathews (2002) views the rapid pace of internationalization by EMNEs as one of their distinctive features, but that feature may in fact be a consequence of internationalizing in a flat world. After all, many "born global" firms in developed economies also internationalized rapidly in the flat world (Knight and Cavusgil, 1996). In other words, inter-temporal comparison of MNEs is potentially confounded by shifts in the macro international context.

A final reason for studying EMNEs is that they remind us of the value of studying internationalization in a more strategic and managerially relevant manner than is normally the case in IB research. Many IB theories look at internationalization in a piecemeal fashion: Work on clusters and the competitive advantage of nations relates home-country characteristics to the CSAs of countries or the FSAs of firms; other works focus on the motivations for internationalization or the costs of internationalization, including the liabilities of foreignness; still others look at the sequence and modes of foreign market entry; and finally there is a vast literature that looks at operational issues, such as international staffing, or international sourcing. But what managers need to know – and therefore IB scholars should be studying – is how these different elements come together to shape the internationalization strategies of firms.

The OLI paradigm, which is perhaps the bedrock of IB theory, connects several islands of IB theory into coherent answers to the question of why MNEs exist, but it, too, is inadequate as a guide for developing internationalization strategies, because it is static, highly abstract, and context-free. Indeed, the latter features account partly for its wide-ranging applicability and longevity (Eden, 2003). The OLI paradigm answers the "why," "where," and "how" questions of internationalization in vertical compartments, taking them one at a time. It does not connect the answers horizontally to propose internally consistent why-where-and-how strategies for internationalization. Research on EMNEs provides the opportunity to make such horizontal connections between islands of IB theory.

There is a well-developed literature on the strategy of single-country firms, as seen in the mainstream strategy literature. There is also a widely accepted taxonomy of strategies for mature MNEs, as seen in the works of Porter (1986) and Bartlett and Ghoshal (1989), which gave us categories such as the multi-domestic, global, and transnational firm. More recently, Ghemawat (2007b) has proposed the Adaptation-Aggregation-Arbitrage model for thinking about the strategic choices facing mature MNEs. But there is as yet no scheme or taxonomy for describing the strategy of infant MNEs as they embark on internationalization. This case falls between the cracks – between mainstream strategy scholars who are hesitant or unable to incorporate international diversification into their models and IB scholars who are preoccupied with the mature MNE. We hope that the generic internationalization strategies identified in this volume can help develop such a scheme for infant MNEs from emerging markets.

References

Amsden, A. and Wan-wen Chu. 2003. *Beyond late development: Taiwan's upgrading policies*. Cambridge, MA: MIT Press.

Bartlett, Christopher A. and Sumantra Ghoshal. 1989. *Managing across borders*. Boston, MA: Harvard Business School Press.

Buckley, Peter J., L. Jeremy Clegg, Adam R. Cross, Xin Liu, Hinrich Voss, and Ping Zheng. 2007. The determinants of Chinese outward foreign investment. *Journal of International Business Studies*, Vol. 38, No. 4 (July): 499–518.

Cheng, Joseph L. 2007. Critical issues in international management research: An agenda for future advancement. *European Journal of Management*, Vol. 1, Nos. 1–2: 23–38.

Eden, Lorraine. 2003. A critical reflection and some conclusions on OLI. In John Cantwell and Rajneesh Narula (eds.), *International business and the eclectic paradigm: Developing the OLI framework*. London and New York: Routledge, pp. 277–297.

Evans, Philip and Thomas S. Wurster. 2000. *Blown to bits: How the new economy of information transforms strategy*. Boston, MA: Harvard Business School Press.

Farmoohand, Ali F. and Phoebe Ho. 2006. *Huwaei: Cisco's Chinese challenger*. Hong Kong: Asia Case Research Center, The University of Hong Kong, Case No. HKU 599.

Farrell, Diana, Christian S. Folster, and Susan Lund. 2008. Long-term trends in the global capital market. *McKinsey Quarterly* (February).

Friedman, Thomas L. 2005. *The world is flat*. New York: Farrar, Straus and Giroux.

Ghemawat, Pankaj. 2007a. Why the world isn't flat. *Foreign Policy*, No. 159 (March/April): 54–60.

Ghemawat, Pankaj. 2007b. *Redefining global strategy*. Boston, MA: Harvard Business School Press.

Huang, Yasheng. 2003. *Selling China: Foreign direct investment during the reform era*. Cambridge: Cambridge University Press.

Hymer, Stephen. 1976. *The international operation of national firms*. Cambridge, MA: MIT Press.

Khanna, T. and Krishna Palepu. 2005. Spotting institutional voids in emerging markets. Boston, MA: Harvard Business School Publishing, Note No. 9–106–014.

Khanna, Tarun and Krishna Palepu. 2006. Emerging giants: Building world-class companies in developing countries. *Harvard Business Review* (October).

Knight, Gary A. and S. Tamer Cavusgil. 1996. The born-global firm: A challenge to traditional internationalization theory. In Tage Koed Madsen (ed.), *Advances in International Marketing*, Vol. 8. Greenwich, CT: JAI Press, pp. 11–26.

Kogut, Bruce. 1985. Designing global strategies: Profiting from operational flexibility. *Sloan Management Review*, Vol. 27, No. 1: 27–38.

Lall, Sanjaya (ed.). 1983. *The new multinationals: The spread of Third World enterprises*. Chichester, UK, and New York: John Wiley, IRM series on multinationals.

Lecraw, D. 1977. Direct investment by firms from less-developed countries. *Oxford Economic Papers*, Vol. 29, No. 3 (November): 442–457.

Luo, Yadong and Rosalie L. Tung. 2007. International expansion of emerging market enterprises: A springboard perspective. *Journal of International Business Studies*, Vol. 38, No. 4: 481–498.

Mathews, John. 2002. *Dragon multinationals: A new model for global growth*. Oxford, UK: Oxford University Press.

Meyer, Klaus E. 2006. Asian management research needs more self-confidence. *Asia Pacific Journal of Management*, Vol. 23, No. 2: 119–137.

Michaels, Ed, Helen Handfield-Jones, and Beth Axelrod. 2001. *The war for talent*. Boston, MA: Harvard Business School Press.

Narula, Rajneesh. 2006. Globalization, new ecologies, new zoologies, and the purported death of the eclectic paradigm. *Asia Pacific Journal of Management*, Vol. 23, No. 3 (June): 143–152.

Palmisano, Sam. 2006. Leading, trust, and the globally integrated enterprise. Speech delivered at INSEAD Business School, Fontainebleu, France (October).

Porter, Michael E. 1986. *Competition in global industries.* Boston, MA: Harvard Business School Press.

Rivkin, Jan. 2000. Imitation of complex strategies. *Management Science,* Vol. 46, No. 6: 824–844.

Tsui, Anne. 2007. From homogenization to pluralism: International management research in the Academy and beyond. *Academy of Management Journal,* Vol. 50, No. 6: 1353–1364.

Vernon, Raymond. 1983. *Two hungry giants: The US and Japan in the quest for oil and ores.* Cambridge, MA: Harvard University Press.

Wells, Louis T. Jr. 1983. *Third World multinationals: The rise of foreign investment from developing countries.* Cambridge, MA: MIT Press.

Wilkins, Mira. 1986. Japanese multinational enterprises before 1914. *Business History Review,* Vol. 60, No. 2: 199–232.

Zaheer, Sri. 1995. Overcoming the liability of foreignness. *Academy of Management Journal,* Vol. 38, No. 2 (April): 341–363.

Index